Mom—

I can't guarantee that this
will be good "beach reading" but
hopefully you'll find it interesting

Enjoy!

AF711360

# Defusing Democracy

# Defusing Democracy

## Central Bank Autonomy and the Transition from Authoritarian Rule

*Delia M. Boylan*

Ann Arbor

THE UNIVERSITY OF MICHIGAN PRESS

Copyright © by the University of Michigan 2001
All rights reserved
Published in the United States of America by
The University of Michigan Press
Manufactured in the United States of America
⊗ Printed on acid-free paper

2004 2003 2002 2001 4 3 2 1

No part of this publication may be reproduced, stored in a retrieval system, or transmitted in any form or by any means, electronic, mechanical, or otherwise, without the written permission of the publisher.

*A CIP catalog record for this book is available from the British Library.*

Library of Congress Cataloging-in-Publication Data

Boylan, Delia M.
Defusing democracy : central bank autonomy and the transition from authoritarian rule / Delia M. Boylan.
p. cm.
Includes bibliographical references and index.
ISBN 0-472-11214-7
1. Banks and banking, Central—Political aspects. 2. Democratization. 3. Banks and banking, Central—Political aspects—Chile. 4. Democratization—Chile. 5. Banks and banking, Central—Political aspects—Mexico. 6. Democratization—Mexico. I. Title.
HG1811 .B69 2001
306.2—dc21 2001000386

*For Lloyd*

# Contents

# Tables and Figures

# Acknowledgments

Among the people whose thoughts have stimulated my own are several professors, colleagues, and friends whose contribution to my work is hard to measure.

I am first and foremost very grateful to my dissertation committee, who supervised this project when it first came into being: Terry Karl (chair), Geoffrey Garrett, Terry Moe, and Philippe Schmitter. This group of individuals brought a rich and diverse set of talents to the table and represents—I believe—the very best of what Stanford University's Department of Political Science had to offer in the 1990s. I thank them for having the confidence in me to back what was at the time an unusual path for a student of comparative politics at Stanford. By throwing their support behind this project, they helped me—and others—to see that some of our discipline's seemingly greatest divides are not so insurmountable after all.

In particular, I thank Terry Karl for her careful and considered knowledge of Latin America and for reminding me, in both her comments and her example, that what we do should always have some bearing on the real world. I am also eternally grateful for her unwavering support through years of grant proposals and job applications, support that reflects her deeply committed and proactive approach to graduate student advising. I thank Terry Moe for those early conversations in which we shaped the broad contours of the argument and for pushing me always to see the project in its biggest light. I am grateful for Philippe's extensive and penetrating comments on draft after draft of dissertation chapters and for his letting me know—early on—that he believed in what I was doing. Finally, I am especially indebted to Geoff Garrett, who did all of the above and then some. Without Geoff, I am quite sure that the entire endeavor would never have gotten off the ground.

Along the way, I also benefited greatly from discussions with various individuals who read or commented on different portions of this project. In particular, I would like to acknowledge the advice and suggestions of Robert Bates, Jorge Buendía, Don Coursey, Alberto Díaz, Jorge Domínguez, Sven Feldmann, Jeffry Frieden, Robert Franzese, Brian Gaines, Charles Glaser, Lloyd Gruber, Stephan Haggard, Jeanne Kinney-Giraldo (several times!), Joseph Klesner, Stephen Krasner, Beatriz Magaloni, Kenneth Oye, Carlos Perez-Verdúa, Peter Smith, Duncan Snidal, Susan Stokes, and Barry Weingast. The argument is all the stronger for their input. I am also deeply indebted to my fine research assistants at both MIT and the University of

Chicago, including Ayhan Akman, Bela Prasad, Jayne Stancavage, Cesar Velásquez, and especially Douglas Bell.

I received material assistance during the course of working on this project from the Social Science Research Council, the Institute for the Study of World Politics, the Institute for International Studies of Stanford University, and the North America Forum at Stanford University. I also thank Stanford University's Center for Latin American Studies for providing me with office space and a congenial work environment during a crucial portion of my initial write-up period, as well as the Irving B. Harris Graduate School of Public Policy Studies at the University of Chicago for similar generosity. Finally, I thank the Department of Political Science at MIT for providing me with the space and time to finish the first draft of this book free of other obligations.

During my year at MIT, I benefited greatly from the rich and vibrant academic community that defines Cambridge. I am especially grateful to those at MIT—Steve Ansolabehere, Ricky Locke, Ken Oye, and Jim Snyder—who made a major effort to smooth my way into my first year of professional teaching and research, as well as to those at Harvard University who involved me in their seminars and gave me a chance to present my work. Since I have come to Chicago, my work has continued to profit enormously from the unique intellectual experience that is the University of Chicago. In this regard, I would like to recognize first and foremost my colleagues at the Irving B. Harris Graduate School of Public Policy Studies, who have taught me again and again the value of interdisciplinary exchange, while not allowing me to get away with any "hand waving" in my arguments. I have also benefited tremendously from the workshops around campus that form the core of the intellectual enterprise at the University of Chicago and that have sharpened my own analytical skills considerably. Here I would like to single out the Workshop on Comparative Politics, which has exposed me on a weekly basis to some of finest talent in our subfield among both faculty and graduate students alike.

As is often the case in a project of this sort, some of the most helpful comments I have received have come in the wake of various conferences, seminars, and presentations along the way. While I cannot hope to thank everyone who has influenced my work in this regard, I am grateful to those who sparked my thinking in the wake of various APSA and LASA panels, as well as to participants at seminars I have given at the Harvard-MIT Research Training Group and the David Rockefeller Center for Latin American Studies at Harvard University, the Kellogg Institute at Notre Dame University, various venues at the University of Chicago, the Department of Political Science at the University of Illinois at Champagne-Urbana, the Department of Political Science at the University of Michigan, and the Department of Political

Science at the University of Rochester. They, too, have had an impact on the final product.

While in the field, I benefited from the help of a number of institutions and individuals. I am particularly grateful to the Center for Latin American Monetary Studies (CEMLA) in Mexico for offering me office space and extensive institutional support with which to carry out my research, as well as to the Autonomous Technological Institute of Mexico (ITAM) for lending me access to its library and e-mail facilities. Special personal thanks go to Luis Alberto Giorgio (CEMLA) as well as to Federico Estevez (ITAM) for facilitating these exchanges. I would like to express my gratitude to the United Nations Economic Commission on Latin America (CEPAL) in Chile for providing me with office space and institutional support and to Ricardo Ffrench-Davis for making this affiliation possible. One of the most rewarding aspects of fieldwork is those contacts one meets inadvertently along the way who subsequently blossom into lifelong friends and colleagues. In this regard, I would also like to acknowledge the help and friendship of Celso Garrido and Marco Riveros Keller.

In closing, I would like to recognize the most important contributor to my personal and professional well-being lo these many years, my husband and colleague, Lloyd Gruber, who has been both my best friend and most ardent supporter from the very earliest stages of this project. Without him, I am convinced that I would never have made it through any of this, and I thank him for bearing with me and for providing me—through his own example—a model of scholarly and personal integrity.

CHAPTER 1

# Introduction

## The Challenge of Democratic Consolidation

The tide of countries making the transition from authoritarian rule in the late 1980s and early 1990s was initially greeted with euphoria. It was taken as a hopeful sign that the post–cold war era would be characterized by a community of nations—developed and developing alike—with a commitment to democratic institutions and democratic values (Fukuyama 1991). Nonetheless, as countries move from the installation of democracy to its consolidation, optimism has faded. While it is true that many countries have succeeded in moving away from their authoritarian pasts, few seem poised today to assume the mantle of a fully democratic future.

Any number of factors have worked to thwart the consolidation of democracy in third world polities. Many countries are riven by economic crisis, prompting political polarization, declining participation, and an escalation of crime and civil violence (Londregan and Poole 1990; Edwards and Tabellini 1991). In other countries, ethnic rivalries have come to the fore, calling preexisting boundaries of political community into question (Horowitz 1985; Young 1993). Finally, many states lack even the basic institutions of a modern democratic polity and are locked into a historical pattern of patron-client relationships and personalistic rule (Sandbrook 1985; Van de Walle 1994).

But the constraint that this study will focus on is of a different order. It stems from the fact that in many of these new democracies, newly empowered leaders are operating within institutional forms and structures that they did not create. Rather, they find themselves trapped within an institutional environment that is designed and controlled by their authoritarian predecessors.

This book offers an explanation for the existence of these authoritarian institutional legacies. It develops a systematic logic of "institutional insulation" that links the incentives and constraints facing power holders in the transition to the nature of the institutions that subsequently emerge. Specifically, I trace these vestigial institutions to strategic behavior by previous authoritarian elites seeking to guard against the inevitability of democracy. By entrenching their preferences in institutional footholds, the authoritarians ensure that the kinds of policies they favor will continue to be pursued long after they have left office. A defining feature of these enclaves of de facto authority is thus their potential to compromise the power and policies of successor governments.

Exiting authoritarian elites may employ any number of institutional strategies in order to protect their interests. For example, military regimes frequently set up mechanisms that allow for military representation in top policy-making bodies and/or shield military officials from dismissal or oversight (Stepan 1988; Agüero 1992). Electoral rules may also be designed to disproportionately advantage certain partisan interests over others (Geddes 1995; Londregan 2000). Or the authoritarians might try to cement in place certain social privileges before leaving power, such as institutionalizing the gains from land reform.

Another way that authoritarians can seek to protect their interests is to increase the autonomy of institutions that would otherwise be subject to the vicissitudes of the democratic political process. In the realm of the economy, one institution that lends itself to such insulation is the central bank. As the agency empowered to administer the country's currency, the central bank plays an important role in shaping the overall direction of the economy. By making the central bank autonomous, control over monetary policy is effectively removed from the hands of politicians.

At first glance, central bank autonomy might seem to offer a somewhat unconventional lens through which to explore this line of reasoning. After all, an autonomous central bank is generally seen as an unmitigated "good." On the theoretical front, it is thought to enable governments to credibly commit to macroeconomic stability. On the empirical end, there is a demonstrated relationship between central bank autonomy and low inflation. This study departs from the received wisdom and offers an alternative, less uniformly benign interpretation of central bank reform. Its starting point is the observation that all political actors should not value central bank autonomy equally. Rather, central bank autonomy is likely to be a source of conflict between those groups that favor low inflation and those who wish to use the economy for political ends. This assertion thus sets the stage for a redistributive perspective on central bank reform, in which central bank autonomy serves as a strategic tool through which conservative governments seek to limit the policy choices of their successors. I argue that where authoritarian elites fear the populism that may be endemic to new democracies and know that a change of regime is imminent, they can be expected to create an autonomous central bank to lock in a commitment to price stability over the long haul.

To lend support to this argument, the study draws upon evidence from the so-called third wave of democratization sweeping the globe over the past twenty-five years. It focuses primarily on two Latin American countries—Chile and Mexico—both of which undertook central bank reforms amid a transition from authoritarian rule. The study concludes by suggesting how this framework might be extended to institutional contexts beyond Latin America and to insulation strategies other than central banks.

At the broadest level, then, this is a book about efficiency versus redistribution in institutions. It is about how people in power protect their interests against subversion in the future. At a more pragmatic level, it is also an attempt to grapple with a recurring feature of the institutional landscape of the contemporary developing world. As I will be at great pains to show, the institutional constraints that new democracies face as they emerge from authoritarian rule are neither accidental nor surprising. Rather, they are the inevitable by-product of the very logic of the transition itself.

## Theorizing Insulation in Transitional Democracies

For students of transitional polities, the observation that new democracies are frequently constrained by the institutional choices of former leaders is hardly novel. Contributors to the "transitions" literature have long recognized the continuing influence that previous authoritarian rulers can exert over certain areas of substantive policy-making. Valenzuela, for example, highlights a number of "reserved domains" that governmental officials "would like to control in order to assert governmental authority . . . but are prevented from controlling by veiled or explicit menaces of a return to authoritarian rule" (Valenzuela 1992, 65). Garretón similarly devotes an entire chapter to the myriad "political proscriptions and exclusions that limit the democratic game," coining the term *authoritarian enclave* to underscore their birthplace in the previous regime (Garretón 1989, 52).[1]

Scholars of democratization have also speculated about the general processes producing these authoritarian institutional legacies. We know, for example, that during the negotiations that may precede the transition, the interests of the outgoing authoritarians are of paramount importance. More specifically, the "king and queen" of the transition game (propertied classes and armed forces) cannot be placed in direct jeopardy (O'Donnell and

1. Note that authors differ in their conceptualizations of this phenomenon. Valenzuela confines his definition of reserved domains to the loss of governmental authority over specific policy domains, while treating informal oversight functions accorded previous rulers (tutelary powers) and biased electoral rules as separate instances of what he calls "perverse institutionalization." In contrast, Garretón has a much broader definition of authoritarian enclave, one that encompasses not only institutional mechanisms that favor authoritarian interests but symbolic legacies (e.g., human rights violations) and privileged socioeconomic and political classes as well. My own definition includes any formal rule or procedure set up by the former regime to favor previous rulers and their allies. It thus encompasses all three of Valenzuela's spheres but corresponds to only the first of Garretón's.

Schmitter 1986, 69). Absent certain guarantees that their interests will be protected, these elites may fail to support a democratic alternative (Przeworski 1991).

The pace and duration of the transition are also thought to bear on the authoritarians' ability to affect the substantive and procedural landscape of the new regime. Where political change is so sudden and sweeping that incumbent elites are caught off guard, they are less likely to play a role in shaping the parameters of what is to follow. But where the transition is more gradual and protracted, elites have more time to set the terms of their withdrawal. The implication is that exiting elites are more likely to leave a strong imprint on the transition in the latter set of "top down" elite-dominated transitions than those "bottom up" transitions led by the masses (Karl 1990; Karl and Schmitter 1994).

Despite these useful insights, however, the transitions literature has yet to offer an overarching explanation for the origins of these institutional holdovers and the conditions under which they are likely to arise. Absent any explicit analytical link between the nature of the authoritarians' interests, the pace of the transition process, and the subsequent appearance of these biased institutional forms, we are at best left with a series of correlations. When all is said and done, how and why these institutional enclaves come about remains a mystery.

In part, this theoretical lacuna is attributable to the fact that authors writing in this tradition have generally been more concerned with exposing the perverse implications of these institutional structures than with exploring their foundations (Karl 1986; Linz 1990; Sørenson 1993). Because of this overriding preoccupation with the "effects" question, the discussion of such insulation tactics has tended to be largely descriptive. This remains true, despite recent contributions where authors have speculated more precisely as to the conditions under which such insulation is likely to occur. In keeping with their broader arguments about regime change, for example, Haggard and Kaufman (1995, 109–39) maintain that the degree of economic crisis is likely to be an important factor in determining how much control exiting military elites are likely to retain under democratic rule. But given that such economic crises are in many cases caused by the very regimes whose behavior these authors seek to analyze, their argument is vulnerable to an endogeneity critique, similarly compromising any speculation about attendant insulation strategies. For their part, Linz and Stepan (1996, 66–71) suggest that we are most likely to see this sort of insulation behavior carried out by hierarchical militaries, followed by nonhierarchical militaries, civilian leadership, on down to sultanistic regimes. While this typology may be accurate, it fails to offer much in the way of a generalized rationale for the presence or absence of these authoritarian enclaves.

In addition to this descriptive bias, a more comprehensive explanation for these authoritarian enclaves has also been limited by a fundamental assumption underlying much of the transitions literature. According to this body of work, the transition is a time of great uncertainty with a large quotient of unpredictability and accident (O'Donnell and Schmitter 1986, 4). Actors may not know their preferences, and even if they do, their actions may have unforeseen consequences that prevent them from realizing their goals. The bottom line is that because of the uncertainty that pervades transitions, we as analysts cannot ascribe purposeful intent to the actions of actors in any systematic fashion.

This study questions the uncertainty assumption. Or at least it questions that assumption where an important set of actors is concerned: authoritarian elites who know that they are losing power to democratic forces. For these elites, the world is not so uncertain. Indeed, precisely because exiting elites can foresee the impact that democracy is likely to have on their interests, they act strategically to make sure that these are not placed at risk. In the chapters that follow, I use this assertion about actors' behavior to generate predictions about how exiting authoritarian elites use institutions to fend off the threat of democracy. I suggest why authoritarian elites choose to deploy institutions defensively; under what conditions they are likely to succeed; and why, once created, "their" institutions are likely to endure.

## Insulation Strategies: Central Bank Autonomy

The starting point for this argument is the literature on bureaucratic insulation in the advanced industrial world. Contemporary theories of bureaucracy offer powerful insights into why an anticipated turnover in power may prompt politicians to use institutions defensively. In brief, the claim is that turnover matters because it signals that politicians cannot enjoy the perquisites of office forever. It also means that their opponents will someday be in power and are likely to pursue policies that work to their disadvantage. Recognizing that their days in office are numbered, incumbent politicians thus have incentives to create institutions that protect their interests from their opponents, who may, as a result, be left worse off (McCubbins, Noll, and Weingast 1987; Horn and Shepsle 1989; Moe 1990a).

It is easy to see how the thrust of this literature might accurately capture the distorting effects of the more obvious perverse institutional forms that tend to accompany transitions, such as biased electoral laws or veto powers for the military. It is admittedly more difficult to see its ready application to central bank reform.

After all, the conventional wisdom now holds that insulated bureaucracies are an essential component of successful economic reform in developing countries (Bates and Kreuger 1993, 464–65; Nelson 1993, 436; Geddes 1994a). By providing policymakers with protection from their political constituencies, such insulation is thought to facilitate the government's ability to use bureaucratic capabilities effectively without "threatening the economic logic of the adjustment process" (Callaghy 1989, 120). This is considered particularly important in new democracies where the reemergence of social demands heightens distributive pressures (Haggard and Webb 1994, 13–15). Central bank autonomy in many ways epitomizes the virtues attributed to such bureaucratic insulation.

And yet, it is precisely because this technocratic interpretation of central bank reform is so widely accepted that autonomy is rendered such an interesting candidate through which to explore the insulation dynamic at hand. For as I argue subsequently, there may be another story to tell in which the Pareto-improving nature of central bank reform is not a given. Rather, politicians have incentives to feel differently about the relative merits of central bank autonomy. The autonomy question is thus transformed from a simple efficiency story into a redistributive struggle over macroeconomic policy.[2]

## The Argument

### Rethinking the Credibility Literature: The Logic of Tying Successors' Hands

Most research on central bank autonomy falls into the category of the "credibility" literature.[3] In a nutshell, this literature argues that governments create autonomous central banks in order to "tie their own hands." Models build from the premise that all politicians have the ability to use surprise inflation to generate short-term gains in output (Kydland and Prescott 1977; Barro and Gordon 1983a, 1983b). As a result, even when governments may pledge a commitment to macroeconomic stability, domestic economic agents know

2. For a partisan take on insulation that is more in keeping with the logic of credible commitment, see Bates 1994.

3. For a thorough review of this literature, see Blackburn and Cristensen 1988; Persson and Tabellini 1994.

that politicians will always be tempted to inflate to improve their electoral fortunes.

In order to solve this commitment problem, politicians take monetary policy out of their own hands and place it under the charge of an autonomous central bank. Precisely because the central bank does not have to respond to voters' interests, it is thought to be more likely to pursue policies conducive to macroeconomic stability (Wooley 1984; Cukierman 1992). The bottom line, then, according to the credibility literature, is that central bank autonomy enables governments to credibly commit to low inflation. And while autonomy is generally thought to come at the cost of greater output variability, on net, society is left better off by delegating monetary policy to a more conservative central banker (Rogoff 1985).

In addition to generating more than a decade's worth of research in the field of economics, the credibility hypothesis has become the received wisdom in political science. Its influence has been particularly strong on a small but growing body of literature that attempts to explain the recent trend toward central bank reform in developing countries. Maxfield (1997), for example, argues that developing country governments make their central banks autonomous in order to signal a commitment to low inflation before international creditors and investors. She thus modifies the conventional wisdom to underscore the important role that international economic actors play as an audience for developing country reforms. The basic intuition, however, is exactly the same: central bank autonomy is executed as a means of demonstrating a credible commitment to low inflation.

Despite the widespread currency of credibility-based reasoning within the fields of economics and political science, this study suggests three reasons that it needs to be nuanced with a more distinctly political orientation. Consider first the empirical evidence from the less developed countries (LDCs). There is no doubt that international economic pressures inevitably play a role in pushing developing country governments toward central bank reform. But if these pressures were the sole determinant of central bank autonomy, then virtually all developing countries would have autonomous central banks. And yet, as we will see in chapter 2, this is simply not the case. Variation is readily apparent whether one chooses to employ formal/legal or more behavioral measures of central bank independence. Even in the face of overriding economic incentives to delegate authority over monetary policy, then, some governments must find it advantageous to maintain political control over the central bank.

The observed empirical variation on central bank autonomy ties to a second weakness in the credibility literature: its underlying premise that all politicians have the same incentives to inflate. Partisan theories of political economy have long argued precisely the opposite. They suggest that parties of the left and right, for example, differ systematically over the mix of inflation and unemployment they prefer (Hibbs 1977). Early variants of these theories were discredited for their assumption of a permanently exploitable Phillips curve (the trade-off between low inflation and low unemployment). More recent work has demonstrated, however, that in the wake of uncertainty surrounding elections, politicians can capitalize upon a short-run Phillips curve in order to manipulate the economy temporarily to their advantage, whether toward low inflation (in the case of the right) or toward low unemployment (in the case of the left) (Alesina and Rosenthal 1995).

While some models of central bank reform do incorporate a short-run Phillips curve (Alesina 1988; Alesina and Gatti 1995), they typically assume that the inflationary variance generated by these short-term partisan cycles renders central bank autonomy equally attractive to all political actors. And yet, there is no reason to presume this necessarily to be the case. To the extent that left-leaning politicians can engineer these short term postelectoral booms—and voters are willing to reward them for this behavior—it is not at all clear why such politicians would want to relinquish this flexibility in favor of the long-run credibility benefits of an autonomous central bank. And to the extent that these parties also place greater weight on real outcomes than they do on inflation, they are also more vulnerable than parties on the right to the output stabilization costs assumed in most standard models of central bank independence. In short, there are sound theoretical reasons to suspect that politicians who attach different values to inflation versus other macroeconomic outcomes are likely to disagree over the desirability of central bank reform.

A third and final reason to question the credibility literature is its assumption that central bank reform is necessarily "cost free." While a growing body of research demonstrates an empirical association between the presence of a central bank and low inflation (Grilli, Masciandaro, and Tabellini 1991; Alesina and Summers 1993), the jury is still out as to how central bank autonomy affects other long-term macroeconomic outcomes such as growth, deficits, and unemployment (Pollard 1994; Eijffinger and DeHaan 1996). And additional empirical work suggests that central bank autonomy may, in fact, increase the short-term trade-off between output and inflation (Debelle and Fischer 1994; Walsh 1995a). If the effects of central bank autonomy on these other macroeconomic variables are unknown or, indeed, adverse, this would seem to be yet another reason for left-leaning politicians to be wary of central bank autonomy.

The basic thrust of chapter 2, then, is that what is lacking in the credibility literature is politics. When the idea of an autonomous central bank is subjected to closer scrutiny, it becomes increasingly clear that all political actors should not value this institutional change equally. Rather, those who favor low inflation should welcome autonomy with open arms, while those who prefer more political control over the economy have incentives to oppose it. In light of these claims, we can at least cast doubt on the credibility literature's claim that where divergent ideological preferences exist, central bank independence represents a mutually beneficial compromise between opposing forces (Alesina and Gatti 1995). Rather, building on the work of Goodman (1992) and Cukierman (1994), it seems at least plausible to suggest that central bank autonomy may also serve as a means through which conservative governments—fearing the prospect of a leftward rotation in power—impose this institutional structure on their unwilling successors.

If the literature on partisan political economy lends plausibility to this more conflictual view of central banks in the advanced industrial world, a similar argument should also hold true for the developing world. To be sure, the redistributive "game" surrounding autonomy looks somewhat different. On the one hand, because the number one cause of inflation in developing countries is not employment but deficit spending (Cukierman 1992, 47–82), the political struggle is much more likely to center around those who stand to win or lose from the central bank's inability to monetize deficits. On the other hand, the financial liberalization that tends to accompany autonomy will also find supporters and detractors, as it eliminates the traditional role of the central bank in the LDCs as a vehicle of preferential credit (Haggard and Lee 1993). Once we account for these adjustments, however, there is every reason to believe that the "tying successor hands" argument advanced in this chapter can serve as a plausible explanation for central bank reform in the developing world.

## Central Bank Autonomy in the Transition from Authoritarian Rule

In chapter 3, I argue that the transitional political environment constitutes particularly fertile ground for extending this sort of redistributive logic. After all, the key issue on the table is really turnover of power and how such turnover affects the expectations of incumbent politicians as to how their preferred policies are likely to fare in the future. One would be hard pressed to find a political context where turnover assumes greater relevance than in the case of regime change, for it is precisely at the moment of the transition that authoritarian elites realize that they will not rule indefinitely. And while they do not know exactly what is coming their way, they do know that the situation does not look good for them. On the one hand, as previously marginalized groups gain a voice in the political arena, the potential for a radical change in policy must increase. On the other hand, unlike their counterparts in first world democracies who can expect one day to return to power, this may well be their last chance to influence the future course of events. Fearful of these risks inherent in regime change, the authoritarians should logically seek protection. By safeguarding their interests in well-insulated institutions, they can maintain influence over those arenas of policy they care about most.

Naturally, not all transitions will be equally threatening or—by extension—warrant the same degree of insulation. In addition to spelling out a general logic of transitional insulation, then, chapter 3 suggests the conditions under which it is likely to occur. How much insulation the authoritarians will be willing to undertake, I argue, depends on two factors. First, this is likely to be affected by the *intensity of threat,* as determined by the extent to which the preferences of exiting authoritarians and incoming democrats are expected to diverge. Second, the *proximity of threat,* or the relative imminence of the transition to democracy, should also condition insulating behavior. The incentives to insulate are expected to be stronger the more the preferences of the authoritarians differ from those of their likely democratic successors and the closer the onset of democratization.

With this general argument about transitional insulation as a backdrop, I then apply its logic to central bank reform. The central intuition driving the model presented in chapter 3 is that democracy offers different distributional incentives than authoritarian rule. If nothing else, the onset of elections means that politicians need to be more sensitive to voters' needs (Garrett and Lange 1996, 61–63). In particular, there are incentives for newly elected politicians to choose policies that benefit social groups who recently obtained a voice in the political arena (Alesina 1994, 45–47). Politicians in the developing world are also more susceptible to the "time inconsistency" problem—both because they are more vulnerable to being overthrown (Ames 1987, 25–27) and because voters typically have shorter time horizons (Haggard and Kaufman 1995, 157–58). Even where the democrats are not rabid populists, then, we can still safely say that politicians in emergent democracies are likely to want greater flexibility in the short term to appeal to different constituencies via increased social spending (Haggard and Kaufman 1989; Hunter and Brown 1998).

This more interventionist economic scenario does not always constitute a threat to outgoing authoritarian elites. That depends on the economic policy preferences of the authoritarians, which are determined here by the interests of dominant economic actors (capital). My assumption is that while democratically elected politicians are forced to balance the competing demands of business and voters when designing economic policy, authoritarian governments are free to respond entirely to the concerns of business. Drawing on Frieden (1991a), the model then posits two types of authoritarian regimes. For those more protectionist authoritarian regimes that cater to the interests of "sheltered" and asset-specific capital, those in power have no reason to fear the future in a strictly economic sense. After all, their constituents (import competing industries and nontradables) stand to benefit from the sorts of increased spending and preferential credit policies likely to be associated with democracy. These authoritarian governments thus have no incentive to limit the central bank's ability to monetize government deficits or to act as a development bank. To the contrary, they represent those sectors that have historically benefited from the lowered cost of capital entailed in the more lax fiscal and credit policies associated with dependent central banks in the developing world (Haggard and Maxfield 1993).

But there is also a set of important cases where the preferred policies of the authoritarians will not mirror those of the democrats. These are of course those authoritarian regimes that cater to a different type of capital—predominant in the "exposed" and non-asset-specific sectors of the economy (financial capital, foreign capital, and tradables). For these sectors of the economy that value macroeconomic stability, economic openness, and financial liberalization, the specter of intervention inherent in democratization does constitute a "strong threat." Accordingly, the creation of an autonomous central bank should be a very attractive strategy. Because an autonomous central bank views credit policy through the lens of macroeconomic management, it is likely to resist policies that result in excess spending, loose monetary policy, and high inflation. By establishing a monetary regime where populist economic alternatives are virtually off the agenda, conservative authoritarian regimes can also set up powerful constraints over the types of policies that democratic governments can pursue in the future.

The model yields three basic outcomes that can be thought of as points along a continuum. Where there is no clash between the economic policy preferences of the outgoing regime and the incoming democrats (i.e., the intensity of threat is weak) and/or democracy is a good way off, there should be no change to the legal status of the central bank. This set of outcomes corresponds to—among other things—the transition from a protectionist authoritarian regime, and it accounts for those *null* cases where a transition occurs but no autonomous central bank is created. In contrast, where there is a sharp preference divergence and regime change is imminent, the authoritarians will have strong incentives to insulate, and autonomy should be *full.* This set of cases encompasses those market-oriented regimes where democracy does represent a potential threat to the economic interests of the outgoing elites. In between, we should expect a set of middle-range outcomes to occur when the policy divergence between the exiting authoritarians and incoming democrats is lower and/or the democratic threat is more distant. In this last set of cases, autonomy should only be *partial.*

In all cases, autonomy is measured using the four sets of formal indicators developed by Cukierman (1992). These include the relative stringency of the terms affecting central bank lending to the executive, the extent to which the central bank is given control over the formulation of monetary policy, the degree to which the objectives of the central bank are centered on the goal of price stability, and the scale of executive influence over the composition and tenure length of the central bank's governing board.

## Explaining Institutional Persistence

In sum, this book suggests why credibility explanations may be inadequate for understanding the process through which autonomous central banks are created and why an alternative more political logic may also be at play. But while I privilege this more political explanation, I do not claim that credibility explanations never matter or do not capture part of the story. In fact, this study brings in credibility at the end of the story to explain why, once these autonomous central banks are established, we can expect them to remain.

After all, central bank autonomy only serves as an effective insulation strategy insofar as it is difficult to undo. If the authoritarians had no reason to believe that their institutional creations would last, they would be loath to undertake the effort to build them in the first place. How, then, can they be so sure that these central bank reforms will not be overturned?

The explanation I offer is rooted in the concept of reputation. Reputation is the view formed of an individual or organization by another based on past experience and that is subsequently used as a basis for forecasting future behavior (Kreps 1991). Once established, an autonomous central bank acquires tremendous reputational value in the eyes of international creditors and investors as a symbol of commitment to macroeconomic stability. Regardless of their policy preferences, new governments should thus be reluctant to tamper with autonomy. To do so would be to risk the massive outflow of foreign capital, with disastrous consequences for the economy. While incoming governments may not like living with an institution that denies them short-term flexibility over the economy, the instantaneous costs associated with abolishing an autonomous central bank autonomy are sufficiently dramatic—and politically salient—to make this a moot point (Calvo and Mendoza 1996).[4] While my argument thus shares with Maxfield

4. While I posit the international constraint as the overriding source of institutional persistence, it is buttressed by a host of domestic factors described in chapter 3.

(1997) an emphasis on international capital as a powerful force in shaping central bank reforms in the developing world, we differ critically in how we assess its significance and implications.

The thrust of my persistence argument, then, is that politicians in new democracies who inherit autonomous central banks are likely to view these as a liability. This does not mean that these politicians are impervious to the long-run destabilizing effects of inflation. To the extent that central bank autonomy is associated with macroeconomic stability over time, it may come to serve as a valuable institutional anchor in countries otherwise prone to volatile inflationary cycles. Indeed, central bank autonomy may have a number of positive long-run externalities (for economic stability, political stability, etc.) that leave these new democracies better off. My purpose, however, is not to evaluate autonomy's virtues from the standpoint of a given nation's long-term social welfare. It is to suggest the potential costs it may have for the short-term interests of political leaders in office and the constituencies they represent. To the extent that it deprives these politicians of a crucial lever of economic control with which to respond to pent-up societal demands, they may view autonomy as compromising their short-term office-seeking objectives.

When all is said and done, the question really comes down to how we choose to understand institutions. Do we assume an efficiency-based view in which institutions reflect mutually beneficial bargained agreements (cf. Williamson 1985; Milgrom and Roberts 1992), or do we adopt a more redistributive perspective in which institutions embody a set of interests that one group of more powerful actors imposes on another with concomitant costs (Levi 1990; Moe 1990a; Knight 1992)? If one takes the latter tack, then I am agnostic about whether or not central bank autonomy is ultimately "good" for these new democracies. What I do claim is that it might be potentially bad for the democrats whose control over the economy is sharply decreased just when flexibility is needed most.

## Research Design

As a vehicle for exploring some of the theoretical points made in this book, chapters 4 through 7 are devoted to a paired comparison of two transitional democracies where central bank reforms were undertaken—Chile (1989) and Mexico (1993). In order to undertake this comparison, I employ a comparable case methodology (Lipjhardt 1975).[5] The idea is to focus on cases that are

5. This method is also referred to elsewhere as "systematic comparative illustration" (Smelser 1968), "controlled comparison," and "most similar systems design" (Przeworski and Teune 1982).

similar in a large number of important characteristics but dissimilar with respect to the variables with which a relationship is hypothesized. The overriding virtue of such a strategy is that it offers a large measure of control, thereby circumventing the "many variables, small number of cases" problem that tends to plague comparisons among a handful of countries.

To this end, I privilege the two dimensions of the threat variable thought to influence central bank reform in the transition from authoritarian rule: the intensity of threat (as measured by the sectoral support base of the authoritarian regime and the democrats' economic agenda) and the proximity of threat (as measured by the relative strength of the incoming opposition). And since a major rival hypothesis explains this outcome as a function of the need for international economic credibility, I also assess the relative plausibility of this international explanation for each of the countries in question. By focusing on key variables and subjecting each case to the same data requirements, this study meets the prerequisites of George (1982) for a structured, focused comparison intended to sharpen the theoretical rigor of small-*n* studies and to improve their potential for generalizability.

As noted earlier, my argument is meant to hold for all transitions except those where political change is so sudden and so sweeping that incumbent authoritarian elites lack both the time and the ability to enact this sort of self-serving institutional reform.[6] This study traces the course of central bank reform within two "top down" transitions: Chile (1980–89) and Mexico (1988–93). While there is no logical imperative for focusing exclusively on two Latin American countries, Mexico and Chile lend themselves to the comparison at hand.

At the time of the reform in question, both countries could lay claim to a powerful capitalist class with a vested interest in central bank autonomy. Both were more or less equally vulnerable to the international economy. And they each had authoritarian regimes facing a major domestic political challenge and/or the advent of democratization. In spite of these relatively parallel economic and political contexts, Chile opted for a fully autonomous central bank, while Mexico created a partially autonomous institution. By controlling for both powerful capitalist actors and international economic context, I thus show how variation on the proximity of democratization in turn yielded variation on the corresponding degree of autonomy afforded the central bank. The implicit null hypothesis is that where central bank autonomy is absent, it

6. In a sense, one could thus consider the pace of the transition to constitute what Smelser refers to as a "parameter" in this research design: for example, "a condition that is known or suspected to influence the dependent variable but which, in the investigation at hand, is made or assumed not to vary" (Smelser 1968, 70).

is due either to the extremely distant nature of the transition or to a lack of significant difference in the economic policy preferences of the authoritarians and the democrats. Such a case is considered briefly in chapter 8.

A comparative case methodology is particularly suited to a study of this nature, which relies heavily on such inherently qualitative phenomena as the "fear of impending democratization" and the "proximity of threat" that would be difficult to measure in the context of a large-*n*, quantitative study. In order to adequately capture such concepts I need to re-create the decision-making calculus of policymakers with respect to how they viewed the options before them at the time of the reforms in question. This requires close and detailed attention to the two cases at hand, which can only be achieved through extensive field research. Such field research entails detailed journalistic accounts; archival research at on-site university libraries and policy-research organizations; and extensive interviews with government officials, academics, and representatives of the media and private sector.

This intensive form of data collection is useful on two levels. On the one hand, it facilitates assessment of the validity of alternative explanations. On the other hand, by employing the within-case formula of George (1982) for process tracing, historical archives and interviews can be used in order to specify more explicitly the intervening steps between my hypothesized causal mechanisms and resultant institutional outcomes. Such process tracing is particularly useful where the Mexican case is concerned, as the incomplete nature of the Mexican transition obscures clear-cut inferences with respect to the reform in question.

By thus combining a controlled case comparison with a research design that allows for both positive and negative instances of the phenomenon under study, I am able to isolate the independent effect of my independent variable on the institutional outcome at hand, thereby replicating—where possible—a quasi-experimental research design. As with any methodology, there are some drawbacks. First, as is often the case in small-*n* studies, the observations used for analysis were deliberately selected. The explanatory reach of this sort of "retrospective research design" is inherently limited, as it is much more dependent on my preconceived notions about the empirical world than what might have emerged were my observations drawn from a large, random sample of cases (King, Keohane, and Verba 1994, 141–42). Moreover, because only high and medium values of autonomy are examined in detail, the conclusions are vulnerable to selection bias (correlation between selection rule and dependent variable) (King, Keohane, and Verba, 1994, 130).

While problematic, these methodological weaknesses do not, in my view, constitute a serious problem. Of necessity, qualitative studies almost never employ a random selection rule. While in an ideal world I would be able to select cases exclusively on the basis of explanatory variables, the present research design moves me in the direction of such a goal while in the meantime allowing for a well-controlled comparison. The study also both allows for and is premised upon a dependent variable that actually varies, thereby distinguishing it from a great deal of allegedly comparative research in comparative politics. Finally, undertaking a subsequent case analysis where observations are selected only on the basis of the central independent variable can also mitigate any problems associated with selection bias. Chapter 8, "Central Bank Reform in Comparative Perspective," begins to do precisely this.

A second methodological issue raised by this study relates to the microfoundational nature of the argument at hand and the fact that I assign a set of preferences to the actors in the model I develop. I believe this approach is justified on two grounds. First, I ascribe what I believe to be reasonable preferences to the actors in question: greater flexibility over the economy (in the case of the democrats) and the interests of dominant capitalist actors (in the case of the authoritarians). The idea is to employ a weak assumption about what motivates actors in order to generate a strong conclusion. Second, since actors frequently act strategically when relaying their preferences with regard to a specific event, it is often difficult to take them at their word. More objective—albeit indirect—indicators of their preferences can often provide a more accurate reflection of their state of mind. Finally, I also attempt—where possible—to provide independent evidence for my assessments of actors' preferences in the case studies themselves.

A third issue concerns the determination of the appropriate "cutoff" points for the different variables in play. The key challenge here is how to code a "strong" versus a "weak" threat and, similarly, how to distinguish between "high" and "low" autonomy. While the latter can be assessed using widely accepted measures (i.e., the Cukierman index), the former is much more difficult to specify. Because it is not possible to establish explicit boundaries for these "threat" thresholds, they must be determined empirically. While this arguably generates a somewhat subjective evaluation of this variable, it is also the case that even if this were a quantitative study, these parameters would need to be established empirically.

A final concern arises from the partial nature of the Mexican case analyzed herein. For unlike the full or no insulation variants in which the relationship between the independent variable and the outcome is fairly straightforward, partial insulation is—by definition—an inherently murky concept to get one's hands around. But rather than abandoning the case altogether—or forcing it into a box where it does not belong—I chose instead to work from the basic theory that I have developed in this book and use it to explore the interesting nuances of a particular case. To the extent that we can think of

Mexico as a point on a continuum, it offers a nice point of comparison with Chile within the same overall theoretical rubric. In keeping with the recent trend toward analytic narratives (Bates et al. 1998), I am thus able to use my argument to shed light on an important case in new and interesting ways, while at the same time allowing the case to enrich the underlying theoretical model.

This book unfolds as follows. Part 1 amplifies some of the main theoretical points highlighted in this introduction. Using the literature from American politics on bureaucratic insulation as a backdrop, chapter 2 counters traditional efficiency-based views of central bank reform that emphasize improved welfare with a more redistributive perspective that emphasizes autonomy's potential costs. In chapter 3, I suggest how such an approach might be extended to a transitional political environment.

Part 2 bolsters these theoretical claims with empirical evidence. I begin with an in-depth examination of two transitional democracies in which central bank reform took place—Chile and Mexico—in order to highlight how variation in the proximity of the democratic threat yielded correspondingly different levels of central bank autonomy. The Chilean central bank reform of December 1989—examined in chapters 4 and 5—presents an almost textbook case of the sort of institutional insulation we should expect to see in the wake of a transition to democracy. In the presence of an imminent threat of regime change under the leadership of the center left, authoritarian elites with a vested interest in macroeconomic stability responded by creating a highly autonomous institution. And despite vociferous criticism from the regime's opponents prior to the passage of this legislation, it has persisted under democratic rule without modification.

In contrast, the Mexican central bank reform of December 1993—considered in chapters 6 and 7—better exemplifies a case of what one might call "partial insulation." As in Chile, reform impetus in Mexico grew from a baseline concern over how the incumbent government's economic policy interests might be compromised by future left-leaning rulers. But because the democratic threat facing the authoritarian regime was still distant, the resultant autonomy afforded the central bank was less than complete. Chapter 7 ends with a postscript explaining the reform's relevance to the dramatic events of 1994 and noting the argument's implications for Mexico's ongoing process of democratization.

Part 2 concludes with chapter 8, "Central Bank Reform in Comparative Perspective," in which I examine three cases of central bank reform in transitional political settings similar to Chile and Mexico: two where reforms succeeded (South Africa and Pakistan) and one case of failed reform (South

Korea). Part 3 elaborates on possible empirical extensions of the argument and returns to the "big picture" questions of the relationship between democratization and institutional change.

## Conclusion

It is important to emphasize that this study does not try to provide a comprehensive explanation for central bank reform in all developing countries. As noted previously, the argument is strictly delimited to that class of cases commonly referred to as transitions from authoritarian rule. While I believe that the argument can speak to a number of important cases—elaborated in chapter 8—I do not suggest that mine is the only—or even necessarily the most prevalent—means through which central bank reforms are likely to surface in the third world.

Nor does this study try to establish a lexical ordering of preferences as to which—of several potential contenders—is likely to be the most important insulation strategy for a given authoritarian government. An authoritarian regime in the twilight of its rule might reasonably attempt to insulate its preferences in the military, electoral, and economic spheres. Rather than attempting to catalog and prioritize the variety of options available, this book instead highlights one specific insulation strategy—central bank autonomy—and explains under what conditions the onset of democratization may lead to its appearance.

That said, this study has three much more fundamental objectives. First, I hope to use the specific institutional case of central bank reform in order to illuminate a much more widespread insulation phenomenon. This illustrative research design is thus meant to serve as the first step in the development of a theory to explain one of the most pervasive—and potentially consequential—institutional phenomena confronting third world democracies today. Down the road, it might serve as a theoretical basis for understanding the origins of a variety of authoritarian enclaves—not just central bank autonomy but civil-military relations, electoral laws, and the other biased institutional forms featured in the transitions literature, as I suggest in chapter 9.

Second, I also hope to make a contribution to the burgeoning literature on central bank autonomy by suggesting an alternative, more political logic to the conventional credibility-based wisdom. The "free lunch" mentality that has pervaded the credibility literature for nearly two decades has gone unchallenged far too long. As theoretical and empirical developments increasingly point to the short-run costs that may be attendant upon central bank reform, it is time to rethink our assumptions to cultivate a more nuanced, redistributive understanding of this institutional outcome.

Finally, this work is intended to enrich the literature on institutions more broadly by extending a redistributive approach to the institutional landscape of the third world. For just as political scientists have been all too willing to embrace an economic rationale for central bank reform, so too have they tended to employ similar reasoning in their analysis of institutions. As I argue in chapter 9, however, it is not at all clear that such an approach is the only—or even the most appropriate—way to understand institutions, particularly in new democracies. After all, these are polities that tend to be characterized by large asymmetries of power, where certain actors—by virtue of the resources they possess coming into the transition—are in a position to impose certain institutional outcomes on other players in the "democratic game." Knowing this, we need to discriminate more carefully in our application of the institutionalist literature coming out of the first world. This book can thus also be read as a normative plea for a more textured political analysis of all institutions—central banks and otherwise.

PART 1

# Theory

CHAPTER 2

# Central Bank Autonomy

## A Redistributive Perspective

The introductory chapter laid out the general contours of this book. The general theme is one of institutional autonomy as a form of political insulation. The setting is democracies in transition from authoritarian rule. And the specific institutional form in question is central bank autonomy.

The nuts and bolts of this argument are presented in chapter 3. In order to set the stage, this chapter provides some theoretical background. Above all, this entails a more detailed discussion of the literature on central banks.

Central banks are essentially government banks. First and foremost, they govern monetary policy, controlling how much domestic currency will circulate in a country's economy at any given time. They also act as financial agents for governments, managing and disbursing liquid funds. Third, they may play an international role in setting a country's exchange rate and/or managing its foreign reserves. Finally, they also have a number of supervisory and regulatory duties to ensure the ongoing stability of the private banking sector.[1]

Central bank autonomy refers to the extent to which the central bank carries out these functions independent of executive and legislative control. In recent years, central bank autonomy has assumed growing empirical and analytical significance. On the one hand, the number of countries undertaking central bank reform has gradually increased over the last two decades, escalating dramatically in the early 1990s (Maxfield 1997, 50–70). On the other hand, this more visible and powerful role for the central bank has been accompanied by a large literature in both economics and political science as to the causes and consequences of autonomy.[2]

This study focuses primarily on the decision by politicians to cede authority over monetary policy to an independent agency. The conventional view holds that politicians do so as a means of binding themselves against the temptation of generating inflationary surprises in the future. As a result, society as a whole is said to benefit.

1. For a detailed description of what central banks do, see Downes and Vaez-Zadeh 1991.

2. There is also a separate literature that explores the conditions under which central banks are established. See, for example, North and Weingast 1989; Maxfield 1994; Broz 1998.

This chapter offers a different explanation. Drawing on discussions of bureaucratic design in the American politics literature, I raise the possibility that politicians who create autonomous central banks may be more concerned about their successors' inability to commit to low inflation than their own. As a result, they may design central banks not so much to limit their own freedom of maneuver as they do to bind the policy choices of future governments. Viewed from this more political perspective, central bank reform may shift from being a story of welfare improvement to one of redistribution, wherein those actors who favor low inflation stand to win from autonomy, while those with a more interventionist policy agenda stand to lose.

The chapter is organized as follows. I begin by reviewing contemporary theories of bureaucracy to suggest why the onset of political change may provide incentives for incumbent politicians to imbed their policy preferences in institutions, and I explain the corresponding welfare implications that flow from such a model of institutional choice. Next, I demonstrate how this "tying successor hands" logic might be fruitfully applied to the literature on central bank reform in the advanced industrial countries. I conclude by suggesting why a similar approach should prove equally valid in the developing world.

## Bureaucratic Design: The Politics of Insulation

Contemporary theories of bureaucracy offer powerful insights into the relationship between institutional choice and political change.[3] The basic problem can be cast in terms of the principal/agent literature. This literature refers to a class of problems in which one actor—the principal—considers entering into a contractual relationship with another—the agent—with the expectation that the latter will choose subsequent actions that produce outcomes desired by the principal (Jensen 1983). Within the literature on American politics from which most examples are typically drawn, members of Congress and the president are principals in an agency relationship with an executive bureau, whom they depend upon to execute policies in keeping with their wishes.

In addition to the standard moral hazard and adverse selection problems that typically plague this sort of control relationship,[4] the principals also need to worry about what happens when a new set of principals takes over in the

3. For a more thorough review of the literature on this topic—as well as various critiques that have been leveled against it—see, among others, Mashaw 1990; Huber and Shipan 2000.

4. "Moral hazard" refers to a problem of hidden action (i.e., principals cannot observe the behavior of their bureaucratic subordinates), while "adverse selection" concerns hidden information (i.e., bureaucratic agents know more than their political principals do).

future. For even if the authors of a particular piece of legislation manage to structure incentives and/or employ monitoring techniques to ensure that the agency does exactly what they want during the current period, new coalitions may come into power who fail to respect these arrangements. Politicians currently in office thus need to worry about how they can control policy outputs by government agencies in an environment characterized by political uncertainty (Moe 1990a, 122–25).

This problem of "legislative drift" (Horn and Shepsle 1989) gets resolved in the literature in a variety of ways. McCubbins, Noll, and Weingast (1987, 1989) focus on various "deck stacking" strategies that politicians can employ to influence the process through which agencies make decisions.[5] They suggest that by incorporating specific procedural arrangements (e.g., public notification and participation requirements), politicians can shape agency decision making in a way that privileges those interests who were actively involved in the creation of the original legislation and most affected by the resultant policy. The beauty of this approach—so the story goes—is that these rules need not dictate specific policy outcomes. Rather, they are intended to make sure that the agency will act on "autopilot," so that as preferences of the initial constituencies enfranchised in policy-making change, so too should policies reflect such changes, making new legislation unnecessary.

Moe (1990a, 1990b) offers a similar analysis of agency structure. He identifies a variety of means through which incumbent politicians can manipulate diverse features of bureaucratic structure—for example, introducing sunset provisions, housing an agency in a "safe location," front-loading the benefits of agency mandates—to make it difficult for their opponents to undo their desired policies in the future. In both cases, the basic idea is that politicians can—and do—structure bureaucratic agencies to favor both constituent interests and substantive policy outcomes that the legislation's original framers deemed important, even when this enacting coalition is no longer around.[6]

In addition to exposing the political strategy that underlies such institutional choices, this literature is also explicit about the welfare effects that flow from them. This is particularly true of Moe's work. For Moe, the defining feature of political office is that it is imbued with a preexisting authority. Officeholders thus enjoy a de facto structural advantage over their opponents

5. While McCubbins, Noll, and Weingast are more directly concerned with problems of so-called bureaucratic drift, their framework is equally applicable to control problems arising from changing legislative coalitions. See Horn and Shepsle 1989.

6. The delegation literature has been extended to provide more carefully specified empirical propositions about how different features of the political environment influence both the choice and type of control instrument. See especially Epstein and O'Halloryn 1994; Bawn 1997; and de Figuereido 1998.

in the process of institutional creation, as while in power, they have virtual carte blanche to design institutions as they see fit. And their opponents, like it or not, have little choice but to accept what they create.[7] In this way, Moe suggests, politicians have both the incentive and the ability to use the power of office to impose their policy preferences on their successors. The main implication of his work is that the resultant institutions—far from benefiting all actors equally—may well leave certain actors worse off. At the very least they are likely to introduce a redistributive bias into the resultant policy (McCubbins, Noll, and Weingast 1989, 443).

While varying in their specific emphases, what each of these writings has in common is an emphasis on turnover of power as a key motivation behind institutional design. Turnover matters because it signals to politicians that they are vulnerable to a change of policy in the future and must thus seize the moment to protect their interests while they still have the institutional wherewithal with which to do so. And while the institutions born of this insulation dynamic will not necessarily lie outside the Pareto frontier, they may well generate winners and losers.

This study extends this redistributive view of institutions to the realm of central banks. As noted in the previous chapter, this is not a readily obvious application. But a closer look at this literature suggests that it is entirely plausible. In order to see this, however, we must first review standard accounts of why politicians create autonomous central banks.

## Central Bank Autonomy: The Developed Countries

### The Credibility Literature

Over the last two decades, research on central bank autonomy in the advanced industrial countries has mushroomed under the umbrella of the "credibility" literature.[8] Models build from the premise that unexpected monetary expansion can generate short-term gains in output. As a result, pol-

7. Because he is analyzing agency design within the U.S. political context—where the passage of legislation per force requires negotiation among groups with diverse interests—Moe incorporates an element of political compromise into his theory. But such compromise only serves to further load down the bureaucracy with excessive rules and does not change the essentially coercive nature of the dynamic he describes.

8. In singling out the credibility literature, I am focusing on what I consider to be the conventional wisdom regarding central bank autonomy. In so doing, I do not address another important research tradition that claims that it is the structure of existing political institutions—and their effect on the number of actors in the policy-making process—that makes autonomy more or less likely to occur and/or guarantees its effectiveness. See, among others, Banian, Laney, and Willet 1986; Johnson and Siklos 1992; Lohmann 1998a.

icymakers have the ability to use surprise inflation to stimulate the economy in order to improve their electoral fortunes (Kydland and Prescott 1977; Barro and Gordon 1983a, 1983b).[9]

The problem is that in attempting to fool the public in this fashion, the government produces an inflationary outcome that is suboptimal for all concerned. This situation arises because private economic agents understand the incentives facing politicians. They know that although a government may announce an anti-inflationary policy in one period, it has an incentive to renege on this commitment by generating surprise inflation at some point in the future. Anticipating such inflationary behavior, domestic economic actors build this calculation into their nominal wage contracts and adjust these upward accordingly. The net result is an inflationary spiral with no corresponding gains in employment.[10]

In order to overcome this "time inconsistency" problem, policymakers must devise a means through which to credibly commit to low inflation. One way they can do this is to take monetary policy out of their own hands and place it under the control of an independent agency—an autonomous central bank.[11] Central bankers are thought to be inherently more conservative than politicians and thus less willing to sacrifice low inflation for short-term real economic gains (Wooley 1984; Goodman 1992, 7). And because they do not have to respond to voters' interests, they are also said to evaluate policies in a more technocratic manner than do officeholders (Cukierman 1992, 351–59). Finally, because they are not responsible for fiscal policy, central bankers have little incentive to collect the seignorage ("inflation tax") derived from deficit spending (Grilli, Masciandaro, and Tabellini 1991, 365–66). As independent central banks acquire a reputation for anti-inflationary policies over time, the

9. This can be done for a variety of reasons: to stimulate employment (as described previously), to finance the deficit (through the seignorage revenues derived from increasing the monetary base), or to avoid excessive deficits in the balance of payments (by devaluing the currency to increase exports). For a more detailed discussion of all three motives and their specific relationship to the "time inconsistency" problem noted subsequently, see Cukierman 1992, chaps. 2–5.

10. In the argot of the credibility literature, this dilemma is commonly referred to as the "time inconsistency" problem. This refers to those situations where the best plan made for some future period by an agent is no longer optimal when that period arrives. The time inconsistency problem results because monetary policy is chosen after expectations and actions based on those expectations by private actors have already been determined. Had the government credibly precommitted to an inflation rate of zero, nominal wage contracts would have been settled on the assumption that inflation would be zero, and actual inflation would thus be zero as well. Instead, monetary policy is tinged by an inflationary bias.

11. This is not the only policy alternative available. Other options entail legislating some form of monetary policy rule such as a *k* percent monetary growth rule, establishing a currency board, developing incentive contracts for central bankers, or tying policy decisions to some external commitment such as the gold standard or a fixed exchange rate regime.

public's expectations should eventually converge to this equilibrium, thereby eliminating monetary policy's inflationary bias.

By delegating monetary policy to a conservative central banker who places greater weight on price stability than does the median voter, politicians can thus make good on their promise not to engage in inflationary opportunism in the future. The central bank thus acts as a benevolent social planner, and society, for its part, is left uniformly better off (Rogoff 1985). It is true that in the original Rogoff model, the low inflation yielded by central bank independence is thought to come at the cost of greater output variability. This is because an absolute commitment on the part of the central banker to refrain from using monetary policy to boost output also sacrifices its use as a stabilization device (Lohmann 1992). Thus, for example, in the wake of an exogenous productivity shock, society can be expected to incur large output losses. But because the credibility gains from low inflation are thought to offset losses arising from such output variance, on net, society is still thought to benefit.[12]

Building as they do on early models of opportunistic business cycles (Nordhaus 1975; McRae 1977), many models of central bank reform assumed that all politicians have the same incentives to inflate. The logic behind such models is that preelectoral inflation is merely a tool for generating votes and that politicians can be expected to return to a norm of price stability once they have been elected. Over time, this literature has also expanded to incorporate the notion that politicians of different ideological stripes may differ in the relative weight they place on inflation versus real outcomes. While parties of the left are thought to emphasize low unemployment, government intervention, and the redistribution of income to favor lower socioeconomic groups, right-leaning parties pursue low inflation, a greater role for the market, and distributive policies favorable to business and higher socioeconomic strata (Hibbs 1977).

Early variants of these partisan theories of political economy were discredited for their assumption of a permanently exploitable Phillips curve, which implied that governments could indefinitely skew macroeconomic outcomes to favor their core constituencies. These earlier theories failed to recognize that if economic agents were perfectly informed about the objectives of different parties, they would eventually adjust to changes by bringing wage contracts—and hence employment—in line with existing inflation. But while the notion of a long-run Phillips curve is no longer theoretically

12. In order to correct for this loss of flexibility, Lohmann (1992) introduces the possibility that the government agent can override the central banker at a positive but finite cost. For an argument suggesting that the inflation/output variance trade-off will only occur above a certain level of independence, see Jordan 1997a.

viable, most economists do believe that there is a short-run trade-off between inflation and unemployment (Bernanke and Blinder 1992; Sims 1992). And a fairly sophisticated body of theoretical work has emerged that demonstrates how politicians can take advantage of this short-run Phillips curve in order to favor their preferred set of economic outcomes. More specifically, in the wake of the uncertainty surrounding electoral outcomes, politicians are afforded a brief window in which they can either stimulate the economy or generate a recession before economic agents adjust.[13] And the greater the policy distance between two competing parties, the more pronounced the effect on output is likely to be (Alesina 1988; Alesina and Sachs 1988; Alesina and Rosenthal 1995).

Rational partisan models of political economy have recently been extended to account for central bank reform. In such models, politicians of different partisan hues engage in a preelectoral bargain in which they agree to forego their partisan objectives and install a more independent central bank. Not only is such an agreement said to reduce inflation variance (Alesina 1988), it is also thought to eliminate the politically induced output variability stemming from short-term electoral cycles (Alesina and Gatti 1995).

In short, whether one assumes politicians to be strictly office seeking or intent on delivering benefits to targeted constituencies, the credibility literature views an independent central bank as a uniformly beneficial outcome. Unable to credibly commit to low inflation on their own, politicians instead delegate authority over monetary policy to an independent agency that can do this for them. And because this commitment yields credibility, central bank independence is thought to yield anti-inflation policies at—on average—no real costs.

This "efficiency" view of central bank autonomy has been bolstered in recent years by numerous empirical studies revealing an inverse relationship between central bank independence and inflation (cf. Bade and Parkin 1980; Alesina 1988; Cukierman 1992; Alesina and Summers 1993), as well as autonomy's ability to reduce preelectoral manipulation of the economy (Beck 1982; Clark et al. 1998). Without extensive empirical work to the contrary, many economists have come to conclude glibly that "having an independent central bank autonomy is like having a free lunch; there are benefits but no

13. In these so-called rational partisan models of macropolitical economy, economic agents set wages in the period prior to the election. But because they cannot know with 100 percent certainty which party is going to win the election, they cannot be sure about the expected rate of postelection inflation. The best they can do is to base their wage calculations on a weighted average of the expected inflation rates of both parties competing for office. Should a left-leaning party win the election and pursue a rate of inflation higher than the weighted average, there will therefore be a lag before the public adjusts, allowing for the temporary increase in output.

apparent costs in terms of macroeconomic performance" (Grilli, Masciandaro, and Tabellini 1991, 375).

## The Redistributive Challenge

The bottom line according to the credibility literature is that politicians create autonomous central banks in order to solve a commitment problem, with the result that society is left unambiguously better off. The validity of this perspective hinges critically on the assumption that central bank reform is necessarily cost free. Recent work in economics and political science challenges this assumption, opening the door for a more contentious—and in my view, more compelling—interpretation of central bank reform.

There are two reasons to question the validity of the credibility hypothesis as the sole explanation for central bank reform. The first is theoretical. The credibility literature assumes that all politicians have the same incentives to undertake central bank reform. This is true even in some of the more recent work that explicitly incorporates partisan disagreements over the ideal mix of inflation and unemployment. And yet, it is not immediately obvious why one should necessarily assume such symmetry on the part of political actors. The implicit assumption behind the rational partisan models is that the long-term credibility benefits that flow from central bank independence should outweigh any short-term benefits to be derived from manipulating the Phillips curve. But why should this necessarily be the case, particularly for parties on the left?

After all, while inflationary variance is surely costly to any sitting government, as these models suggest, one must evaluate this cost against the potential political gains to be had from being able to engineer these short-term postelectoral booms. As long as voters are willing to reward left-wing political parties for such behavior, it is not at all clear why these parties would want to sign on to an institutional arrangement that removes this resource from their political arsenal. And even if we were to accept the additional claim that left-leaning political parties value an independent central bank's ability to reduce politically induced output variability, these models say nothing about the Rogoff-style output variability that is due to unforeseen productivity shocks. Given differing weights on nominal and real outcomes, there is no question that the greater real variance induced by such economic shocks should be more painful to the left than to the right. The overall effect of central bank independence on output stabilization is thus at best ambiguous—if not out-and-out costly— for the parties of the left.

In addition to this theoretical rationale, there is a second, more empirical reason to suspect that not all political actors are likely to share the same enthusiasm about central bank reform: the noninflationary consequences of central bank independence are still remarkably unclear (Pollard 1994; Eijffinger and De Haan 1996). Despite its reputation as a "free lunch," we still know very little about autonomy's long-term impact on growth, unemployment, and budget deficits. And what we do know suggests that central bank independence may actually prove costly for more left-leaning actors, at least under certain circumstances.

Of these, growth is the most benign case. Most empirical studies have found that a higher degree of central bank independence is generally not associated with greater variation of economic growth, thus confirming the view that independent central banks are less likely to engage in stop-and-go cycles (Alesina and Summers 1993; Eijffinger and Schaling 1993; Walsh 1994). But while it may be tempting to further assume that—because of its related effects on inflation—independence should also lead to higher long-term growth rates, the empirical evidence seems to show that it is not associated with either higher costs or greater benefits in terms of economic growth (cf. Grilli, Masciandaro, and Tabellini 1991; De Haan and Sturm 1992; Alesina and Summers 1993).[14] Although far from an indictment of autonomy, the lack of a significant positive relationship between central bank independence and growth is likely to leave most left-leaning politicians indifferent, rendering their views of autonomy much more contingent on how it impinges upon other important macroeconomic variables.

In this regard, a far more compelling case about autonomy's potential real costs can be made in the realm of unemployment. While Alesina and Summers (1993) have argued that central bank independence has no adverse unemployment effects, their evidence is statistically quite rudimentary, based solely on correlations among a handful of industrial nations. More sophisticated empirical studies reveal that even where central bank autonomy has been shown to have a positive relationship with low unemployment over time, this has not been due exclusively to the independence of the central bank. It instead hinges on the interaction of central bank independence with other variables such as government partisanship (Way 2000), the sectoral employment structure (Franzese 1994), and/or the structure of coordinated wage bargaining in a given country (cf. Hall 1994; Hall and Franzese 1998; Iversen 1998). While the theoretical specifications and empirical conclusions

14. There are two exceptions. De Long and Summers (1992) find evidence in favor of a positive relationship between central bank autonomy and growth, while Cukierman et al. (1993) come to the same conclusion for LDCs when the relationship is measured with behavioral indicators.

differ across these models, all concur that central bank independence does not necessarily come free of adverse employment effects—a result that cannot be overlooked in the context of redistributive struggles over the economy.

If left-leaning governments have reason to be suspicious of central bank autonomy with respect to its impact on growth and unemployment, this is all the more true of budget deficits. For to the extent that an independent central bank can credibly threaten to make issuing government debt more costly (Franzese 1996) this would seem reason alone to bias left-leaning governments against autonomy. While it is difficult to pull anything systematic out of the empirical research to date, it does seem to be the case that while an independent central bank cannot prevent a government from creating a budget deficit, it may have some restraining influence on fiscal policy (Eijffinger and De Haan 1996, 40). At the very least, its ambiguity on this front is likely to engender caution.[15]

Finally, in addition to the uncertainty surrounding the long-term real effects of central bank reform, there is also the possibility that increased autonomy may actually yield short-term output losses. This is at least the thrust of a growing body of literature on the so-called sacrifice ratio, which suggests that changes in the degree of central bank independence affect the Phillips curve in a manner that exacerbates the short-term trade-off between output and inflation (Ball, Mankiw, and Romer 1988; Ball 1994; Walsh 1995a).[16] Recent work on the European Community (EC) has confirmed that those EC countries with greater central bank independence have also experienced higher short-run costs of disinflation (Debelle and Fischer 1994; Walsh 1995a; Jordan 1997b). This distinction between the short run and the long run is not trivial, since while most economic arguments are about the long run, politics is about the short run. Knowing that central bank autonomy brings with it the promise of output penalties, left-leaning politicians may not wish to endure these short-term political costs of an independent central bank.

---

15. For example, Parkin (1987) and Masciandaro and Tabellini (1988) find some tentative correlational evidence for a negative relationship between central bank autonomy and the level of budget deficits in the advanced industrial countries, but Grilli, Masciandaro, and Tabellini (1991) find no such relationship when they include political variables in their regression equation. Pollard (1994) finds no significant relationship between independence and the level of government deficits but does find a significant negative relationship between independence and variance of budget deficits as a percentage of GDP.

16. The sacrifice ratio can be defined as output loss because of inflation reduction. It is generally thought to be affected by the degree of wage rigidity in the economy (higher levels of wage rigidity lead to a slower adjustment of wages, thus raising the costs of disinflation) and by the average inflation rate (at lower levels of inflation, less frequent price and wage adjustments induce a higher output loss per percentage point disinflation).

In light of these theoretical and empirical considerations, we see how central bank autonomy shifts from being an issue of valence to one of positions (Butler and Stokes 1974). Rather than being something that all actors welcome equally, central bank autonomy might instead be perceived as benefiting those actors who prefer low inflation and disadvantaging those who favor more political control of the economy. Once we accept this more differentiated view of politicians' inflationary motives, our expectations about the incentives to undertake central bank reform shift accordingly. Instead of reflecting some sort of preelectoral compromise between parties with divergent ideologies—as Alesina and Gatti (1995) suggest—central bank autonomy may instead serve as a means through which incumbent politicians with conservative policy preferences seek to limit the policy choices of future governments.[17]

## Central Bank Reform Reconsidered: The Logic of Imposition

The notion that the tenure security of officeholders might affect their propensity to undertake central bank reform is not new to the literature on central bank autonomy. Goodman (1991, 1992), for example, argues that the more incumbent leaders fear that their grip on government is vulnerable, the greater the incentive to increase the independence of the central bank and thereby institutionalize a bias toward monetary restriction in the future. Cukierman (1994) has also argued that incumbent politicians may seek to impose a higher level of central bank independence as a means of limiting the opposition's ability to spend on public goods that the incumbent does not prioritize. The implication behind both of these arguments, as with my own, is that politicians are more likely to cede control over monetary policy when their time in office is limited.[18]

17. Alesina and Tabellini (1990) make this sort of argument to explain how a conflict between opposing parties over spending priorities induces incumbents to use public debt as a device for restricting the composition of future government spending, while Persson and Svensson (1989) develop a similar model to explain the level of such spending. These so-called replacement risk models (Franzese 1996) analyze the case where more conservative governments engage in a behavior that is otherwise anathema to their policy goals—that is, inflation—in order to force successor governments to bring debt back to the socially optimal level. In contrast, I suggest that conservative incumbents will use a policy instrument that is otherwise consistent with their policy preferences to affect the policy choices of future rulers. See the subsequent discussion.

18. Both Posen (1993) and De Haan and Van't Hag (1995) reject the importance of government instability on central bank independence in empirical tests on the advanced industrial countries. But since they do not examine the interactive effects between partisanship and government turnover, it is unclear how their results impinge upon the present argument.

Where I part company with these authors is in their assumption that such an argument should hold regardless of the macroeconomic preferences of the party in power.[19] Such a claim implies that facing an imminent loss of power, politicians attach the same price to being denied such flexibility through an autonomous central bank. But precisely for the reasons outlined earlier, parties of different ideological stripes should not value the trade-off between rules versus discretion equally. Rather, governments can be expected to differ systematically in their relative willingness to incur the costs of creating an autonomous central bank.[20]

Consider the case of right-leaning parties. In normal times, it seems unlikely that they would need to create an autonomous bank in order to secure their preferred policies. After all, they already share a natural bias toward monetary conservatism. But once we add political turnover to the equation, their decision-making calculus should change. Aware of the left's ability to generate short-term expansionary cycles, right-leaning politicians might begin to worry about the prospect of such inflationary bouts in the future. Fearing the use of monetary policy for political ends, they are likely to view central bank autonomy as a welcome opportunity to safeguard a set of outcomes associated with macroeconomic stability.[21]

In contrast, parties of the left facing the same threat of "replacement risk" should have less incentive to insulate the central bank or perhaps no incentive at all. They are instead likely to view autonomy as a liability to the extent that it is likely to augment the costs of generating short-term expansionary cycles and in that it may also have other adverse long-term real effects on the economy. The best they can do is to try to maintain perfect discretion and hope that left-leaning governments are elected to office from time to time.[22]

19. It is true that Goodman (1991, 1992) also emphasizes the importance of a conservative societal coalition in explaining the likelihood of central bank reform. But he fails to link the presence of such interests to the policy preferences of incumbent politicians.

20. For a similar line of reasoning, see Zielinsky 1995. Clark (1994a) also notes the importance of both party competition and incumbent party preferences for the creation of an autonomous central bank. But since he fails to specify whether or not the politicians in his model are Downsian vote maximizers or are differentiated along more traditional left/right lines, it is difficult to interpret his results. An interesting adaptation of this sort of approach that emphasizes how informational asymmetries between parties of divergent ideological stripes may condition central bank reform can be found in Bernhard 1998.

21. Franzese (1999, 32–33) has speculated that a similar fear may have driven the recent spate of central bank reforms in Europe by governments that do not otherwise seem to suffer from a credibility shortage.

22. To be sure, one might argue that precisely because of their tendency to privilege electoral and constituency considerations over low inflation, left-leaning governments are most in need of the credibility boost supplied by an autonomous central bank (Simmons 1996). I address this point in the next chapter.

Viewing the situation from this more political perspective, we can at least cast doubt on the credibility literature's claim that governments choose central bank autonomy exclusively to tie their own hands. Rather, it seems at least plausible that they may also seek to tie the hands of their successors. In keeping with Moe (1990a, 1990b), then, right-leaning governments might use the power of office in order to impose their inflationary preferences on their successors. And future governments would have no choice but to reluctantly accept this set of economic outcomes.[23]

## Central Bank Autonomy: The Developing Countries

### Old Wine, New Bottles: Credibility Arguments in the Developing World

If the literature on macropolitical economy lends plausibility to this more conflictual view of central banks in the advanced industrial democracies, a similar argument should also hold true for the developing world. Unfortunately, the redistributive perspective has yet to take hold. While there has been comparatively little research on the politics of central bank reform in developing countries to date, what does exist largely echoes the themes of the literature in the developed world.

One twist is that there is more emphasis given to the international environment (Siklos 1995; Maxfield 1997). Maxfield (1997), for example, argues that developing countries are likely to undergo central bank reform in order to shore up credibility with foreign creditors and investors. According to this logic, the amount of independence afforded the central bank should vary with governments' perceptions of their need for international finance. Maxfield thus offers a slight modification to the conventional credibility literature in that the economic audience to whom governments signal is no longer domestic but international. When all is said and done, however, the basic intuition is exactly the same: governments choose central bank autonomy to signal a credible commitment to low inflation.

The influence of the credibility literature has been equally strong among those arguments privileging domestic variables. Maxfield (1997, 46–47) argues that where national leaders are insecure in office, they have incentives to wrest control from the central bank in order to buy political support, even when this may militate against their ordinary creditworthiness objectives. And regime change is only thought to exacerbate this dynamic by providing

23. Chapter 3 explains why such reforms should be difficult to undo.

incentives for elites to stay in power as long as possible by manipulating the central bank (Cukierman 1992, 445–47; De Haan and Siermann 1994; Cukierman and Webb 1995). Whether the relevant political event is an election or a transition, then, the conventional wisdom thus suggests that central bank autonomy should be less likely to occur in the prior period. Like many of their counterparts in the literature on the advanced industrial countries, such arguments are predicated on the notion that all politicians have the same incentives to inflate when confronted with the prospect of political turnover.

Despite efforts to tailor explanations for central bank reform to the distinctive contours of the developing world, the familiar adage "old wine, new bottles" seems all too apt. The principal motivating force is still one of signaling a commitment to low inflation, albeit to an international audience. And when pressed to explain exactly how domestic factors come to bear on central bank reform, authors simply revert to the opportunistic business cycle logic characteristic of much of the credibility literature.

## An Alternative Approach: Distributional Conflicts in the Developing World

There are several reasons to find this credibility-based reasoning suspect in a developing country context. Let us examine first the empirical evidence. It is difficult to argue with the fact that developing countries face severe external constraints that make them vulnerable to the whims of the international economy. In the last two decades, the third world has witnessed a debt crisis of massive proportions and an unprecedented movement of capital and goods across borders. If LDC governments are to attract foreign capital and reap the rewards of a liberalized trade regime, they can ill afford to ignore demands by powerful economic actors for institutional guarantees of price stability (Dornbusch and Marcus 1991; Stallings 1992). Maxfield's point is thus well taken: credibility arguments are persuasive when applied to the LDCs.

But if these international economic pressures were the sole determinant of central bank autonomy, then virtually all developing countries would have autonomous central banks.[24] When the empirical data are examined, how-

24. This assumes that these pressures have been more or less constant across countries. This is clearly not always the case, and we can expect that some countries—such as those that have experienced bouts of hyperinflation—have been more vulnerable to outside pressures than others. Such exceptions notwithstanding, it seems reasonable to posit that at least since the onset of the debt crisis in 1982, international economic forces have played an increasingly strong and more or less uniform role in encouraging pro-market economic reforms in developing countries.

ever, it is clear that they do not. As is the case with the advanced industrial countries, we observe instead tremendous variation. As table 2.1 shows, this variation is readily apparent whether one chooses to employ formal/legal or behavioral measures of central bank independence.[25]

Consider the case of four of the most commonly studied Latin American countries—Brazil, Chile, Mexico, and Peru—all of which faced strong international economic pressures at various times since the early 1980s. While both Chile and Mexico increased the autonomy of their central banks in the last decade, Brazil and Peru continue to have highly dependent central banks. Nor does Maxfield's (1997, 50–70) cross-national empirical chapter provide convincing support that international credibility motives are the sole factor driving what variation does exist. The treatment of data is highly sketchy, and there is no evidence for a causal link between the extent of international integration and the move toward increased autonomy across continents. At best, the chapter serves to confirm the fact that central bank reforms in LDCs have increased considerably in recent years, concurrent with an international economic environment in which developing countries are in greater need of creditworthiness. While an important contribution, Maxfield's work should serve as the starting point—and not the denouement—for further research on this subject.[26]

In short, while international credibility is surely part of the story in explaining the recent trend toward increased autonomy in LDCs, the empirical data do not bear out the thesis that international credibility alone can explain variation across countries. What the evidence instead suggests is that some developing country governments must find it preferable to maintain political control over the central bank. A second reason to question the conventional credibility-based wisdom, then, is that it is also guilty of the efficiency logic noted earlier. Whether the context is a fully established democracy or a fledgling neo-democracy, it is questionable that central bank independence will have the same appeal for all politicians.[27]

---

25. Formal measures of independence involve the legal relationship between central bank decision makers and the government, while behavioral indicators attempt to capture the less visible aspects of the central bank's actual behavior. See chapter 3.

26. The same can be said for arguments that might attribute central bank reform in developing countries to the force of international ideas. According to this line of reasoning, powerful international institutions—such as the World Bank and IMF—foster and fund the spread of market-oriented ideas (such as central bank autonomy) to decision leaders in developing countries (Sikkink 1991; Dominguez 1996). Like the international credibility argument, however, an international ideas argument also fails to account for the cross-national variation we observe. International support for a conservative monetary regime dates back to well before 1980 (Drake 1990) and has only increased subsequently. And yet some countries have changed the legal status of their central banks while others have not.

27. Clark and Maxfield (1996) have developed an international signaling model that

**TABLE 2.1. Alternative Measures of Central Bank Independence, 1980–89**

| Country | Behavioral | Formal |
|---|---|---|
| Greece | 0.8 | 0.55 |
| Egypt | 0.7 | 0.49 |
| Turkey | 0.6 | 0.46 |
| Chile | 0.2 | 0.46 |
| Nicaragua | 0.6 | 0.45 |
| Kenya | 0.8 | 0.44 |
| Honduras | 0.9 | 0.43 |
| Philippines | 0.8 | 0.43 |
| Peru | 0.7 | 0.43 |
| Venezuela | 0.5 | 0.43 |
| Portugal | 0.7 | 0.41 |
| Ethiopia | 0.9 | 0.40 |
| Argentina | 0.0 | 0.40 |
| Israel | 0.8 | 0.39 |
| Uganda | 0.8 | 0.38 |
| Nigeria | 0.9 | 0.37 |
| Malaysia | 0.8 | 0.36 |
| Mexico | 0.7 | 0.34 |
| India | 0.7 | 0.34 |
| Botswana | 0.6 | 0.33 |
| Zambia | 0.5 | 0.33 |
| Ghana | 0.8 | 0.31 |
| Romania | 0.8 | 0.30 |
| Singapore | 0.4 | 0.29 |
| Thailand | 0.9 | 0.27 |
| Indonesia | 0.8 | 0.27 |
| Colombia | 0.8 | 0.27 |
| Korea | 0.5 | 0.27 |
| South Africa | 0.8 | 0.25 |
| Uruguay | 0.7 | 0.24 |
| Poland | 0.5 | 0.24 |
| Panama | 0.8 | 0.22 |
| Taiwan | 0.8 | 0.21 |
| Pakistan | 0.7 | 0.21 |
| Brazil | 0.2 | 0.21 |
| Zimbabwe | 0.9 | 0.20 |
| Yugoslavia | 0.8 | 0.17 |
| Morocco | 0.8 | 0.14 |
| Hungary | 0.9 | 0.10 |

*Source:* Cukierman, Webb, and Neyapti 1993, 364-65. Reprinted with permission.

*Note:* Formal measures are based on the index presented in Cukierman 1992. Behavioral measures are based on central bank governor turnover rates. Note that in order to facilitate comparison between the two measures, the behavioral measures have been transformed so that higher numbers indicate greater central bank independence.

To be sure, the redistributive game surrounding autonomy should look somewhat different in the developing world. For starters, the central inflationary motive is likely to shift from increasing employment to generating revenue so as to redistribute wealth and/or stimulate demand (Cukierman 1992, 47–82). Because LDC governments lack well-functioning capital markets and/or an effective system of taxation, they tend to rely more heavily on the central bank's ability to print money as their primary source of revenue. By printing money, the central bank is able to extract real purchasing power from the public (seignorage). And the way the government collects this hidden source of revenue is through deficit financing via the central bank, which constitutes the main source of inflation in the developing world (Fry 1997). At a first cut, then, the political struggle in LDCs is likely to center around who wins and loses when the central bank is no longer able to freely monetize government debts.

But it is also the case that central banks have traditionally served as a sort of "development bank" in the third world. Through the use of targeted credits, interest rate ceilings, and other forms of financial repression, central banks have historically been used to prop up certain firms, sectors, and industries favored by the state (Haggard and Lee 1993). The creation of an autonomous central bank typically does away with such practices. On the one hand, it allows interest rates to be freely determined by the market (Haggard and Maxfield 1993, 305). On the other hand, it also puts an end to the deficit spending that has often financed such subsidies, whether directly (through budgetary transfers) or indirectly (through the rediscounting operations of the central bank in which seignorage gains are passed on to favored borrowers through the commercial banking system) (Haggard and Maxfield 1993, 315). A second dimension to the political struggle in LDCs is thus likely to take shape around the financial liberalization that tends to accompany autonomy and around who stands to win or lose when the central bank terminates its role as a vehicle of preferential credit.

Once we account for these adjustments, however, there is no reason to think that the potential for conflict over central bank autonomy should be any different in the developing world. And once we incorporate this redistributive dimension into the study of central bank reform in LDCs, we can also consider the plausibility of the sorts of insulation arguments advanced earlier in this chapter as an explanation for its occurrence. At the very least,

recognizes that states may differ in the relative weight they attach to price stability (and, as such, the desirability of having an independent central bank). But the overall thrust of the paper is still one of trying to determine the conditions under which signaling to international investors by either type of state is likely to result in a foreign capital inflow, rather than the prior—and arguably more fundamental—question of why some LDC states are willing to forego central bank autonomy entirely.

the "tying successor hands" logic ought to be relevant in one political context of considerable importance in the developing world: democracies in transition from authoritarian rule.

Returning to the delegation literature with which we began this chapter, the key issue on the table is turnover of power. Normally, we associate turnover with democratic societies, where the existence of regularly scheduled elections provides the mechanism for the turnover of power between opposing forces. We do not think much (by definition) about turnover in the context of authoritarian societies. But there is a moment in authoritarian rule where turnover does become relevant, and that moment is the transition to a more democratic polity. For it is at this point when authoritarians need to begin to think about the possibility of change and what this change will mean for how their preferred policies are likely to fare in the future.

For a variety of reasons enumerated in the following chapter, I will argue that democratization brings with it the prospect of a more interventionist economic future. To the extent that this proves threatening to the interests of certain authoritarian elites, the exaggerated nature of turnover entailed in a regime change ought to increase autonomy's value as a strategic instrument.[28] Rather than focusing on the short-term support they can buy through the manipulation of the economy—as the existing literature suggests—those elites who fear losing power permanently might well seek to tighten their control over monetary policy. In this way, central bank autonomy may serve as a means of insuring against the threat and uncertainty of democracy itself.[29]

28. Lohmann (1997) makes an analogous argument to suggest why Japan was likely to create an autonomous central bank post-1993, after the end of nearly forty years of single-party rule in Japan.

29. As noted earlier, what little empirical work has been carried out on the relationship between political instability and central bank independence in the developing world would seem to lend provisional support to the opposite conclusion: that greater political instability leads to less independence on average (e.g., Cukierman 1992; De Haan and Siermann 1994; Cukierman and Webb 1995). But this work is far from conclusive, relying as it does on different groups of countries, divergent measures of central bank independence, and various proxies for political instability. And, more important, none of these works controls for the policy preferences of the regime in power.

CHAPTER 3

# Preemptive Strike

## Central Bank Autonomy in the Transition from Authoritarian Rule

The previous chapter provided an extensive discussion of current thinking on central banks in the advanced industrial democracies. To date, the conventional wisdom has posited autonomous central banks as structures of mutual advantage and efficiency. In contrast, I argued for a more explicitly political view of central bank autonomy that emphasizes policy conflict and the unequal distribution of costs and benefits. I concluded by noting the relevance of this more redistributive perspective for the study of central bank reform in the less developed countries.

But even if this alternative paradigm is generalizable to the countries of the developing world, a straightforward application is not as simple as it seems. Rather, this perspective must be modified to accommodate the distinctive institutional context in question. For the study at hand—which focuses on the "moment" of a transition from authoritarian rule—this means that a few quite fundamental changes are in order.

First, the central actors are invariably different. In the advanced industrial democracies, the politicians in various models tend to be presidents, legislators, and/or political parties. In a transition to democracy, the central divisions are much more rudimentary: the authoritarians presently in power and the democrats who challenge their continued hold on office.[1] The relationship between turnover and insulation also shifts accordingly. The normal turnover characteristic of regularly scheduled democratic elections also no longer applies. We are instead concerned with the incentives facing incumbent elites when the much more dramatic prospect of regime change is on the horizon. Finally, some thought must be given to the sorts of distributional conflicts that central bank autonomy is likely to engender in the third world. As noted at the end of chapter 2, it seems unlikely that this battle will take the form of the well-known inflation versus unemployment debate. The political struggle in developing countries is more likely to center around the central bank's role in facilitating or impeding deficit spending and preferential credit policies.

1. For simplicity's sake, I treat both the authoritarians and the democrats in this model as unitary actors, recognizing that in reality, there are likely to be divisions within each. Where relevant, such divisions are taken up in the case studies.

While such changes are meant to capture the distinctive institutional environment of the transition from authoritarian rule, the basic ideas remain the same. The overall environment is one of uncertainty about the future state of the economy. Incumbent elites are motivated not by credibility concerns but by fear of what their opponents might do once elected to office. And the power holders' response to this fear is to design structures that protect their interests against the vicissitudes of domestic political change.

To address some of these points in a more systematic fashion, this chapter develops an argument to explain the choice and persistence of central bank autonomy in the transition from authoritarian rule. This argument is presented in four stages. I begin with a general model of transitional insulation in which I outline the relationship between democratization and institutional change. This argument then is applied to the realm of central banks. I explain why democracy may prove threatening to the economic interests of certain authoritarian rulers, when this might prompt them to delegate authority to an independent central bank, and why, once created, these autonomous institutions are likely to remain. This chapter concludes with a discussion of how the independent and dependent variables will be operationalized in this study.

## Transitions and Turnover: The Insulation Incentive

### The Drive to Insulate

The previous chapter suggested why an anticipated turnover in power might prompt politicians to use institutional reform to protect their interests. The claim here is that a change of regime drastically increases this insulation incentive. This implies that the turnover entailed in a regime change is more threatening than routine democratic turnover. Why is this so?

To begin with, this is not an everyday loss of power. While incumbent politicians never welcome defeat, releasing the reins of power is likely to be particularly momentous for authoritarian elites who have had an entire state apparatus at their fingertips. For unlike their counterparts in first world democracies, who can expect someday to return to power, this may well be the last "hurrah" for exiting authoritarian elites. If they want to influence the future course of policy, the time to do so is now or never.

Second, a regime transition also heightens the climate of overall uncertainty (Przeworski 1986, 1991). While shifts between governing coalitions within advanced industrial democracies occur within some known (if varying) parameters, there is no blueprint for change between two forms of rule.

In the words of two famous scholars of transitions, authoritarian elites cannot be sure "how—or for that matter, by whom—the normal political game will be played in the future" (O'Donnell and Schmitter 1986, 66).

Above all, however, a regime change is threatening insofar as it jeopardizes the authoritarians' preferred policy outcomes. The hierarchical nature of decision making under authoritarian rule means that, ceteris paribus, these governments are more or less free to make policy choices as they see fit. Democracy, in contrast, requires that more groups will obtain a voice in the polity. In particular, previously marginalized groups whose demands have been limited or repressed can be expected to try to shift policy to their favor. By definition, then, the onset of democracy offers greater opportunities for a change in the direction of policy.

In the wake of this heightened climate of threat, authoritarian elites have an incentive to think about how the onset of democracy is likely to affect their interests in the future. One might be inclined to ask why authoritarian rulers should care about the future at all. If it is true that they are losing power, and may never again regain it, what are their incentives to care about what happens once they are gone? I argue that such skepticism reflects an excessively narrow view of the incentives facing authoritarian leaders and of what happens to them when they lose power.

Short of the rare case of violent revolution, most exiting authoritarian leaders do not disappear entirely. Rather, they can expect to be citizens in the new polity. They will therefore retain an interest in the system and be vulnerable to how that system affects them. This could be due to a variety of reasons. For example, the authoritarians might be concerned about their professional future or their personal economic well-being. They might also be beholden to certain special interests whose welfare will be affected by democracy. Or they might have a collective investment in the particular merit of a certain set of policy ideas. The relevant question is thus not why they should care about the future but rather what they plan to do about it.

In normal times, we would not expect authoritarian regimes to delegate authority as a means of protecting their interests. Given the choice between a constrained and an unconstrained equilibrium, they should always choose the latter and wait until the final period before giving up any power. There are several reasons to believe that insulation should not be a dominant strategy for authoritarian elites.

First, the nature of hierarchy is such that the creation of an independent agency is inevitably characterized by principal-agent problems (Jensen 1983). Even under the most carefully monitored circumstances, some degree of slippage inevitably occurs. As long as the authoritarians are secure in their hold on power, they should therefore want to structure an agency in the most transparent way possible to allow for smooth, easy political oversight down the road. That way, they can make sure that the agency does not get off track and pursue its own objectives rather than those of the politicians who designed it. Absent a threat from their political opponents, it is not clear why an authoritarian government would want to deny itself this important degree of institutional leverage. After all, insulation only comes at the cost of ineffective organization and reducing their own ongoing control over the agency (Moe 1990a, 132–35).

In addition to these monitoring problems, agency independence also limits flexibility. Committing oneself to follow the dictates of a formal set of rules invariably entails a certain loss of discretion on the part of the government. In particular, those in power lose the ability to use the agency to respond to unforeseen contingencies. This observation is, of course, at the heart of the debate over "rules versus discretion" that first surfaced in the wake of the early credibility literature (Kydland and Prescott 1977). It is again unclear why an authoritarian government would want to risk this loss of responsiveness unless it faced a worse alternative—control by someone else.

A third and final reason to expect that the basic incentive for insulation should be absent without the threat of regime change has to do with the expectations effects that flow from institutional creation. Once established, rules create expectations in the minds of other actors, who conduct themselves on the basis of the existence of a certain set of procedures. It thus becomes quite costly for governments to violate such rules without incurring the wrath of their partners in exchange (Milgrom, North, and Weingast 1990; Lohmann 1998b). The authoritarians are likely to factor in such expectations effects before they choose to institutionalize a set of guidelines in the first place (Cukierman, Kiguel, and Liviatan 1992). Knowing that they may be obliged to respect the rules of whatever they create, they should be reluctant to cede authority to an independent agency unless they have no choice.[2]

For all of these reasons—political control problems, the loss of discretion, and the binding nature of rules—an authoritarian government should not want to risk creating an independent agency prior to realized concerns about a transition. Our story, however, begins at a point in time when authoritarians know that they are likely to lose control of the polity at some point in the future. This knowledge changes the decision-making calculus of authoritarian leaders with respect to insulation. For once we add political

2. To be sure, fewer veto players to check their arbitrary use of authority clearly affords authoritarian regimes greater leeway to violate existing arrangements when it suits their interests (North and Weingast 1989). But precisely because they are aware of the reputational costs attached to violating an established set of rules, they are unlikely to act on these incentives, or at least they risk punishment when they do.

turnover to the equation, the authoritarians begin to fear what will happen to their preferred policies when their enemies are in charge. Since their first best alternative is no longer an option—to stay in power and rule—they instead focus their energy on those aspects of the public domain they can hang on to under the new regime. They should logically choose those policy arenas that matter to them most.

In this way, insulation—while previously unpalatable—can become strategically desirable for exiting authoritarian rulers as a means of protecting their interests. By freezing their preferences in institutional structures before they leave office, the authoritarians attempt to maintain de facto influence—if not control—over certain spheres of policy once they are gone. In so doing, they deny their opponents a substantial niche of power under the new regime, thereby constraining the democrats to move within a set of preexisting programmatic parameters.

## Introducing Variation: The Intensity and Proximity of the Democratic Threat

The previous discussion suggests why the onset of democracy is likely to lead to insulating behavior on the part of exiting authoritarian elites. That said, not all transitions are going to be equally threatening or, by extension, warrant the same amount of insulation. We must, therefore, unpack this notion of threat in order to determine the different values it can take and its corresponding effects on the likelihood of insulation.

At a first cut, one factor likely to affect the incentive to insulate is the *intensity of threat,* or the extent to which the preferences of exiting authoritarian elites and incoming democrats are expected to diverge. As a general rule, we can think of the democrats' preferences as falling within a band of policy outcomes, centered on a point prediction of distance. This band is similar to a confidence interval. Sometimes, the successor government can be expected to be friendly. Future democratic leaders in such cases are likely to continue the policy preferences of previous rulers, and the corresponding incentives to insulate should be weak. In many cases, however, successors will be perceived as hostile and can be expected to pursue policies that deviate sharply from those of their predecessors. Where such marked preference incongruencies are expected to exist, the onset of democracy represents a strong threat. Under these circumstances, officeholders have a more powerful incentive to cement their interests in an institutional form.

But even where successor governments do have different policy priorities, it is not clear that the transition will always be met with an insulation response. Insulation will also depend on the *proximity of threat.* This dimension of the threat variable attempts to measure the relative imminence of the transition to democracy. In those cases where the authoritarians believe that they will never lose power—or will do so only at a relatively distant point in the future—they are unlikely to insulate at all. Rather, because of the various costs to insulation identified earlier (e.g., opportunities for slippage, expectations effects, etc.), the authoritarians are unlikely to bother assuming these costs unless the costs are "worth it." Conversely, if they face an imminent threat of democracy, then the authoritarians are more likely to discount such trade-offs and respond with a highly insulated institution.

In sum, the incentives to insulate will vary in accordance with the expected policy distance between the authoritarians and the democrats and the relative immediacy of democratization (see fig. 3.1). We should expect to witness no insulation when there is considerable policy affinity between the outgoing authoritarian and incoming democratic rulers and/or when the transition is sufficiently distant. In contrast, insulation is most likely to occur when there is strong preference divergence and regime change is looming. Note, however, that neither the intensity of threat nor its proximity is dichotomous in nature. Rather, both of these dimensions can assume a range of continuous values. This suggests that the resultant threat that they yield and the concomitant insulation are not "either/or" categories. The model can thus also account for instances of partial insulation.

To be sure, there will also be cases where the sudden and violent nature of the transition triggers a "flight" instinct on the part of incumbent elites. After all, one cannot expect to insulate overnight: it takes some time to design an institution that can effectively protect one's policy interests. Where they lack sufficient time, rather than insulate, the authoritarians are instead likely to take what they can get to maximize their personal safety and wealth before they are run out of town. This class of cases corresponds to a subset of those "mass ascendant" transitions in which sweeping change from below catches elites off guard (Karl 1990). As noted earlier, however, violent revolutions from below are rare. In most cases, exiting authoritarian elites can be expected to have some margin of maneuver within which to act defensively. These instances of unanticipated shock thus constitute an exception to the argument at hand, not the norm.

In short, expectations about the likely impact of turnover are important because they influence the extent to which incumbent elites need to worry about the future and, consequently, the degree of insulation they seek to obtain. Institutional outcomes are likely to be particularly affected by anticipation of a change in policy and the pace at which the transition takes place. These arguments should always hold—regardless of the specific insulation strategy at hand.

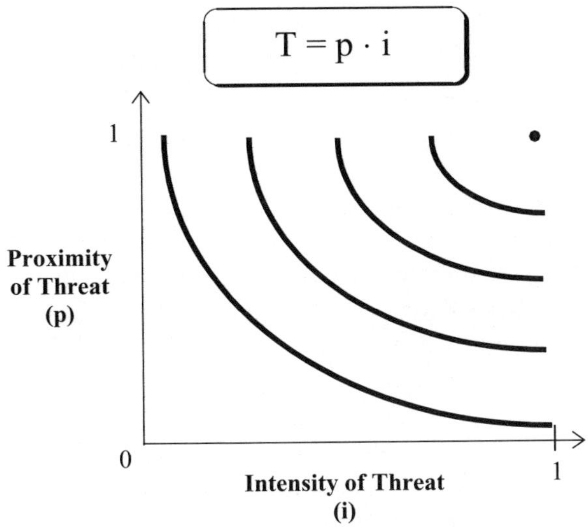


**Fig. 3.1. The degree of threat (*T*)**

## An Application: Actors, Interests, and the Demand for Autonomy

With this basic logic of transitional insulation in place, we can now examine the specific insulation strategy with which this book is concerned: central bank autonomy. In order to elucidate the insulation logic surrounding this institutional form, I begin by identifying the intensity of the threat: how the expected preference divergence between incoming democratic and outgoing authoritarian governments affects incentives regarding central bank reform. This requires an understanding of who the democrats are, what they want, and why this might be threatening to incumbent authoritarian elites.

### The Democrats

In this model, the democrats are the political parties of the democratic opposition around whom the democratizing coalition clusters once the transition is under way (O'Donnell and Schmitter 1986, 57–64). If all goes well, they can expect to be the incoming governments of the future democratic regime. Regardless of their ideological stripe, we can expect these opposition politicians to care about their prospects for election. They have, after all, been excluded from the political arena for a considerable period of time. They now have the opportunity not only to voice their opinions but also to govern.

Because they care about getting elected, the democrats have an incentive to respond to constituency concerns and to attempt to garner favor by pursuing policies that will receive a positive response from the electorate. This electoral motive has implications for the sorts of economic policies that they can be expected to endorse.

As a general rule, we should expect the democrats to favor policies that enable them to use the economy for political ends, ranging in scale from modest forms of intervention to more extreme populist measures. While this may seem like a somewhat controversial claim in light of the current era of neoliberal economic restructuring, we can delineate several theoretical and empirical reasons why this might be the case. By definition, the convocation of elections forces politicians to be more sensitive to unemployment and the redistribution of wealth and risk (Garrett and Lange 1996, 61–63). The increased level of political mobilization in new democracies leads to heightened social and economic expectations and increased distributional demands from all sectors of society. No matter who the relevant political actors are, they have incentives to choose policies that benefit social groups who recently obtained voice in the political arena and to redistribute wealth downward (Alesina 1994, 45–47). As one moves from no elections to elections, then, changes should occur in the amount of government spending (increases), in the type of spending (more welfare-oriented expenditures), and in the structure of taxation (a more progressive system).

A second reason to expect politicians in new democracies to favor maintaining some degree of discretion over the economy is their vulnerability to the risk of being overthrown. This is especially true in those cases where groups and constituencies who support the old regime have a voice and a political-military presence. Newly minted politicians are likely to try to use macroeconomic policy to buy out public support by distributing benefits to general allies, rather than risking more austere policies that might further alienate the public (Haggard and Kaufman 1989, 59–60; Ames 1987, 25–27, 42). At the very least, the possibility of a military coup is likely to give them shorter time horizons where the economy is concerned (Geddes 1994a, 13).

A final reason to think that politicians in new democracies may be more interventionist than their first world counterparts has to do with the time horizons of voters. Because they live in countries characterized by low levels of income, extreme poverty, and the absence of extensive social welfare systems to shield them from economic downturns, voters in the developing world typically have shorter time horizons (Haggard and Kaufman 1995, 157–58). This assumption underlies most contemporary models of policy reform in the developing world, which are predicated on what is known as the "*J*-curve" (Hellman 1998, 206–8). According to this model, even while neoliberal reforms may be good for the majority in the long run, they impose a variety of costs in the short run such as rising unemployment, falling wages, and higher prices on state-subsidized goods (Przeworski 1991, 136–262; Bresser Pereira 1993, 60–62). And because economic agents are presumed to be myopic, they will tend to focus on the short-run costs of such policies, rather than their long-term benefits (Edwards 1990, 5; Sachs 1990). This literature therefore predicts that voters should rationally resist market-style reforms, either because they know that they stand to lose from such policies (Bresser Pereira, Maravall, and Przeworski 1993, 2; Piñera 1994, 227; Nelson 1994, 476–77) or because they are uncertain of how these costs will be distributed and/or fear that they may be in the "losing" group (Alesina and Drazen 1991; Fernandez and Rodrik 1991).

Recent work has challenged the assumptions behind the *J*-curve, suggesting that voters may in fact be more "intertemporal" than they are myopic and hence willing to trade off short-term costs for the promise of long-term gains (Stokes 1996) or at least to view stabilization as a necessary evil (Rodrik 1996). But precisely because democracy is so new, politicians may not know where voters fall and thus may assume them to be less conservative than they actually are.[3] And even where voters have shown themselves to be willing to support neoliberal reform, that support has been highly conditional, dependent on sustained economic improvement (Nelson 1992, 256; Stokes 2001, chap. 5). Where market-oriented reforms have not led to improved economic performance, voters have been all too willing to punish incumbents, as the elections in Venezuela (1993, 1998) and Poland (1995) attest. Such data suggest that even where politicians do embrace market-oriented reforms, they should be reluctant to do so too wholeheartedly lest they deprive themselves of crucial levers of control with which to guarantee their survival.

In brief, there are a variety of theoretical reasons to believe that newly empowered democratic leaders should favor a more interventionist economic agenda. There will naturally be variation, and not all democrats will be equally motivated to intervene in the economy to the same extent. It is also true that in today's international economic environment, it is increasingly unlikely that any new government would try to pursue an extreme populist program that might trigger capital flight and/or discourage private sector investment. But even where the democrats are not rabid populists, we can still safely say that politicians in emergent democracies are likely to want greater flexibility over the economy in the short term to appeal to different constituencies.

3. The fact that where left-leaning politicians have chosen to undertake neoliberal reforms in Latin America they have frequently concealed their programmatic agendas suggests that politicians believe voters are shortsighted (Stokes 2001).

At the very least, this hypothesis seems borne out by the empirical evidence available. There is no question that in recent years, radical trade liberalizations, fiscal adjustments, and institutional reforms have been implemented by democratic regimes around the globe, often by what were historically populist and interventionist parties (Remmer 1990; Bates and Kreuger 1993; Geddes 1994b). Many have concluded that left-leaning democrats may actually have a comparative advantage at implementing neoliberal reforms precisely because their historical opposition to such policies allows them to more credibly signal to voters why it may be necessary to endure these policies' short-run costs (Cukierman and Tomassi 1998). But while this "it takes a Nixon to go to China" logic may well be an explanation for why left-leaning governments are well positioned to undertake painful adjustment measures, it says nothing about the extent to which they actually carry out those measures. As in the advanced industrial world, the seeming convergence toward markets across the ideological spectrum may mask some important underlying nuances (Rodrik 1997; Garrett 1998).

We know, for example, that historically democratic regimes have spent consistently more than their authoritarian counterparts, particularly on social programs (Ames 1987). We also know that politicians in transitional democracies are more likely to resort to deficit spending and expansionary policies than are politicians in established democracies (Haggard and Kaufman 1989). And even in those Latin American cases where politicians have embraced radical market-oriented reform programs, these leaders have frequently reverted to more classically populist measures in order to obtain electoral victory in the second round of elections (Roberts 1995). In short, democratic governments may not be any less equipped to impose costly neoliberal adjustment packages than their authoritarian counterparts. But they do appear less likely to cut social spending for the sake of reducing the public deficit, even when controlling for the exigencies of the post–debt crisis era (Hunter and Brown 1998). This last finding, in particular, is relevant to the argument advanced in this chapter.

## The Authoritarians

Regardless of where the democrats actually fall on the interventionist continuum, equally important for the argument at hand is what the authoritarians believe about what the onset of democracy is likely to mean for the future of the economy. In other words, we are as much interested in what the democrats want in objective terms as in what the authoritarians fear that they want and in how this fear conditions the likelihood of central bank reform. In order to assess why the "specter of intervention" inherent in democratization might be threatening to existing authoritarian elites, we need to turn now to consider the policy preferences of the authoritarians.

In this model, the economic preferences of the authoritarians are determined by the interests of dominant economic actors (capital)—whether market oriented or protectionist. As Linz (1975) notes, authoritarian regimes must accommodate the interests of some constituency in order to survive; they are accountable to someone, if only the military establishment or other sectors within the state elite. In positing that this constituency is capital, I am merely adapting Lindblom's famous "privileged position of business" argument about capitalist democracies to an authoritarian setting (Lindblom 1977).[4] But whereas under democratic rule, voters' needs and interests often mitigate the power of business, this tension is considerably diluted under authoritarian rule. In effect, capital becomes the government's constituency.

Naturally, the "democratic" economic scenario described previously will not always constitute a threat to outgoing authoritarian elites. This should depend upon the type of capital that they represent. Drawing on Frieden (1991a) and Frieden and Rogowski (1996), the model posits two types of capital. For those authoritarian regimes that cater to the interests of sheltered and asset-specific capital, for example, there is no reason to fear the future in a strictly economic sense. Sheltered sectors contain those firms that produce for the country's internal consumption and whose productive activity is predominantly affected by domestic economic policies. Asset-specific firms are those holders of fixed assets that can only shift their production from one activity to another at great cost. In both cases, these types of capital encompass the protectionist sectors of the economy: import-competing industries and nontradables (retail, construction, and public services) for which it is hard to create international markets. These are firms that seek protection from international competitors and who are vulnerable to changes in government policy.[5]

Like the democrats, the authoritarian governments who represent these sectors of the economy have no incentive to limit the central bank's ability to monetize government deficits and to dole out subsidies and credits. To the contrary, their economic constituents should favor everything that an

4. Lindblom argues that the well-being of a capitalist economy in a democracy hinges primarily on the profits and sales of business. Governments are thus obliged to cater to business interests via various policy "inducements" (tax breaks, investment incentives, etc.) to compensate the risk assumed on the part of investors.

5. Within this group of firms in developing countries, a particularly powerful block is constituted by the state-owned industries, which have traditionally been more dependent upon special favors from the state in order to survive (Haggard and Maxfield 1993, 299).

autonomous central bank is designed to counteract. These are, after all, the sectors that have traditionally benefited from the lowered cost of capital entailed in interest rate ceilings and preferential credit policies (Clark 1994b). To the extent that financing for such policies was historically supplied via various direct and indirect government subsidies to financial intermediaries, the fiscal constraints implied by an autonomous central bank should work directly against these groups' interests (Haggard and Maxfield 1993, 314–15). The elimination of exchange controls that often accompanies autonomy—and which effectively constitutes a tax on export earnings—similarly removes yet another crucial subsidy for imported inputs for domestic industry (Maxfield 1991, 426). Finally, in Latin America at least, labor unions have also tended to be strongest in the protected and nontradable sectors of the economy, particularly in government services and state-owned industries. To the extent that autonomy brings with it the risk of higher unemployment, firms in these industries are also likely to oppose autonomy on the grounds that it threatens the livelihoods of their workers.

But there is also a set of important cases where the preferred policies of the authoritarians will not mirror those of the democrats. These are of course those authoritarian regimes that cater to a different type of capital—predominant in the exposed and non-asset-specific sectors of the economy. Exposed sectors are those economic actors for whom increased international exchange is beneficial (exporters and importers). Non-asset-specific capital encompasses those sectors of the economy based in liquid or mobile assets who can easily shift their assets from one activity to another (domestic financial capital, the financial services industry, and foreign capital). The former prefers a macroeconomic environment that enables it to realize the fullest possible benefits associated with broadened economic horizons (Frieden and Rogowski 1996). The latter welcomes policies that enable its holders to move their funds to whatever activity is earning the highest rate of return (Frieden 1991a, 1991b). Together, they constitute a powerful market-oriented constituency for whom democracy—and its accompanying economic agenda—constitutes a strong threat.

For these market-oriented authoritarian regimes, the creation of an autonomous central bank is a very attractive strategy. Above all, central bank autonomy increases the costs of borrowing for incoming democratic governments (by raising interest rates), while at the same time lessening the effectiveness of doing so (by eliminating the expansionary effects of borrowing stemming from seignorage). Autonomy thus promises an end to the inflationary consequences of deficit spending, the hallmark feature of Latin American populism (Dornbusch and Edwards 1991). Low inflation is highly valued by exposed sectors and foreign capital seeking to expand opportunities for international trade and investment, who need macroeconomic stability in order to adequately forecast investment decisions. Banks and other financial institutions whose real interest rate earnings are eroded by surprise inflation also prize stability (Maxfield 1991, 425; Posen 1993).

A second reason that autonomy should be appealing to these authoritarians is that it institutionalizes a policy of financial liberalization. By removing the allocative inefficiencies and sectoral biases that characterized the era of "financial repression" (McKinnon 1973, 1991), an autonomous central bank frees financial policy of its political underpinnings that are thought to be a disincentive to savings and growth (Fry 1982, 1984). Without such barriers to investment, those who hold non-asset-specific capital are free to move their funds to wherever they see fit. The reduced reliance on reserve requirements will similarly afford private banks greater discretion in administering their funds (Maxfield 1991, 427).

Finally, central bank autonomy also has important implications for exchange rate policy. First, autonomy is generally accompanied by the gradual elimination of exchange controls, which, in reducing the red tape required to move foreign exchange in and out of the country, facilitates the free flow of capital to productive domestic investment opportunities (Frieden 1991b; Maxfield 1991, 426). Foreign capital holders, in particular, are likely to welcome this aspect of central bank autonomy, as well as the more dynamic export-oriented sectors of the economy that stand to benefit from an infusion of foreign investment. Second, to the extent that an autonomous central bank can prevent substantial currency volatility, this is also likely to be favored by internationally oriented investors, financiers, and traders, for whom such uncertainty is costly (Frieden 1998, 85).[6]

Briefly, for those authoritarian regimes that are beholden to exposed sectors and non-asset-specific capital, central bank autonomy offers several distinct advantages. By impeding a government's ability to costlessly finance its deficits, autonomy helps to eliminate the primary cause of inflation in LDCs. And because an autonomous central bank views credit policy through the lens of macroeconomic management, it also hinders a government's ability to distort financial policy for political ends. By establishing a monetary regime

6. It is true that there is often a trade-off between price stability and exchange rate stability. While the financial sector should have a preference for a stable currency, exporters are likely to prefer some measure of devaluation to make their products more competitive in home and foreign markets. But since this conflict has less to do with preferences over the level of the exchange rate than it does with central bank autonomy per se, it is only of secondary importance to the argument here.

where populist economic alternatives are virtually off the agenda, conservative authoritarian regimes can thus set up powerful constraints on the types of policies that governments can pursue in the future.[7]

## Autonomy Observed: Hypothesizing Insulation Outcomes

The previous section outlines how the onset of democracy should affect the baseline preferences of actors in a transition with respect to the creation of an autonomous central bank. Our next task is to identify the conditions under which this outcome is likely to be observed.

As we have seen, the amount of autonomy afforded a central bank should hinge critically on two factors—one dependent upon the preference differences between the actors (the intensity of threat) and one dependent on how soon democracy is likely to occur (the proximity of threat). Neither of these factors is sufficient in and of itself. Rather, in order for central bank autonomy to occur, it is important that both conditions be present.

Taken together, these two dimensions of threat yield three sets of potential outcomes. Where there is no clash between the economic policy preferences of the outgoing regime and incoming democrats and/or democratization is sufficiently distant, there should be no change to the legal status of the central bank. Among other things, this corresponds to the transition from a protectionist regime. For these elites, democracy is not likely to constitute an economic liability, and so the demand for central bank autonomy should never even arise in the first place. But where there is a sharp preference divergence and regime change is imminent, the incentives to insulate will be strongest. These cases encompass those market-oriented regimes where the onset of democracy does constitute a strong threat to the economic interests of the outgoing authoritarians and autonomy should be full. In between, we should find a range of outcomes that we can term *partial autonomy*. These are

7. To be sure, one might reasonably argue that market-oriented authoritarian regimes would have an even stronger incentive to leave the economy in utter disarray, so as to have a ready-manufactured justification for coming back into power and fixing democracy's "mess." While this is an interesting theoretical possibility, there are several reasons to believe that it is unlikely to be the strategy they adopt. First, these authoritarians (and the capitalist factions they represent) are presumably already privileged and powerful anyway. Were they to deliberately wreak havoc on the economy, not only might they jeopardize their own positions, but the general populace might also want to hold them accountable. Second, there are no guarantees that such a strategy would ultimately prove functional, as many events might ensue in the interim that might preclude them from returning to office. Finally, to the extent that the authoritarians were driven by office-seeking motives and the economy were to perform well over time, they could claim credit subsequently for having acted in the best interests of the country.

cases where the preference divergence is lower than in the full case and/or the democratic threat is more distant.

## Why Insulation Matters: Explaining Institutional Persistence

We now know why authoritarian governments have incentives to create autonomous central banks and when they are likely do it. But before this discussion is concluded, a final theoretical puzzle hangs in the air. The thrust of the argument presented in this chapter is that central bank autonomy should run counter to the interests of the democratic opposition to the authoritarian regime. If this is the case, then why do the democrats not simply turn around and reverse this legislation once they are elected to office? We have already noted that the transition is a moment of institutional flux, where rules are created "on the fly" (O'Donnell and Schmitter 1986). Institutional reversal would thus seem to be perfectly in keeping with such a fluid political environment. If so, then how can the authoritarians be so sure that what they create is going to last?

The short answer is that they can't. Insulation is really only the best that the authoritarians can do, and they have no formal guarantee that this effort will not be in vain. I argue, however, that the authoritarians can be reasonably confident that their institutional creations will survive and even thrive into the future. How can we explain this seemingly counterintuitive outcome?

### Evaluating Theoretical Alternatives: Are the Democrats Worse Off?

One potential explanation is that despite their public protestations to the contrary, incoming democratic governments are secretly delighted with autonomy. The logic here is similar in flavor to those arguments that suggest that international financial institutions provide a convenient scapegoat for painful economic reforms that governments would prefer to enact but are otherwise prevented from doing for fear of domestic political reprisals (cf. Agénor 1994; Giavazzi and Giovannini 1989, 111, 126; Giavazzi and Pagano 1994). Much in the same way that LDC governments can credibly claim to domestic audiences that the International Monetary Fund (IMF) "forces" them to undertake costly adjustment measures (Cotarelli and Giannini 1998), so too could one argue that autonomy permits these same governments to absolve themselves of all responsibility for anti-inflationary policies (Kane 1980).

A second explanation for persistence is much more straightforward. It argues that precisely because the democrats may lack credibility with various capitalist audiences, they eagerly welcome central bank independence as an early deal to signal their own macroeconomic solvency. This sort of argument is consistent with recent claims that left-leaning governments actually stand to benefit most from the credibility boost afforded by an autonomous central bank (Simmons 1996).

Both of these arguments suggest that, far from harming the interests of the incoming governments, central bank autonomy would actually leave the democrats better off. While compelling in their reasoning, both arguments suffer from the same fundamental weakness: they assume politicians with very long time horizons who are willing to look beyond the next election by implementing policies that are politically costly to their constituencies. As noted earlier, this is not a realistic portrayal of these politicians, particularly for newcomers to the political arena who face unusually high redistributive demands. Without denying the host of benefits an autonomous central bank might afford the democrats in the long run, in the short run they are more likely to be concerned with getting elected. And to the extent that things such as the sacrifice ratio preclude them from achieving this goal, an autonomous central bank is likely to be perceived as a constraint, not as a godsend.

But just because the democrats would prefer not to have an autonomous central bank does not mean that they are free to ignore markets entirely. There are, however, a variety of other ways that they can demonstrate their credibility short of delegating authority to an independent agency. They might, for example, choose to enact some sort of corporatist wage bargaining between business, government, and labor in which various interest groups choose to forsake distributive conflict in the name of promoting both lower inflation and higher unemployment (Lange and Garrett 1985; Alvarez, Garrett, and Lange 1991). Or they might design an incentive contract through which the central bank commits to a quantitative inflation target that is then enforced through some sort of reporting requirement (Walsh 1995b; Persson and Tabellini 1993). They could also delegate budget preparation responsibility to a bureaucratic agency that ultimately reports to politicians (Hallerberg and Van Hagen 1997) or enact numerical limits on fiscal deficits or public sector borrowing (Poterba 1994; Bohn and Inman 1996). Precisely because the preceding devices entail less absolute loss of discretion than an autonomous central bank, they may constitute a welcome alternative for politicians wishing to retain a greater degree of flexibility over the economy. The point, then, is not that the democrats should eschew credibility entirely but that they should logically prefer mechanisms that are less costly than creating an independent agency.

In what follows, I offer a third and more comprehensive explanation for institutional persistence whose logic would hold even in the absence of the other two theoretical possibilities. Unlike either of these two efficiency-based alternatives, my argument suggests that the democrats need not be pleased with this institutional legacy but, rather, may have no choice but to accept it.

## International Constraints: The Logic of Reputation

My explanation for the persistence of central bank autonomy in new democracies is rooted in the concept of reputation. Reputation is the view formed of an individual or organization by another based on past experience that is subsequently used as a basis for forecasting future behavior. The idea is that as actors interact with each other over time, they build a reputation for a certain type of behavior. This reputation then conditions the extent to which others will bargain with them in the future. This mechanism works because it is accompanied by a built-in punishment mechanism: failure to live up to one's reputation precludes the opportunity to make profitable deals in the future. Reputation thus serves as an informal norm that fortifies existing institutional arrangements and can even serve as a proxy form of commitment itself (Kreps 1990).

My basic claim is that, once established, international investors come to count on central bank autonomy as a guarantee of a secure investment climate. Regardless of how it got there, new governments are going to be reluctant to tamper with autonomy lest they pay the high costs associated with transgressing this sort of reputational mechanism: the massive outflow of foreign capital from their economies. This logic is very similar to that invoked in the first section of this chapter to explain why the authoritarians only create insulated agencies when they know that they are losing power. There, I argued that because rules create expectations, violating them is very costly. Absent the threat of turnover, authoritarian governments should thus be reluctant to commit themselves to an overly binding set of constraints lest they be obliged to respect them. But it is for the very same reason—the costs attached to violating an established set of rules—that once established, these autonomous agencies are likely to remain.

The analogy here is to the costliness of devaluations. One feature common to many exchange rate–based stabilizations is that once a government decides upon a given peg, it will generally do whatever it takes to maintain parity, even long after it becomes clear that a devaluation is necessary. This is because deviations from committed exchange rates are perceived to be very costly, even if the currency is subsequently repegged at some other level (Cukierman, Kiguel, and Liviatan 1992). In addition to whatever electoral losses may be attendant on such behavior, financial markets can also be expected to engage in destabilizing speculation, capital flight, and so on (Lohmann 1998b, 11). If reneging on a preestablished currency peg has thus been shown to have a variety of negative political and economic consequences, a similar story should also hold true for other commitment devices such as an autonomous central bank.

To be sure, if the reputational value of an autonomous central bank is so high, we must also ask ourselves why the democrats would not have an incentive to set one up on their own. Two explanations prove relevant in this regard, both of which require us to think about the nature of international investors. First, there is a big difference between not having an institution in the first place and destroying one that already exists. Markets may well be willing to tolerate the absence of an autonomous central bank, as long as a given LDC government has some other means of demonstrating credibility. In contrast, the literature on "herding behavior" suggests that even tiny changes in a country's policy behavior may drive large waves of capital to exit (Calvo 1995; Calvo and Mendoza 1996). Abolishing an independent central bank would be a highly transparent signal that a government intended to inflate the economy, thus triggering immediate capital flight.

Second, even if one wanted to argue that central bank autonomy would eventually bring all sorts of positive externalities for the democrats, the coordination required to build a favorable foreign investment climate emerges only gradually over time (Stone 1996). To the extent that my earlier portrayal of the democrats is correct, we might believe that incoming democratic governments would be willing to forego the discounted future benefits of creating an independent central bank in order to enjoy the short-term benefits of greater flexibility over the economy. But we might also believe that they might be willing to relinquish such flexibility rather than pay the immediate costs associated with eradicating an autonomous central bank that already exists.

The logic I offer for why central bank autonomy is not overturned thus bears some resemblance to the notion of "audience costs" in the sanctions literature. Audience costs are those costs associated with failing to make good on threats or promises. Once an actor has made a public institutional commitment to a given action, reneging on this commitment causes it to lose face with other members of the international community (Martin 1993). But while the literature on audience costs implies that actors deliberately invest in costly signals as a means of making commitments credible, I propose that in the case at hand, the commitment is thrust upon them. All things equal, the newly elected democratic governments would rather not inherit an autonomous central bank from their authoritarian predecessors. Once the bank is there, however, the costs of exclusion are higher than those associated with having "joined" in the first place (Gruber 2000). As a result, the democrats have little choice but to abide by the central bank's new rules. Though this is not their first best alternative, they are obliged to grin and bear it.

Ultimately, it is impossible to definitively prove why autonomous central banks persist under the new regime. Not only does this constitute a counterfactual, but even if the democrats do oppose autonomy, they are not likely to openly admit it in light of the reputation considerations noted earlier. There is, however, some suggestive evidence that the institutional persistence argument I offer is at the very least plausible. While a variety of central bank reforms were undertaken in the developing world between 1989 and 1993, no country took steps to decrease its autonomy (Maxfield 1997, 50–70). While this is not conclusive proof that an international constraint is in operation, it does suggest that in an age of increasing global capital mobility, few developing countries are willing to tempt fate. Stronger evidence in this regard comes from Venezuela. In early 1994, a populist administration elected on an anti-neoliberal platform announced that it was going to reduce the autonomy of this country's central bank. Within hours after the announcement, the stock market plummeted, and capital began flowing out of the country at a massive rate.[8] International investors were simply not willing to run the risk of staying in a country where they could no longer have the financial guarantees that an autonomous central bank provides. Venezuela's attempt to buck the system was thus met with an automatic, market-based penalty.[9]

In short, as long as the international economic environment continues to favor the policy outputs of an autonomous central bank, it is likely to reinforce the longevity of this institutional form. For once this institution is up and running, it is easier for the democrats to keep it than to pay the sudden and certain costs of demolishing it.

## Bolstering the International Constraint: Domestic Strategies for Entrenchment

It would be a mistake, however, to attribute the persistence of central bank autonomy entirely to international forces. In addition, one can point to a variety of domestic factors that might serve to further lock in this institutional

8. *Latin American Weekly Report,* May 12, 1994.

9. It is true that the newly elected Caldera administration was not initially deterred by this capital flight and stuck by its intention to force out the president of the central bank. The argument here does not predict what all governments will do under all circumstances. It merely underscores the rational incentives they face given the costs attached to overturning a preexisting set of rules.

reform. Taken together, these constitute a powerful set of reasons to believe that the authoritarians' attempts to insulate the economy will prove a resounding success.

One domestic factor likely to enhance the persistence of an autonomous central bank is the fact that powerful actors associated with authoritarian rule—such as business and the military—may have a stake in its continued existence. As Przeworski (1992, 122) notes, "decisions made ex ante create conditions that are difficult to reverse ex post, since they preserve the power of forces associated with the ancien regime." No one would go so far as to argue with the claim that changes to central bank statutes are likely to incite a military coup. But the implicit threat of force and/or capital flight by such powerful constituencies may be sufficient to ward off any would-be effort to tamper with the authoritarians' preferred institutional forms (Valenzuela 1992; Loveman 1998, 128). This would seem to be particularly true to the extent that the authoritarian regime has deliberately strengthened certain capitalist groups prior to leaving office who then threaten to destroy the economy unless the democrats respect the rules (such as central bank reform) that ensure its operation (Bates 1991).

One might argue that such a constraint is epiphenomenal, in that it will last only as long as the current balance of power persists. But even if the influence of these "inherited" constituencies fades, the central bank is also likely to generate a new clientele over time who will come to benefit from its policies and thus have a significant stake in autonomy remaining (Bates 1994, 32; Rodrik 1994, 83–84; Tornell and Esquivel 1995). As Geddes (1995) notes, periods of rapid institutional change occur only rarely; once a given institution is created, the vested interests that emerge behind it tend to reinforce the status quo. That autonomous central banks promote the securitization of assets that in turn makes possible their rapid exit gives this sort of capital both a stake in and the power to defend this institution. Central bank autonomy may thus become embedded in a certain form of interest group politics over time.

But even if we were not to assume that the central bank would develop a constituency of its own, there is still good reason to believe that this institutional form will not be easily reversed. Precisely because the authoritarians know societal support for autonomy may not last indefinitely, they are likely to employ some sort of domestic entrenchment strategy before leaving power to make sure that a reversal is next to impossible. They might, for example, lodge a rule in the constitution that makes it necessary for a two-thirds legislative majority to approve any changes to the central bank. This sort of device was used amply by the outgoing authoritarian elites in the Chilean transition as a means of protecting their interests. To the extent that democratization is all about the move toward the rule of law, the democrats will have incentives to respect these rules in order to give legitimacy to their newly minted democratic polity. They are thus likely to heed the rules governing the autonomy of the central bank, even when they might have preferred to avoid it entirely.

Even without these sorts of legal constraints, however, there are a variety of other reasons to believe that a democratic political environment will serve to guarantee institutional compliance. As Tsebelis (1997) has shown, the responsiveness of policy to a change in societal preferences is inversely related to the number of formal veto players in the political system—for example, the number of institutional actors whose assent is required for a policy change. One of the defining characteristics of democratic rule is precisely that decision making involves more institutional actors than is the case under authoritarian rule. At the most basic level, then, the greater number of veto players under democratic rule will automatically make shifting the status quo more difficult (North and Weingast 1989). Particularly where such checks and balances are complemented by ideological polarization—in which some members of the enacting coalition retain veto power under future governments—this is all the more reason to think that central bank autonomy should endure (Keefer and Stasavage 1998, 1999).

In turn, more sociological factors may also play a role in preserving the central bank's autonomy. Once an institution is in place—and regardless of how it got there—it tends to generate shared expectations. Over time, these become a force for stability as domestic actors get used to abiding by its rules and making decisions based upon its existence (Moe 1987, 255–56). Simply because they reflect the common experience of actors, these shared expectations are likely to reinforce the autonomy of the central bank, even among those who might otherwise oppose it.

A final reason to think that central bank autonomy is unlikely to be overturned stems from the notion of path dependence (David 1988). As institutions unfold over time, they acquire an institutional momentum of their own: other institutions form around them, and they come to generate increasing returns to scale (Arthur 1989). A given system becomes entrenched, not because it is necessarily the most efficient for those involved but because it becomes locked in by a series of small initial choices. Once these choices are in place, there is no incentive to change the initial institutional framework, even though more attractive arrangements might have been selected at the outset from the point of view of the incoming power holders.

Whatever the dominant constraint at work—whether international or domestic—the bottom line is that there are any number of reasons to think that, once created, an autonomous central bank is likely to last. And none of them requires that the democrats be left better off. Rather, incoming governments will have little choice but to accept the institutional legacy with which they are confronted.

## Measurement and Operationalization of Variables

This chapter concludes with a discussion of how the independent and dependent variables will be operationalized in this study.

### The Independent Variable: The Degree of Threat

*The Intensity of Threat*

In keeping with the earlier theoretical discussion, the threat variable is made up of two component parts. The first dimension corresponds to what I call the *intensity of threat.* In the model at hand, this threat is determined by the distance between the ideal points of the outgoing authoritarian and incoming democratic governments, as measured by the sectoral support base of the authoritarian regime and the democrats' economic agenda. Let us consider these in turn.

I have argued that the onset of democracy constitutes a strong threat for those authoritarian regimes where non-asset-specific capital and exposed sectors are dominant. The stronger this market-oriented capital base, the greater the resultant incentive should be to create an autonomous central bank. At its most basic level, the strength of non-asset-specific and exposed capital should be reflected in its economic power. Percentage contribution to gross domestic product (GDP), annual growth rates, and percentage share of exports in GDP should all serve as indicators of the power these capitalists can be expected to wield. In order to evaluate more precisely which groups within this capitalist block are driving economic policy, I divide them into their sectoral components (e.g., finance, manufacturing, etc.).[10]

In addition to the sheer economic might of these economic actors, I also consider their political power. A measure of the formal political power of the financial, foreign, and export-oriented sectors is first necessary. In those cases where a peak organization exists, the relative weight given to these sectors on its governing board should serve as a reasonable proxy for their formal business power. Political power can also be imputed to these sectors to the extent

10. It is possible that the sectoral distinction I employ here may be highly correlated with other more salient distinctions such as firm size and/or region. For example, larger firms may find it easier to integrate into the international economy, while smaller firms may face greater hurdles in adjusting their production for the international market.

that their business organizations are given an official role in the policy-making process. A second measure of the political power of business is informal and attempts to measure influence. One indicator of influence is the extent to which certain types of capital do not have to go through business organizations at all but are instead afforded direct access to high-level government ministers or even the president. The existence of small groups or clubs of very powerful market-oriented capital with whom the government consults on an informal basis is often indicative of their political clout. Reputational indicators can also be illustrative in this regard, in that they suggest the extent to which these capitalists are perceived to command influence over government policy.

As a general rule, however, we should expect traditional strategies of collective action to be less relevant when assessing the strength of the non-asset-specific and exposed sectors of the economy. By definition, non-asset-specific capital is not tied to any one country or industry. Those who hold it are therefore free to leave their country of origin and invest this capital elsewhere if they are not content with the economic policies of a given government. This permanent exit option enables this type of capital to maintain permanent leverage over government policy (Offe and Wiesenthal 1980). As a result of this silent clout, the first set of economic measures of power may in some ways be the most telling when evaluating the importance of non-asset-specific capital.

Finally, because the intensity of threat is meant to capture the expected policy distance between the authoritarians and the democrats, we must also know something about the economic policy preferences of the democrats. As noted earlier, some democrats will clearly be more populist than others and will—by extension—be more threatening to the interests of outgoing authoritarian elites. It is therefore important to look at the expected nature of the democrats' economic agenda in evaluating the intensity of threat. Opposition party platforms, mobilization activity, and statements to the press should all prove helpful in assessing where the democrats actually fall on the ideological spectrum. The attitudes and beliefs that the authoritarians and their constituents hold about such preferences, as measured through press statements, opinion polls, and elite interviews, should also give us some purchase on what the authoritarians perceive about the interventionist content of the democrats' economic message.

### *The Proximity of Threat*

Even if the demand for central bank autonomy is dictated at a first cut by the intensity of the democratic threat, this economic incentive is necessary but not sufficient. As noted earlier, the demand for central bank autonomy is also a function of the proximity of the democratic threat. While the latter notion is conceptually clear, it is difficult to measure directly.

Ideally, we could assign a time-based metric to evaluate the proximity of the transition. Were the authoritarians to expect the transition to occur in, say, fifty years, we would probably not expect them to insulate at all. Conversely, if they anticipated a regime change within the next year, they would be likely to undertake full insulation. In between these two extremes, however, lies an array of outcomes that might be closer to high, low, or medium threats. But how to establish the appropriate temporal cutoff through which to code, say, a medium threat? Is it two years? Four years? Ten years? Since it is almost always impossible to identify the precise time at which democratization will occur ex ante, we need to measure the proximity of threat in a more tractable fashion. The empirical measure used for the proximity of threat is thus the strength of the democratic opposition, on the assumption that this should reveal something about the relative imminence of democratization. The presumption is that the stronger the democratic opposition, the closer the onset of regime change and the more immediate the consequent need to insulate.

Since the opposition has been defined as the political parties of the opposition, the first measure of their strength should be the degree of fragmentation that exists among them. To the extent that the parties of the opposition are united under one umbrella, they are likely to be stronger and more threatening to exiting authoritarian elites. If they are instead divided and competing, they pose less of a political risk to incumbents. The ideological distance between opposition political parties is thus likely to be a good indicator of the opposition's relative strength, as reflected in the degree of overlap or convergence in the parties' programmatic agendas. If all parties are more or less in agreement on a range of policy issues, they are more likely to find common ground and unite. If sharp divisions exist within the polity over major spheres of policy, then they are less likely to cohere.

A second measure of opposition strength is the degree of popular support that opposition parties enjoy. To the extent that the opposition block has a relatively high degree of support from the populace, it can be expected to have more leverage in combating the authoritarian rulers. If elections exist and are reliable, percentage vote share should be a good indicator of the popularity of opposition parties. If there are no elections and/or these are not reliable, then other signals of popular approval can be utilized, such as mass attendance at public rallies sponsored by the opposition, public opinion polls, and/or the degree of engagement in informal partisan activity.

But since power is a relational concept, a second measure of the power of the democratic opposition should be reflected through the strength of the outgoing authoritarian elites. The key issue here is the internal cohesion of the regime. This is defined as the state's ability to overcome internal principal-agent and collective action problems to pursue coherent policies (Donor 1992). Where authoritarian states are tightly organized and united, this should facilitate the leadership's ability to pursue its policy goals. In contrast, if multiple factions exist within the ruling elite, this should undermine the authoritarians' effectiveness. Such divides not only hinder the leadership's ability to execute policies in a timely fashion, they also open up opportunities for alliances between liberalizing factions of the authoritarian regime and its opposition (O'Donnell and Schmitter 1986). While internal cohesion is difficult to operationalize, it should be indicated by the extent to which there exists a unity of views among the ruling elite, as reflected in the continuity of personnel, common professional or educational training, and/or similar socioeconomic origins. Evidence of any open disagreements within the ruling elite should similarly attest to the regime's vulnerability.

A second indicator of the strength of the authoritarians should be captured in their external popularity. Even the most repressive authoritarian regimes face a legitimacy constraint. If there are thus widespread signs of citizen dissatisfaction with the ruling elite, this is likely to make it increasingly difficult for the regime to stay in power. Because an authoritarian regime can typically repress its opposition and/or mobilize artificial support, it is difficult to measure its true popularity. Accordingly, vote share (where elections exist) and/or the existence of antiregime activities such as strike activity, popular protests, armed insurgencies, and so on, should serve as reasonable proxies.

It is worth noting that this entire argument is predicated on the assumption that all authoritarians that wish to insulate are empowered to do so. To be sure, some authoritarian regimes are weaker than others are, and on occasion this may disrupt their ability to pass laws as they see fit. Earlier in the chapter, for example, I referred to those "overnight" transitions where the authoritarians are caught off guard and lack the time or ability to dictate the institutional framework that follows. Absent this set of circumstances, however, it seems reasonable to presume that even in an authoritarian regime with severe internal collective action problems, the organizational threshold to pass a new law must be lower than in a democracy.[11]

11. Take the case of Argentina, which is generally recognized as a case where exiting elites were less able to control the terms of the transition than most. Even there, the military was able to stay in power for a year after its defeat in the Falklands/Malvinas conflict and to pass protective legislation making subsequent civilian attempts to control the military more difficult than they might have otherwise been (Agüero 1992, 168).

## The Dependent Variable: Central Bank Autonomy

The literature on central bank independence has identified two distinct dimensions of autonomy: formal/legal and informal (behavioral). Formal measures of autonomy involve the legal relationship between central bank decision makers and the government. They tend to emphasize factors such as the appointment and composition of the central bank board, the extent to which the government has financial and/or budgetary control over the central bank, and whether or not the central bank is legally obliged to accommodate the government's fiscal policy.[12] Informal measures attempt to gauge less visible aspects of central bank behavior. Unofficial arrangements between the central bank and various parts of the government, the quality of the bank's research department, and the personalities of key individuals in the central bank are all variables thought to affect behavioral autonomy.

Neither of these measures is without its problems. Although perhaps a better reflection of the day-to-day reality, behavioral indicators are inherently difficult to quantify in an impartial manner. For example, while one would ideally like to measure the extent to which monetary and fiscal authorities consult with one another on an informal basis, this information is not likely to be readily available or easily scored. Most studies thus develop indices of central bank independence based upon their legal attributes, although there is some variability with respect to which features ought to be included in these indices and how they should be weighed.[13] Even with such discrepancies, however, the correlation among various formal/legal indices is typically quite high (Walsh 1995a).

As a general rule, formal/legal measures of central bank autonomy have been significantly correlated with low inflation in the industrialized countries (Grilli, Masciandaro, and Tabellini 1991; Cukierman 1992; Alesina and Summers 1993). The third world presents a less clear-cut picture. In light of the more fluid legality that tends to characterize developing country polities, formal/legal indicators are thought to be a poor measure of independence. Nor have they shown any empirical effect on inflation (Cukierman 1992; Cukierman, Webb, and Neyapti 1993). This has prompted most empirical analyses

12. See, among others, Bade and Parkin 1980; Alesina 1988; Masciandaro and Tabellini 1988; Cukierman 1992.

13. Note, for example, that while Belgium is ranked fifth among advanced industrial countries in the scale used by Alesina (1988), it is ranked fourteenth according to the scale of Cukierman (1992). Japan illustrates a similar point. For a discussion of various measurement-related problems associated with formal/legal indices, see Pollard 1994; Eijffinger and De Haan 1996.

of central bank independence in the developing world to rely instead on behavioral indicators.[14]

But it is not clear that existing behavioral measures are much better, despite their statistically significant relationship with low inflation in this set of countries (Cukierman, Webb, and Neyapti 1993; Cukierman and Webb 1995). For example, in order to capture the political instability of LDCs, Cukierman (1992) has used governor turnover as a behavioral measure of central bank independence. The assumption is that autonomy should be positively correlated with the experience and prestige of the governor. As Maxfield (1994, 560) has pointed out, however, using turnover rates as proxies for independence is not ideal, since a governor may enjoy a long tenure period precisely because he or she is more politicized. More recently, Cukierman and Webb (1995) have attempted to develop a measure of the "political vulnerability" of the central bank, as measured by the fraction of political transitions that is followed within six months by a replacement of the central bank governor. While their evidence seems to confirm the intuition that political instability is likely to be correlated with changes in the head of the central bank, they do not examine the extent to which such instability is itself a product of larger swings in the economy (Cukierman 1996, 15). The possibility of such reverse causality makes any claim about the causal relationship between central bank autonomy and economic outcomes based on this measure speculative at best.

Just what ought to serve as the best measure for autonomy in developing countries is thus not clear, rendering this a ripe avenue for future research. This study will focus primarily on formal/legal measures of autonomy, although behavioral indicators will also be considered in the case studies where relevant. While recognizing the demonstrated shortcomings of this approach for the class of countries at hand, there are several arguments that weigh in its favor.

First, unlike behavioral indicators that are difficult to measure and highly idiosyncratic, formal indicators favor systematic comparisons across countries. Second, it is entirely possible that the observed difficulties in employing formal/legal measures within LDCs may have less to do with their inherent unsuitability than with the fact that the measures themselves are not appropriate. Third, if what precludes formal indicators from serving as an adequate measure is, in fact, a question of tenuous legality, then we are likely to find tremendous variation across both countries and regime types. Since this study is concerned with how such rules hold up under democratic

14. Keefer and Stasavage (1999) have suggested that formal legal indicators of central bank independence do hold up as a reasonable predictor of inflation in LDCs, as long as there are a sufficient number of veto players and a sufficiently high degree of ideological polarization.

regimes, the formal/legal indices may be presumed to hold more sway.[15] Finally, to the extent that LDC governments face an increasingly internationalized economic environment, their incentives to comply with existing rules should thus be all the greater. This was not the case during the bulk of the time period that the Cukierman, Webb, and Neyapti data set covers (1950–88), when the forces of international integration were on average considerably weaker.

In what follows, I elaborate upon four broad sets of rules that facilitate the creation of an autonomous central bank (Cukierman 1992). It is important to underscore that autonomy does not hinge on just one of the following dimensions but rather on how they combine as a whole. In all cases, a central bank's autonomy is enhanced to the extent that political influence over monetary policy is minimized or eliminated entirely.

## Limitations on Lending

The first formal dimension thought to affect a central bank's autonomy has to do with the limits placed on central bank financing to the government.[16] As a general rule, the more legal constraints there are on such financing, the more autonomous the central bank is thought to be. The logic here is straightforward: limits on central bank lending to the government impede the latter's ability to use the proceeds of monetary expansion (seignorage) to monetize government debt. More autonomous central banks on this dimension tend to be those, such as in Germany and Switzerland, where there are strict limits set on direct central bank credit to the government. A more lax set of rules is found in the Bank of England, where there are no special legal limits on the amount of credit the central bank can give to the government.

In addition to the overall amount of lending allowed, there is a series of more technical criteria that affect the relative severity of the terms attached to such lending.[17] In all cases, the greater the role given the executive in

15. This assertion is based on the assumption that, all things equal, we should expect greater violation of existing rules under authoritarianism than under democracy. When we bear this in mind, it is perhaps less surprising that legal indicators have done a relatively poor job of predicting actual central bank independence in the developing world. The most widely cited index—Cukierman, Webb, and Neyapti 1993—is based on decade-long averages of central bank autonomy for fifty-one developing countries during 1950–88, a time when many of these countries underwent significant periods of authoritarian rule.

16. The central bank can extend credit to the government in one of two ways: through its direct credit facilities or by buying public debt in the primary market (indirect financing).

17. Relevant indicators here include the extent that limitations on financing are expressed in fixed cash amounts rather than as percentages of revenues or expenditures, who controls the terms of lending to the government (e.g., the maturity, interest, and amount of loans), and the breadth of potential recipients of such loans (e.g., federal government, state governments, or public enterprises).

influencing the amount, conditions, or extent of the financing the government receives, the more autonomy is potentially compromised. In the Cukierman index, this measure has greater proportional weight than the others do, suggesting that this is a very important component of autonomy.

## Formulation of Monetary Policy

A second dimension of autonomy pertains to the process through which monetary policy is formulated. While some degree of coordination between the executive branch and the central bank is generally thought to be prudent, a central bank should be given complete or near complete discretion over the formulation of monetary policy if it is to be truly insulated from political control.

At one extreme there are those counties, such as Germany, where the central bank has an extraordinary amount of control over how monetary policy is made and carried out. The Bundesbank not only has full responsibility to determine monetary policy but is also obliged to support the general economic policy of the government only to the extent that such policy is compatible with its own statutory objectives. On the other extreme, there are countries such as Japan, where—at least until 1997—monetary policy was either explicitly or implicitly in the hands of the minister of the economy (treasurer). Countries such as Switzerland fall in between these two limits. In Switzerland, the central bank and the government are legally obliged to consult one another before implementing policies, although executive approval is not necessary for the enactment of actual policy decisions.

One indicator of the degree of control the central bank exerts over monetary policy formulation is reflected in the relative veto power granted to the executive branch on the central bank board. In countries such as the United States and New Zealand, the executive branch is explicitly prohibited from attending central bank board meetings. In other countries, such as Germany, the executive branch is permitted to attend the meetings of the central bank board and can even request that a measure be temporarily deferred but has no voting privileges. Also significant in this regard are those rules governing conflict resolution in the event of a policy disagreement between the central bank and the executive. Where such mechanisms exist, they are also thought to be conducive to autonomy as they decrease opportunities for behind the scene influence by the government.[18]

18. As a general rule, most countries do not have any explicit arrangements for the resolution of conflicts. There are exceptions. In both the Netherlands and New Zealand, for example, the government and the central bank have the ability to make disagreements public, although to date, neither country has resorted to this practice. Other countries embed dispute resolution mechanisms in the veto power afforded the executive branch over monetary policy decisions, as I note in my discussion of the Chilean case.

## Central Bank Objectives

A third component of autonomy derives from the statutory objectives that the central bank is obliged to pursue by law. The more the central bank's goals are centered on maintaining price stability, the less room it is thought to have to use monetary policy to achieve political ends such as growth or unemployment. The Bundesbank, for example, is legally obliged to make safeguarding the stability of its currency its number one priority. In contrast, the Bank of England's legislation only requires that it "promote the public good," leaving the actual interpretation of such an objective open to speculation. While rare, there are also cases such as Switzerland where despite considerable latitude in the phrasing of monetary policy objectives—"to pursue a credit and monetary policy serving the interests of the country as a whole"—quantitative monetary stock targets are rigidly pursued in order to ensure that price stability is in fact achieved (Central Bank of Chile 1989, 27).

An important informal indicator of the strength of the central bank's objectives is thought to be the corresponding strength of the central bank's accountability mechanisms. The underlying premise is that a commitment to a given objective is not enough to guarantee autonomy. Rather, the public needs evidence that those making monetary policy are actually carrying out their job.[19] But even the most independent central banks are not generally characterized by strong accountability measures, a testimony to the "secretiveness" that is often said to characterize these institutions. This is likely to be particularly true in the cases with which this book is primarily concerned—democracies in transition from authoritarian rule—where it seems unlikely that exiting rulers would be interested in setting up such checks and balances before leaving office. After all, subjecting the central bank to scrutiny only opens up an avenue of potential control by the democrats. The authoritarians thus have strong incentives to design an institution that limits such accountability to the greatest extent possible.

## The Central Bank Board: Term Length, Appointment, and Dismissal

A fourth and final formal dimension of central bank autonomy pertains to the rules surrounding the central bank's governing board. Several different

19. There are a variety of ways to augment a central bank's accountability. In New Zealand, the central bank is obliged to publish policy targets agreed upon in advance by the central bank governor and finance minister. In the United States, accountability assumes the form of semiannual reports to Congress and regular appearances by members of the Federal Reserve before congressional committees. The very structure of the central bank board itself can also serve as a form of accountability insofar as it allows for a system of checks and balances on the execution of central bank functions, as occurs in the federalist countries of Switzerland, Germany, and the United States.

issues come into play here. First, there is the question of term length. The conventional wisdom is that the longer the term of appointment, the less likely it is that prevailing political trends and ideas will influence members of the board. The United States, where the governors of the Federal Reserve serve for fourteen years, is a good example in this regard. Even more important than the actual length of board member terms, however, is the extent to which these overlap with those of elected officials. The eight-year terms of Bundesbank board members are deliberately staggered to avoid the influence of four-year parliamentary sessions on board selection. This arrangement contrasts starkly with the pre-1993 French system, where board members were appointed for indefinite terms that in practice frequently coincided with those of French presidents (Swinburne and Castello-Branco 1991, 431).

Second, the procedures governing the appointment and dismissal of central bank governors are also thought to be relevant to autonomy. The less discretion afforded the executive in choosing or removing members of the board the more independence is favored, as this is thought to give precedence to more technical criteria regarding board composition. Since there is no country in the world where the central bank is exclusively empowered to choose its own members, the important distinction for appointment procedures is how much discretion the central bank enjoys. In Switzerland and Germany, central bank councils are consulted in nominations that are ultimately made either by the legislature (Switzerland) or the executive (Germany). In other more classically dependent central banks such as that of Japan, the head of state makes all appointments in consultation with the cabinet. Autonomy is also enhanced to the extent that technical—as opposed to policy-based—criteria are invoked for the dismissal of governors. In Germany, for example, governors can only be removed for technical causes such as bankruptcy, criminal offenses, and major conflicts of interest. Contrast this with the situation in France prior to 1993, where there was no limit on the president's ability to remove incumbent governors, rendering the central bank no more than an arm of the presidency.

In addition to how appointments are made, who is chosen for these positions is also significant. In many countries, the composition of the board provides an avenue of potential influence for different groups in the formation of policy. In Germany and the United States, where the central bank is based on a series of decentralized reserve banks, regional influences are felt. In New Zealand, financial and/or private sector experience is prioritized as a criterion in the selection of board members. However such representation is ironed out, the key point to underscore is that central bank board composition can be used to shape decisively the tenor of monetary policy.

This dimension of independence assumes particular importance in a regime change. Rather than limiting their executive discretion over board composition, conservative authoritarian regimes should logically create rules that give them as much input as possible. Particularly since the first central bank board will protect their interests during the first—and potentially most "dangerous"—phase of democratic rule, appointment power should be employed as a means of safeguarding their economic policy preferences. The authoritarians are therefore unlikely to select a pluralistic governing board with a wide range of sectoral or regional interests. They instead have incentives to handpick a small group of technocrats and/or members of the financial community whose preferences closely align with their own.

In short even among what are generally considered to be the world's most autonomous central banks—those of Germany, the United States, and Switzerland—there is no blueprint for the optimal way in which to secure independence. As this brief discussion reveals, there are any number of different combinations of features that can collectively yield an autonomous central bank. But with these general guidelines in place, we have a baseline from which to evaluate the nature of the dependent variable privileged in this study.

With this theoretical model in place, the next section of the book provides an in-depth exploration of the events surrounding the central bank reforms in Chile (1989) and Mexico (1993). This is followed by more examination of a variety of other cases in the developing world. My main objective is to explain some of the observed variation surrounding central bank autonomy in the developing world through the lens of the argument presented in this chapter. More generally, I also hope to elucidate the broader phenomenon of institutional insulation of which central bank reform serves as an important instance.

PART 2

# Empirics

CHAPTER 4

# Authoritarians under Siege

## Chile's Democratic Rebirth

For anyone well versed in Chile's much-heralded transition from authoritarian rule in 1989, the allegation that this was a well-insulated transition will hardly come as a surprise. Such insulation was in many respects the hallmark feature of this country's political changing of the guard (Valenzuela 1992; Arriagada and Graham 1994). Indeed, the very term *authoritarian enclave* had its genesis in the numerous pockets of de facto control that General Augusto Pinochet's military government retained after leaving formal power (Garretón 1989).

But although it is now virtually de rigueur to invoke the Chilean case when noting the institutional irregularities characteristic of new democracies (Karl and Schmitter 1994; Haggard and Kaufman 1995), analyses of their origins are few and far between. While many scholars recognize the onset of democracy as the triggering event, there is no comprehensive explanation linking specific features of Chile's democratization process to the extent of insulation observed.

Accordingly, chapters 4 and 5 represent a departure from previous scholarship on the Chilean transition on two grounds. First, my objective is not to describe but rather to explain the forces that gave rise to these biased institutional forms. I elucidate why—not just empirically but also theoretically—Chile constitutes a baseline case for our understanding of insulation in the transition from authoritarian rule.

Second, rather than privileging the military sphere in my analysis, I instead turn to the economic arena and, specifically, to central bank reform. For while central bank autonomy invariably makes it onto the "top ten list" of major institutional reforms enacted in the twilight of Chile's authoritarian rule, there have been no detailed political studies of how this reform evolved. In light of the central bank's pivotal role in ensuring, or imposing, the basic pillars of Chile's much-touted economic model, it would seem to be a particularly worthwhile candidate through which to trace the course of the authoritarians' institutional legacy.

With these objectives in mind, in the next two chapters I apply the theoretical argument developed in previous chapters to the Chilean central bank reform of 1989. While chapter 4 sets the stage for the reform by documenting the intensity and proximity of the democratic threat, chapter 5 evaluates the magnitude and persistence of the insulation response. I contend that the perceived threat to Chile's incumbent authoritarian elites was sufficiently strong and immediate to warrant the creation of one of the most autonomous central banks in the developing world.

The present chapter unfolds as follows. The first section, "Reform Background: Chile's Neoliberal 'Revolution,' " provides an overview of the neoliberal economic project carried out by Chile's authoritarian regime and the nature of the capitalist support base underpinning this model. Having established the authoritarians' vested interest in a set of market-oriented policies, in the second section, "Reform Timing: Questioning the Credibility Logic," I examine the 1989 Chilean central bank reform as an expression of these interests. Here, I dispute the official economic arguments invoked to explain this reform in order to provide evidence that its motive and timing were political. The third section, "Reform Motive: Transition, Fear, and the Drive to Insulate," documents the nature of the political threat to which I attribute the decision to insulate. Faced with the prospect of an imminent transition and the resurgence of a powerful center-left opposition, exiting authoritarian elites began to fear for the fate of their economic project under democratic rule.

## Reform Background: Chile's Neoliberal "Revolution"

Before we enter into a detailed analysis of the events surrounding the Chilean central bank reform of 1989, a word is in order on the broader economic context in which it was carried out. For to understand the impetus behind the reform, it is important to establish both the profoundly pro-capitalist nature of Pinochet's economic project and those specific interests that it sought to protect.

### The Economic Model: Pinochet's Foundational Project

The military government of General Augusto Pinochet came to power in September 1973 amid a crisis of massive proportions. Three years earlier, Salvador Allende's left-wing Popular Unity (Unidad Popular [UP]) government had been elected to office and had initiated a transition toward socialism. Under Allende, the banking system and all major copper mines were nationalized, while the expropriation of large manufacturing firms and agrarian reform were accelerated. But the socialist experiment quickly soured. Classically populist economic policies yielded soaring inflation rates of over 600 percent and growing fiscal deficits (see table 4.1), while massive strikes, extensive shortages, and plummeting investment all led to a collapse in production. As economic tensions grew, Chile's classically tripartite political system became increasingly radicalized. In this climate of profound macroeconomic imbalances, political polarization, and increasing violence, the Chilean military staged a coup to overthrow the Allende government.[1]

In the short run, the military's objective was to restore order to the country. But it was quickly evident that this was not merely a short-term coup d'état designed to wrest power from the left but, rather, a long-term "foundational" project to fundamentally restructure Chile's economy and society (Moulian 1992). In the economic realm, this meant transforming an import-substituting, regulated, statist economy into an export-oriented, free-market economy. In political terms, it translated into prolonged authoritarian rule,

**TABLE 4.1. Selected Domestic Macroeconomic Indicators for Chile, 1971–89**

| Year | Growth in GDP | Unemployment | Inflation | Fiscal Deficit as as % of GDP[a] | Investment as % of GDP |
|---|---|---|---|---|---|
| 1971 | 9.0 | 3.9 | 28.2 | 10.7 | 18.3 |
| 1972 | –1.2 | 3.3 | 255.4 | 13.0 | 14.8 |
| 1973 | –5.6 | 5.0 | 608.7 | 24.7 | 14.7 |
| 1974 | 1.0 | 9.5 | 369.2 | 3.5 | 17.4 |
| 1975 | –12.9 | 14.8 | 343.3 | 0.9 | 15.4 |
| 1976 | 3.5 | 12.7 | 198.0 | –0.6 | 12.7 |
| 1977 | 9.9 | 11.8 | 84.2 | –0.1 | 13.1 |
| 1978 | 8.2 | 14.2 | 37.2 | –1.5 | 14.5 |
| 1979 | 8.3 | 13.6 | 38.9 | –3.3 | 25.6 |
| 1980 | 7.8 | 10.4 | 31.2 | –4.5 | 17.6 |
| 1981 | 5.5 | 11.3 | 9.5 | –0.8 | 19.5 |
| 1982 | –14.1 | 19.6 | 20.7 | 3.5 (8.8) | 15.0 |
| 1983 | –0.7 | 14.6 | 23.1 | 3.2 (7.5) | 12.9 |
| 1984 | 6.3 | 13.9 | 23.0 | 4.3 (9.1) | 13.2 |
| 1985 | 2.4 | 12.0 | 26.4 | 2.5 (9.8) | 14.8 |
| 1986 | 5.7 | 8.8 | 17.4 | 2.1 (5.0) | 15.0 |
| 1987 | 5.7 | 7.9 | 21.5 | 0.2 (1.5) | 16.4 |
| 1988 | 7.4 | 6.3 | 12.7 | –0.1 | 17.0 |
| 1989 | 10.0 | 5.3 | 21.4 | –1.2 | 18.6 |

*Source:* For growth in GDP, unemployment, inflation, and fiscal deficits data, the source is Corbo and Fischer (1994, 32). For investment data, the source is Dornbusch and Edwards 1994, 112.

[a]A minus sign indicates a surplus. The figures in parentheses include an estimate of the quasi-fiscal subsidies channeled though the central bank (Larrañaga 1989).

1. For a detailed account of the breakdown of democratic rule in Chile, see Sigmund 1977; Valenzuela 1978.

which was seen as the only way to achieve a "technical firmness in decision-making" that would ultimately pave the way for a society rooted in "individual freedoms" (Valdés 1995, 30–31). The goal in both cases was to rout out any vestige of the country's previous economic model and democratic political system, which were seen as having led to economic mismanagement and political demagogy (Valdés 1995, 29). One cannot underscore enough the importance of Allende's three-year socialist experiment for understanding subsequent political events in Chile: it furnished the rhetorical enemy against which the entire transformational project would be directed over the course of the next seventeen years.

In explaining the authoritarians' "revolutionary" mission to modernize Chile, most authors have tended to emphasize its ideological underpinnings. In particular, they point to the group of U.S.-trained Chilean economists who developed and disseminated the monetarist prescriptions that shaped economic policy under early military rule (Montecinos 1988; Valdés 1995). It is certainly true that within the heterogeneous coalition of civilians, economists, and business elites who advised the military regime during the first decade of authoritarian rule, the so-called Chicago Boys held a particular pride of place (Valenzuela 1991, 54–60). To the extent that they offered a development model that was distinct from the traditional marxism or interest group politics of Chile's past, they found a receptive audience within the military leadership, who appropriated the model as their own (Silva 1996, 97–135; Moulian 1992). But while the authoritarians undoubtedly believed in the scientific correctness of their neoliberal project (Valdés 1995, 31–32), it would be a mistake to separate the technical logic of this economic model from the capitalist interests underlying it. Rather, the two were intimately intertwined.

In their effort to safeguard a functioning market-based economy, the authoritarians sought first and foremost to make the resurgence of a powerful anti-capitalist movement unlikely—if not impossible—in the future (Garretón 1986, 154). Despite the regime's universalistic rhetoric in which it presented itself as existing over and above the interests or pressures of any specific group or sector, there is no question that this model fundamentally benefited—and held its key constituency within—the Chilean business class (Moulian 1992). The central role accorded the private sector in the new model was clearly visible during the 1973 coup, when business groups conspired with the Chicago Boys in drafting the blueprint document that would serve as the basis for the initial set of reforms (Valdés 1995, chap. 11; Silva 1996, 85–88). Even in subsequent periods where economic policy ran directly counter to the interests of specific sectors, business would remain a consistent ally of the military government. In effect, Chilean entrepreneurs established a tacit quid pro quo with the Pinochet regime: a blank check of political support in exchange for the assurance that they would never again revisit the rampant violation of property rights witnessed under Allende (Frieden 1991a, 143–77).

In addition to assuring the continued well-being of the private sector, Chile's authoritarian government also had a more direct personal interest in securing the success of a market-oriented economic model. As Silva (1991, 99–100) notes, the Chicago Boys themselves—or entrepreneurs closely linked to them—were the top executives of the vast financial-industrial conglomerates that expanded rapidly between 1974 and 1978, gaining control of some of the country's most dynamic economic sectors.[2] This economic relationship was further soldered through the free flow of personnel between the public sector and these so-called economic groups (*grupos*) (Meller 1984). Because of these strong links to the country's main centers of financial and industrial power, the government thus had a vested interest in implementing a set of policies that would enable the groups to prosper. More to the point, Chile's extensive state-owned natural copper endowment also meant that the military government would be a direct beneficiary from a program of economic adjustment based in the liberalization of trade (Geddes 1994b, 207).

In sum, Pinochet's neoliberal economic project was executed both in benefit of and in tandem with powerful capitalist actors inside and outside the state. In what follows, I describe in more precise terms the nature of this support base. While the exact composition of dominant capital interests changed over the course of Chile's seventeen-year military rule, the regime can be consistently classified as "market oriented" by the criteria established in chapter 3.

## The Interests behind the Model: Economic Actors under Military Rule

The economic policy program of Chile's authoritarian regime is generally divided into two periods. During the first phase of so-called radical neoliberalism (1975–82), the government pursued a two-pronged agenda that combined orthodox stabilization with profound economic restructuring.[3] Without a doubt, the government's principal economic support bases during this initial reform process were the large financial-industrial conglomerates noted

2. By 1978, the three conglomerates to whom many top policymakers were linked—Cruzat-Larraín, Banco Hipotecário de Chile (BHC), and Edwards economic groups—controlled 53 percent of the private sector banking system's total assets and 42 percent of its dollar credit, as well as 71 of the 250 largest Chilean firms, which amounted to 40 percent of those firms' total assets (Silva 1991, 100).

3. I borrow this term from Montero (1993). Other authors use the terms *authentic* (Silva 1991) or *internationalist* (Muñoz 1992) to refer to this phase of neoliberalism. It has been examined in detail by a variety of authors. See, among others, Cieplan 1982; Vergara 1985; Foxley 1986; Edwards and Edwards 1991.

earlier. Because of their privileged access to foreign credit, these groups were well positioned to benefit from the liberalization of the economy. In particular, they were able to use their domination of the financial intermediation of foreign loans to expand the growth of the financial sector and to modernize selected industries (Frieden 1991a; Hastings 1993).

Three areas of the economy benefited during this early phase of liberalization: banks; non-traded-asset markets such as financial services and real estate; and traded goods where Chile had a clear comparative advantage but had previously faced negative effective protection, such as primary production and some traditional manufacturing industries. In contrast, the regime's reversal of previous import substitution and regulation had a negative impact on those sectors that had come to rely on protectionist programs, especially within the manufacturing sector (see table 4.2). The net balance of these winners and losers within the industrial sector at the end of the 1970s is seen in figure 4.1. Not surprisingly, the economic groups and their conglomerate affiliates tended to dominate ownership within the economy's most successful sectors.[4]

**TABLE 4.2. Chile: Sectoral Economic Trends, 1974–82 (sectoral output and employment as % of total)**

| | 1974 | 1979 | 1982 |
|---|---|---|---|
| Primary | | | |
| Output | 17.7 | 17.1 | 13.3 |
| Employment | 25.6 | 24.0 | 23.5 |
| Manufacturing | | | |
| Output | 29.5 | 21.2 | 18.9 |
| Employment | 19.5 | 16.7 | 14.1 |
| Commerce | | | |
| Output | 14.1 | 16.7 | 15.6 |
| Employment | 11.6 | 15.6 | 16.8 |
| Financial Services | | | |
| Output | 5.3 | 8.1 | 11.2 |
| Employment | 1.9 | 2.7 | 3.6 |

*Source:* Frieden 1991a, 163. Copyright © 1991 by Princeton University Press. Reprinted by permission of Princeton University Press.

4. Note, for example, that in 1978, the Cruzat-Larraín group had 33 firms in real estate, construction, and investment companies; 6 in financial services; 10 in commerce; 16 in agriculture, forest products, and mining; and 34 in industry—especially wood products, pulp, and paper; copper products; seafood; food products; and beverages. In the same year, the Vial/BHC group had 20, 9, 3, 9, and 15 firms, respectively, while its manufacturing affiliates were primarily in metalworking, appliances, and food products (Frieden 1991a, 166–67).

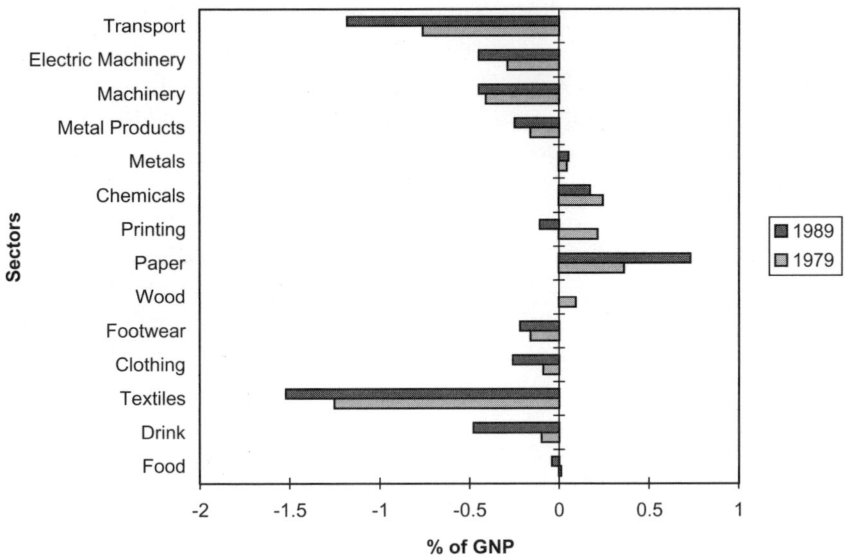


**Fig. 4.1. Chile: Industrial restructuring by sector (% of GNP). (From Valdes 1992, 65.)**

At the end of the first phase of neoliberal economic reforms, the military regime appeared to have achieved what it had set out to do. The economy had been radically transformed from one where public ownership was dominant to one where nearly all economic activity was in the hands of the private sector. At the same time, growth had fluctuated consistently between 5 and 10 percent from 1977 to 1981, and inflation—once as high as over 600 percent—was down to under 10 percent in 1981. But all was not as it seemed. Chile's "boom" in the 1970s had been sustained largely through a heavy reliance on foreign savings. In 1981–82, Chile's total foreign debt represented 50 percent of GDP, and amortizations plus interest payments were approximately 85 percent of Chilean exports, compared with 42 percent for 1975–80 (Arriagada and Graham 1994, 246). In 1982, a combination of recession, the abrupt termination of external credit, and a major devaluation of the currency weakened the repayment capacity of large segments of Chilean borrowers, erupting into a financial crisis of massive proportions (Muñoz 1985; Arrellano 1988; Larraín 1989).

The 1982 crisis had pronounced and immediate economic effects. GDP growth fell by 19 percent, and unemployment skyrocketed to nearly 20 percent. In order to salvage the severely overindebted financial sector, the government took over 70 percent of the Chilean banks, absorbing all of their debt

(Frieden 1991a, 61). It also repurchased approximately 50 percent of the enterprises that had been privatized in the 1970s. For the first time since the military took power in 1973, there were massive public protests, as organized labor, middle-class groups, and resurgent political parties took to the streets to rally forces against the economic and political project of the authoritarian regime (Huneeus 1985; Garretón 1986).

For our purposes, however, the 1982 crisis was significant because it triggered a pronounced shift in domestic economic policy coalitions. With the collapse of orthodox monetarism and abundant foreign finance, the large financial conglomerates of the 1970s lost much of their momentum, many entering into bankruptcy. In their place, a new coalition for "pragmatic neoliberalism" surfaced, whose major protagonists were drawn from the more traditional business associations (Montero 1993, 52–54; Silva 1996, 173–213). As the regime gradually recovered from the economic crisis of 1982–83, this group of capitalists became the motor behind a new economic model: one anchored in the orthodox stabilization and economic restructuring of its more radical predecessor but peppered with selective inducements and mild forms of protection.[5]

In particular, the second phase of neoliberalism generated a core constituency of large-sized firms with substantial ties to international markets. Over a twenty-year time span, Chile's export sector had more than doubled its relative size, climbing from 12 percent of GNP in the decade of the 1960s to nearly 30 percent of GNP in the mid-1980s (Ossa 1993a, 387). Within the tradables sector, the locus of economic dynamism was its natural resource sectors (mining, forestry, fishing, and nontraditional agriculture). Over the course of the 1980s, natural resource–based exports expanded their productive potential by more than 16 percent of what would have occurred without trade liberalization.[6] In contrast, those branches of industry previously associated with import substitution industrialization (ISI) in Chile (e.g., textiles, automobile parts, and electronic parts) suffered a contraction equivalent to

5. Pragmatic neoliberalism softened its predecessor by offering price protection for some depressed areas of agricultural production, encouraging a preferential exchange rate for exports, and helping banks to repatriate their assets while at the same time drafting much more restrictive bank regulations. For a more detailed discussion of the policies of this period and their effects, see Fontaine 1993; Wisecarver 1993; Bosworth, Dornbusch, and Labán 1994.

6. By 1985, these sectors accounted for approximately 85 percent of the country's total exports. While Chile's natural copper endowment was pivotal in this regard, the real source of the economy's dynamism lay in nontraditional natural resource exports. Nontraditional exports in the agriculture, forest, and fisheries sectors rose from 3.7 percent of total exports in 1970 to 30 percent in 1990, while copper's participation declined from 75 percent to 45 percent during the same period (Meller 1992, 39).

nearly 60 percent of what their productive potential had been before liberalization occurred (see fig. 4.2). To provide some idea of the magnitude of this change, the intrasectoral shift within the country's productive apparatus was on the order of 5 percent of GNP (see fig. 4.3).

By the end of the 1980s, these exposed sectors of the economy were prospering within an exceedingly favorable macroeconomic environment. A realistic exchange rate had been maintained through successive devaluations to encourage the use of resources in producing tradable goods. With the onset of an ambitious debt conversion program in 1985, total debt service declined from 49 percent of exports in 1985 to 25 percent in 1988 (see table 4.3). Many of the enterprises bought back by the state were privatized again but this time without the concentration of ownership that had characterized the first wave of privatization (Luders 1991). Growth picked up steadily, averaging 6 percent between 1985 and 1989, and unemployment dropped to 5 percent in 1989. In short, after many fits and starts, it appeared that the neoliberal economic experiment had borne fruit, at least where the private sector was concerned.

Over time, the military regime's liberalizing experiment thus created a set of powerful economic interests that prospered in the Chilean economic environment and owed their success to the dictatorship. While during the first period of radical neoliberalism this coalition was comprised primarily of financial and international capital, in the second phase of pragmatic neoliberalism it was rooted in productive capital within the country's traditional areas of comparative advantage. In both cases, the existence of these powerful economic constituencies led to a societal demand for a set of market-oriented policy outcomes conducive to economic openness, private property, and macroeconomic stability. In other words, throughout the course of its seventeen years in power, the military government of General Augusto Pinochet acted as an advocate for the types of capital that would both lend their support to and benefit from a central bank reform.[7]

7. Frieden (1991a) maintains that the salient division among Chilean capitalists under military rule was not sector but class. But as this analysis and Frieden's own both reveal, one can clearly delineate winners and losers in both periods of authoritarian rule that break down along sectoral lines. The fact that this economic distinction does not readily translate into obvious political differences should not be taken as evidence that the more protected sectors of the economy did not lose out under authoritarian rule. In the first period (1975–82), their quiescence can be explained by the fact that they still saw neoliberalism as the price they had to pay to prevent a reversion to socialism. In the second period (1983–88), their lack of vocal protest over economic policy reflects the fact that the losers within the smaller, more sheltered firms were not politically active or savvy, as will be noted subsequently.

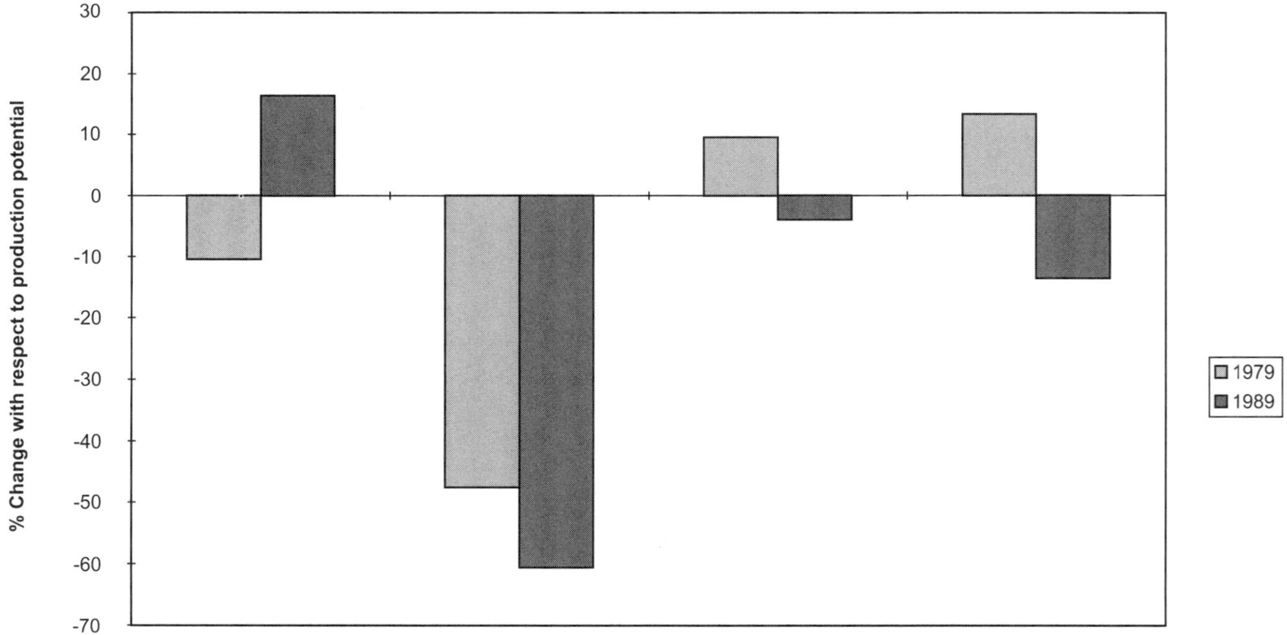


Fig. 4.2. Chile: Industrial restructuring (% change with respect to production potential). (From Valdes 1992, 64.)

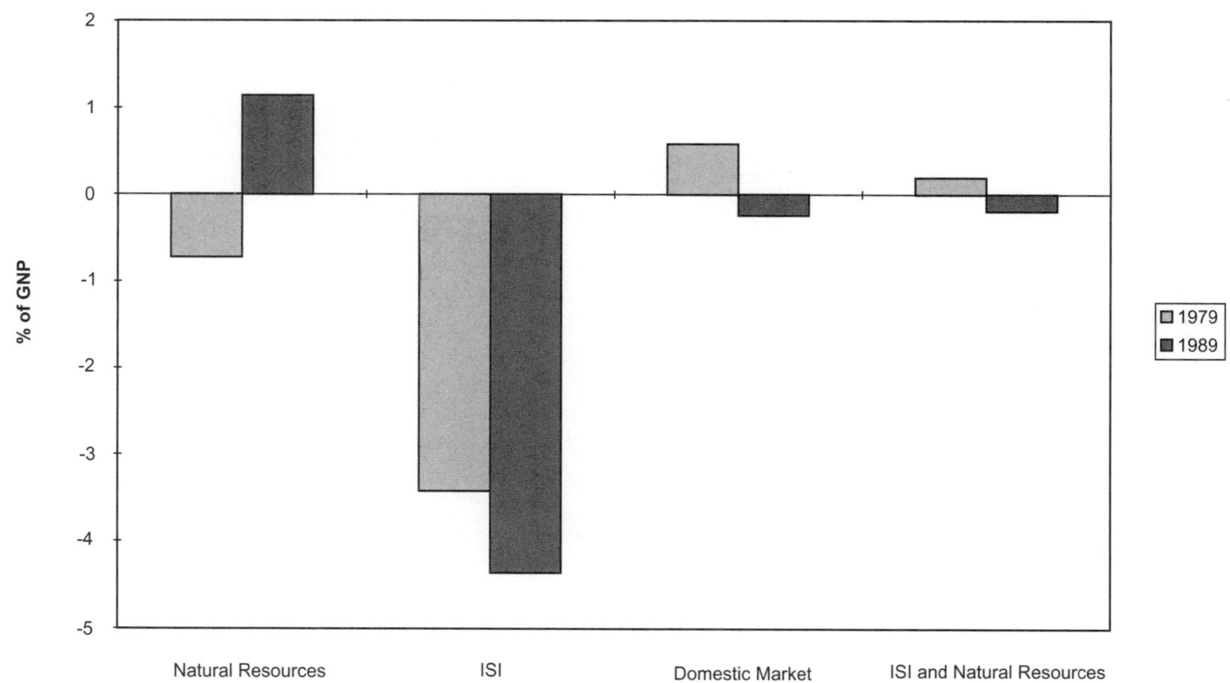


Fig. 4.3. Chile: Industrial restructuring (% of GNP). (From Valdes 1992, 64.)

**TABLE 4.3. Chile: Selected International Economic Indicators, 1970–89**

| Year | Real Exchange Rate Index | Trade Deficit[a] | International Reserves (millions of U.S.$) | Balance of Payments[b] | Ratio of Debt Service to Exports | Import Cover[c] |
|---|---|---|---|---|---|---|
| 1971 | 85.6 | 1.0 | 162.7 | n/a | n/a | n/a |
| 1972 | 64.7 | 3.5 | 75.8 | n/a | 9.9 | 1.5 |
| 1973 | 74.4 | 1.9 | 121.6 | –21 | n/a | n/a |
| 1974 | 122.7 | –0.7 | 41.1 | –55 | 9.9 | 1.4 |
| 1975 | 147.1 | 2.0 | 55.9 | –344 | n/a | n/a |
| 1976 | 124.1 | –4.3 | 405.1 | 414 | 31.1 | 3.0 |
| 1977 | 100.0 | 1.8 | 426.5 | 113 | 33.8 | 2.4 |
| 1978 | 111.4 | 3.3 | 1,090.1 | 712 | 40.7 | 4.0 |
| 1979 | 112.2 | 2.8 | 1,938.3 | 1,047 | 26.5 | 5.4 |
| 1980 | 97.2 | 4.2 | 3,123.3 | 1,244 | 43.1 | 5.9 |
| 1981 | 84.5 | 10.3 | 3,213.3 | 70 | 65.0[d] | 4.5 |
| 1982 | 94.2 | 1.9 | 1,815.0 | –1,165 | 71.3 | 4.1 |
| 1983 | 113.1 | –2.7 | 2,036.3 | –541 | 54.5 | 5.2 |
| 1984 | 118.2 | 1.1 | 2,303.2 | 17 | 59.9 | 4.9 |
| 1985 | 145.2 | –2.8 | 2,449.9 | –99 | 48.6 | 5.8 |
| 1986 | 159.7 | –3.8 | 2,351.3 | –228 | 41.5 | 5.4 |
| 1987 | 166.6 | –4.1 | 2,504.2 | 45 | 36.5 | 5.2 |
| 1988 | 177.6 | –7.2 | 3,160.5 | 732 | 25.2 | 5.2 |
| 1989 | 173.5 | –3.6 | 3,628.6 | 439.7 | 27.5 | 3.9 |

*Source:* For real exchange rate index and trade deficit data, the source is Corbo and Fischer 1994. For international reserves, the source is World Bank, *World Tables* (Washington, DC: World Bank, various years). For balance of payments data, the source is Edwards and Edwards 1991; and Central Bank of Chile, *Boletín Mensual* (Santiago, Chile: Central Bank of Chile, various years). For debt service to export ratios and import cover data, the source is International Monetary Fund, *World Debt Tables* (Washington, DC: International Monetary Fund, various years).

[a]Percentage of GDP, computed with national account information at current prices; a minus sign indicates a surplus.

[b]A minus sign indicates a deficit.

[c]Total reserves over imports of goods and services per month.

[d]Estimate.

## Reform Timing: Questioning the Credibility Logic

In light of the decidedly market-oriented nature of Chile's authoritarian regime, it is perhaps not so surprising that the government would have chosen to enact a central bank reform. The relevant question to ask, however, is not why the regime chose to undertake a central bank reform at all but, rather, why it chose to do so when it did.

When the Pinochet government enacted legislation granting autonomy to its central bank in December 1989, the official rationale was twofold. First, central bank autonomy would aid in preserving a climate of macroeconomic stability. Many in the military government attributed Chile's inflationary history to the pervasive control that the executive branch had wielded over the central bank under democratic rule (De la Cuadra 1987). The authoritarians wanted Chile to avoid the macroeconomic imbalances that were said to result from the pursuit of short-term objectives such as output and employment in search of political dividends (Rosende 1993, 296). In order to do this, they argued, future governments could not rely on mere concertation among societal actors. Rather, they would need to "institutionalize mechanisms to ensure macroeconomic stability" (Fontaine 1989, 66). By making the effects of fiscal deficits transparent, an autonomous central bank would "sound the alarms . . . at this non-legal tax called inflation" (Fontaine 1989, 66). In short, the government invoked standard credibility arguments in its explanation for this reform initiative.

In addition to this more conventional credibility-based explanation, the reform was also justified on legal grounds. The 1980 Chilean political constitution had defined the Central Bank of Chile as "an autonomous entity of technical character that possesses its own assets" (Political Constitution of the Republic of Chile 1980, Article 97). Beyond defining these quite general parameters, however, the 1980 Constitution said very little about the technical basis for such autonomy.[8] Rather, the Constitution authorized the execution of a subsequent organic constitutional law, in which the composition, organization, and attributions of the central bank would be established in order to give more precise meaning to its putative autonomy. The existence of this clause effectively constituted a legal obligation to enact a more fully detailed central bank reform at some point in the future (Figari Oxley 1989, 1).

8. Article 98 of the Constitution did contain two clauses that would serve as important guidelines for the central bank law that would eventually be passed in 1989. First, it prohibited the central bank from financing any public expenditure or loan of the government either directly or indirectly. Second, it established a legal precedent of "no discrimination" with respect to the regulations or requirements pertaining to any individual, institution, or entity with which it conducted business. I will discuss these features of autonomy—and their relative significance under authoritarian rule—in more detail in chapter 5.

There is, however, good reason to question both of the government's avowed motives. A closer look at the central bank autonomy initiative as it evolved over the course of authoritarian rule suggests a much more political explanation for the timing of this reform.

### Pre-1980: The Chicago Boys and Early Reform Efforts

The first thing to note in the Chilean case is that the original idea for central bank reform actually dates back to the mid-1970s, when the Chicago Boys first attempted to make the central bank autonomous. While the proposed setup was not identical to the reform that was eventually passed in 1989, what is striking is how many of the ideas that found their way into the 1989 organic law were also present in the original version.[9] If this is the case, then one must question why the government did not go ahead and enact a central bank reform when the idea first surfaced.

One explanation—consistent with a credibility-based account— is that the macroeconomic environment simply did not call for a central bank reform at this point in time. While the credibility literature does not specify an optimal time to undertake central bank reform, it seems most likely that commitment devices are most called for during times of economic crisis. Under conditions of fiscal imbalances and strong inflation, "the best antidote might be to adopt a permanent institutional change that eliminates legally the central bank's ability to finance the government" (Roubli-Kaiser 1996, 13). A severe crisis also opens up a political window of opportunity in which to introduce dramatic changes, break a policy stalemate, and put reform opponents on the defensive (Balcerowicz 1995). As Williamson and Haggard aptly note, "the worst of times give rise to the best of opportunities for those who understand the need for fundamental economic reform" (Williamson and Haggard 1994, 565).

The evidence from this period is somewhat difficult to interpret on this

9. Those closely involved with the first reform initiative swear that the two initiatives were almost identical, and portions of the proposed law discussed in meetings of the constitutional commissions during the late 1970s also lend support to this claim (Briones Espinosa 1989). The most striking difference between the two reform initiatives appears to have been in the area of exchange rate policy. While the earlier initiative subscribed to a fixed exchange rate regime (which largely reduced the central bank's role to one of carrying out exchange operations), the latter initiative was enacted under a crawling rate regime and thus, by definition, afforded the central bank a broader range of powers (interviews by the author, tape recordings, Santiago, Chile, with Pablo Baraona, former minister of the economy under Pinochet, April 21, 1995; Jorge Cauas, former minister of the economy and vice president of the Chilean Central Bank under Pinochet, May 3, 1989; Hernán Errázuriz, former legal adviser to the Pinochet government, April 26, 1995; Daniel Tapia, former central bank economist under Pinochet, April 20, 1995).

point. When discussions about central bank reform first began to incubate within the military regime in 1974–75, one could reasonably claim that the country was still in the midst of a macroeconomic crisis that warranted extreme anti-inflationary measures: inflation was still close to 400 percent, and the country was exhibiting a balance of payments deficit.[10] But by the time these discussions actually came to a head as part of a broader set of internal negotiations over constitutional reform in 1979, such need was less clearly visible: inflation had diminished considerably, and the regime was actually showing a fiscal and balance of payments surplus. In short, depending on when one chooses to date the timing of the central bank reform initiative, it was more or less necessary from a credibility standpoint.

If we reject the credibility hypothesis as a clear-cut explanation for the fate of the first initiative, perhaps its demise can be attributed to the lack of sufficient interest on the part of the private sector. It would be difficult to argue, however, that there was not a powerful capitalist constituency in place by the late 1970s that would have strongly favored a central bank reform. As noted earlier, the government's sectoral support base in the 1970s was quite conducive to central bank reform: financial conglomerates with considerable ties to international capital. There was also considerable momentum for central bank autonomy among the conglomerates' chief representative within the regime: the Chicago economic team. Its leading spokesman at the time, Sergio De Castro, contended that it was "fundamental to have a system that impedes the President of the Republic from imposing policies contrary to monetary stability on the central bank" (Briones Espinosa 1989, 40). The Chicago Boys even went so far as to consult with IMF officials as to how they might go about putting this idea into practice.[11] At their behest, discussion ensued within the regime over whether or not an autonomous central bank ought to be incorporated into the upcoming 1980 Constitution.

But despite these explicit pressures for central bank reform by powerful economic actors, the initiative encountered considerable resistance from Pinochet's political and legal advisers. The reluctance to endow a state body with so much independent power was evident in the legislative commissions that were established to evaluate proposed changes to the constitution. In the words of one member of these commissions, "a conflict between the presi-

10. Exactly when these informal discussions began with respect to central bank reform is unclear. Most of those interviewed, however, placed these discussions toward the middle of the decade. For example, Pablo Baraona, who was in many ways the intellectual father of the early initiative, claims that discussions began shortly after the military coup in early 1974 and that the crucial elements were in place by 1976 (Baraona, interview).

11. It was then that they discovered that their desires to limit central bank financing to the government and create a nonpoliticized central bank board were echoed in an emerging school of economic thought: the credibility literature (Errázuriz, interview).

dent of the republic . . . and a totally autonomous power that controls the monetary system would simply produce a catastrophe" (Briones Espinosa 1989, 39). This sentiment was echoed by another individual who commented, "such an organ would be absolutely incompatible with a presidential regime" (Briones Espinosa 1989, 39). Yet another member warned of the dangers that might ensue were a sitting president to be denied sufficient veto power over the central bank board. He described such an arrangement as "politically inconvenient," referring to autonomy as "an iron belt . . . that inevitably invites the possibility of breaking the very purpose it is meant to underlie" (Briones Espinosa 1989, 37). Ironically, the objections to central bank autonomy voiced by the government's political advisers were in many ways prophetic of the objections that would be raised ten years later by its democratic opposition when the initiative was finally unfurled.

As a result of this political resistance, the first attempt to grant autonomy to the Central Bank of Chile floundered. The "consolation prize" was the inclusion of three more general clauses in the Constitution rendering the central bank nominally autonomous, with the promise of a more detailed organic law to follow. But the vagueness of their terms was indicative of the profound disagreements that had taken place within the regime as to whether—and how much—autonomy was ultimately desired (Briones Espinosa 1989). For the time being, it was clear that autonomy was considered antithetical to the regime's political interests and that the Pinochet government did not have any intention of enacting an organic law at any point in the near future. Indeed, when some of the economists approached the new minister of finance about moving ahead with the organic law shortly after the 1980 Constitution had been ratified, they were told that it was "the last thing on the government's agenda."[12]

Chile's early battles over central bank reform are instructive. While it might be the case that the government balked because the idea was too novel or too untested, I would offer a different explanation that is consistent with the general thrust of this book: an authoritarian regime will choose to cede authority to an autonomous institution only when its hold on power begins to loosen. As one of the principal economic advisers involved in this early initiative noted when explaining its demise, "it is hard for governments to yield power. . . . the military government had lots of support then. It simply did not look like this government could end."[13]

The demonstrated opposition to early efforts at central bank reform thus casts doubt on the government's claim that the 1989 reform was driven

12. Former "Chicago Boy" economist closely identified with the first reform initiative, confidential interview by the author, tape recording, Santiago, Chile, April 28, 1995.

13. Ibid.

sheerly by economic motives. Absent a compelling political reason to do so, the government was simply unwilling to cede authority over monetary policy to an independent agency. In spite of explicit signs of support for an autonomous central bank among its economic advisers, it would seem that an additional political incentive was needed before the government would be prompted to act.

## Post-1980: Big Business and the Economic Demand for Autonomy

Economic explanations for the reform's timing appear even more suspect in the period after 1980. If the constitution stipulated a legal mandate for central bank reform as early as 1980, why did the Pinochet government wait nine years to implement it?

The government claimed that the reform initiative had been stymied by Chile's 1982 economic crisis. According to the government, the crisis was such that it could not have prioritized a reform of this magnitude, and it waited instead for a more stable macroeconomic environment in which to move ahead.[14] What this really meant—as opposition economists would subsequently point out—was that the government needed a dependent central bank in order to bail out insolvent private commercial banks (Arrellano 1989, 93; Zahler 1989a, 100–101). As a result, it was simply not a propitious moment for the government to establish an autonomous institution purportedly rooted in the nondiscriminatory treatment of private lending institutions (Ossa 1993b).

One can question whether the 1982 financial crisis might, in fact, have provided the most favorable macroeconomic environment for central bank reform from the standpoint of gaining external credibility. This hypothesis will be considered in the next section of this chapter. But there is an additional, even more compelling reason to think that the government might have acted sooner. By the mid-1980s, extensive privatization and an atomized labor movement associated with pragmatic neoliberalism had combined to yield a powerful capitalist class with a vested interest in the policies guaranteed by an autonomous central bank (Silva 1996; Rehren 1995). We have already commented on the economic power of this exposed capital located within the country's areas of comparative advantage. Here, a word is in order on its political power.

As Campero (1991) notes, Chile's entrepreneurial class under military

14. See comments by various regime officials in "Autonomía del Banco Central es Mandato Constitucional," *El Mercurio*, November 25, 1988.

rule could essentially be broken down into two main groups: the "neoliberals"—large enterprises with a liberal capitalist vision of development—and the "corporatists"—small and medium-sized firms predominantly oriented toward the internal market. While the small and medium-sized firms dominated in numerical terms, they lacked economic and political might.[15] They thus had little influence on shaping the course of economic policy, and their pleas for greater protection and selective credit policies fell largely on deaf ears.[16] In contrast, the political dominance of the more internationally oriented, "neoliberal" faction was readily apparent.[17]

With the shift in domestic economic policy coalitions that took place following the 1982 crisis, there had been a corresponding shift in the role that capitalists played in the construction of economic policy. Business-government relations evolved from a behind the scenes, tacit alliance characteristic of the 1970s to one of active business participation in the policy agenda in the 1980s. The peak organization for large firms—the Confederation of Production and Commerce (Confederación de Producción y Comercio [CPC]) played a major role in redefining key parameters of the "pragmatic" neoliberal economic model that ensued (Silva 1991, 110–14; Campero 1991, 138–43). Important businesspeople were also named to ministerial posts in the economic agencies of the government (Silva 1991, 112–13). By 1984, large firms began to enjoy direct access to the policy-making process through their participation in various legislative and economic commissions, as well as a presidential consulting body—the Economic and Social Council (Dugan and Rehren 1990).

15. Of some 276,000 entrepreneurs in the late 1980s, about 240,000 owned small businesses (Campero 1991, 129). These firms tended to be concentrated in the less internationally competitive sectors, where 93 percent found their livelihood in transportation, traditional agriculture, or small-scale commerce and artisanry (Campero 1988, 48). Politically, they were weak and marginalized. Voluntary membership in business organizations deprived their peak organization—CONUPIA—of an important source of funding that might otherwise have been used to mobilize support for their preferred policies. And unlike the peak business association representing large firms, this organization was rarely consulted by the government on major policy initiatives (Juan Morales, president of Conupia, interview by author, tape recording, Santiago, Chile, June 5, 1995).

16. Note, for example, that the members of ASIMET—the business organization including small merchants and the transportation sector under military rule—felt that the economic reactivation did not favor national industry and that small and medium-sized firms continued to operate under depressed conditions. In June 1985, these sectors attempted to reconstitute a new confederation in order to advance their views. But they were unable to achieve substantial results and were thus overshadowed by the policy preferences of the large firms (Silva 1991, 142). For more on the economic policy preferences of small and medium-sized firms under military rule, see also Ortega Riquelme 1985; Pardo V. 1989.

17. This is not to suggest that there were no protectionist interests in the neoliberal coalition. But such large, protectionist firms were clearly dominated by the free-marketeers (Silva 1991, 117).

Above all, however, the political power of big business was reflected in the fact that it increasingly came to project itself as a sociopolitical actor independent of the government or political parties. By transferring so much control over economic activity to the hands of the private sector, Pinochet's economic program had endowed the Chilean business class with a tremendous amount of structural power and influence. Powerful capitalists gradually came to recognize that this privileged position gave them an automatic role in the decision-making process, such that they, together with the state, constituted the leadership of the system (Montero 1993, 53). As one Chilean businessman phrased it, "Governments can change, but none will produce a tenth of the well-being if capitalists do not produce it. It is important that politicians see this clearly—because it gives us more power than ever before" (Montero 1990, 112).

By the mid-1980s, entrepreneurs from large firms began putting such autonomy to use to defend their policy interests. Indeed, "there was a strong identification between the policies of the Pinochet government and the aspirations of a group of businesses that valued external opening, competition, and the role of cutting-edge technology" (Montero 1990, 110). A poll conducted of leading business elites in 1986 lends credence to this claim. The poll showed that they felt that the economic policies of the authoritarian regime mirrored their economic policy preferences almost perfectly (Campero 1988, 51). In 1986, they began employing mass gatherings as a vehicle for promoting this neoliberal ideology. Declaring themselves to be the "motors of development," the business class embarked upon a self-proclaimed "battle of ideas." This new discourse vaunted a market-oriented economic model as "the only one capable" of overcoming underdevelopment, advancing the idea of the "freedom to undertake economic activity as the foundation of modernization and progress" (Campero 1991, 144).

It is of particular note that business groups lent their enthusiastic support to the central bank autonomy initiative. They called publicly for a central bank with "maximum independence from the government and political power" (Garretón 1989, 101), which was seen as "an indispensable pillar for the development of any society that aspires to be truly free."[18] Business groups were also among those consulted by regime officials to express their views on early drafts of the legislation when the idea first resurfaced in the mid-1980s. Once a draft document was circulating in 1988, business leaders created a commission within the CPC to study the initiative and propose specific

18. Editorial statement by Fernando Agüero, president of the industrial sector's business association, SOFOFA (Sociedad de Fomento y Fábril [Organization of Industry and Manufacturing]) in *Industria,* June 1989, 6.

changes.[19] Perhaps most significantly, when the military government ultimately selected the individuals who would be on the first central bank board in late 1989, large firms were given the right to vet potential candidates.[20]

In brief, as early as 1986, the Chilean economy was dominated by a set of free-market economic actors who enjoyed considerable influence over economic policy-making and who demonstrated interest in an autonomous central bank. And yet, the government chose to overlook this obvious economic incentive to undertake central bank reform. It is true that the reform was actually reactivated as early as 1986.[21] But an adviser close to the team in charge of the initiative affirmed that this was more because the Constitution required it than because the regime felt that it needed a central bank reform at this point in time.[22] In support of this hypothesis, note that this legislation's evolution was exceedingly slow during this period and that key components—such as who would serve on the first central bank board—had been left incomplete. Rather than being a high priority for the regime, the law seemed destined to be indefinitely "in committee."

## International Explanations: The Need for International Credibility

If domestic economic pressures do not seem to provide a satisfactory explanation for this reform's timing, perhaps a plausible motive can be found in

19. While the CPC enthusiastically endorsed the central bank legislation, it also had a number of specific differences with the government. For example, it favored greater accountability procedures especially over the central bank's management of its assets, fewer exchange rate controls, and the inclusion of a representative from the financial sector on the central bank board. Most of these changes were not ultimately included in the final legislation, although a few minor accountability procedures were included (interviews by the author, tape recordings, Santiago, Chile, with Manuel Feliú, former president of the CPC [in the late 1980s], May 30, 1995; Alfredo Gutierrez, professor of law at the University of Chile and head of the CPC study commission, May 31, 1995).

20. Former economic adviser to a leading business association, confidential interview by author, tape recording, Santiago, Chile, June 1995.

21. In 1986, a small commission of four or five individuals was formed to study previous central bank reform efforts in Chile as well as various models of autonomy from other countries. On the basis of these studies, it was to develop a draft of the new autonomy legislation. This committee worked on the legislation over the course of several years, refining and rewriting portions of the text and also circulating it to various members of the military regime and the Chilean business community for comment (interviews by the author, tape recordings, Santiago, Chile, with José Antonio Rodriguez, former legal adviser at the central bank under Pinochet, May 2, 1995; Jorge Cauas; Juan Andrés Fontaine, former director of studies at the Central Bank of Chile and principal author of the 1989 organic law, May 10, 1995).

22. Confidential interview by the author, tape recording, Santiago, Chile, April 28, 1995.

Chile's international economic environment. Here again, however, the evidence is dubious. By 1989, when the reform was finally undertaken, Chile failed to meet any of Maxfield's (1997) conditions for times when central bank autonomy is likely to be employed as a signaling device to the international community. First, despite a balance of payments deficit in 1985–86, Chile was running a balance of payments surplus by 1987. Nor did the predominant form of asset flow conform to the expectations about central bank reform held by Maxfield (1997, 45–54). In the latter half of the 1980s, Chile experienced an enormous influx of net foreign direct investment while indirect portfolio investment was negligible. According to Maxfield, such developments rendered central bank autonomy virtually "unnecessary" in the eyes of the government (Calderón and Griffith-Jones 1994, 5).

When we turn to Maxfield's third indicator—the extent of financial regulation—we see that Chile again defied the international credibility logic. According to Maxfield (1997, 44–46), greater financial regulation should make a country a less likely candidate for central bank autonomy, since it can arguably rely more on domestic sources for financing. But precisely because of the 1982 crisis, Chile's national capital account was heavily regulated, indeed, much more so than those of many other LDCs (International Monetary Fund 1992; Haggard and Maxfield 1996). Finally, other indicators of the need to compete for international capital simply fail to confirm the international credibility hypothesis: the ratio of debt service to exports had been virtually cut in half from close to 50 percent in 1985 to 25 percent in 1988; import cover had returned to its pre-1980 levels; and international reserves were steadily increasing (see table 4.3). To the contrary, what these indicators suggest is that Chile was in quite good shape vis-à-vis its external creditors when the central bank reform was enacted.

The same cannot be said for the period seven years earlier. Recall that the government attributed the delay in the central bank reform in the early 1980s to the enormity of the 1982 financial crisis. But if one accepts the proposition that central bank reforms are most necessary—in credibility terms—during periods of economic crisis, then there was arguably no better time for the Chilean government to have implemented the autonomy initiative than in 1983–84. Indeed, the external macroeconomic environment suggested that the country was ripe for a reform of this nature at that time.

Consider Maxfield's indicators. Unlike in the period when the reform was actually undertaken, in the early 1980s Chile was in the midst of an acute balance of payments crisis: the balance of payments deficit in 1982 was nearly equal in magnitude to what the surplus had been in 1980. Foreign capital inflows should also have militated in the direction of central bank reform. It is true that what little foreign capital did enter the country was almost entirely in the form of medium- and long-term credits—providing only a moderate incentive for central bank reform (Maxfield 1997, 41–42). But given that the net resource flow during this period was actually negative, this was arguably even more of an incentive to entice renewed lending through the establishment of an autonomous central bank. Finally, it was precisely the liberalization of capital controls that contributed to the speculative behavior and subsequent collapse of the banking system in the early 1980s (Hastings 1993). According to Maxfield, this lax regulatory environment should have rendered Chile a prime candidate for central bank reform.

Other indicators also suggest that the early 1980s would have been a propitious time for the Pinochet government to enhance the credibility of its monetary policy. By the end of 1982, international reserves had dropped nearly U.S.$1.4 billion from the previous year. Concurrent with the sharp decline in international lending, foreign investment as a percent of gross capital formation also slumped, totaling in 1983 almost a third of what it had been before the 1982 crisis (Calderón and Griffith-Jones 1994, 6). The drying up of foreign capital inflows that took place in Chile in late 1981 was not entirely due to exogenous international forces. Rather, it was in many ways a reaction on the part of international bankers to the deteriorating domestic conditions and policy mistakes associated with the late stages of radical neoliberalism (Edwards and Edwards 1987, 196). As the real exchange rate appreciated, foreign funds had begun to head for more secure investments in dollar-denominated assets (Hastings 1993, 220). In the wake of plummeting foreign investor confidence, central bank reform would have been an obvious means through which the regime might have bolstered its flagging international image.

Briefly, if economic credibility had been the issue, there were any number of junctures in the seventeen-year span of the Pinochet regime when the government had sufficient economic incentives to make the central bank autonomous. It might have responded to domestic pressures when the idea first surfaced in the mid-1970s. Alternatively, it might have chosen to enact central bank reform following the 1982 financial crisis, as a signal of its commitment to macroeconomic stability before a skeptical international audience. Finally, it might easily have implemented the autonomy initiative in the mid-1980s, in light of its compatibility with the macroeconomic policy demands of powerful capitalist classes. The fact that the government chose to wait until 1989 suggests that its motive and timing were not strictly economic but also political.

## Reform Motive: Transition, Fear, and the Drive to Insulate

Neither the concerns of powerful domestic economic actors nor the exigencies of international capital were sufficient to warrant central bank reform in the 1970s and 1980s. Rather, the government needed to perceive that its hold on power was in jeopardy. Prior to 1988, there was no incentive for central bank reform precisely because Pinochet himself enjoyed a tremendous amount of power and security that enabled him to defend the neoliberal model and those interests behind it with impunity. In 1988, all of this would change, and the authoritarians would begin to have reason to rethink their strategy.

### Pre-1988: Pinochet's Iron Hold on Power

Over the course of his seventeen-year rule, Pinochet had acquired numerous powers that placed him at the center of the Chilean political system. The military coup of 1973 eradicated all democratic political institutions and replaced these with a military junta that assumed all executive, legislative, and constituent duties, including the power to override the 1925 Constitution where it saw fit.[23] While government responsibilities were initially divided evenly among the four commanding officers of the junta, Pinochet moved quickly to centralize power in his own hands. Through a series of decrees, Pinochet catapulted himself from chief of the armed forces to "first among equals" in this governing body, ultimately proclaiming himself president of the republic. As the undisputed leader within Chile's strongly presidentialist political system, he was able to intervene directly in the design of laws and to exercise appointment powers across all spheres of the federal government. This concentration of power within the executive branch was matched by the progressive marginalization of the junta, which was increasingly relegated to a legislative rubber-stamp role, beholden to the whims of Pinochet (Arriagada 1985, 28–134; Valenzuela 1991, 36–40).

Pinochet's role as the commander in chief of the armed forces fortified his political power. His unilateral control over promotions and retirements within the army proved to be very effective both in eliminating rivals and in securing the loyalty of his subordinates (Arriagada 1985, 125–28). By infusing all levels of the government with military appointees—particularly from the army—Pinochet also ensured that his political authority was reinforced by his military seniority (Huneeus and Olave 1987; Huneeus 1988a). In this way, Pinochet was said to be imbued with a "dual legitimacy" deriving from his twin roles as president of the republic and its chief military commander (Huneeus 1988b). These two roles were synthesized in 1982 when his politi-

23. Prior to the coup, Chile had a separation of powers system. Following the coup, a state of siege was declared that suspended all individual rights. The legislature was closed down, political parties that had participated in the previous democratic government were banned, the free press was curtailed, and military appointees replaced all elected municipal authorities.

cal and military advisers were unified under one body—the secretary of the presidency, which cemented the centralization of power in one individual.

The final pillar of power within Pinochet's personalized dictatorship was its legal status in the 1980 Constitution. As the decade of the 1970s wore on, it became increasingly clear that if Pinochet were to justify his right to remain in power, he would need to institutionalize both a rationale and a modus operandi for protracted military rule (Garretón 1986, 160–63). The 1980 Constitution did this through two constitutional orders. The first served to extend Pinochet's extraordinary concentration of power through 1988.[24] The second corresponded to a second eight-year period, beginning in 1989, when Chile would shift from military rule to a protected democracy in which the armed forces would play a guardian role. In the short run, the 1980 Constitution thus enabled the governing block to "legitimately" continue military authoritarian rule for eight more years.[25] In the long run, it imbued the authoritarians' political project with a considerable degree of permanence.

Above all, the 1980 Constitution entailed a variety of features that were designed to afford the military a privileged position under the eventual democracy that would result. For example, the military was given a vaguely worded constitutional mandate to "guarantee the institutional order of the republic," without defining either how this function would be exercised or what was meant by "guarantee" (Valenzuela 1992, 64). The armed forces were also given predominant representation on a National Security Council with the ability to oversee national security and monitor the actions of elected officials, in addition to widespread appointment powers. Finally, the Constitution denied democratic presidents the power to remove or freely choose armed forces commanders. Regardless of what political events might transpire in the future, Pinochet would thus remain as commander in chief of the armed forces.

In contrast to its strengthening of the military's role, the Constitution sought to circumscribe the authority of the political sphere, particularly that of the president and the legislature. Some political features of this protected

24. The first period had its legal basis in a series of transitory constitutional articles. These articles abolished habeas corpus and gave Pinochet complete latitude to declare states of emergency and to impose drastic curbs on individual liberties and rights without appeal to courts. While Pinochet was removed as an official member of the junta, he obtained the right to a self-appointed representative who reported directly to him. Since the junta continued to operate under a unanimity rule, Pinochet thus continued to enjoy (indirect) veto power over the junta's proceedings.

25. The 1980 Constitution was ratified with a landslide victory in a constitutional plebiscite held the same year, which the regime officially won with 67 percent of the vote. But in light of opposition repression, government counting of ballots, and the lack of electoral registers, few observers considered this to have been a legitimate show of popular support (Valenzuela 1991, 54).

democracy included: an exceedingly difficult constitutional amendment procedure, a legislature in which a third of the Senate would be appointed by the military regime through the establishment of the so-called designated senators, and a supreme court whose power lay in a constitutional tribunal with a strong military presence. In effect, many powers commonly held by the president were disbursed to bureaucratic state entities that were granted both autonomy and tutelage over the system: the military, the designated senators, and the supreme court (Arriagada and Graham 1994, 252). Toward the end of the decade, all of this would be buttressed by a series of additional organic laws and electoral reforms that would strengthen even further the outgoing regime's stranglehold over an eventual transition to democracy (see chap. 5).

## The Proximity of Threat: The 1988 Plebiscite

In sum, Pinochet had amassed a tremendous amount of power—political, military, and legal—during the course of his rule, with which he was able to promote and defend the interests of dominant economic actors as he saw fit. The only potential source of uncertainty in this iron hold on power was contained in the succession mechanism governing the transition between the two constitutional orders noted earlier. According to the 1980 Constitution, the political leadership during the second phase of "protected" democratic rule would be determined by a popular plebiscite to be held in 1988. In this plebiscite, the electorate would choose between allowing Pinochet to continue to rule Chile for another eight-year term or holding a popular election to select a new president. If all went according to plan, the plebiscite would merely provide a popular mandate for eight more years of authoritarian rule. In the event of a victory of the "no," presidential elections would be held on December 14, 1989.[26]

On the eve of the plebiscite, both subjective and objective indicators made it seem unlikely that the government would lose its bid to remain in

26. One can of course question why the regime created a constitution that contained the seeds of its own demise. A number of potential explanations have been offered. Most authors emphasize that at the time it created the Constitution, the regime was running out of legitimacy both with domestic audiences and abroad and needed to show that it was capable of political flexibility (Garretón 1986, 158–63; Valenzuela 1991, 50–54; Varas 1987). Others emphasize the fact that the regime was riding on an economic boom at the time of the 1980 Constitution and thus saw the plebiscite as no more than a "rubber stamp" (Arriagada and Graham 1994, 251). An alternative and potentially more compelling argument is that in addition to the reasons noted previously, the Constitution (and the plebiscite) was an effort by certain groups within the regime who feared a populist threat either by Pinochet himself or by another future government. In response to this fear, they wanted to establish clearly defined rules that would guarantee the preservation of certain political and economic assurances, regardless of who was in power (Moulian 1992).

power. To begin with, Pinochet saw himself as endowed with a historic mission to continue in office until his death. In the years leading up to the plebiscite he was quoted as saying, "the government of the armed forces has never been conceived of as a parenthesis in the civic history of the country. No one cannot recognize the legitimate right that we have to extend our project beyond 1989" (Varas 1987, 196). He additionally warned that "We will not turn over power just for fun; the first eight years served to dictate laws that complemented the 1980 Constitution, and the eight years that follow [are meant] to apply these in real form" (Huneeus 1986, 61). The quite prosperous state of the Chilean economy only made such an outcome seem all the more likely. Finally, the government's ability to use government ministries to target various social groups also gave it a considerable resource edge over its opponents. For all of these reasons, the vote was construed by the regime as no more than a legitimating device for maintaining power until the end of the century (Constable and Valenzuela 1991, 297).

This confidence exploded overnight, however, when the "no" vote won by a margin of 55 percent against Pinochet to 43 percent in favor. It is clear in retrospect that the regime overestimated its ability to win the plebiscite and, in so doing, unwittingly contributed to its own demise. On the one hand, the government went out of its way to ensure conditions for a "fair fight."[27] When the opposition actually won, the government thus had no choice but to accept the outcome, as a series of international and domestic pressures obliged it to do so.[28] On the other hand, the regime was also blinded by its own success in fostering growth and private investment. It dismissed opposition polls as biased and relied instead on reports from local government and army officials that were uniformly favorable (Constable and Valenzuela 1991, 304–5). In particular, it ignored its own poor record on social justice (see the following discussion). This played directly into the hands of the opposition, who ran an effective campaign indicting the regime for its neglect of the bottom 40 percent of the population (Arriagada and Graham 1994, 263–67).

The watershed defeat of Pinochet in the plebiscite had a number of

27. During the campaign itself, the government lifted states of exception, allowed for a fair and public registration process, and granted the opposition limited access to television. On the night of the actual vote, the opposition was allowed to set up an independent system to monitor elections and vote counting, with three poll watchers at each voting establishment as well as a sophisticated computerized vote counting system.

28. These included pressures from the U.S. government and the international financial institutions; the existence of moderate pro-democratic forces on the political right; and the nature of the armed forces itself, which—while loyal to their commander and chief—were also a highly professional institution strictly committed to constitutional rule (Constable and Valenzuela 1991, 302–5). With respect to this final point, note that it was a member of the ruling junta, General Fernando Matthei, who first declared the victory of the "No" campaign.

significant consequences. First, it was a visible signal that the Pinochet regime did not enjoy the widespread popular legitimacy that its leaders had imagined. It was particularly clear that the government's neoliberal economic program had worked against it in the electoral sphere. While the Chilean economic model had been widely praised for outstanding growth performance, the vast majority of the country's population had not reaped the rewards of such success (Ffrench-Davis 1991). In a post facto analysis of the plebiscite vote, 72 percent of those who voted "no" did so primarily for economic reasons, of which 38 percent saw the poverty question as the prime motivation behind the need for a change of government. Economic justice was prioritized even ahead of such concerns as human rights, general disapproval of the military government or Pinochet himself, or the need for a return to democracy (Méndez et al. 1989, 96).

In addition to revealing the regime's "redistributive illegitimacy" (Varas 1991, 75), the plebiscite also put an end to Pinochet's efforts to perpetuate his personal dictatorship through the end of the century. While he would remain as commander of the armed forces, his days of dual domination in both political and military spheres had come to an end. In this way, the plebiscite signaled the beginning of a shift in the internal balance of power within the regime, from a reactionary faction identified with maintaining Pinochet in power at all costs to a more moderate, negotiating faction open to the idea of a transition to democracy (Moulian 1993, 15–20).[29] The triumph of this more moderate faction would be definitively revealed when the government agreed to engage in negotiations over the Constitution in July 1989.[30]

Third, the plebiscite defeat also pointed to a well-organized opposition coalition under the leadership of the major parties of the center and left—the Concertation of Parties for Democracy (Concertación de los Partidos por la Democracia [Concertación]). Despite a decade of infighting and programmatic divides, these parties had been able to overcome their differences to successfully unite behind the singular goal of defeating Pinochet. Their success in this endeavor can be attributed to three separate learning processes

29. I refer here to the classic "hard-liner versus soft-liner" split (O'Donnell and Schmitter 1986). The "hard-liners" corresponded to the army and a conservative right-wing political party, the Independent Democratic Union (Unión Democrática Independiente [UDI]), while the "soft-liners" were represented by the other branches of the armed forces of the military and a moderate right-wing National Renovation Party (Renovación Nacional [RN]).

30. In the course of these negotiations, the government agreed to a number of changes to the Constitution: the quorum for a constitutional amendment was diminished from two-thirds of two consecutive Congresses to two-thirds of both legislative bodies; the veto power of the National Security Council was reduced in part; the presidential term following the transition was shortened from eight to four years; and the number of elected senators was increased from twenty-six to thirty-eight. For more on the events leading up to these negotiations, see Moulian 1993.

that took place in the years leading up to the plebiscite (Garretón 1991, 1992; Puryear 1994; Kinney-Giraldo 1996). First, they came to recognize their own role in bringing about the political gridlock that had culminated in a military coup twenty years earlier. They vowed to avoid a repetition of such polarization and sought instead to use the party system to restore consensus as both an ideal and a mechanism of democracy (Correa 1993).[31] Second, they also recognized that if they were going to end authoritarian rule, they would need to beat the regime at its own game. Despite their initial reticence to do so, the parties of the opposition ultimately decided to work within the confines of the framework of the 1980 Constitution—and the plebiscite in particular—as the forum for their fight. Finally, a third factor enhancing their success was their decision to unite in a strictly operational sense for the plebiscite, postponing the more potentially divisive issues of programmatic message and presidential candidate until they had first succeeded in ousting Pinochet.

By shifting the relative balance of power away from outgoing authoritarian elites and in favor of the incoming democrats, the plebiscite thus unleashed a process of transition to democracy. To be sure, this transition would unfold within the parameters set by the regime itself. But there was no question that it would take place as scheduled. The victory of the "no" was thus an unequivocal indication that democracy was not only an inevitability but also an event to which the country could attach a precise date and time.

## The Intensity of Threat: The Specter of a Center-Left Future

The only remaining question was who would take Pinochet's place: a right-wing puppet government comprised of the parties that had supported him in the plebiscite and could be expected to continue his programmatic agenda; or the center-left coalition that had united to bring about his downfall in the plebiscite? While there was no way of knowing for sure, the results of the plebiscite suggested the latter. This scenario provided sufficient reason for the government and its powerful business allies to begin to worry about how such an outcome might affect their interests in the future.

It is certainly true that the opposition did make a concerted effort to repeatedly stress its intention of maintaining macroeconomic stability under democracy. Many authors have pointed to the moderate nature of the Concertación's economic message as a crucial factor in securing its victory in the 1988 plebiscite, particularly among undecided voters (Angell and Pollack 1990, 4–5; Arriagada and Graham 1994, 264–65). It is also true that Alejandro

31. On the notion of "consensus building" as a means to execute socioeconomic and political policies, see Foxley 1985; also *Revista Cieplan* 1988.

Foxley, who was widely expected to be finance minister in the event of a Concertación victory, repeatedly reassured the Chilean economic elite that he would respect private property, would exert fiscal responsibility, and would not dismantle Pinochet's economic reforms (Kinney-Giraldo 1996, 252–54).

But collective memories combined with poor communication links meant that, ex ante, such promises fell on deaf ears. As far as powerful economic actors were concerned, the political class of the left and center had not evolved since 1973 (Bartell 1992). As the president of the peak business organization declared at the time, "We do not perceive that the opposition political groups of the center or center-left have incorporated into their economic and social thought that the best economic system is that of the market" (Rehren 1995, 12). A prominent businessman similarly noted that "most of the guarantees of macroeconomic stability come from economists and not from political leaders or formal statements by opposition parties. . . . [This] strongly diminishes their credibility, since one could treat these as expressions of good will that, later on, will be overtaken by political events."[32] Such mistrust was reflected in the fact that when Alejandro Foxley went to address a business gathering four days after the opposition's victory in the plebiscite, he was booed publicly by members of the business community who stood up and shouted, "We don't believe a word that you say" (Cavallo 1992, 149)! It is perhaps not surprising that in the two days following the victory of the "no," the stock market dropped by 11 percent and 16 percent, respectively (Campero 1991, 149).

It would be a mistake, however, to emphasize exclusively the role of private sector skepticism in generating an atmosphere of fear. The truth is that there was also a series of objective indicators that stirred up uncertainty regarding the future economic situation of the country. To begin with, we must recall that the Concertación coalition was by no means composed solely of moderates. In addition to its leadership within the centrist Christian Democrats, this seventeen-party coalition also included several parties and political movements from the Chilean left, many of whose leaders had held prominent positions within the socialist Allende government of the early 1970s.

Much of the Chilean left had undergone a fundamental process of ideological renovation over the course of the 1980s, renouncing its previous commitment to armed struggle and embracing a path of moderation and compromise (Silva 1992; Loveman, 1993). But a variety of individuals from the more hard-line faction of the Socialist Party also formed part of the opposition coalition. Only years earlier, this movement had called for a "revolution

32. "El Futuro de la Política Económica," *Industria*, October 1988, 7.

of the proletariat," and its continuing ties to militant far-left groups led to allegations of secret pacts between the Concertación and the Marxists in the period following the plebiscite (Angell and Pollack 1990, 6).[33] It was no secret that the Christian Democrats needed an alliance with the left in order to obtain an electoral majority in the parliament (Moulian 1993, 34). If they wanted to keep this unwieldy coalition alive, they would have to heed some of the demands of the more extremist elements, particularly since all important decisions had to be made through negotiations between leaders of the various parties.

In addition to the presence of radical elements within the Concertación alliance, another objective threat to continued macroeconomic stability was the popular mandate for a more actively redistributive economic program. As noted earlier, the primary stimulus behind the victory of the "no" had been the perceived failure on the part of the Pinochet regime to respond to pent-up social demands. Polls conducted at the time suggest that there was a widely held view among the working-class and middle sectors that the economic situation under Aylwin would change considerably in their favor (Hojman 1990, 26). Such polls also revealed that the majority of the population preferred policies that did not correspond to those advocated by the neoliberal status quo. To the contrary, in a series of polls carried out between 1986 and 1991, 70 percent of the persons polled opted for health care and education managed by the state; 57 percent felt that the state should own the most important companies; and 80 percent believed that foreign investment should be subjected to greater controls, if not nationalized (Arriagada and Graham 1994, 265).

While Foxley was acutely sensitive to the dangers of generating populist policy cycles (Foxley 1990, 118), business groups had to worry about the government's ability to withstand popular pressures for a profoundly redistributive economic agenda. Few had forgotten the recent experience in Argentina, where a newly democratic government advancing a platform of economic restructuring ultimately caved in to interest group demands (Acuña 1994; Flisfisch 1994). Despite whatever moderate discourse Foxley and others might have put forth publicly, it was thus common knowledge that with nearly 5 million people below the poverty line in a country of 13 million, "Chile's return to democracy can only survive if it responds to popular demands for redistribution and greater social expenditure" (Angell and Pollack 1990, 21).

33. Indeed, while the Christian Democrats successfully opposed including any avowedly Marxist movements in their electoral coalition for the 1989 presidential elections, several individuals held joint membership in both the Concertación and the far left coalition—the Broad Party of the Socialist Left (Partido Amplio de la Izquierda Socialista [PAIS]).

A third factor exacerbating the overall atmosphere of uncertainty was the internal divisions within the Concertación leadership itself regarding what sort of economic policy to pursue under democratic rule. There were considerable differences among the various party elites over issues such as the optimal tariff regime and level of industrial protection, the size and nature of state intervention, the role permitted foreign investment, and even the desirability of enacting another agrarian reform (Hojman 1990, 41). Such discrepancies came to the fore in a much-publicized incident that took place in March 1989 surrounding a draft document for the Concertación's economic program. On this occasion, Foxley personally vetoed the initial document drawn up by the technical committees of the Christian Democratic and Socialist Parties. He argued for a less regulatory role for the state on no less than twenty different points concerning foreign investment, the system of tariffs, the tax structure, and the privatization of public enterprises.[34] While the program was ultimately revised to a milder, albeit still ambiguously interventionist version (see the discussion that follows), this version emerged only after Foxley threatened to quit the economic team entirely (Cavallo 1992, 150–52; Kinney-Giraldo 1996, 250–52).

The significance of such an incident cannot be understated. Note in particular that the draft was not the product of the extremists in the Concertación rank and file but rather reflected a consensus position taken after intense negotiations among the coalition's moderate vanguard.[35] Such an act suggests that there was considerable support within the opposition leadership for a much more decidedly statist economic policy orientation.[36] And because the draft document—and the dispute itself—was quickly circulated to the press, these internal programmatic tensions were widely known. Such an overt internal conflict made it clear that even if Foxley was personally committed to macroeconomic stability, there was no guarantee that he would be able to stem the tide of more populist currents within his own coalition.

Such doubts were not alleviated by the final version of the Concertación's proposed economic program. While the final draft was considerably muted compared with its predecessor, it did not remove these ambiguities entirely. As Loveman (1995) notes, "the Concertación program was

34. For the actual contents of this draft document, see *Hoy* 608 (March 13–19, 1989): 39–41.

35. I refer here to the Christian Democratic Party and the more market-friendly "Renovated" (PS-Nuñez) wing of the Socialist Party.

36. As a leading member of the opposition's political team noted when reflecting on this period, "in 1989 the climate of economic ideas that were being nurtured within the Concertación were—in the best case scenario—in transition" (Flisfisch 1994, 25). Indeed, it was not until 1991 that the Christian Democratic Party explicitly endorsed the role of the market and private property as part of its development strategy (Rehren 1995, 22).

ambitious—indeed, too ambitious" (Loveman 1995, 306). In the economic realm, it promised social and economic policies to mitigate income inequality, reduce unemployment, provide educational and economic opportunities, and reduce extreme poverty, while sustaining economic growth, technological innovation, and modernization of the public sector (Aylwin 1990). In particular, the opposition had made "growth with equity" the centerpiece of its economic platform, promising to redress the "social debt" left by the military government through tax increases on business, increased labor rights, and the creation of a solidarity fund in which public defense expenditures would be reassigned to social spending (Aylwin 1990). While the proposed economic agenda could hardly be termed radical, it was both sufficiently vague in specifics and progressive in spirit to excite the concern of its conservative opponents (Rehren 1995, 44–47).

For example, the president of the CPC referred to the Aylwin program as "quite ambiguous; it allows as much for a government that is interventionist, structuralist, and statist as it does for a government that is free, market-oriented, and open, like that of today."[37] A businessman in the right-wing RN party similarly queried, "it is not clear what will be the role of the market and what will be the role of central planning in the assignment of resources . . . which will be the role of the private sector and which the role of public sector in development. . . . will we have to relive the past? Return to . . . 1970?"[38] Business reacted particularly strongly to the proposed changes in labor legislation: "Can one believe that the fruit export sector will survive and continue its expansion with strikes during crop season, obligatory work stoppages . . . and ports controlled by union monopolies?"[39] A policy research organization favorable to the military government even went so far as to project the expected economic costs attendant on a Concertación victory in the presidential elections, predicting that a victory of the "no" would lead to an initial expansionary bonanza (Cheyre 1988).

While it is certainly true that, once elected, the Concertación did go on to pursue an economic program that continued the principal pillars of the military regime, this should not be confused with the mixed signals that were sent in the months prior to its taking power. Ex ante pledges to maintain macroeconomic stability notwithstanding, I would question how much this message ever registered upon the upper echelons of the entrepreneurial class in the twi-

37. Felia, Manuel. "Crecer en Democracia," interview by Andrés Adler, *Ercilla,* November 15, 1988, p. 18.

38. "Programa de Gobierno de la Concertación: Cree en el Estado y sus Burócratas y Desconfía de las Personas," *Renovación Etapa* 2, no.32 (July–August 1989): 9.

39. Commentary from the conservative magazine *Economía y Sociedad,* as quoted in "Se Dijo," *Industria,* December 1988, 11.

light of authoritarian rule. Rather, due to a combination of objective socioeconomic realities coupled with the actions and statements of the opposition itself, the authoritarian regime and the powerful capitalist actors behind it still feared a resurgence of the populist economic policies that had inspired the military coup of 1973. As one author summed it up, "democracy represented a dual threat for the business class: on the one hand, the possible destabilization associated with excessive participation, and on the other hand, the fiscal imbalance associated with populist fiscal measures" (Montero 1993, 54).

In this way, the 1988 plebiscite signaled to Chile's authoritarian government the onslaught of a democratic threat that was not only intense but also proximate. After seventeen years in which they had enjoyed free rein to impose their policy preferences at will, the authoritarians could not take a chance. If they wanted to take action to protect their interests, they would have to move quickly. The next chapter documents the nature of their response.

CHAPTER 5

# Imminent Threat, Ironclad Response

## The 1989 Chilean Central Bank Reform

The previous chapter established the motive for Chile's 1989 central bank reform. Following the outcome of the 1988 plebiscite, the authoritarian regime and its powerful economic constituencies confronted a political future in which they would no longer be in charge. As it became increasingly evident that their heir apparent would hail from the center left, they began to fear what democratization might mean for the fate of their economic interests.

With this transitional political context as a backdrop, this chapter examines the nature of the authoritarians' response. Fearing the prospect of a "hostile takeover" by the Concertación, the Pinochet government sought to safeguard its economic interests by enacting a constitutional amendment to create a highly autonomous central bank.

The primary objective of this chapter is thus to illustrate the strong case of the argument presented in this book, one where the intensity and proximity of the democratic threat are both sufficiently pronounced for a highly insulated institution to result. But in addition to describing the reform outcome, this chapter also has two additional objectives. First, I argue that the extreme nature of this reform left the regime's democratic opposition worse off. Second, I explain why, despite their vocal opposition to the reform in 1989, incoming democratic governments have nonetheless maintained it intact.

I proceed in three steps. First, I show how the government's decision to enact the reform only after its loss in the plebiscite illustrates its role as an insulating device whose primary intent was to constrain the policy choices of future democratic governments. I then confirm this assertion by detailing the specific features of the reform's contents that render the Chilean central bank one of the most autonomous in the developing world. Second, I document the democrats' reactions to the reform in order to underscore its adverse welfare effects. Through a careful examination of their objections to both the content and process of the central bank law, I demonstrate why the democrats would have preferred a very different institutional outcome than the one with which they were ultimately confronted. Finally, I show why, despite the fact that this institution ran counter to the interests of subsequent democratic governments, they were nonetheless powerless to overturn it. In addition to a series of domestic political obstacles, the democrats were fundamentally constrained in their desire to change the law by the knowledge of the severe economic costs that would attend such an action in today's world economy.

In advancing these arguments, I refute much of the conventional wisdom on the Chilean transition. It is certainly true that one of the most distinguishing features of Chile's transition to democracy has been the continuation of neoliberalism under democracy. In interpreting this turn of events, however, many analysts have concluded that the democrats learned to value the economic model that they once decried and, by extension, the institutional accoutrements (such as central bank reform) that anchored it in place (cf. Hojman 1990; Arriagada and Graham 1994; Weyland 1997). Stated somewhat differently, the assumption behind much of the contemporary scholarship is that the continuation of market-oriented reform in democratic Chile was more by choice than by constraint.

This chapter challenges that view. I build from the premise that far from welcoming the neoliberal policy agenda with open arms, democratic governments in Chile had no other alternative. At least where monetary policy was concerned, they resigned themselves to taking their cues from the institutional legacies of their authoritarian predecessors.

## Responding to the Threat: The Reform Resurfaces

### After the Plebiscite: The Authoritarians Mobilize

After the opposition's victory in the plebiscite, military officials argued that it had been a "personal defeat for Pinochet, but not for the political and economic system that they had created" (Hojman 1990, 26–27). In light of the extensive range of enclaves embedded in the 1980 Constitution, the authoritarians certainly had the institutional wherewithal to make this a reality. In addition, the authoritarians used their final year and a half in power to even further entrench the central pillars of their authoritarian project. It was clear that they intended to leave the incoming government "todo atado y bien atado" (tied, and well-tied) (Loveman 1995, 309).

In its final months in office, the junta decreed a series of new organic laws to constrain incoming governments in the political and military spheres (Valenzuela 1992; Arriagada and Graham 1994, 250–53). Permanent tenure in office was afforded to civil servants of the military government—particularly in local government—thereby severely limiting the new government's ability to restaff the public administration. In turn, limited presidential appointment and removal power over military commanders was reinforced, and the military was also guaranteed minimum military budget levels.[1] An autonomous national television council was also created to oversee radio and television programming and the licensing of new stations. Finally, the regime cemented in place an electoral system that was deliberately structured to favor the regime and its supporters in an eventual transition to democracy. This system allowed the right—a minority—to secure representation in Congress far beyond its share of the popular vote. Following the plebiscite, electoral redistricting was further enacted to facilitate the representation of pro-regime supporters in the rural countryside.

In addition to these more decidedly political insulation tactics, the government also enacted a series of measures to cement a market-oriented bias within the economy. First, it passed the Banking Law in mid-1989, which converted all outstanding governmental loans to private commercial banks held over from the 1982 crisis into so-called subordinated debt with the central bank. By renegotiating this debt on exceedingly generous terms, this law served as a guarantee to a powerful group of investors that the government would neither control nor intervene in their banks in the future (Batarce 1993).[2] Second, the government also established a set of budgetary procedures that empowered the president to selectively veto specific spending provisions proposed by the legislature while limiting the ability of Congress to amend items upward (Baldez and Carey forthcoming). Finally, the government also began to legislate a state entrepreneurship law, which placed strict limits on the productive activities of the state. Through such a bill, Pinochet was able to dramatically accelerate the pace of privatization during his final year in power, divesting the government of even formerly strategic state enterprises such as one of the major TV channels and the national airline.

But by far the most significant of these economic insulation strategies was the constitutional law to grant autonomy to the central bank. As noted earlier, the central bank reform had actually been in preparation since mid-1986. But just how much of the law was actually written prior to the plebiscite is subject to some debate. Some members of the government's economic team swear that the central bank reform was all set to go months in advance and merely needed Pinochet's authorization; others close to the president maintain that the reform was done "at midnight" on the eve of the govern-

1. More specifically, a clause was introduced into the Constitution guaranteeing the military 10 percent of all proceeds from Chile's state-owned copper revenues.

2. The subordinated debt issue became a major source of controversy in Chile between the government and private commercial banks in the early 1990s but was ultimately resolved through negotiations between the central bank and the major indebted commercial banks in June 1996.

ment's departure from power.[3] Regardless of which version is correct, what is clear is that one of its crucial elements—the makeup of its incoming governing board—was delayed until after Pinochet's loss in the plebiscite. Its last-minute nature is reflected in the fact that the bill was not passed in the legislature until October 10, 1989, and did not go into effect until December 10, 1989, just four days before the presidential elections were to be held.

The fact that the regime waited until it had been defeated in the plebiscite before it ratified the central bank reform lends plausibility to the argument that the legislation's timing was dictated by political reasons. For if this had been a purely technical initiative, the logical strategy would have been to name the board members and sign the central bank law into practice prior to the plebiscite. That way, the government would have had an institutional guarantee regardless of who won the referendum. This is certainly the order of events that the regime's technical staff would have preferred, and a number of them were disillusioned when Pinochet chose to postpone the central bank initiative until after the plebiscite. As one such individual who worked closely on the initiative commented with regret, "we had discussed the importance of doing this legislation before the plebiscite 10,000 times. But for whatever reason, it just wasn't sent. This was a huge mistake."[4] Instead, just as had occurred some ten years earlier when the Chicago Boys first raised the idea of central bank reform, political calculations again outweighed economic expediency.

One can imagine that Pinochet had two reasons for biding his time. On the one hand, since this was an election year, the government stood to benefit from a dependent central bank. The last thing in the world that it would have wanted was to be saddled with an autonomous institution that might prevent it from engaging in "political business cycle" behavior. And, in fact, during the final year before the plebiscite, the government did introduce a series of measures designed to stimulate the economy by expanding expenditure and consumption, reflected in the fact that growth soared to 10 percent in 1989, 4.5 percent higher than forecasted (Ffrench-Davis and Muñoz 1990, 142).

On the other hand, and in keeping with the argument presented in chapter 3, the government should also have been reluctant to assume the risks entailed in creating an autonomous agency unless it had no choice. It would thus require a loss in the plebiscite before the regime would deem the creation of an autonomous agency necessary. As a weekly political magazine noted at the time, "it is curious that Pinochet has not yet pushed this law through,

3. Based on confidential tape-recorded interviews by the author with economic advisers in the military regime, Santiago, Chile, April–June 1995.

4. Prominent economist formerly associated with the military regime, confidential interview by the author, Santiago, Chile, May 11, 1995.

despite the fact that it is ready. This would seem to reflect that . . . he does not want to tie up everything before he has the certainty that he will have to succumb."[5] A former Chicago Boy noted when commenting on the timing of the initiative, "it was not until 1988 when the government knew that it was going to have to turn the government over to another group that it sped this organic law up. If they hadn't had to hand over the government, they would have never pulled this thing off the shelf."[6]

Suggestive evidence for how the onset of democratization might have influenced the reform's timing is implied in select comments made by various government officials both during and after its legislation. While these officials were never willing to admit an exclusively political motivation, there was often a not-so-veiled link made between the prospect of impending economic chaos and the need for central bank reform. For example, the principal author of the initiative expressed skepticism about the opposition's willingness and ability to preserve macroeconomic stability under democracy, charging that "the acid test . . . [will be] its adhesion to the concept of an autonomous central bank" (Fontaine 1989, 66). And the commander in chief of the Chilean navy, Admiral Merino, was purported to have gone so far as to claim that autonomy "would prevent a socialist economy from being introduced in Chile."[7] Such sentiments were perhaps best summed up by a former official in the Pinochet regime who confessed that "we all had a fear of democracy in mind when we did this."[8]

The political motive I impute to the reform was certainly reflected in the comments of the regime's opposition. In undertaking the reform at this time, opponents charged that the government was motivated by its fear that any future economic team would not be fully convinced of the "virtue and need to protect macroeconomic balance in general and to minimize the inflation rate, in particular" (Zahler 1989a, 101). In this way, the reform was seen as a clear attempt to "freeze monetary policy at the constitutional level" (Zahler 1989a, 101) by establishing a "parallel economic team . . . to perpetuate the Chicago Boy scheme"[9] that would deprive the new government of the "ability . . . to bring about its own economic programs" (Zahler 1989a, 102). As the Concertación's chief legal adviser commented, "it is evident that this is being legislated at the last minute to guarantee a technical-financial enclave that assures . . . groups of power within the present regime a situation of

5. "La Dictadura: Así Gobierna Pinochet," *Análisis,* August 15–21, 1988, 7.

6. Confidential interview by the author, tape recording, Santiago, Chile, April 28, 1995.

7. "José P. Arrellano Confía que Será Revisada, la 'Privatización' del Banco Central," *La Epoca,* August 20, 1989.

8. Confidential interview by the author, tape recording, Santiago, Chile, April 25, 1995.

9. Comment by Ernesto Edwards in "Se Busca Instalar Equipo Económico Paralelo en el Banco Central," *El Diario,* November 28, 1989.

omnipresent veto and control against any alternative economic policy in the future" (Briones Espinosa 1989, 7). As far as the opposition was concerned, it was "difficult to think of a reason other than the results of the plebiscite of October, 1988 to explain the timing of this reform" (Zahler 1989a, 101). As a result, the reform was taken as "irrefutable proof of [the government's] fear of democracy."[10]

There is no question that the decision to wait until after the plebiscite had taken place was a high-risk strategy, since in the event that the "yes" campaign did not prevail, the government might be forced to negotiate some of the reform's contents. But the fact that Pinochet was willing to take this risk reflects the extent to which he had confidence in his ability to win. Even with hindsight, such confidence does not seem unreasonable, given that he did manage to capture 43 percent of the vote. Had the authoritarians won the plebiscite, we can thus imagine an outcome more like the Mexican case: they would have gone ahead eventually with the reform, particularly given its constitutional mandate. But they would have probably designed its autonomy in a much more cosmetic fashion, to enable the central bank to continue to serve the immediate interests of those in power.

In sum, the events and commentary surrounding the 1989 Chilean central bank reform lend plausibility to the notion that its timing was a response to a politically uncertain future by an authoritarian government under siege. Once the authoritarians knew that they would definitively lose power, they quickly pushed through legislation authorizing an autonomous central bank. As one of the foremost experts on the inner workings of this period in Chilean history concluded, "without the transition, there would not have been a central bank law."[11]

## The 1989 Chilean Central Bank Reform: An Overview

The intensity and proximity of the perceived democratic threat were reflected in the institution that was created. By formal measures, the Central Bank of Chile is widely considered to be one of the most autonomous in the developing world (Swinburne and Castello-Branco 1991; Cukierman 1992).[12]

10. Comment by Ramón Briones Espinosa in "Ley del Banco Central Facilita Fuga de Capital," *El Diario,* October 11, 1989.

11. Ascanio Cavallo, columnist, *La Epoca,* interview by the author, tape recording, Santiago, Chile, May 24, 1995.

12. Note that the central bank had been nominally autonomous since 1953, when the term *autonomous* was first employed in its legal charter. But it is clear that until 1980, the term *autonomy* did not have much legal or practical meaning. In addition to quite vaguely worded central bank objectives, its board of directors had also provided ample representation to various special interests. More importantly, it was also understood that the central

The high degree of autonomy afforded the Chilean central bank was most evident in those provisions pertaining to central bank lending to the government. On this crucial dimension of autonomy, Chile is known to have the strictest limits in the world: the central bank could provide neither direct nor indirect financing of government expenditures, except under wartime conditions (Central Bank of Chile 1990, 16). These restrictions applied not only to the executive but to all state agencies and enterprises as well. While a similar clause impeding central bank loans to the executive had also been included in the articles of the 1980 Constitution, it had not carried much weight under authoritarian rule.[13] In contrast, the new law represented a rigid set of financing constraints.

To be sure, many autonomous central banks place limits on direct forms of central bank financing to the government. For example, the German Bundesbank stipulates such limits in strict cash amounts, which have been maintained at the same level since 1969 (Swinburne and Castello-Branco 1991, 425). But most central banks do allow for indirect financing of the government by permitting the central bank to purchase government bonds in the course of open market operations. By explicitly excluding the possibility of any financing of any type, the Chilean law made deficit spending by future governments extremely difficult and extremely costly.

The independence of the Chilean central bank was also enhanced through a second aspect of its new charter: the unilateral discretion it was afforded over monetary policy formulation. As noted in chapter 3, autonomy is generally thought to be strengthened to the extent that the central bank is granted complete or nearly complete control over monetary and credit policy. In this regard, the 1989 law clearly met these standards: it gave the central bank full authority to conduct open market operations, to determine the discount rate, and to set reserve requirements.

In addition to these normal central bank functions, however, what was

bank would act within general policy lines set forth by the government (Briones Espinosa 1989). Even after its autonomous status was elevated to a constitutional rung in 1980, the fact that there was no accompanying detailed legislation meant that the central bank continued to respond directly to the executive branch. Thus, despite the fact that Cukierman (1992) codes Chile's central bank independence as fairly high relative to that in other countries over the period 1950–88, it was not until 1989 that this autonomy really took shape (Fontaine, interview).

13. In particular, it had been periodically violated through the so-called triangularization of financing. Under this sort of scheme, third parties such as state financial institutions that were exempted from the "no lending" clause would act as financial intermediaries between the central bank and the government. While loopholes of this sort could still arguably be pursued even under the strict conditions of the 1989 law, they would henceforth require the acquiescence of a fully autonomous central bank, as opposed to one that was autonomous merely in name (Fontaine, interview).

striking about the 1989 law was that it also endowed the central bank with several extra policy-making attributes such as external debt management; financial regulation; and various foreign trade, investment, and tariff policies. While many central banks are charged with some mix of such auxiliary powers, few amass them to the degree demonstrated in the Chilean case. It is of particular note that Chile's central bank had the unique distinction of being the only central bank in the world in control of exchange rate policy. Even in the United States, widely considered to have one of the more autonomous central banks in the world, exchange rate policy is determined by the U.S. Treasury. Although these extra powers do not constitute direct indicators of autonomy per se, they do suggest that the Chilean central bank was afforded substantial influence over a broad range of economic policy arenas at the expense of other government ministries (Arrellano 1989, 92–94; Briones Espinosa 1989, 50).[14]

Many of these powers had been granted to the central bank in its previous 1975 charter, albeit in a less clearly delineated format (Figari Oxley 1989, 14). Under the new legislation, however, these were accompanied by explicit provisions to weaken the veto power of the finance minister. As noted in chapter 3, a key determinant of the effective degree of control afforded the central bank in the formulation of monetary policy is the formal role afforded the executive on the central bank board. In this regard, the Chilean reform most closely resembled the German system: while the minister of finance was permitted to attend the meetings of the central bank board and could even request that a given measure be temporarily deferred, he or she had no voting privileges. And in the event of a dispute with the executive, the law gave the central bank the upper hand across a range of policy domains.[15]

In addition to these many provisions designed to increase the power of the central bank over the government, the legislation also featured one provision that would weaken this control. I refer here to the legislation governing exchange liberalization. Under previous legislation, any international exchange operation not authorized by the central bank had been illegal.

14. There are those who argue that this power was somewhat mitigated where the Finance Ministry was concerned by the fact that all of the government's internal debt was held on the central bank's balance sheets rather than those of the Finance Ministry. This was the product of the 1982 crisis when the central bank had to step in and bail out insolvent commercial banks by absorbing their debt. Critics of the Concertación have suggested that because of this "patrimonial situation," the central bank is not fully solvent, since the Finance Ministry might use its financial leverage over the central bank as a means of influencing policy (Rosende 1993, 317–18; Tapia 1993, 353).

15. In the area of monetary policy, for example, a proposed suspension by the finance minister could be overridden if four out of the five board members were opposed. Where exchange restrictions were concerned, the finance minister's objections could also be overridden by the unanimous opposition of the board.

Under the new law, this provision was reversed; all exchange operations were permissible except those explicitly prohibited by the central bank. Moreover, while exchange controls had previously been ongoing, with the new law these had to be renewed annually. While the temporary nature of exchange controls arguably diminished the power of the central bank over the government, it also constituted a not-so-subtle means through which the authoritarians sought to push future governments toward their ideal point of full exchange liberalization. As one member of the Concertación's economic team put it, "while this doesn't impede that restrictions are renewed every year . . . there is an implicit pressure in the law that forces you to progressively eliminate controls until you arrive at total freedom."[16]

A third indicator of the high degree of autonomy afforded the central bank was reflected in the nature of its policy objectives. Under its 1975 charter, the central bank had been given a quite vague mandate: "promoting the ordered and progressive development of the national economy" (Figari Oxley 1989, 14). As noted in chapter 3, vaguely worded objectives are generally thought to compromise autonomy to the extent that they allow for the pursuit of goals that conflict with price stability, such as growth and unemployment. Chile's 1989 central bank law dramatically increased this dimension of autonomy by substituting its ambiguously worded language with a much more narrowly focused objective: "maintaining price stability and due payment of internal and foreign debts" (Central Bank of Chile 1990, 4). By extending the objective of price stability to include the complementary objective of ensuring a sound payments system, the authors of the reform sought to avoid the type of internal financial or external balance of payments crises that had blocked efforts to maintain price stability in the past (Fontaine 1989, 68; Rosende 1993, 299–301).

In contrast to the legislation's precisely worded goals, however, accountability measures to ensure that the central bank would actually meet these objectives were predictably weak. As in Germany, the law did require the president of the central bank to keep the president of the republic informed with respect to its policies and to "consider the general orientation of the government's economic policies" when passing its resolutions (Central Bank of

16. Nicolás Eyzaguirre, former director of studies at the Central Bank of Chile, interview by the author, tape recording, Santiago, Chile, April 24, 1995. One must, of course, ask why the authoritarians did not simply go ahead and legislate total exchange liberalization at the outset, rather than making the controls subject to annual renewal. This was the source of a great deal of internal debate within the regime in the drafting of the legislation, between free-marketeers such as Fontaine, who favored total freedom, and more traditional central bank bureaucrats who felt that a small and open economy could not risk full exposure to the vicissitudes of the international economic environment. The annual renewal clause was thus a compromise between these two positions (tape-recorded interviews by the author with various individuals involved in drafting the 1989 organic law, Santiago, Chile, April–June 1995).

Chile 1990, 9). The central bank was additionally required to produce an annual report summing up the state of its own financial affairs, as well as two annual reports to the minister of finance and the Senate, one that summed up the policies pursued throughout the previous year and another that made projections for the upcoming year. While, in theory, the Senate and the executive would use these opportunities for active debate and public evaluation of the bank's policies (Fontaine 1989, 69), in practice these reports could be of but little concrete use. Unlike in the United States where Federal Reserve Board members can be regularly summoned before the U.S. Congress, in Chile these appearances did not extend beyond the two required annual visits. And since the Senate's role was really only to discuss proposed policies ex post, this limited how much it could really contribute in any substantive sense (Massad 1989, 86–87).

The final area where the government considerably enhanced the autonomy of the central bank pertained to those rules governing the central bank board. Under prior legislation, an executive committee composed of three individuals had governed the central bank: the president, the vice president, and the general manager. These were presidential appointees with indefinite term lengths, who could be removed at the executive branch's discretion.

The new law radically altered this highly politicized board structure. First, it established a governing board of five members who would be named by the president of the republic, with prior approval of the Senate. While it is true that autonomy is thought to be most enhanced where the central bank itself chooses its own governing board, in practice, this never occurs, and input from auxiliary bodies such as legislatures and/or councils is considered to be a reasonable second-best option. By stipulating Senate confirmation of all nominees, the law thus prevented undue presidential discretion in the appointment procedure. To further reduce political influence in board member selection, the new law established long and staggered terms in office (ten-year terms with partial renewal every two years).[17] The only central bank in the world where board members serve for a longer period of time is the United States Federal Reserve, where the term is fourteen years. Finally, rules governing the dismissal of board members were broadly consistent with those of the Bundesbank. Dismissal was made contingent on technical, as opposed to policy-based, criteria—such as conflict of interest, use of public office for personal gain, or failure to comply with one's duties.[18]

17. The president of the central bank was appointed for a five-year period. All terms were renewable.

18. There was one exception. The legislation authorized the president, with prior approval of the Senate, to remove any or all of the board members on the grounds that the council member had voted "in favor of bank resolutions representing a material and clear breach of the purposes of the Bank . . . and that said resolution has been the main and direct cause of a material damage to the economy of the country" (Central Bank of Chile 1990, 12).

In short, through a carefully crafted set of rules, Chile's authoritarian regime was able to safeguard its interests by making monetary policy largely impervious to the influence of future democratic governments. By then entrenching this institution in the Constitution with an organic law that would require a four-sevenths majority in both chambers of the legislature to overturn, Pinochet further sought to ensure that his economic legacy would not be dismantled.[19] At the end of the day, the outgoing government thus emerged with a highly autonomous central bank in hand.

## Reform Reaction: The Opposition Responds

The highly political nature of the reform did not go unnoticed by the regime's opposition, which was exceedingly critical both of its specific components and of its timing. While its unfavorable impact was somewhat mitigated by a set of last-minute negotiations with the government, the net effect of the reform was still resoundingly negative for the regime's opponents.

### Reform Negotiations: The Creation of the "Quota"

The democrats were incensed by the creation of a reform that they perceived as highly political in both design and motivation. In particular, they objected to the way in which the reform was enacted, which they saw as the product not of debate and discussion but rather of imposition. As the then vice president of the Christian Democratic Party argued, "let the sovereign people sanction the government if it carries out bad economic policy. . . . we do not need pre-designed tutelaries from rulers that have already been defeated."[20] The opposition's principal objections accordingly centered around Pinochet's ability to unilaterally appoint the entire five-member board, which was deemed "illegitimate" and "an abuse of power"[21] and seen as an attempt to give "technical justification for practices which are authoritarian in nature" (Zahler 1989a, 105). Perhaps this sentiment was most poetically phrased by another leading economist in the opposition, who commented, "even if autonomy had been a good idea, it was a bad handicap to have been 'illegitimately conceived' under another political system."[22]

19. To further change the three clauses of the Constitution guaranteeing autonomy required a favorable vote by three-fifths of both legislative branches.

20. As quoted in "Andrés Zaldívar Cuestionó Normativa del Banco Central," *El Mercurio,* January 21, 1989.

21. Comment by Ricardo Ffrench-Davis in Ricardo Ffrench-Davis and Joaquín Vial, "Ley del Banco Central Deberá Ser Modificada," *El Mercurio,* August 18, 1989.

22. Eyzaguirre, interview.

That said, because the reform was presented as a fait accompli, it did not look as if the opposition would play any role whatsoever in either its plan or its operation. As it turned out, the opposition was wrong. In the final days before the law was to go into effect in early December, the Pinochet government negotiated a political formula whereby the board would be composed of two appointees from the outgoing regime, two from the opposition, and one independent to be mutually agreed upon by the two sides.

By agreeing to politicize the central bank board in this fashion, the government was effectively consenting to a decrease in the autonomy of the central bank. As I argue in chapter 3, outgoing authoritarian regimes have strong incentives to use the first central bank board to stack the decks with handpicked technocrats in order to ensure that their preferred policies will dominate during the first phases of the democratic regime. But in the case at hand, the Chilean government instead made board composition a point of compromise with its political opponents. Unlike the other dimensions of autonomy where the outcome was largely consistent with the expectations, this was the one area where the authoritarians diverged markedly from ex ante predictions.

The decision to negotiate was not an easy one for the authoritarians. After all, it constituted a virtual admission that they did not believe that their candidate, former finance minister Hernán Büchi, would triumph in the upcoming presidential elections. For had they been confident of a right-wing victory, there would have been no incentive for them to compromise at all: their self-appointed central bank board would have existed in perfect harmony with the incoming economic cabinet. And, indeed, many within the authoritarian camp, not the least of whom was Büchi himself, were angry when this concession was made (Cavallo 1992, 154). These more intransigent, hard-line factions were particularly critical of the government's principal architect in these negotiations, Minister of the Interior Carlos Cáceres, who was seen as having "sold out," thereby compromising the outgoing regime's economic interests.[23]

The negotiation of the first central bank board ultimately represented a risk-averse strategy for the outgoing government, however. The authoritarians knew that in the likely event that the Concertación won the presidential elections, a Pinochet-appointed board would lack widespread legitimacy, only making its job harder to carry out and providing an excuse for the

23. See, for example, Tapia (1993, 350–51); also assorted editorials in *El Mercurio:* "Banco Central Independiente?" March 24, 1990; "Autonomía del Banco Central," *El Mercurio,* November 14, 1993; "Autonomía del Banco Central," *Estrategia,* January 5, 1994. Cáceres was also criticized for these negotiations during confidential tape-recorded interviews by the author with several former officials in the military regime, Santiago, Chile, April–June 1995.

incoming government to dismiss it as an unjust authoritarian legacy. Were public opinion to buy into this sort of rationale, this could also have negative electoral repercussions for the right. The so-called quota thus represented a way for the authoritarians to assure stability in the transition.[24] They could make the reform more palatable to the opposition by compromising on an important feature, while still obtaining the vast majority of what they wanted.

Nor were the negotiations an easy sell within the opposition camp. On the one hand, there were those such as Foxley who thought that the quota would at least afford the opposition a voice in monetary policy. On the other hand, there were also others who opposed the negotiations insofar as these were seen as indirectly legitimizing the autonomy legislation. Indeed, the first opposition economist who was selected to fill a spot on the board, Ricardo Ffrench-Davis, declined on the basis that he did not want to go forward as a Pinochet appointment (Cavallo 1992, 154).

Ultimately, however, the decision to negotiate on the part of the opposition was based on the simple recognition that it was better to have something than nothing. The democrats foresaw that policy coordination between a Concertación executive and a Pinochet central bank would be exceedingly difficult, especially since the rules were biased so strongly in favor of the central bank.[25] Accepting the 2–2–1 formula was really the best that they could hope for under the circumstances.[26] They did, however, manage to score two minor coups in the negotiations. First, they were able to name a member of the Socialist Party to the first central bank board, which had been a major sticking point with Pinochet (Cavallo 1992, 153). Second, they also managed to guarantee that the first individual to be rotated out of office was the so-called independent, thereby ensuring their own ability to rename the president of the board two years later.[27]

In brief, with just days to go before the central bank legislation was to take effect, the democrats found themselves with a new modus operandi—one in which they, too, would assume a role in the institution that they had proclaimed "illegitimate." While their participation on the board undoubt-

24. Carlos Cáceres, former minister of the interior under Pinochet, interview by the author, Santiago, Chile, May 26, 1995. Moulian (1993, 15–20), employs similar reasoning to explain why the outgoing government chose to negotiate the constitutional reforms.

25. Ricardo Ffrench-Davis, chief economist for monetary policy in the Concertación's economic team, interview by the author, tape recording, Santiago, Chile, April 18, 1995.

26. The opposition had to stand firm even to get this much. In previous months, the authoritarians had approached it with other formulas, including four-to-one and three-to-two in favor of the authoritarian government. But the opposition had stalwartly refused to accept participation in a board that put the Concertación at a disadvantage (Ffrench-Davis, interview). See also Cavallo 1992, 152–54.

27. See comments by Alejandro Foxley in "Cambios a la Ley del Banco Central Serán Por Consenso," *La Epoca,* December 7, 1989.

edly constituted an improvement over the status quo, the question we must ask ourselves is whether—from the standpoint of the democrats—the quota obviated the reform's otherwise nefarious effects.

## The 1989 Central Bank Reform: A Critique

It has been argued that the negotiation of the board composition somehow altered the enclave aspect of Chile's central bank autonomy by establishing a norm of multiparty representation within this otherwise authoritarian institution.[28] I contend, however, that such a benign reading of this reform is misguided. Rather, there are many reasons to believe that—even after the quota—the democrats would have chosen to forego inheriting an autonomous central bank altogether.

For one thing, the democrats had virtually no input into the design of the central bank legislation. Negotiations over the composition of its first governing board notwithstanding, the rules governing all other aspects of the central bank's autonomy were never open for debate. Despite an extensive range of objections raised to various aspects of the reform noted earlier, these criticisms were never incorporated into the legislation itself. As a prominent member of the opposition's economic team noted, "until the negotiations of the first board, we were completely shut out."[29] In weighing the net effect of this reform in its totality, it is thus important that the significance of the quota not be overstated. What is relevant is not that the authoritarians chose to negotiate the central bank board but, rather, that this was all that they negotiated.

Whether or not opposition members played a role in the design of this institution would not matter if they felt that they had come away with a good deal. But as one prominent former opposition member confessed, "even after the negotiations, we felt that we had received something very unfair and very unequal."[30] Indeed, if the opposition had been happy with the outcome, one would have to believe that the reams of detailed criticisms and elaborate counterproposals drafted in the months prior to the reform's passage were merely strategic in nature (see the discussion that follows). One would also have to believe that if we were to go back in time and give the Concertación leaders another chance to rechart the course of their future, they would still

28. This line of argument was suggested during a tape-recorded interview by the author with Manuel Antonio Garretón, sociologist and noted political commentator, Santiago, Chile, May 16, 1995.

29. Ffrench-Davis, interview.

30. José Pablo Arrellano, leading economist in the Concertación's first economic team, interview by the author, tape recording, Santiago, Chile, May 2, 1995.

have chosen the autonomous central bank that they have today. The evidence simply does not support this line of argument.

At the time that the initiative was announced, many in the opposition questioned whether a central bank reform was even necessary in the first place. While they agreed with the importance of maintaining macroeconomic stability as a general principle, they argued that "the independence of the central bank is neither a necessary nor a sufficient condition for the stability of prices, and even less so for macroeconomic balance" (Eyzaguirre 1989, 1). Rather, the democrats argued that "low inflation responds more to a coherent, disciplined and coordinated monetary, fiscal and exchange rate policy than it does to an autonomous central bank" (Zahler 1989a, 104). To drive this point home, they pointed to the final years of the Pinochet administration as an example of how a dependent central bank need not necessarily be incongruous with macroeconomic balance. Not only did other alternatives exist for maintaining price stability, such as designing some sort of law to limit government borrowing from the central bank and/or the extent of its internal and external debt, but these were thought to pose considerably less danger to Chile's future democratic rulers (Zahler 1989a, 111).[31] In sum, the prevailing sentiment among the Concertación's leading advisers was thus that the central bank ought to depend politically on the executive (Briones Espinosa 1989; Zahler 1989a).

But even if one wished to argue that the opposition would have chosen to enact a central bank reform in 1989, there is no question that it would have approached the task quite differently. This is readily apparent in the numerous criticisms that the democrats levied against the central bank legislation at the time that the reform surfaced.[32] First, they protested the enormous concentration of power that the initiative conferred to the central bank. Because of the transfer of so many policy-making attributes to the central bank, the opposition feared that the institution would effectively constitute "a fourth power of the state" (Zahler 1989a, 102). The democrats vehemently opposed this extension of central bank functions, arguing that "the larger the independence of the central bank with respect to those organs of power which are generated democratically, the less should be its attributions in areas that do not correspond directly to monetary policy" (Zahler 1989a, 110). Rather than making the central bank independent or more technical, they favored limit-

31. The opposition repeatedly invoked Chile's experiences of 1982–83 as evidence of how an excessively rigid set of rules over monetary policy might preclude the central bank from having the freedom of action it would need to respond to a financial crisis of this order (Arrellano 1989; Zahler 1989a).

32. Note that those listed subsequently represent a summary of the major objections to the law. For more specific criticisms of its individual features, see Briones Espinosa 1989; Eyzaguirre 1989; Ffrench-Davis 1989; Zahler 1989b.

ing its powers and dispersing these among other state agencies so that decentralization would not be employed toward generating "technocratic tutelaries, but rather towards consolidating and strengthening the democratic regime" (Zahler 1989a, 111).

Second, the opposition also objected to the lack of explicit mechanisms for assuring coordination between monetary and fiscal policy. Precisely because of the large number of policy-making faculties accorded the central bank, the democrats feared that the potential for conflict with other economic authorities would increase (Arrellano 1989, 92–94). As one opposition economist noted, "to hand over an enormous power, practically without counterweight, to an autonomous body . . . contains the enormous risk of generating a process of formulation of policies that are inconsistent with one another" (Massad 1989, 86). Particularly in light of the demonstrated link between monetary policy and real economic variables, the opposition questioned "whether or not it is possible and even efficient that there be two independent teams acting simultaneously, especially if they are of different economic ideologies" (Zahler 1989a, 112). In short, the opposition felt strongly that it was important to separate technical from political criteria in the execution of monetary policy but not in its design, which should be instead the product of a coordinated effort among various economic agencies (Massad 1989; Briones Espinosa 1989).

Finally, the democrats also objected to what they saw as the proposal's lack of extensive accountability mechanisms. As one opposition leader starkly phrased it, "Why should a group of technocrats have so much power and control . . . without assuring corresponding political responsibility?"[33] The democrats felt that by failing to establish clear mechanisms for overseeing the central bank's budget and monitoring the actions of its board, the legislation offered few incentives to pursue a policy of sound economic management (Massad 1989, 86–87; Zahler 1989a, 102). There was said to be "no way to check if the policies applied corresponded to those previously announced, if they had realized their expected effect, or if they had unnecessary costs" (Massad 1989, 87). Because of the lack of checks on the central bank's behavior, it was said to threaten to "commit an outrage against the bases of a politically open and democratic society" (Zahler 1989a, 111).

The general tenor of these critiques was reflected in the modifications proposed by the opposition with respect to the existing legislation. On all four of the principal dimensions of autonomy explored in this study, the democrats desisted from creating a fully insulated central bank. For example, while

33. As quoted in "Banco Central no Debe Financiar Déficit Fiscal," *El Mercurio,* June 20, 1989.

the democrats agreed in principle with the idea of closely monitoring government finances, they also felt that rather than prohibiting all borrowing from the central bank, the law ought instead to establish limitations (Zahler 1989a, 111). Where coordination was concerned, the democrats argued for integrating the central bank into other areas of economic policy-making, proposing that the president of the central bank attend meetings of the economic cabinet (Massad 1989, 89). With respect to central bank objectives, they questioned the prudence of privileging the goal of price stability to the exclusion of all other policy objectives, arguing that such rigidity would deny the government sufficient flexibility with which to respond to internal and external shocks (Massad 1989, 78–82; Zahler 1989a, 106–7). Finally, while they supported lengthy terms and Senate confirmation of central bank governors, they also lobbied for a partial replacement of the central bank board with each successive administration at the discretion of the incoming president (Arrellano 1989, 95; Massad 1989, 89). In short, a closer look at history suggests that were they to do it all over, the democrats might never have created an autonomous central bank at all or—had they done so—would have gone about it quite differently.

The Pareto-improving nature of the 1989 central bank reform in Chile thus tends to be overstated. There is no question that once a norm of multiparty representation in this otherwise "authoritarian" institution had been established, the democrats were less dissatisfied with the autonomy legislation than they had been previously. In this way, the quota undoubtedly made the reform more palatable for the opposition by softening the blow of a more comprehensive central bank reform. It would be a mistake, however, to conclude that once the quota was negotiated, the opposition was more or less content with the rest of the reform's contents (Arriagada and Graham 1994, 269). Rather, for all of the reasons previously noted, the democrats felt that they were faced with an institution that was excessively powerful and excessively constraining. As far as they were concerned, this outcome might well have been avoided without sacrificing anything on the economic front and, indeed, gaining a great deal where democratic accountability was concerned. And it is worth pointing out that these criticisms were not coming from the more radical fringe elements at the edges of the coalition but rather from its most prominent—and centrist—economists.

Political negotiations over the bank's first governing board notwithstanding, the central bank reform was thus a resounding success for the outgoing authoritarian government. While it had agreed to carve out a role for the opposition in the administration of its cherished institution, the underlying design of the autonomous central bank would continue to bear the regime's unadulterated trademark.

## The Reform in Retrospect: Explaining Institutional Persistence

### The Persistence Paradox: Alternative Explanations

In the first six years following Chile's transition from authoritarian rule, the autonomy afforded the Central Bank of Chile in 1989 remained unscathed. Nor does a central bank reform of comparable proportions seem likely in the foreseeable future. In light of the considerable controversy that erupted over the reform when it was announced, this outcome might seem somewhat surprising.

After all, the very opposition who once so vociferously criticized this initiative was subsequently elected to office for three successive administrations. Throughout 1989, it had repeatedly affirmed its intention to make the modification of the central bank law a top priority.[34] One opposition member had even predicted that a major legislative conflict would ensue "if there is not a rapid consensus with the sectors of the right to modify this law in the first few days that the future congress is in operation."[35] Such sentiments continued to be voiced even after the 2–2–1 compromise had been negotiated with the outgoing authoritarian government. For example, the day after the agreement was made public, Concertación presidential candidate Patricio Aylwin declared that "we consider it to be indispensable to introduce modifications to this law," noting that "the agreement achieved with respect to the board does not imply that we are renouncing this objective."[36] Various individuals in the Concertación even went so far as to specify which modifications ought to be prioritized when the reform eventually occurred (Ffrench-Davis 1989). Nonetheless, in the months and years that followed, the incoming government never followed through on these proposed revisions.

At the very least, one might have expected subsequent governments to try to staff the central bank board with their own appointees as individual seats on the governing board became available. Instead, despite the fact that it was never written down, the quota persisted under democratic rule. With each successive retirement, an outgoing governor was replaced by someone from the same political party and/or general ideological persuasion, thereby

34. See, for example, comments by Ffrench-Davis and Vial in "Ley del Banco Central Deberá Ser Modificada"; also see the interview with Ricardo Ffrench-Davis in *Informativo: Comercio Exterior* 2, no. 7 (October 1989): 14–15.

35. See comments by Briones Espinosa, "Ley Del Banco Central: Facilita Fuga de Capital."

36. As quoted in "Aylwin y Lagos Satisfechos por Consejo del Banco Central," *La Nación,* December 6, 1989.

maintaining the political balance that was said to characterize the first central bank board.[37] What is more, some of the initiative's most ardent critics went on to assume positions of high leadership in the central bank, including several who became members of the governing board itself.

In light of such apparent anomalies, we must explain why there was no effort to modify this legislation and why, to the contrary, there emerged what seemed to be a tacit acceptance of this institution by the democrats. One potential explanation is that incoming governments were secretly pleased with their institutional inheritance. Despite their public protestations to the contrary, they in fact welcomed central bank autonomy with open arms. By possessing an autonomous central bank of authoritarian origins, they could blame the central bank when they were forced to undertake unpopular economic measures, such as the 1990 adjustment (Arriagada and Graham 1994, 268).

An alternative explanation is that, in the interim, the politicians of the center and left had learned the virtues of macroeconomic stability. This line of reasoning suggests that there had been a convergence of economic thought across the political spectrum about the importance of controlling the money supply in order to control inflation (Weyland 1997). Concertación officials had thus come to appreciate an institution that tied their hands where the economy was concerned, rendering the 1989 Central Bank Law "a blessing in disguise" (Hojman 1990, 33). The implication of both of these arguments is that far from constituting a burden to incoming democratic administrations, autonomy was actually a godsend.

There is no question that in the years since the central bank reform was enacted, Chile's macroeconomic environment continued to flourish. Following an initial adjustment designed to counteract the overheating of the economy in 1989, Chile resumed, and even surpassed, its previous macroeconomic performance over the course of the next several years. Inflation fell from 26 percent in 1990 to 8 percent in 1994; growth averaged approximately 6 percent per year between 1990 and 1994; and the public sector deficit as a percentage of GDP was negative (see table 5.1). Moreover, foreign capital was pouring into the country at record levels (Calderón and Griffith-Jones 1994; Ffrench-Davis, Agosín, and Uthoff 1995). By the early 1990s, Chile was one of but four developing countries that had earned the title "low-risk investment"

37. As noted earlier, the first governor to step down in 1991—outgoing president Andrés Bianchi—was not replaced by another "independent" but rather by the central bank's vice president, Roberto Zahler, one of the original Concertación board appointees. Once this initial change was made, however, and despite occasional controversies, replacements have essentially followed a strict partisan quota.

in the classification scheme developed by the Economist Intelligence Unit (Flaño 1992).

In short, throughout the first half of the decade, Chile was experiencing many of the "goods" commonly associated with an autonomous central bank (Fontaine 1993; Rosende 1993). But the relevant question to ask ourselves is not whether the democrats would have chosen to forego this stable macroeconomic environment but, rather, whether they would have preferred an outcome that would have enabled them to do more to achieve their programmatic agenda. I argue that they would have preferred such an outcome. A closer look at the evidence reveals that the existence of an autonomous central bank did impede the government's ability to redistribute wealth and stimulate demand as it might have wished.

## Revisiting History: Why the Democrats Were Worse Off

There are many reasons to believe that the democrats who came to power on the heels of Pinochet found it costly. Above all, we must recall that this was a coalition that had campaigned—and won—on a platform of promising to bring an end to the profound socioeconomic inequities that had characterized military rule in Chile. Declaring that "there can be no economic progress without social justice,"[38] the democratic opposition had repeatedly underscored its primary objective of "reconciling economic growth with social equity."[39] By looking more carefully at the redistributive objectives of incom-

**TABLE 5.1. Chile: Selected Domestic Macroeconomic Indicators (1990–94)**

| Year | Growth of GDP | Public Sector Deficit[a] | Inflation | Unemployment Rate[b] | Rate of Overall Investment |
|---|---|---|---|---|---|
| 1990 | 3.3 | –0.58 | 25.7 | 5.7 | 26.2 |
| 1991 | 7.3 | –1.81 | 16.5 | 5.3 | 24.8 |
| 1992 | 11.0 | –2.05 | 8.9 | 4.4 | 28.2 |
| 1993 | 6.3 | –1.53 | 6.7 | 4.5 | 29.8 |
| 1994 | 4.2 | –1.36 | 7.8 | 5.9 | 28.9 |

*Source:* Central Bank of Chile, *Boletín Mensual* (Santiago, Chile: Central Bank of Chile, various years).

[a]As percentage of GDP (minus sign indicates a surplus).

[b]Percentage of labor force.

38. Former president Patricio Aylwin, as quoted in "Es Prematuro revisar el ajuste Económico," *El Mercurio,* March 15, 1990.

39. Patricio Aylwin, *Message of the President to the Cámera de Diputados, April 10, 1990, Cámara de Diputados,* Legislatura Extraordinaria, 319a, Session 8a, 376.

ing democratic governments prior to coming to power versus what they were actually able to achieve, one can thus evaluate the extent to which the existence of an autonomous central bank effectively "cramped their style."

Consider first the case of fiscal policy. Upon coming to power, the Aylwin government's first legislative initiative was to enact a tax reform to finance new social programs and make the country's tax structure more progressive. But while this reform was presented as the linchpin in the government's strategy to respond to the needs of the poorest groups in Chilean society, the final product was quite moderate in nature, entailing only a modest extension of tax instruments and social spending practices already in place (Boylan 1996). And although the tax reform did enable the government to increase social spending for the poorest segments of the population by 17.4 percent in 1990 and 12 percent in 1991 (Vergara 1994, 249), for everyone outside this safety net, emphasis remained on the provision of private insurance. Such a system generated a social dualism of sorts, in which those who could afford market-based services could enjoy good care, while those who lacked sufficient resources were forced to rely on inefficient services provided by a shrinking state (Vergara 1993, 1997). In short, far from representing an innovative or dramatic departure from the social spending practices of authoritarian rule, social policy under democratic Chile instead continued to rely on similar programs and organizations and even on the same market-based ideology (Petras and Leiva 1994, 122–35). While it would be difficult to attribute such moderation exclusively to the central bank's inability to finance government spending, there is no question that the central bank's rigid commitment to inflation control restricted a more aggressive social policy that might have benefited a broader swath of Chilean citizens (Vergara 1994, 248).

A similar tale of restraint emerges where labor policy is concerned. Before taking office, the Concertación team had promised "profound changes" in labor legislation, in which the strengthening of labor rights and labor organizations would in turn contribute to the establishment of a more "equitable distribution of the fruits of development" (Aylwin 1990, 25). Four years later, incumbent president Eduardo Frei similarly declared, "Labor policy constitutes an essential component of the modernization of the country in a context of further democratization and socio-economic development" (Frei 1994, 59). But while democratic governments did effectuate some real changes on behalf of labor, including increases in the minimum wage and some improved scope for collective bargaining, labor legislation under both administrations remained heavily tilted toward the interests of business (Frank 1997).

While it is true that workers saw a steady increase in both wages and employment under democratic rule, such favorable trends must be understood within their larger historical context. By 1993, average and minimum wages had not yet returned to their 1981 levels, and only in 1994–95 did they go beyond the levels reached in 1970 (Frank 1997, 26). And even while wages were growing at an average of 3.6 percent per year from 1990 through 1992, productivity grew at a corresponding 3.8 percent, resulting in a productivity/wage gap that grew by 1.7 percent during this period (Petras and Leiva 1994, 168). Above all, however, the labor reforms proved meager insofar as they failed fundamentally to afford labor organizations more effective institutional mechanisms through which to increase their collective bargaining power. At the end of the day, only 75 percent of all organized workers had the right to strike, while but 12.9 percent of all waged labor could negotiate collectively (Frank 1997, 28). To be sure, the lack of significant progress on the labor front was due primarily to the intransigence of business elites, who stalwartly resisted attempts by both Concertación governments to allow for cross-sectoral bargaining and better representation of nonunionized workers. But to the extent that low wages were deemed crucial to maintaining Chile's competitive edge (Petras and Leiva 1994, 170–71), the relentless pursuit of price stability by an autonomous central bank could only serve to reinforce these existing structural income inequalities between capital and labor.[40]

The government's inability to follow through on its avowedly redistributive objectives was also reflected in Chile's income distribution during the period in question. For while the incidence of poverty was cut by nearly a third between 1990 and 1994 and absolute poverty was cut in half, the income share of the lowest 40 percent of the population fell only slightly from 13.3 percent in 1990 to 13.1 percent in 1994 (Sheahan 1997, 19–20). Indeed, Oscar Altimir has calculated that the Gini coefficient of income concentration for 1992 remained 23 percent higher than in 1968 (Altimir 1995, 16). Despite all of the efforts by two successive Concertación governments to prioritize a pro-equity agenda, the distribution in the share of income between the lowest 40 percent of the population and the highest 20 percent remained hardly unaltered from the preceding twenty-five years. While one cannot attribute such inequities to the legal status of the central bank, its implicit restraints on government spending precluded any serious attempts at income redistribution on the part of the democrats.

The manifest tension between the policy objectives of democratic governments and the autonomy of the central bank is further revealed by looking at the nature of various conflicts that arose between the two over the course of the 1990s. While one can trace such strains back to the austerity program

40. Not surprisingly, labor militancy increased considerably during the second period of democratic rule under the Frei government (1994–99), when the country witnessed its first mass labor demonstration since the transition (Loveman 1995, 322).

carried out by the central bank in October 1992,[41] they began to escalate in earnest in late 1995. Following the government's successful negotiation of an 11 percent increase in public sector wages in November, the central bank publicly admonished the Finance Ministry for failing to contribute to the central bank's annual inflationary goal of 6.5 percent.[42] After interest rates again rose in April 1996, Finance Minister Eduardo Aninat responded publicly by saying that he hoped that this adjustment would be "intense, but brief,"[43] to which central bank president Roberto Zahler retorted that the rise "would last as long as necessary to obtain the desired objectives."[44]

Such conflicts ultimately came to a head in June 1996 when Roberto Zahler announced his sudden resignation as president of the Central Bank of Chile after nearly seven years on its governing board. While the proximate cause of Zahler's resignation lay in disagreements with the rest of the board over how to resolve the outstanding debt owed the central bank by several prominent commercial banks, it was no secret that this came on top of a series of disputes between the central bank and the Finance Ministry over the course of macroeconomic policy, in general, and interest rate policy, in particular.[45] More specifically, while Zahler wanted to keep interest rates at their currently high levels, Aninat urged the central bank to ease its relentlessly tight monetary policy to facilitate renewed growth.[46] To be sure, one might be inclined to chalk up such conflicts to the invariable tussles that occur within any system with an autonomous central bank. But the sudden and dramatic nature of Zahler's resignation would seem to lend credence to the notion that the Frei government felt inordinately restricted by the central bank in its ability to pursue a more aggressive growth-oriented policy agenda.

But perhaps the best support in favor of the argument that the central bank legislation was a constraint on incoming governments is the fact that dissatisfaction with its contents persisted well into democratic rule. For

41. In his annual report before the Senate in 1992, the central bank president reiterated the need to have "fiscal policy cooperate in order to maintain the objectives of the central bank" no less than eight times (Rosende 1993, 315).

42. See "Discrepancia por Reajuste Público," *La Epoca,* November 23, 1995. The central bank had made a similar critique one year earlier when the administration had negotiated a 12.2 percent increase in public sector wages, again claiming that such an action put the central bank's inflationary goals at risk.

43. "El Gobierno Espera que Medida del Banco Central Sea de Corto Plazo," *La Epoca,* April 10, 1996.

44. "Zahler Dice que No Hay que Creer que el Alza de Tasas Durará Poco," *La Epoca,* April 11, 1996.

45. See "El Adiós de Zahler," *La Epoca,* July 7, 1996; "La Verdad de la Renuncia," *Hoy* 989 (July 8–14, 1996): 30–32.

46. "Test for Chile's Central Bank: Resignation of Chief Raises Autonomy Questions," *Financial Times,* July 3, 1996.

example, the former head of studies at the central bank under the first Concertación administration openly argued in 1994 that inflationary control should not be the central bank's sole objective but, rather, a means through which to obtain the broader objective of "equitable development."[47] And even those former opposition economists who subsequently went on to form part of the central bank's leadership acknowledged that despite the existence of the quota, the underlying structural power of the central bank remained unaltered and potentially problematic. In particular, they pointed to the inadequacy of existing coordination mechanisms, which enabled the central bank to totally override the Finance Ministry when it saw fit—a concern that was subsequently realized in the wake of the Zahler-Aninat battles of 1996.[48] They also noted that the central bank continued to enjoy an excessive amount of economic policy-making ability. As one prominent central bank official observed, "given the degree of autonomy that the central bank has, it would be better to focus on a few objectives and get rid of the rest. I would take many of these other powers away because they just aren't necessary."[49] Perhaps these lingering doubts were best summed up by one high-ranking economist in the Frei administration who concluded, "I think that autonomy is overrated."[50]

Without going so far as to say that the existing autonomy legislation was uniformly negative, I can state that democratic governments in Chile quickly came to discover that many of their initial fears about central bank autonomy—for instance, the lack of coordination, the "fourth power of the state," and the weakness of accountability mechanisms—had been borne out in practice. More to the point—and to employ the language put forth in chapter 2—autonomy has precluded the democrats from obtaining their ideal point on the short-term Phillips curve. It is, of course, entirely possible that these governments simply did not want to do more, and hence their limited redistributive achievements reflect instead a deliberate effort at self-restraint (Weyland 1997). And yet, such a line of argument is not supported by their behavior in other policy arenas. Note, for example, that in the case of the tax reform, the government initially sought to obtain considerably more than it ultimately got both in terms of the overall amount targeted and the reform's specific components (Boylan 1996, 14). And while the administration was initially aggressive where labor policy was concerned, most of the labor code

47. See comments by Ricardo Ffrench-Davis in "Control de la Inflación No Debe Ser la Única Responsabilidad del Banco Central," *La Voz de la Libre Empresa,* January 26, 1994.

48. Eyzaguirre and Arrellano, interviews.

49. Member of the Central Bank of Chile's governing board, confidential interview by the author, tape recording, Santiago, Chile, May 20, 1995.

50. Arrellano, interview.

reforms found in the Concertación program went unfulfilled (Silva 1996, 233).

Extrapolating from these two experiences—and in light of the Concertación's incentives to respond to the concerns of their support base—one can only infer that the Concertación saw central bank reform as more a constraint than an opportunity. By inheriting an institution that made price stability its number one priority, democratic governments in Chile thus had no choice but to shelve their redistributive objectives or at least tone these down considerably. When all is said and done, the net result is that the country witnessed "economic growth but not the growth of equity" (Frank 1997, 31).

### Domestic and International Constraints: Why Insulation Works

The previous section suggests that the democrats did not grow to embrace the central bank's autonomy but, rather, continued to have serious objections to some of its key features. If this is true, then we must return to the question with which we began this discussion: why did they not attempt to overturn or, at the very least, modify the legislation upon assuming power? In other words, if the two Pareto-improving interpretations of institutional persistence do not seem borne out by empirical reality, then how do we explain the inertia that has characterized this law since its passage? I would submit that there are several explanations for why the legislation was not overturned. All suggest that while the democrats might have wanted to change certain aspects of the central bank legislation, they were powerless to do so, constrained as much by the deliberate lock-in strategies of their authoritarian predecessors as by the nature of the international economy itself.

Recall from our discussion in chapter 3 that authoritarian governments frequently employ a variety of domestic entrenchment strategies in order to make reversal of their enclaves difficult for incoming governments. In the Chilean case, we see a particularly dramatic case of such lock-in tactics at work. As noted in chapter 4, among the enclaves built into the 1980 Constitution were a series of quite difficult procedures for constitutional reform. While these varied across different kinds of reforms, the threshold for a change of any sort was quite considerable. By establishing these quorums, the authoritarians consciously sought to ensure that new governments would not be able to modify existing institutional forms without the blessing of some supporters of the military regime.

For an organic constitutional law, such as that governing central bank autonomy, the Constitution required a four-sevenths majority in both chambers of the legislature. In other words, the Concertación would have needed 69 votes in the Chamber of Deputies and 27 in the Senate in order to have changed this law. While it met such conditions in 1989 in the Chamber of Deputies, where it held 72 seats, it was 5 short of the necessary votes in the Senate, where it held only 22 seats. Naturally, had two complementary enclaves themselves not existed—the designated senators and the electoral system that disproportionately advantaged the parties of the right—one could argue that the government might have easily secured the necessary seats. But because of the existence of the four-sevenths majority clause on top of an already biased electoral system, the incoming government had no choice but to accept defeat. As one member of the incoming economic team noted, "Yes, we thought seriously about changing the law . . . but we were convinced that we couldn't because we lacked the majority in the senate, and we knew that we would lose."[51]

Of course, one might argue that the democrats could have chosen simply to flout the autonomy legislation, ignoring the arguably artificial veto role afforded their opponents. But as we noted in chapter 3, incoming democratic governments have little incentive to break extant laws and practices. Rather, precisely because they need to prove their democratic credentials, they have every incentive to obey existing legislation, even where this runs directly counter to their interests.

Such incentives were particularly strong in the Chilean case. Because the polarization of political parties was widely blamed for having triggered the breakdown of democracy in 1973, the Concertación had a vested interest in showing that democracy could work without producing the instabilities of the past. As Loveman notes, "the Aylwin government was determined to restore legitimacy and credibility to civilian government, prove itself an effective economic manager, and survive four years in office without provoking a military coup" (Loveman 1995, 309). The first challenge facing the new leaders thus consisted in "stimulating . . . rules for political behavior that would allow for the full force of the state of law and civilian institutions" (Huneeus 1994, 14). The democrats also needed to show themselves to be capable of cooperating with the authoritarians and their civilian counterparts: the right and business groups. President's Aylwin's chief adviser and political strategist, Edgardo Boeninger, was convinced that Chile's fundamental political problem was the lack of trust among social and political actors and that reestablishing such trust was a prerequisite for reestablishing democratic rule (Puryear 1994, 93). In light of these multiple exigencies for establishing stable

51. Ffrench-Davis, interview.

and lawful democratic rule, the authoritarians could be fairly sure that the democrats would be unlikely to do anything to tamper with the existing institutional order.

In addition to these legal considerations, one must also factor in a third constraint: those domestic constituencies empowered by the authoritarians to ward off any and all threats to the status quo. Chief among these where the economy was concerned was the existence of a powerful business class. By accelerating the privatization of the economy before leaving power, the Pinochet regime had effectively rendered the private sector an irreversible authoritarian enclave of its own (Rehren 1995, 36). Even with Pinochet's subsequent loss in the plebiscite, "the idea was that the capitalists would still be strong enough to defend the market economy on their own from the social democrats" (Silva 1991, 119).

And this is precisely what they did. As Rehren notes, "from the moment Aylwin took power, the CPC understood that its role before the new authorities was none other than defending the economic system of a free market" (Rehren 1995, 60). This guardian function manifested itself in two ways. First, business groups began to assume a tutorial role vis-à-vis the maintenance of a market economy, constantly reminding the authorities of what had "yet to be done" (Montero 1993, 62). Second, business also took on a much more active role in the policy-making process, replacing its historically intermittent involvement with a "sustained, systemic influence" (Rehren 1995, 56). For example, business groups participated actively in the governmental commissions set up to study the labor reform, steadfastly denouncing all modifications of the existing legislation, which were seen as fomenting unnecessary instability. In what some might interpret as a not-so-subtle threat, the then head of the CPC, Manuel Feliú, charged that "the labor reform will make Chile a mediocre country, impeding its normal development; if this reform does not satisfy us, we will not invest in the country" (Rehren 1995, 72). By virtue of its sheer economic clout, business was thus able to modify most of the government's significant policy initiatives in a direction more conducive to its own interests (Silva 1996, 231). The democrats implicitly understood that tampering with any preexisting arrangements designed to safeguard the market economy—such as the autonomy of the central bank—was similarly "off limits."

Finally, there was an additional, arguably even more important international constraint that made reversal of the central bank legislation unlikely. As noted in chapter 3, the contemporary international economic environment places enormous limitations on the ability of developing country governments to alter extant commitments to macroeconomic stability. In the words of a prominent Chilean economist, "greater international interdependence, greater financial integration of our economy in the rest of the world, and the development of a capital market . . . all make the consequences of an inconsistent monetary policy appear more rapidly and with higher costs" (Arrellano 1989, 94). To the extent that disarming the autonomy of the central bank might be perceived by international investors as tantamount to "inconsistent monetary policy," one can thus reason that the more integrated the developing country economy, the higher the costs associated with this sort of transgression.

The Chilean case readily displays the enormity of such international constraints. Consider the volume and nature of foreign investment. During the period 1990–93, foreign capital inflows, already high, increased by nearly 50% with respect to the period 1986–89 (see table 5.2). While foreign direct investment played a leading role in this surge, portfolio investment (which had been temporarily suspended following the financial crisis of 1982) also came back with a vengeance in the 1990s. In 1993, it represented almost 20 percent of all capital inflows, rising as high as 26 percent in 1993 (Calderón and Griffith-Jones 1994, 6). In 1994, the amount of foreign capital flowing into Chile via secondary ADRs intensified even further, rising as high as U.S.$1 billion and constituting an additional net capital inflow equivalent to 2 percent of GDP (Ffrench-Davis, Agosín, and Uthoff 1995, 109).[52] In turn, speculative short-term capital flows were also strongly positive in the period 1989–92 (Ffrench-Davis, Agosín, and Uthoff 1995, 112–13). Because their highly liquid nature affords them a permanent exit option, both of these types of foreign capital are considered among the most volatile (Maxfield 1997). With their sudden surge in the 1990s, Chile was thus increasingly vulnerable to the whims of international capital markets.

But while all emerging markets were arguably highly sensitive to international capital markets during the early 1990s, Chile was exceptionally so. As Hojman (1990) notes, capital flight from Chile had been remarkably low under Pinochet, due largely to the high degree of confidence that owners of short-term capital placed in this regime's long-term economic strategy. As of the early 1990s, the Aylwin administration had not yet been invested with the same degree of confidence; to the contrary, foreign capital was rather biding its time to see how economic policy would pan out under this center-left administration. Particularly in light of the economic program's demonstrably ambiguous attitude toward foreign investment as well as the historically sta-

52. ADRs are American Depository Receipts, gleaned through the sale of shares by Chilean companies on the U.S. stock exchange.

tist leanings of the Christian Democratic Party, the danger of substantial capital flight under Aylwin at the slightest signal of something going wrong was a strong possibility (Hojman 1990, 35).

In light of this inherent skepticism on the part of international capital, incoming democratic governments were acutely aware of the need to promote an image of political and economic stability. Precisely because Chile had lived through periods of uncertainty in the past, newly elected officials realized that once the fundamental rules of the game were established, any change to them could have disastrous economic effects. Were such sudden and unexpected policy shifts to take place, Chile might be labeled "a high risk

**TABLE 5.2. Chile: Volume and Composition of Medium- and Long-Term Private Capital Flows, 1980–94 (millions of dollars)**

| Average Annual Inflows | 1980–82 | 1983–85 | 1986–89 | 1990–93 |
|---|---|---|---|---|
| A. Foreign investment | 373 | 119 | 879 | 1,131 |
| 1. Foreign direct investment | 332 | 119 | 857 | 663 |
| Direct effective foreign investment[a] | 332 | 92 | 118 | 605 |
| Debt -equity swaps[b] | 0 | 27 | 739 | 58 |
| 2. Portfolio investment | 41 | 0 | 22 | 468 |
| Bonds[c] | 41 | 0 | 0 | 81 |
| Capital | 0 | 0 | 22 | 387 |
| Investment funds[d] | 0 | 0 | 22 | 100 |
| ADR's | 0 | 0 | 0 | 287 |
| B. Medium- and long-term credits[e] | 3,626 | 1,231 | 727 | 1,266 |
| Credits associated with DL 600 | 134 | 53 | 324 | 630 |
| Other credits[f] | 3,492 | 1,178 | 403 | 636 |
| C. Total | 3,999 | 1,350 | 1,605 | 2,397 |

*Source:* Calderón and Griffith-Jones 1994, 5. Reprinted with permission.

[a]Corresponds to the net inflows through Legal Decree 600 and chapter XIV of the Compendium of Norms for International Exchange (CNIE) of the Central Bank of Chile.

[b]Corresponds principally to the net inflows through Chapter XIX of the CNIE.

[c]Bonds emitted exclusively through private companies. In 1991 and 1992, there were emissions of bonds on the part of state entities on the order of U.S.$200 and U.S.$120 million respectively.

[d]Corresponds to the funds created through Law 18657.

[e]Corresponds to the gross flows (disbursements) of private medium- and long-term credits.

[f]Includes disbursements of medium- and long-term credits from creditors; those that came in through Article 15; and those assigned to banks, companies, and individuals by international private commercial banks.

country, with all of the implications that this has for investment, technological innovation and development possibilities" (Cortázar 1990, 70).

The democrats needed only to look to the experiences of their neighbors to realize the costs involved in sudden, unpredictable swings in policy. We have already noted the punishment inflicted on Venezuela by international markets when a neopopulist government attempted to tamper with the autonomy of this country's central bank. The Mexican peso crisis offers a similar lesson. While this crisis was not prompted by a sudden change in monetary policy per se, the mismanagement of the Mexican currency over the course of 1994 triggered a swift and dramatic outpouring of international reserves from this country (see postscript to chap. 7). Such examples served as a potent—if not proximate—reminder of the perils associated with inconsistent policy choices in an era of highly integrated financial markets.

In light of the nature and extent of Chile's international integration in the early 1990s, then, it seems unlikely that incoming governments would not have realized that to place Chile's relationship with foreign capital in jeopardy was to play with fire. Stated somewhat differently, even if incoming governments had won the necessary legislative majorities, they still would have been loath to overturn the existing central bank legislation for international credibility reasons. While talk of an additional reform thus was probably sincere before this legislation was enacted, there is no evidence that the government ever really intended to carry out this threat once the reform had been passed.

Another way of saying this is that had central bank autonomy never existed, the democrats would have been perfectly happy to live without it. Once it was in place, however, any attempt to modify or reverse this legislation would have been costly. The same can be said for the ongoing persistence of the quota. All things equal, democratic governments would have probably preferred to stack the decks with their own people. But once the norm of multipartisan participation became established, it acquired an institutional legitimacy of its own that would be very difficult to undo.

Governments in Chile's incipient democracy have thus been forced to live with this essentially coercive economic institution in their midst. While there was a great deal of programmatic affinity between the central bank and the executive during Chile's first two democratic administrations, this does not alter the essentially imposed flavor of this reform. Indeed, if it was possible to produce a major conflict of interest under allegedly like-minded agencies—as we saw in 1996—one can only wonder what might occur in a more antagonistic political setting. In particular, were a populist government to lock horns with a conservative central bank board in the future, democratic politicians would quickly discover that in many respects, their economic policy choices had already been made for them.

With the more paradigmatic Chilean case as a backdrop, the next two chapters consider the Mexican central bank reform of 1993. While sharing a number of basic features with the Chilean reform of 1989, the Mexican case differs in one key respect. Specifically, it demonstrates that the amount of autonomy an authoritarian government will cede to an independent agency hinges critically on the relative proximity of the democratic threat. In this way, it furnishes us with excellent grounds for comparison for the argument at hand.

CHAPTER 6

# Technocracy under Threat

## Mexico's Democratic Awakening

The previous chapter presented the Chilean central bank reform of 1989 as a strong case of institutional insulation in the transition from authoritarian rule. Faced with an impending regime change under the helm of the center left, conservative authoritarian elites insulated monetary policy against the threat of an interventionist future. By creating a central bank with considerable authority across a series of policy domains, they attempted to bind successor governments to a neoliberal policy agenda.

The Mexican case illustrates a different dynamic. Like Pinochet's Chile (1988–89), Mexico under Carlos Salinas de Gortari (1988–93) can also be classified as a conservative authoritarian regime confronting a democratic opposition with populist overtones. As in Chile, the ruling elite would respond to this challenge by safeguarding its preference for macroeconomic stability in the form of an autonomous central bank. But while a transition to democracy was virtually a given in the Chilean case, in Mexico this threat was considerably more tenuous. While the authoritarians in Chile thus had incentives to create a fully autonomous central bank, the autonomy afforded the Mexican central bank was only partial.

Chapters 6 and 7 elaborate upon this comparison. While chapter 6 establishes the similarities between the Mexican and Chilean cases, chapter 7 underscores their differences. The present chapter thus examines the origin of the democratic threat prompting Mexico's authoritarians to insulate, while the following chapter looks at its magnitude and corresponding consequences for the 1993 central bank reform.

This chapter unfolds as follows. The first section, "Reform Background: Mexico's Neoliberal Revolution," offers an overview of the economic project enacted under the Salinas administration and the capitalist constituency underlying it. After a vested interest in macroeconomic stability on the part of the ruling elite has been demonstrated, the second section, "Reform Timing: Challenging the Conventional Wisdom," considers the timing of the 1993 central bank reform in light of these policy preferences. While many have attributed the timing of the reform to the government's need to demonstrate its credibility both domestically and internationally, I show why a straight credibility story would have argued for implementing the reform much earlier. Having thus cast doubt on the singular ability of various economic arguments to explain the reform's timing, in the third section, "Reform Motive: The Onset of the Democratic Threat," I attribute its motive to more decidedly political factors. I argue that after the extraordinary political events surrounding the Mexican presidential elections of 1988, the Salinas government realized that it was only a matter of time before democracy made its way to Mexico. Recognizing that its days in power were numbered, the Salinas clique began to worry about how an eventual transition to democracy might compromise its neoliberal economic project in the future.

As noted in chapter 1, any depiction of a partial insulation outcome is inherently murky, as—by definition—partial insulation only occurs at that "in-between" stage where a democratic threat is present but not yet overwhelming. While the 1993 Mexican central bank reform thus represents a much messier case than that in Chile, the ways in which it deviates from the full autonomy baseline are both interesting and important—particularly for a more complete understanding of the political and economic events that ensued in Mexico throughout 1994. A closer look at this case thus allows us to explore some interesting permutations on the central insulation theme advanced in this book without abandoning its fundamental logic.

## Reform Background: Mexico's Neoliberal Revolution

Before entering into a detailed analysis of the events surrounding the Mexican central bank reform of 1993, it is important to begin by identifying the authoritarians in question and those interests they sought to protect. Accordingly, this section will establish the profoundly market-oriented nature of Mexico's authoritarian regime and the capitalist support base underlying it.

### The Economic Model: The Origins of Salinastroika

Most analysts date the current era of Mexican economic policy to the financial crisis of 1982. Like so many of its Latin American counterparts, the Mexican government took full advantage of the flush international economic environment of the 1970s to finance large fiscal deficits at home. But as was also the case for so many other developing country governments, the unsustainability of this situation eventually came home to roost. In the early 1980s, high world interest rates together with a sharp decline in the price of oil combined to create much less hospitable external conditions. No longer able to count on cheap and abundant credit or its principal export to generate much needed foreign exchange, the government responded in 1982 with a large-scale devaluation. When this also failed to stem the tide of falling foreign reserves, the government resorted to more draconian measures. In August 1982, the government declared an involuntary moratorium on its foreign debt payments, which was followed by the nationalization of its entire banking industry.[1]

The 1982 crisis had a daunting effect on the Mexican economy as inflation soared, production halted, and growth rates turned negative (see table 6.1). For our purposes, however, the crisis was significant because it marked the advent of a new era of policymakers—and policy-making—within Mexico. Upon assuming office in 1982, incoming president Miguel De la Madrid expunged advocates of expansionary policies from positions of leadership within the ruling Institutional Revolutionary Party (Partido Revolucionario Institucional [PRI]) (Hernandez Rodriguez 1988). In their wake, a new cohort of young, predominantly professional economists emerged with deep commitment to the principles of a free-market economy (Camp 1990, 1995; Golob 1996). Over the course of the 1980s, this technocratic vanguard gained a virtual monopoly of control within the Mexican state, permeating all

**TABLE 6.1. Mexico: Selected Domestic Macroeconomic Indicators, 1980–93 (%)**

| Year | Growth in GDP | Urban Open Unemployment | Inflation | Deficit (as a % of GDP) | Investment (rates of growth)[a] |
|---|---|---|---|---|---|
| 1980 | 9.1 | 4.3 | 29.8 | –7.5 | |
| 1981 | 8.8 | 3.9 | 28.7 | –14.1 | 13.9 |
| 1982 | –0.6 | 4.0 | 98.8 | –16.9 | –17.3 |
| 1983 | –4.2 | 6.3 | 80.8 | –8.6 | –24.2 |
| 1984 | 3.6 | 5.8 | 59.2 | –8.5 | 9.0 |
| 1985 | 2.6 | 4.5 | 63.7 | –9.6 | 12.2 |
| 1986 | –3.8 | 5.1 | 105.7 | –15.9 | –10.4 |
| 1987 | 1.9 | 4.4 | 159.2 | –16.1 | 6.4 |
| 1988 | 1.2 | 4.4 | 51.7 | –12.5 | 10.2 |
| 1989 | 3.3 | 3.7 | 19.7 | –5.6 | 7.5 |
| 1990 | 4.5 | 3.2 | 29.9 | –4.0 | 13.3 |
| 1991 | 3.6 | 3.0 | 18.8 | –1.5 | 13.0 |
| 1992 | 2.8 | 3.3 | 11.9 | 0.5 | 15.8 |
| 1993 | 0.4 | 4.0 | 8.0 | 0.7 | –0.4 |

*Source:* For growth in GDP, inflation, deficit and investment data, the source is Banco de México 1994. For unemployment data, the source is Información Básica Anual 1994 (Mexico City, Mexico: Centro de Estudios Económicos del Sector Privado, 1994).

[a]Reflects private sector investment at 1980 prices. Note that 1981–85 is taken from Lustig 1992, although based on Banco de México statistics.

1. For a detailed account of the 1982 crisis and the events leading up to it, see Gonzáles Casanova and Aguilar Camín 1985; Ros 1987; Buffie and Sangines Krause 1989; Bazdresch and Levy 1991.

levels of the Mexican bureaucracy and securing key posts within national political office (Centeno and Maxfield 1992; Centeno 1994). Under its leadership, Mexico experienced a dramatic about-face in its economic policy that would shape the tenor of economic and political events over the course of the fifteen years that followed.

The economic program implemented by the so-called técnicos proceeded on two tracks (Weintraub 1990; Lustig 1992; Córdoba 1994). First, it entailed a series of measures to restore macroeconomic stability, with particular emphasis on lowering inflation and protecting the country's international reserves. Second, it sought to replace six decades of inward-oriented, state-led development in Mexico with an outward-oriented development strategy that privileged the private sector. While De la Madrid initiated the bulk of these reforms, Salinas consolidated the inroads made by his predecessor by deepening them.

The road to recovery was not an easy one. Throughout his term in office, De la Madrid was able to maintain a trade surplus, largely due to a deliberate policy of peso undervaluation (see table 6.2). He also shepherded Mexico's entry into GATT (General Agreement on Tariffs and Trade) in 1985. But progress was less visible on other fronts. Despite repeated attempts at orthodox stabilization programs, macroeconomic stability was only achieved at the very end of the decade with a social pact between business, labor, and the government (Whitehead 1989).[2] While a debt rescheduling agreement adopted in 1986 helped to facilitate some new lending, the government failed to redirect the reverse resource transfer out of the country that had taken place over the course of the 1980s (Lustig 1992, 55–59). By 1988, when Salinas took office, he still faced an upward battle: inflation remained at over 50 percent, foreign reserves stood at but a little over U.S.$6 billion, and growth rates had stagnated at below 2 percent.

But Salinas rose to the occasion. Under his administration, the country witnessed an international debt relief agreement under the so-called Brady plan; the privatization of all major industries (including the reprivatization of the banking system); the reduction of inflation to one digit; and the liberalization of trade, investment, and agricultural policies, culminating in the signing of the North America Free Trade Agreement (NAFTA). Midway through his term in office, these policies appeared to be realizing their expected payoffs. For the first time since the reforms were initiated in 1982, growth rates in 1989 had been positive for three successive years, climbing as high as 4.5 percent in 1990. Total external debt as a percentage of GDP was

2. This agreement—commonly referred to as the "Pact"—was a tripartite agreement among the government, business, and labor groups to adopt orthodox fiscal adjustment measures, concerted income and price controls, and accelerated trade liberalization.

**TABLE 6.2. Mexico: Selected International Economic Indicators, 1980–93 (in millions of dollars unless otherwise noted)**

| Year | Real Exchange Rate Index[a] | Balance of Payments (current account) | Balance of Payments (capital account) | International Reserves | Ratio of Debt Service to Exports | Import Cover[b] |
|---|---|---|---|---|---|---|
| 1980 | 100.00 | –10.72 | — | 4,175 | 49.5 | 1.5 |
| 1981 | 118.72 | –16.56 | — | 4,971 | 53.2 | 1.3 |
| 1982 | 86.80 | –6.27 | — | 1,778 | 56.8 | 0.6 |
| 1983 | 79.63 | 5,860 | 339 | 4,793 | 51.7 | 2.4 |
| 1984 | 97.20 | 4,183 | 306 | 8,019 | 52.1 | 3.4 |
| 1985 | 100.94 | 800 | –316 | 5,679 | 51.5 | 2.3 |
| 1986 | 69.15 | –1,374 | 2,716 | 6,674 | 54.2 | 3.1 |
| 1987 | 63.64 | 4,239 | –1,188.8 | 13,692 | 40.1 | 5.0 |
| 1988 | 77.74 | –2,375.7 | –1,163 | 6,327 | 48.2 | 1.7 |
| 1989 | 83.50 | –5,821.2 | 3,175.9 | 6,740 | 41.1 | 1.5 |
| 1990 | 83.05 | –7,451 | 8,163.6 | 10,217 | 25.9 | 1.9 |
| 1991 | 91.12 | –14,892.4 | 24,940.1 | 18,052 | 29.6 | 3.0 |
| 1992 | 96.77 | –24,804.4 | 26,542.3 | 19,171 | 44.3 | 2.7 |
| 1993 | 102.08 | –23,393 | 30,882.4 | 25,299 | 42.3 | 3.0 |

*Source:* For real exchange rate data, the source is Banco de México 1994. For balance of payments data (current account and capital account), the sources are Banco de México, 1993, and *Información Básica Anual 1994.* Mexico City, Mexico: Centro de Estudios Económicos del Sector Privado, 1994. For international reserves, debt service to exports and import cover data, the source is the International Monetary Fund, *World Debt Tables* (Washington, DC: The International Monetary Fund, 1994, 1996.)

[a]Real effective exchange rate estimated on the basis of consumer prices for 133 countries weighted by GDP.

[b]Ratio of reserves to imports.

cut in half, dropping from 73.7 percent in 1987 to 35.7 percent in 1992 (Banco de México 1994, 275). In its wake, foreign capital began to flow into Mexico at an unprecedented pace. To be sure, there was also cause for concern, including slowing growth rates after 1991, low domestic savings rates, and a growing trade deficit that, by 1993, was on the order of U.S.$25 billion (Dornbusch and Werner 1994; Ros 1994; Ramírez de la O 1995). But the expectation was that larger infusions of foreign capital would stimulate the growth of exports and the trade deficit would eventually disappear (Lustig 1992, 11).

Over the course of the 1980s and 1990s, economic policy in Mexico thus fell into the hands of a technocratic nucleus with a deep commitment to neoliberal economic reforms. Under their tutelage, the Mexican economy witnessed considerable change such that, by the mid-1990s, Mexico seemed poised for economic takeoff. In the words of two prominent Mexican government economists looking back on Salinas's six-year term in office (*sexenio*), "by the end of 1993, all pieces of the jigsaw puzzle seemed to be falling in place" (Gíl Díaz and Carstens 1997, 167).

## Interests and Influence: The Economic Power behind the Salinas Regime

In explaining the wave of neoliberal reforms in Mexico that took place in the 1980s, many analysts have underscored the role of ideas. Lauded by the *Economist* in 1991 as "the most economically literate group that has ever governed any country anywhere,"[3] the técnicos unquestionably shared a common vision in which free markets and international integration were the only solution for Mexico (Golob 1996). This ideological cohesion was honed through a common career track within Mexico's public finance ministries, graduate training in prestigious economics departments abroad, and considerable ties to domestic think tanks associated with orthodox economic thought (Camp 1990; Centeno 1994). It would be a mistake, however, to attribute the momentum behind this economic project sheerly to the force of ideas. Rather, ideas become salient at specific historical junctures because society demands them.

In Mexico, the onset of neoliberal policy reforms stemmed in large part from the demands of the business community. Business confidence had been severely damaged by the debt crisis and ensuing bank nationalization of 1982 (Escobar Toledo 1987; Luna, Tirado, and Valdés Ugalde 1991; Valdés Ugalde 1996). If it were to be successful in reinitiating the productive development of

3. *Economist*, December 14, 1991, p. 19.

the country, the government knew that it needed the support of the business class. Indeed, former Mexican finance minister Jesús Silva Herzog later confessed that during this period, economic policymakers felt that they needed to improve relations with the private sector any way they could (Schneider 1997, 9). The overall program of austerity implemented in the 1980s, as well as the dramatic expansion of the nonbanking financial sector noted subsequently, reflected this effort by the government to court the private sector (Heredia 1992, 1996; Puga 1993a). As business support for a more export-oriented and internationalist agenda grew over time, government policy followed suit (Frieden 1991a, 220–22). These efforts culminated in the signing of the "Pact" in 1987—which is often interpreted as a formal sign that a new era of business-state cooperation had begun (Kaufman, Bazdresch, and Heredia 1994).

But while De la Madrid's market-oriented policy reforms were largely successful in mending fences with business elites, many entrepreneurs still feared a return to populism in the early 1990s. The additional economic restructuring undertaken by Salinas constituted an attempt to convince the private sector—once and for all—that the Mexican government was committed to the neoliberal ideas it espoused. By addressing issues such as the cleanup of public finances, the expansion of opportunities for private investment in agriculture, and the Free Trade Agreement, the government was in effect responding to long pent-up demands from the Mexican business community (Valdés Ugalde 1994, 231). As testimony to this emerging business-government partnership, major economic policies came to be implemented through a series of elite negotiations between the government and important business groups, marginalizing Mexico's traditional systemwide corporatist forms of business-government relations (Luna 1995, 85; Heredia 1996, 148; Valdés Ugalde 1996, 142; Gibson 1997, 356).[4]

Who were these capitalist interests that were so closely allied with the neoliberal reformers? One quite visible pocket of economic power during this period was the financial sector (Garrido 1994a, 1997). Its strength stemmed initially from a series of measures to fuel the growth of nonbank financial

4. This "high tech clientelism," as one author called it (Quintana 1992, 181–88), was best exemplified in the wake of the privatization of the Mexican banking system, in which the banks were auctioned off in a highly secretive process to the country's most powerful economic actors (Elizondo 1993). It is true that among those capitalists that stood to benefit most from such privatization efforts, many were individuals directly associated with the ruling family itself, and this group included, most notably, the president's own brother, Raúl Salinas (see "A Mexican Mover and Shaker and How His Millions Moved," *New York Times*, June 5, 1996). I choose to treat this "personal enrichment" line of reasoning as a subsidiary—and not a rival—hypothesis to my own, as the personal enrichment of the ruling family can be understood as part of the authoritarians' broader pro-capitalist agenda.

institutions following the nationalization of the Mexican banks in 1982. Over the course of the 1980s, the growth of this parallel financial sector was spectacular, generating extraordinary rents, particularly for the brokerage houses (Heyman 1991; Mansell Carstens 1992). Between 1985 and 1990, the stock market index grew by 347 percent in real terms, while the capital gain in dollar terms was 752 percent (Natella and Manson 1991, 17). Following the extensive program of financial liberalization initiated in the early 1990s, private financial activity flourished even more (Maxfield 1993; Ortiz 1994). Of particular note, the internationalization of government debt securities led to a dramatic expansion of the money market, which increased fourfold from 1989 to 1993 (Mansell Carstens 1994, 23). In turn, the lack of competition together with large increases in the demand for credit allowed the newly privatized banks to generate high interest rate spreads, enabling them to realize profits well above those of comparably sized countries (Peñaloza and Garrido 1994, 49–53; Gruben and Welch 1996). The depth of financial penetration that took place over the course of these two sexenios is reflected in the ratio of the monetary aggregate M4 to GDP, which rose from 31.3 percent in 1980 to as high as 52.7 percent in 1993 (Banco de México 1994, 225).

A second source of economic power during this period was the export sector, whose sales doubled from U.S.$25.9 billion in 1983 to U.S.$51.8 billion in 1993. Throughout the De la Madrid and Salinas sexenios, the Mexican government sought to simultaneously reduce its dependence on the state-owned oil sector and accelerate trade liberalization. As a result, there was a dramatic increase in the growth of non-oil exports and in manufacturing exports in particular. The latter averaged an annual growth rate of 24.2 percent during 1982–87 (Dussell Peters 1996, 78)—a trend without parallel even among the Asian Tigers. To provide some idea of their importance within the economy, note that while the index for GDP as a whole in 1988 was 101 (1980 = 100), the index for manufacturing was 109 and for manufactured exports 355 (Weintraub 1990, 11). While the growth of the manufacturing sector as a whole began to slow in the early 1990s, those branches with strong ties to international markets continued to excel (see table 6.3).[5] Not surprisingly,

5. Indeed, the fastest growing manufacturing branches in this table (group IA) also exhibited the highest average annual export growth in the early 1990s, which grew from 11.9 percent of the total share of total exports in 1988 to 19.4 percent in 1992 (Dussell Peters 1996, 78). The dynamism of manufacturing sector exports in this strata was in no small measure due to the presence of the so-called maquiladoras—foreign-owned assembly plants located along the U.S.-Mexico border that imported inputs from the United States duty free, assembled products in Mexico, and exported these abroad. While accounting for about 25 percent of Mexico's manufactured exports in the late 1980s (Weintraub 1990, 10), the maquiladoras accounted for approximately 40 percent of that sector's export growth between 1988 and 1992 (Dussell Peters 1996, 78).

**TABLE 6.3. Typology of Mexico's Manufacturing Sector**

| | GDP Growth (1988–92) | Capital Intensity (1988–92) |
|---|---|---|
| Group I | 10.4 | 0.26 |
| Subgroup IA | 14.7 | 0.69 |
| Automobiles | 22.8 | 0.68 |
| Basic petrochemicals | 9.6 | 2.11 |
| Beer and malt | 7.5 | 0.42 |
| Glass and products | 7.5 | 0.29 |
| Electrical equipment | 6.9 | 0.31 |
| Subgroup IB | 8.0 | 0.11 |
| Fruits and vegetables | 11.3 | 0.06 |
| Alcoholic beverages | 10.9 | 0.20 |
| Metal furniture | 9.0 | 0.09 |
| Structural metal products | 8.9 | 0.11 |
| Electronic equipment | 8.8 | 0.16 |
| Household appliances | 8.2 | 0.08 |
| Machinery and electric equipment | 7.6 | 0.09 |
| Cleaning and toilet preparation | 7.6 | 0.20 |
| Meat and milk products | 7.5 | 0.07 |
| Motors and auto parts | 7.2 | 0.12 |
| Other food products | 6.9 | 0.11 |
| Group II | 4.5 | 0.24 |
| Subgroup IIA | 4.0 | 0.92 |
| Medicinal products | 5.5 | 0.55 |
| Basic inorganic chemicals | 4.8 | 1.15 |
| Cement | 4.1 | 1.29 |
| Rubber products | 3.5 | 0.23 |
| Plastic resins, synthetic fibers | 3.2 | 0.57 |
| Petroleum Refining | 2.9 | 1.84 |
| Subgroup IIB | 4.7 | 0.09 |
| Other Manufacturing Industries | 6.5 | 0.07 |
| Soft drinks and flavorings | 5.7 | 0.07 |
| Plastic products | 4.8 | 0.11 |
| Other chemicals | 4.6 | 0.20 |
| Printing | 4.5 | 0.08 |
| Apparel | 4.5 | 0.04 |
| Other metal products | 4.4 | 0.14 |
| Ceramics | 4.4 | 0.05 |
| Other textile industries | 4.1 | 0.04 |
| Non-electrical machinery | 4.1 | 0.19 |
| Fats and oils | 4.0 | 0.18 |
| Food for animals | 3.3 | 0.04 |
| Group III | –0.5 | 0.17 |
| Subgroup IIIA | 0.3 | 0.66 |
| Steel and iron | 2.3 | 1.15 |
| Paper and paperboard | 1.5 | 0.35 |

TABLE 6.3.—*Continued*

| | GDP Growth (1988–92) | Capital Intensity (1988–92) |
|---|---|---|
| Coffee | –1.0 | 0.24 |
| Pesticides and fertilizers | –7.4 | 0.42 |
| Jute, rough textiles | –31.4 | 0.49 |
| | | |
| Subgroup IIIB | –1.0 | 0.07 |
| Tobacco | 1.9 | 0.11 |
| Corn milling | 1.3 | 0.02 |
| Other wood products | 0.8 | 0.02 |
| Sugar | 0.5 | 0.17 |
| Wheat milling | 0.3 | 0.05 |
| Nonferrous metals | –0.3 | 0.19 |
| Leather and footwear | –1.2 | 0.02 |
| Lumber, plywood | –2.7 | 0.03 |
| Cotton, wool, synthetic textiles | –4.6 | 0.13 |
| Other transportation equipment | –9.0 | 0.08 |
| | | |
| Agriculture | 0.9 | — |
| Mining | 1.2 | 0.35 |
| Manufacturing | 4.9 | 0.22 |
| Services | 3.7 | 0.11 |
| | | |
| Total | 3.6 | 0.13 |

*Source:* Dussell Peters 1996, 76–77. Reprinted with permission.

*Note:* This typology classifies the sector and its 49 branches according to their level of economic activity. Branches have been classified into three groups based on their average annual growth rate (AAGR) in terms of GDP for the 1982–87 boom and the postliberalization period of 1988–92. Each branch in group I accounts for an AAGR of GDP of at least 2% higher than the manufacturing's average (4.9%), while each branch in group II accounts for an AAGR of GDP that falls between 2% of manufacturing's average and –2% of the overall average. Each branch in group III shows an AAGR of GDP 2% below manufacturing's average. Furthermore, subgroups within each of the groups have been established. Thus, the branches with a capital intensity (net capital stock/employment) higher than manufacturing's average during the period 1988–92 (0.22) are in the respective subgroups A, and the branches with a capital intensity lower than manufacturing are in subgroups B. High and increasing capital intensity reflects the potential modernization of the respective activities and a higher potential for facing increasing competition as well as for realizing higher profit rates. From this perspective, it is anticipated that group I with its 16 branches, particularly the 5 branches of subgroup IA, will represent the "leading" branches of the Mexican manufacturing sector with the highest growth potential and the highest probability of achieving successful integration into the world market (Dussell Peters 1996, 77).

these winning branches tended to be dominated by large-scale firms, who were best equipped to reorient their production toward external markets and who consequently led the push for further trade liberalization in the early 1990s (Alba Vega 1993a; Puga 1993b; Heredia 1996, 144–45).

The growth of export and financial capital during this period was also accompanied by the concentration of its profits in the hands of a very small economic elite: the economic groups (*grupos*). By 1987, the country's top 101 economic groups controlled 365 of the country's top 500 companies in sales, accounting for 38 percent of output by the manufacturing sector alone (Garrido 1993, 26). By 1992, this trend had accelerated, as the country's 10 largest private economic groups generated 56 percent of total sales, mobilized 61 percent of total assets, and represented 53.7 percent of employment.[6] The dominance of the groups within the country's most dynamic industries is evident in table 6.4. The most powerful conglomerates also tended to dominate the financial sector, playing a preponderant role in the acquisition of privatized state-owned firms—including the banks (Garrido 1997, 7; Heredia 1996, 145; Teichman 1995, 152–53; Valdés Ugalde 1994, 234). Because of their control over a large portion of the most profitable sectors of the economy as well as their substantial ties to foreign capital, private national groups came to assume a position of leadership within the new economic model (Garrido 1994b).

In contrast, the losers in this development model were those areas of the economy that had failed to successfully restructure their production in the wake of the trade liberalization of the 1980s. These were the "sons and daughters" of import substitution industrialization—those industries that produced traditional consumer goods for the domestic market. Unlike the modern, large-scale manufacturing industries such as chemicals and plastics, whose productivity soared, traditional industries such as tobacco and footwear were badly hit by the reduction in trade barriers (see table 6.3). Not surprisingly, these less dynamic industries also tended to be dominated by small firms and microenterprises (Pastor and Wise 1997, 432–36; Alba Vega 1993b, 471). Although some of these "losing" branches such as textiles and paper were able to improve their export performance significantly over the course of the 1980s, output and wages stagnated, and by the early 1990s, they were thought to have exhausted their potential (Bizberg 1996, 92–95; Pastor and Wise 1997, 435–36). While these more typically sheltered sectors were also constituents of the ruling party, their interests were increasingly marginalized in favor of the more economically powerful exposed and non-asset-specific sectors of the economy (Frieden 1991a, 221; Luna 1994).

In sum, while De la Madrid bore the burden of healing business-government wounds, Salinas used this newfound alliance with important sectors of capital to deepen these reforms. The principal beneficiaries of this reform agenda were the financial sector, large export firms, and the financial and economic groups that united them. In other words, the Salinas and De la Madrid administrations presided over an economy dominated by precisely the sort of economic actors that stood to benefit from the creation of an autonomous central bank.

6. *Expansión,* September 4, 1991, p. 139.

TABLE 6.4. **Mexico: Indicators for the Ten Largest Private National Groups and Their links with the Large Firms, 1992**

| Grupo | Position of Group | Sales (millions of dollars) | Total Number of Firms | Total Number of Firms Included among the Top 500 | Principal Firm of the Group Included within the Top 500 | Position within the Top 500 | Type of Firm | Position within this Branch | Position among the 500 largest Export Firms |
|---|---|---|---|---|---|---|---|---|---|
| Vitro | 1 | 3,308.90 | 92 | 47 | Vidrio Plano | 76 | glass | 1 | 24/55/80 |
| Carso | 2 | 2,554.42 | 6 | 6 | Telmex | 1 | communication | 1 | 4 |
| Alfa | 3 | 2,492.75 | 10 | 10 | Hylsa | 8 | iron and steel | 2 | 43 |
| | | | | | Petrocel | 41 | petrochemical | 5 | 14 |
| | | | | | Sigma | 49 | food | 6 | |
| Cemex | 4 | 2,213.20 | 42 | 18 | Empresas Tolteca | 20 | cement | 1 | 52 |
| Visa | 5 | 2,100.10 | 106 | 7 | Cervecería Cuauhtémoc | 17 | beer | 1 | 53/58 |
| | | | | | Ind. Embotelladora de México | 95 | beverages | 4 | |
| Desc | 6 | 1,654.20 | 124 | 13 | Novum | 27 | petrochemicals | 2 | 27 |
| | | | | | Spicer | 17 | auto parts | 1 | 13 |
| | | | | | Univasa | 73 | food | 8 | 5/9/12/48 |
| Minera México | 8 | 937.35 | 40 | 6 | Ind. Minera México | 21 | mining | 1 | |
| La Moderna | 9 | 921.57 | 15 | 2 | La Moderna | 16 | tobacco | 1 | 75 |
| Peñoles | 14 | 732.80 | 30 | 18 | Met-Mex Peñoles | — | mining | 2 | 74 |

*Source:* Garrido 1994b, 166. Reprinted with permission.

## Reform Timing: Challenging the Conventional Wisdom

With this clearer picture of Mexico's authoritarians in mind, we are now in a position to examine their motivations for undertaking central bank reform. At first blush, the Mexican government's decision to make its central bank autonomous in 1993 should not seem at all surprising. In light of the government's demonstrated commitment to macroeconomic stability, an autonomous central bank would seem a perfectly logical component of its neoliberal reform agenda. But as was the case in Chile, the relevant question to ask is not why the authoritarians chose to undertake a central bank reform per se but, rather, why they chose to do so at this particular moment.

When the Salinas administration unveiled its constitutional amendment to make the Bank of Mexico autonomous, the reform was presented as the crowning event in a decade-long effort to bring Mexico's public finances under control (Ortiz 1994). Consider the case of inflation. From 1987, when the Pact was initiated, to 1993, when the central bank reform was announced, annual inflation had dropped from 159.2 percent to under 10 percent—reaching single digits for the first time in more than two decades. The same was true of budget deficits. Following large-scale privatization of its public enterprises and an aggressive effort to increase tax revenues, the Mexican government had registered a budgetary surplus in 1992 for the first time in decades, equivalent to 0.5 percent of GDP. According to Finance Minister Pedro Aspe, it was only now, "having achieved these solid bases for fiscal restraint," that the economy was finally "in condition for an autonomous central bank."[7] To undergo fiscal and monetary reform in the reverse order, Aspe argued, would have been "to engage in an act of pure voluntarism."[8]

By waiting to undertake this reform until after it had succeeded in attaining single-digit inflation and a budgetary surplus, the government's objective was thus less one of establishing credibility than of entrenching it. Rather than being a mere by-product of the Salinas administration, such policies would now "transcend individuals and transform themselves into institutions" (Aspe 1993, 5). By separating the function of creating money from the other tasks of the state, the government would effectively establish "an institutional counterweight to the rest of the public agencies in which there are continual demands to increase spending" (Aspe 1993, 6). In this way, central bank autonomy would serve as living proof that the country that had set off the debt crisis but a decade earlier was now willing to renounce permanently its inflationary past.

7. Pedro Aspe, interview with Jacobo Zabuldovsky, *Televisa,* May 17, 1993.

8. Pedro Aspe, Mexican finance minister (1988–94), interview by author, tape recording, Mexico City, Mexico, January 30, 1995.

And yet there is good reason to question the government's avowed need to delay central bank reform until after fiscal reform had been completed. A closer look at the evidence suggests that, if anything, the government had incentives to undertake this reform much earlier.

### Domestic Demand for Autonomy: The Optimal Time for Commitment

One must begin by questioning how much added economic value a central bank reform could realistically have had in Mexico in 1993. As argued in the discussion of the Chilean case in chapter 4, central bank autonomy would seem most necessary from a credibility standpoint when private sector confidence is lowest. But precisely because of the Salinas administration's demonstrated success in stabilizing the macroeconomic environment, there is little evidence to suggest that such a costly signal was in order. To the contrary, private sector optimism with respect to the future had been rising steadily ever since Salinas took office, reaching an all-time high of 94 percent by July 1992.[9] In the first semester of 1993—just before the central bank reform was announced—it was still as high as 82 percent.[10] Indeed, the rapid recovery of business confidence was one of the defining features of the Salinas administration (Valdés Ugalde 1994, 231).

The same cannot be said for the period a decade earlier. Following the debt crisis of 1982, inflation soared to nearly 100 percent, while fiscal deficits as a percentage of GDP climbed to a record level of 17 percent. As the debt service to exports ratio climbed to 62 percent, the country entered into a profound balance of payments crisis. In the wake of this macroeconomic disarray, investor confidence followed suit. In 1982 alone, investment rates as a percentage of GDP were negative on the order of 17 percent and dropped to 24 percent the following year. During the first two years of the De la Madrid administration, an estimated U.S.$17.7 billion worth of capital fled Mexican borders (Centeno 1994, 70). Throughout the rest of the decade, capital continued to hemorrhage at a net rate of $5 billion per year, and net repatriation did not begin until after 1990 (Oks and Van Wijnbergen 1993, 206, 219). If credibility were at issue, there was arguably no better time for the Mexican government to have implemented a central bank reform.

In addition to macroeconomic circumstances, political considerations should also have militated in favor of enacting the central bank reform well before 1993. As noted earlier, business groups had been quite active in pres-

9. As noted in a biannual poll of business elites in the magazine *Expansión,* July 21, 1993, 51.

10. Ibid.

suring the government to show a deeper commitment to neoliberal reforms following the nationalization of the banks in 1982 (Millán 1988; Maxfield 1989; Luna, Tirado, and Valdés Ugalde 1991). By the time Salinas assumed power in 1988, an economic constituency of financial and export-oriented capital that would have benefited from an autonomous central bank was already securely in place. We have already noted the economic power of the brokerage houses and large export firms. Here, a word is in order on their political power.

Most authors divide the Mexican business community in the 1980s into three main factions.[11] The first—the "liberal conservative" wing—was composed largely of medium-sized firms based in the country's industrial north. Known for its political activism, this faction had championed the opposition to government economic policy in the early part of the decade. A second so-called technocratic faction centered around the insurance industry, the brokerage houses, and the large economic groups. While historically more accommodationist in its dealings with the ruling party, this group shared the conservative economic policy orientation of the liberal conservatives. Finally, a third and considerably weaker faction represented more protectionist forces in the economy, particularly those small and medium-sized businesses that had traditionally been under the protective wing of the state.

By the end of the 1980s, Mexico's formal structure of business representation was squarely in the hands of the technocratic faction (Luna and Tirado 1992). Its influence was most visible within the peak business organization—the Business Coordinating Council (Consejo de Coordinadores Económicos [CCE]). Because the CCE's organizational structure privileged sector, rather than membership size or geographical region, its governing board accorded disproportionate weight to the less numerically strong members of the body—the insurance industry, the brokerage houses, and the economic groups.[12] While these three organizations together accounted for 42 percent of the representation within the CCE, together they comprised only 121 (barely 1 percent) of the more than 900,000 CCE members (Luna and Tirado 1992, 95).

11. Business-government relations in Mexico have been the subject of numerous studies. Puga (1993a) provides a succinct history of business-government relations over the course of the twentieth century, while Camp (1989) offers a detailed sociological profile of Mexican business groups, and Garrido (1992) quantifies their economic activity. An excellent overview of business-government relations in the 1980s can be found in Maxfield and Anzaldúa Montoya 1987.

12. The CCE was made up of seven principal affiliate organizations: the business chambers of the country's five main economic sectors (agriculture, industry, commerce, finance, and insurance) as well as a northern-based business union, Confederaciá Patronal de la República Mexicana (COPARMEX), and a small club of elite businessmen representing the country's largest economic groups (CMHN).

This structural bias in favor of powerful capitalist actors was particularly acute where the country's largest economic groups were concerned. Of the seven main affiliates within the CCE board, one corresponded to a private club of businessmen—the Council of Mexican Businessmen (Consejo Mexicano de Hombres de Negocios [CMHN])—representing the economic groups. While composed of only 37 individuals, this so-called peak of peaks carried the same voting weight within the CCE as the commerce chamber with some 200,000 members. Because of its sheer economic might, the CMHN was able to impose its preferences on the "collective" decisions made by the CCE. This was not a luxury afforded the small and medium-sized firms in the CCE, who were instead at the mercy of decisions made by the grupos and large firms.[13] In turn, the CMHN also benefited from what is known as "door-knocking privileges" (derecho a picapuerta), or direct access to the upper echelons of the government in order to lobby for its preferred policies. As evidence of its integral role within the policy-making process, note that the CMHN was able to screen potential PRI aspirants to the presidency.[14]

By the end of the 1980s, it was clear that this politically powerful economic oligopoly not only favored continuing the process of market-oriented reform initiated under De la Madrid but wanted to deepen it. Recall that despite De la Madrid's bold efforts at liberalization, the business community continued to be wary of the government's resolve in the economic arena. As late as December 1987, businesspeople were still not satisfied with the program for reprivatization outlined by the De la Madrid administration and had not discarded the notion that something like bank nationalization could still occur (Valdés Ugalde 1994, 231). On the eve of the presidential elections of 1988, the then president of the CCE commented, "populist decisions have hurt the country. . . . it is necessary to return to economic orthodoxy. . . . the next sexenio must continue the policies of privatization as part of the strategy

13. The relatively weak position of the smaller and medium-sized firms within the CCE was reinforced at the level of the individual, sectorally based chambers, where leadership also tended to be dominated by large firms. The government was thus able to ignore the demands of small and medium producers, even when they were numerically a good deal stronger. In the wake of the Pact negotiations noted previously, for example, Confederaciá de Cámaras Industriales de los Estados Unidos Mexicanos (CONCAMÍN) was dominated by large manufacturing companies in sectors such as automobiles, fibers, and steel that generally favored trade liberalization. This in turn muted the impact of its member organization, Canacintra, which typically represented small manufacturing companies more inclined toward protectionism (Kaufman, Bazdresch, and Heredia 1994, 391–92). Smaller and medium-sized firms also traditionally lacked the technical information necessary to provide an informed opinion on government policies—particularly of a macroeconomic nature. As a result, they typically relied on chamber leadership to inform them of such matters, which also served to dampen their influence (Carlos Alba Vega, economist, El Colegio de México, interview by author, tape recording, Mexico City, Mexico, January 11, 1995).

14. " 'Afinidad y Afecto' de Empresarios Para Aspe y Camacho," *El Financiero,* January 20, 1993.

of modernization" (Centeno 1994, 13). Indeed, the choice of Salinas as candidate within the PRI was said to be the result of "private sector forces associated with multinationals who desired the development of a privatizing, monetarist and free trade PRI" (Puga 1993a, 183).

In light of such public proclamations at the end of the 1980s, it would not be far fetched to suggest that in addition to, or even instead of, the 1987 stabilization pact, the authoritarians might have enacted a central bank reform to reassure investors of their commitment to macroeconomic stability. As one member of the Mexican financial community so eloquently phrased it, central bank autonomy was a "no brainer" for business groups, as "leaving the central bank in the hands of government was like leaving Dracula in charge of the bloodbank."[15] Notwithstanding their own coincidence of interests with those of the Salinas government, the private sector welcomed any and all institutional changes that might thwart any backsliding on the part of future governments (Valdés Ugalde 1996, 142). Indeed, when Aspe came to discuss the autonomy initiative with the CCE before unveiling it publicly, he is said to have told the assembled members that he was "giving them something that they'd been asking for a long time."[16] And yet, in spite of these overriding economic incentives for central bank reform as early as 1987, the technocratic faction waited six more years before it would act.

In short, a more careful analysis of the De la Madrid and Salinas sexenios suggests that there were incentives for a central bank reform at various points during the 1980s. The government might have undertaken the autonomy initiative following the economic crisis of 1982, as part of broader efforts to win back investor confidence. They might also have acted in the late 1980s, when the demands of powerful economic actors also favored a more explicit commitment to macroeconomic stability and economic liberalization. To therefore argue—as the Salinas government did—that this reform would not have been credible at an earlier point in time simply does not make sense. Rather, the appropriate political question to ask is why the Mexican government undertook this reform when it did, given that the relevant economic preconditions existed well before 1993.

## International Explanations: The Need for Foreign Capital

One set of potential explanations attributes the reform's timing to international factors. According to these hypotheses, the 1993 central bank reform

15. Timothy Heyman, Mexico representative for Barings Securities, interview by author, tape recording, Mexico City, Mexico, February 2, 1995.

16. Francisco Calderón, former general director of CCE, interview by author, tape recording, Mexico City, Mexico, January 16, 1995.

represented a deliberate attempt by the Salinas administration to shore up credibility with foreign investors.

The notion that this reform was undertaken largely to cater to a foreign audience was very much the received wisdom outside official government circles. A member of the country's leading left-wing party argued, for example, that the reform was done in part as a way for the "group in government to send a message to the international community about its commitment to stability beyond this sexenio."[17] This sentiment was echoed in the words of a prominent Mexican economist, who attributed this reform to the government's desire to "reinforce the idea of Mexico being a 'first world' country."[18] As one economist at the Mexican stock exchange glibly summarized this view of the reform's motives, "the government wanted to be seen as the 'nice kid' in the hemisphere."[19]

In academic circles, this argument has been most forcefully articulated by Maxfield (1997, 102–4), who links Salinas's support for central bank independence in 1993 to a multifaceted effort to increase foreign financial inflows to Mexico. Specifically, Maxfield argues that when it looked as though the passage of the North American Free Trade Agreement (NAFTA) might be in jeopardy, Salinas instead pushed through a statutory increase in central bank authority in order to lessen potential investor uncertainty. According to Maxfield, the central bank reform essentially served as a contingency measure for foreign capital in the event that the free trade agreement did not pass.

But even while the time-sensitive nature of the NAFTA hypothesis offers a plausible credibility-based explanation for the 1993 reform, a closer look at the evidence reveals that it is not sufficient on its own to explain the reform's timing. Consider first the indicators that Maxfield (1997) uses to suggest the need for such credibility, beginning with the balance of payments criterion. It was true that the country had a large current account deficit in 1993 (see table 6.2). But high and increasing levels of foreign reserves—which had risen from a low of approximately U.S.$6 billion in 1988 to a high of U.S.$25 billion in 1993—had helped largely to compensate for the trade deficit. Her second indicator, the state of financial regulation, is also open to differing interpretations. As noted earlier, the country witnessed a substantial deregulation of the domestic financial market early on in the Salinas administration (Maxfield

17. Jorge Calderón, former deputy and senior economic adviser to the Party of the Democratic Revolution (Partido Revolucionario Democrático [PRD]), interview by author, tape recording, Mexico City, Mexico, December 5, 1994.

18. Victor Urquidi, economist, El Colegio de México, interview by author, tape recording, Mexico City, Mexico, January 9, 1995.

19. Confidential interview by the author, tape recording, Mexico City, Mexico, January 31, 1995.

1993; Ortiz 1994). That said, Mexican banks sought—and achieved—a considerable degree of protection in the wake of subsequent NAFTA negotiations that protected them from undue foreign competition (Mansell Carstens 1994, 29–41; Kessler 1998).

Maxfield's third indicator—the predominant form of asset flow—is perhaps the most convincing of the three where the Mexican case is concerned. At the time that the reform was undertaken, the lion's share of incoming foreign investment was in the form of foreign equity and bonds (Mansell Carstens 1994, 8). This would seem to lend support to Maxfield's claim that central bank reform is most necessary when the predominant type of asset flow is highly liquid in nature. When evaluated in the context of a series of other indicators, however, it is not so clear that Mexico needed to signal its credibility to the international community in 1993. Rather, as Maxfield herself readily concedes, several objective measures of international creditworthiness were strong and improving (Maxfield 1997, 94–104).

Note, for example, that from 1988, when Salinas took office, to 1993, total external debt as a percentage of GDP had declined from 58 percent to 36 percent (Banco de México 1994, 275). And while not nearly as dramatic as the growth of portfolio investment, direct foreign investment had also reached an all-time high, largely as a result of a 1989 law liberalizing Mexico's historically protectionist foreign investment regime.[20] By 1993, total foreign investment in Mexico in 1993 had climbed to a record 33 billion dollars—up from a mere 3.6 million in 1989. This total was nearly 49 percent higher than government projections for the sexenio as a whole and almost 35 percent higher than all foreign investment accumulated between 1973 and 1988 combined.[21]

In the wake of such trends, it would seem difficult to argue that Mexico still felt obligated to prove itself before the international economic community. Rather, as a country risk assessment carried out by a foreign investment agency noted in August 1993, "since 1982 the government has done virtually everything that foreign creditors have asked by way of imposing austerity policies and liberalizing the economy."[22] A series of qualitative indicators lends support to this assertion.

20. I refer here to the 1989 Law on Foreign Investment. Prior to this law, the foreign investment regime had been highly restrictive, stipulating those activities reserved exclusively for the state, those activities reserved exclusively for Mexicans, those activities in which foreign investment could not exceed a certain percentage set below the maximum 49 percent, and those activities where foreign investment could be no greater than 49 percent. The new law expanded a range of operations open to 100 percent foreign ownership and, provided certain conditions were met, did not require investors to seek approval from the regulating body (Lustig 1992, 125–30).

21. "Inversión Extranjera: Carrera Contra Reloj," *Expansión,* February 2, 1994, p. 21.

22. *International Country Risk Guide,* August 1, 1993.

In the 1991 *International Country Risk Guide,* Mexico received a score of 68.5 on a scale with a high of 92 and a low of 21, falling just behind Venezuela, South Korea, and Thailand in the developing world (Natella and Manson 1991, 66). The Mexican stock exchange's "designated market" status by various security and exchange boards in Britain, the United States, and Japan was also a sign of outside faith in the Mexican financial system. In May 1993, Mexico became the twenty-fifth member of the Organization for Economic Cooperation and Development (OECD), suggesting that Mexico's efforts at economic liberalization had not only won it recognition but, in this case, equal status among this "club" of first world countries. Finally, it is worth noting that uncertainty surrounding the passage of NAFTA did not seem to have had any appreciable effects on the behavior of foreign capital during the relevant time period. As an economic analyst noted at the time, the U.S.-Mexico interest rate differential would prove to be a consistent draw for foreign money even if a NAFTA delay or defeat in the U.S. Congress were to cause a temporary drop in the stock market.[23]

This is not to suggest, of course, that international factors played no role whatsoever in influencing the reform's timing. When questioned as to the motivation behind the central bank autonomy initiative, a variety of individuals closely involved in the initiative acknowledged that the government was concerned in part with promoting a set of favorable expectations with respect to the future of the economy, especially before foreign investors.[24] And there is no doubt that the uncertainty surrounding the passage of NAFTA in late 1993 made this a particularly propitious moment to do so. As the following chapter of this book will reveal, however, talk of a central bank reform was under way within the upper echelons of the Mexican government well before the passage of NAFTA was ever in doubt. What such evidence suggests is that while government officials were surely concerned with enhancing Mexico's international credibility, they were equally if not more preoccupied by a series of domestic political events that impinged critically upon the reform's evolution, timing, and content.

In brief, while the NAFTA negotiations did coincide with central bank reform, it seems unlikely that they were its exclusive motivation. In light of Mexico's international reputation for macroeconomic stability, it is doubtful that foreign investors needed a central bank reform to convince them further.

23. Note, for example, that when anti-NAFTA statements from U.S. representative Richard Gephardt and Ross Perot caused pessimism in the Mexican markets in September 1993, the government responded by raising interest rates. Financial analysts considered this a move to prevent short-term foreign capital from fleeing an uncertain stock market ("Making Money in Difficult Times," *Business Mexico,* November 1993, 7).

24. Based on confidential tape-recorded interviews by the author in Mexico City, Mexico, July 1997.

In making this argument, I do not mean to suggest that Mexico was not vulnerable to the international economy in 1993, as the subsequent events surrounding the 1994–95 peso crisis would reveal in bold relief. What I am suggesting is that in addition to international economic pressures, other factors were at work in influencing this decision.[25]

## Reform Motive: The Onset of the Democratic Threat

If the 1993 central bank reform was not motivated exclusively by domestic economic demand, or by international economic pressures, then what was driving it? In order to develop a plausible alternative logic to explain this reform, I turn to the domestic political environment. We have already noted that at the time the reform surfaced, the Mexican president was supported by a baseline constituency that favored a "privatizing, monetarist, and free trade" ruling party (Puga 1993a, 183). Historically, the Mexican president had no trouble pursuing policies that benefited the constituency. With the onset of the 1988 national elections, however, it became clear that this luxury would not continue indefinitely.

### Pre-1988: Mexico's "Perfect Dictatorship"[26]

The contemporary Mexican political system dates to the early part of the twentieth century, when a violent social revolution led to the overthrow of Porfirio Díaz's personalistic authoritarian regime (1876–1911) and the establishment of a new, postrevolutionary order. The 1917 federal Constitution established a tripartite separation of powers system, dividing decision-making responsibil-

25. In the years since the reform, rumors have also surfaced that the central bank initiative was part of an explicit agreement between the U.S. and Mexican governments in the wake of the NAFTA negotiations that Mexico would maintain exchange rate stability over the medium term. Once again, the fact that the central bank autonomy initiative predated the NAFTA negotiations by several years calls such logic into question. And when asked point blank about the existence of such a "deal," a chief negotiator of the trade agreement was resolute in affirming that there was absolutely no demand for an autonomous central bank in Mexico on the part of the United States (Patricia Armendariz, interview by author, tape recording, Mexico City, Mexico, August 22, 1997). But even if the Americans had pressed for such an arrangement—whether tacitly or otherwise—it is not clear how such a turn of events would challenge the fundamental argument put forth in this chapter and the next. If the U.S. government was indeed looking for some assurances about the long-term stability of the economy, that was because it was concerned with precisely the same scenario that I will argue preoccupied the Mexican government: the long-term economic consequences of domestic political change.

26. I borrow this term from the Peruvian novelist Mario Vargas Llosa, who thus described the Mexican political system during an interview on *Televisa,* August 30, 1990.

ity among executive, legislative, and judicial branches.[27] It also created a federal system in which states' rights and municipal autonomy were explicitly recognized. Finally, this system was also strongly presidentialist, placing jurisdiction over a series of policy arenas in the hands of the executive. But despite the fact that its formal trappings seemed to mirror those of the United States, in reality the president also enjoyed an unusually broad range of informal powers that enabled him to dominate the country's political system.[28]

To begin with, he served as the "supreme head" of Mexico's hegemonic, multisector "official" political party—the PRI. This position empowered the president to choose party leaders, shape the party's internal governance, and impose his personal choices for the PRI's gubernatorial and congressional candidates, as well as for the leaders of powerful state-run unions (Cornelius 1996, 34). Of particular note, through the unwritten norm of "finger-pointing" (*dedazo*), the president was able to control unilaterally selection of the ruling party's next presidential nominee. In the PRI-dominated party system (see the discussion that follows), this essentially amounted to the ability to name his own successor. Despite the PRI's heterogeneous composition, its hierarchical chain of command thus meant that the party served at the beck and call of the president (Weldon 1997).[29]

In addition to controlling the ruling party's internal organization, the president could also rely on the PRI as a tool of far-reaching political support. Since its inception in 1929, the PRI had sought to incorporate the broadest range of social, economic, and political interests under its wing.[30] Through a combination of extensive state patronage and occasional repression, the party was able to secure the loyalty of mass actors to the regime (Heredia 1994). Because of its privileged relationship with the state, the "official" party also

27. The federal legislature was bicameral in nature. Originally, it was made up of a 64-member senate (2 from each of Mexico's thirty-one states plus 2 from the Federal District) and a 300-member chamber of deputies, selected on majority vote in single-member districts.

28. For general discussions of Mexico's unique brand of authoritarianism, see, among others, Cornelius, Gentleman, and Smith 1989; Collier and Collier 1991; Molinar Horcasitas 1993. The "bare essentials" can be found in Cornelius 1996.

29. It is interesting to note that while the president has served as de facto party leader since the presidency of Lázaro Cárdenas (1934–40), the office of party leader is not technically an attribute of the presidency. As Weldon (1997) convincingly argues, a great deal of the authority afforded the president thus stems not so much from the Constitution or from any inherent centralism in the Mexican political system but rather from a role that the party has historically delegated to the president.

30. The official party was divided into three sectors: the peasant sector, the labor sector, and the "popular" sector (representing most government employees, small merchants, private landowners, and low-income urban neighborhood groups). Each sector was dominated by one mass organization: the National Confederation of Peasants (Confederación Nacional Campesina [CNC]), the Mexican Worker's Federation (Confederación de Trabajadores de México [CTM]), and the National Confederation of Popular Organizations (Confederación de Organizaciones Populares [CNOP]).

enjoyed financial, campaign, and media resources that gave it a tremendous advantage over its competitors.[31] Although the political system did entail competitive elections, these held more symbolic value than anything else, serving to reinforce the legitimacy of the ruling elite (Wiarda 1989, 6). Where ample access to government personnel and financial resources proved insufficient, the PRI was able to ensure its dominance over electoral opponents through its ability to commit electoral fraud with virtual impunity (Reding 1991). As a result of these multiple built-in advantages, between 1929 and 1988, the "official" party never lost an election for the presidency, state government, or federal senate.

Finally, the president's supreme authority within the PRI also afforded the chief executive a considerable degree of control over the rest of the country's political institutions (Garrido 1987; Weldon 1997). For example, the president effectively served as the country's chief legislator, imposing his agenda on a PRI-dominated congress that served as a rubber stamp for presidential initiatives. Among other things, this allowed the president to modify the Constitution as he saw fit, a prerogative of which all presidents since 1917 have availed themselves (Garrido 1989, 422).[32] It also meant that his widespread appointment and removal powers would go unchallenged—especially those over high cabinet ministers and high-level bureaucrats. With each successive administration, the president could thus reinforce his policy preferences by infusing all levels of the bureaucracy with members of his *camarilla,* or political clique (Cornelius and Craig 1991, 45–53). Because its members were all handpicked, the president could also rely on the Supreme Court to uphold all presidential decrees and legislation. As a result of its absolutist nature, many have argued that the only limit on presidential power in Mexico was the fact that the president could not be reelected.[33]

31. For example, the ruling party enjoyed virtually unlimited access to government funds for campaign financing. It was the only political party that possessed a truly nationwide network of campaign organizers and poll watchers. And because the television station was state owned, it would typically devote 90 percent or more of its coverage to the campaigns of the PRI (Cornelius and Craig 1991, 61–62).

32. Note that this is not a power that is legally afforded the president, as constitutional amendments required a two-thirds majority in both chambers of the legislature. By virtue of Article 71 of the Constitution, however, which grants the president the authority to introduce bills to Congress, most constitutional amendments have initiated in the executive branch (Weldon 1997, 235).

33. There are two interpretations of the relationship between the party and the executive in Mexico. Traditionally, it was assumed that the party's submissive role vis-à-vis the president was but one of the president's many informal powers (Garrido 1989; Aguilar Camín and Meyer 1993). A more recent challenge to this view holds that the executive's power depends instead on unified partisan control of both chambers of Congress, the president's ability to discipline the "official" party, and continued PRI dominance over opposition parties (Molinar Horcasitas 1994; Weldon 1997). While this debate is not relevant to the period described here (pre-1988), events under the Zedillo administration seem to lend more credence to the latter interpretation.

Given that PRI electoral victories and PRI support for the president were virtually preordained, Mexican politics was historically characterized by a great deal of stability. The only real source of uncertainty in this system stemmed from the president's choice of successor, and even that was quite low (the successor was handpicked and could virtually always be assumed to be like minded). This stability was reflected in the extraordinary policy continuity observed between 1930 and 1982 and in the fact that there were no major institutional reforms during this period. Thus, despite the popular saying in Mexico that "there is a revolution every six years"—implying an incentive to undo the policies of one's predecessor—the empirical record suggests otherwise.[34] Even after the dramatic shift in policy following the 1982 debt crisis, the fact that the political system remained intact meant that the president could still pursue his policy interests at will.

## The 1988 Elections: The Threat of Democracy Surfaces

This "pleasant" state of affairs came to an abrupt end in 1988. Like the plebiscite in Chile, Mexico's 1988 national elections served as the first visible signal that the future of the world's longest ruling political party was in jeopardy after almost sixty years of uninterrupted power.

The 1988 presidential elections were an unexpected watershed event in Mexican political history (Cornelius, Gentleman, and Smith 1989). While the official results showed Salinas narrowly winning with just over 50 percent of the vote, few believed that the results had not been doctored, prompting accusations of electoral fraud for the first time in history (Reding 1988a).[35] The pronounced drop in support for the PRI presidential candidate constituted a marked departure from historical trends (see fig. 6.1). At the time, the election results were widely interpreted as a vote of "no confidence" in the austerity measures initiated under De la Madrid, which had produced a decline in living standards over the course of the 1980s (Weintraub and Baer

34. It is true that incumbent presidents have often sought to differentiate themselves from their predecessors by pursuing abrupt changes in policy. Prior to 1982, however, all such "revolutions" took place within the parameters of an overarching consensus on a populist developmental model, such that even when one could detect palpable shifts between left-leaning and right-leaning administrations, these were always within the rubric of a large and ever-expanding state. Indeed, it was precisely because of the existence of this constantly expanding pie that political leaders could employ a variety of political and economic concessions in order to purchase the temporary loyalty of whichever group found itself temporarily excluded from power (Smith 1989, 396).

35. The official results showed 51 percent for the PRI, 31 percent for the left-wing Democratic Current (Frente Democrático Nacional [FDN]), and 17 percent for the right-wing National Action Party (Partido Acción Nacional [PAN]).

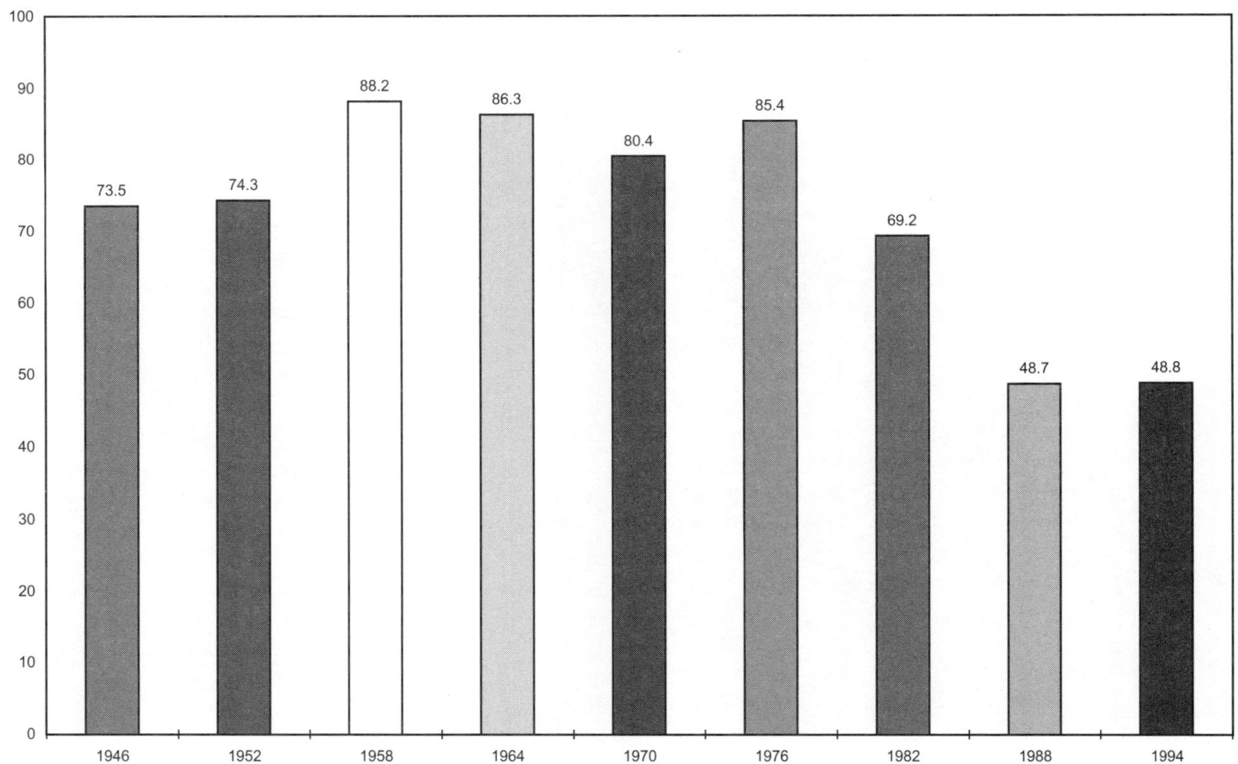


**Fig. 6.1.** **Mexico: Support for ruling party's presidential candidate, 1946–94. (From Cornelius 1996, 64.)**

1992, 193–97).[36] While subsequent analyses have shown that the number one determinant of voter defection in the 1988 presidential elections was not economic policy but, rather, attitudes toward the political regime, there is no question that a series of underlying ideological cleavages had emerged that might easily lend themselves to an electoral realignment in the future (Domínguez and McCann 1996, 110–12; Klesner 1994,180).[37]

In turn, Salinas's candidacy also brought deep fissures within the ruling party to the surface. From the 1950s onward, the PRI was characterized by a long-standing divide between the so-called nationalists and the neoliberals (Cordera and Tello 1981). While the former had advocated classically protectionist policies to increase public investment and stimulate domestic demand, the latter weighed in favor of controlling inflation and dismantling Mexico's elaborate system of import substitution industrialization to open up Mexico's borders. The two groups had historically coexisted in relative harmony within the Mexican state, alternating in their influence (Smith 1979; Camp 1985). But with the decided shift toward a neoliberal economic model beginning in 1982, it was clear that there was only room for one faction to exert its leadership (Ronfeldt 1989).

The rise of the neoliberal faction over the course of the 1980s had a splintering effect on internal party unity. First, it revealed the profound dissatisfaction with economic liberalization at the party's base. Cornerstone policies of the neoliberal reform agenda, such as the privatization of state-owned enterprises and cuts in government subsidies, were directly damaging to the core interests of organized PRI support—workers and peasants (Weintraub and Baer 1992; Dresser 1994a; Middlebrook 1995). In the months leading up to the 1988 elections, strong internal opposition emerged from these more traditional sectors of the party, who viewed the Salinas candidacy within the PRI as a decisive blow to the party's historic origins (Smith 1989). This was followed by the collapse of the PRI's so-called sectoral vote in 1988, as official party candidates affiliated with the party's traditional peasant and labor organizations failed to deliver their customary number of votes. It is no secret, for

36. In a Gallup poll conducted just before the 1988 elections, 74 percent of respondents said that the country's economic situation was bad or very bad, and 81 percent of those who actually defected from the PRI in the November elections also categorized it as such (Domínguez and McCann 1992, 213).

37. Domínguez and McCann (1996) propose what is essentially a two-step model to explain voting behavior in this election, in which voters decided first on their view of the ruling party. If they were favorably predisposed toward the PRI, seeing it as a party that both was likely to strengthen over time and was likely to improve the country's economy, then they voted for the PRI. If, on the other hand, they were critical of the ruling party and its ability to manage the economy, then they supported an opposition party based on their policy preferences and social cleavage attachments.

example, that many members of the state-controlled petroleum worker's union were actively engaged in the Cárdenas campaign (see "The Cárdenista Challenge," which follows), providing both organizational and financial support (Cornelius and Craig 1991, 78; Teichman 1995, 175; Middlebrook 1995, 293–94).

Second, the rise of the technocratic faction within the PRI also blocked the political mobility of more statist elements within the party leadership. In 1986, dissident elements associated with the party's left wing formed a protest movement within the PRI calling for greater internal democratization of the party and less commitment to a single economic dogma (Carr 1989; Bruhn 1996). When it was unsuccessful in its bid to recover party leadership, this faction broke with the ruling party in an unprecedented move and formed an independent left-wing political movement (see the discussion that follows). This rift was by far the most significant in the PRI's history and made it clear that the growing disparity between the "haves" and "have-nots" within its ranks was beginning to take its toll.[38]

In addition to these obvious signs of ruling party decline, the 1988 elections also signaled the rise of a political opposition in Mexico. Throughout most of the PRI's history there had been no effective opposition to speak of in Mexico. Rather, the main function of opposition parties had been to indirectly legitimize the ruling party by providing it with nominal competitors. But when popular discontent began to surface with regard to the government's austerity policies after 1982, opposition parties were the main beneficiaries (Molinar Horcasitas 1989, Molinar Horcasitas 1991; Klesner 1994).[39]

While the growth of the opposition had taken place primarily at the local level over the course of the 1980s, following the 1988 elections, opposition

38. One must of course ask why the técnicos would choose to pursue a set of economic policies that would per force undermine their political support. One possibility is that when they first began the liberalization of the economy, they simply did not anticipate its political fallout with certain support groups. This interpretation seems unlikely, however, given the foresight otherwise attributed to them. A second position holds that the authoritarians understood full well that economic liberalization would in turn engender political liberalization but they thought that they could sequence economic and political freedoms à la Gorbachev (Rubio 1993; Coppedge 1993). While the latter interpretation seems more plausible, it also suggests implicitly that Salinas was guiding the country toward democracy. In keeping with Dresser (1994a) and Craske (1996), it seems more likely that while Salinas was laying the groundwork in the country for political change, it was not toward eventual democratic rule. Rather, he was laying the foundation for a new brand of Mexican authoritarianism whose organizational structure and constituency bases would be brought in line with Salinas's own economic project. I return to this point in chapter 7.

39. The increasing strength of the opposition was also fueled by a series of electoral laws introduced in order to quell antisystem activities, which lowered the legal mandate for party registration, increased the total number of seats in the Chamber of Deputies from 400 to 500, and introduced proportional representation for 200 of those seats.

parties obtained a national presence (Alcocer V. 1994; Reyes del Campillo 1996). For the first time in history, the PRI lost its two-thirds dominance in the lower chamber of the legislature and, with it, the ability to unilaterally reform the Constitution. For the 1988–91 period, the PRI was thus reduced to a working majority in the Chamber of Deputies, where it held but 260 out of 500 seats. This effectively made Salinas the first president in Mexican history who would be forced to negotiate with the opposition in order to enact major legislative initiatives. Also for the first time since the ruling party was founded in 1929, opposition party candidates were elected to the Senate, gaining 4 out of 64 seats. While the ruling party's need to rig elections had arguably increased as a result of this more competitive environment, the cost of doing so had also risen (Molinar Horcasitas 1993).

The 1988 national elections thus made clear that the days where a PRI victory could be taken as a given had officially come to an end. Not only was the ruling party itself increasingly polarized, but it also now faced a newly invigorated opposition. In the words of one political analyst, the 1988 elections "made opposition legitimate and democracy possible" (Pastor 1990, 8).

## The Cárdenista Challenge

But while the regime had broader reasons to fear these signs of democratization, it also had a very specific cause for alarm. For the first time in history, the principal challenge to the PRI did not come from the right but rather from the left.

At the time of the 1988 elections, the opposition clustered around two poles: the right-wing National Action Party (Partido Acción Nacional [PAN]) and the left-wing National Democratic Front (Frente Democrático Nacional [FDN]). While the former was a conservative, predominantly middle-class party with a support base drawn heavily from the industrial north, the latter was a coalition of disparate left-wing groups that traditionally drew the bulk of its support from the urban upper and middle classes (Klesner 1994, 163–81). In the early and middle part of the 1980s, the PAN had capitalized on the growing discontent within the middle class to win a series of electoral contests in northern Mexico at the local level (Loeza 1989). But in 1988, the left-wing alliance seized center stage in national politics under the leadership of breakaway populist candidate Cuauhtémoc Cárdenas.

A former leader of the PRI who left the ruling party amid the internal disputes noted earlier, Cárdenas ran for president on a decidedly anti-neoliberal platform. Highly critical of the speculative economy that had grown up around the Mexican stock market, Cárdenas called instead for a revitalization of domestic production geared for internal market consumption (Reding

1988b, 334). Viewing a mixed economy as "essential in order to properly orient economic development and preserve national self-determination" (Reding 1988b, 335), Cárdenas was particularly intent on providing political and economic support for Mexico's collective farm (*ejido*) system. In this more classically social democratic, Keynesian vision of economic growth, international debt repayment would take a backseat to stimulating domestic economic growth and satisfying social needs. In particular, job creation would be made a top policy priority to increase the purchasing power of Mexican workers. And while not denying the importance of expanding exports, Cárdenas also felt that there ought to be continued controls on foreign investment (Reding 1988b, 340). In brief, his movement represented everything that the técnicos did not.

Cárdenas's staunchly anti-neoliberal message resonated with large segments of the Mexican population. While he officially garnered only 31 percent of the popular vote, he was widely believed to have been the real winner in the 1988 presidential elections (Reding 1989). As noted earlier, he generated considerable support among the PRI's rank and file union members and peasants, who had benefited greatly from social reforms under Cárdenas's father, Lázaro, in the early years of the party's creation. Many of the PRI's base-level militants were also sympathetic to the nationalist-populist rhetoric that Cárdenas advanced. In short, one thing that the 1988 elections had made abundantly clear was that the PRI and the left were now competing for the same "market share" (Klesner 1994, 174; Magaloni 1998).

With the 1988 elections, the left thus gained a permanent place on the political map in Mexico (Castañeda 1993; Bruhn 1996). In the wake of Cárdenas's newfound electoral strength, the ruling elite—and the powerful capitalist actors it represented—began to worry about how this turn of events might affect their interests in the future. In the words of one author, "except for death, nothing strikes greater fear in the heart of Mexican big business than the specter of Lázaro Cárdenas" (Valdés Ugalde 1994, 229). Frightened by the prospect of a reversion to populism, the technocratic faction of organized business threw its support solidly behind Salinas (Puga 1993a, 202; Luna 1995, 83). Even the more traditionally confrontational radical business faction ceased its previous campaign against the concentration of power within the political system and assumed a more accommodationist position toward the government (Kaufman, Bazdresch, and Heredia 1994, 398). Faced with the possibility of a center-left future, powerful business groups recognized their incentives to close ranks behind a business-friendly neoliberal government.

In sum, the results of the 1988 elections sent out shock waves within Mexico's ruling elite. Not only were the traditional sources of ruling party power in jeopardy, but there was also a direct programmatic threat to the interests of its market-oriented leadership. The events surrounding the 1988 elections thus provided the first concrete evidence that the clock was ticking for authoritarian rule in Mexico.

This chapter has situated the Mexican central bank reform of 1993 within the broader economic and political context in which it took place. Until now, the events described in this chapter have borne a great deal of resemblance to those in the Chilean case. First, as in Chile, a government of a decidedly neoliberal bent carried out the reform. Second, also as in Chile, this was a case where prevailing economic explanations alone could not account for the reform's timing. Finally, as was the case in Chile, the stability of Mexico's authoritarian rule was rocked by an unexpected and cataclysmic event that placed the threat of democratization squarely on the table.

And yet, despite what appeared to be similarities between these two cases on a series of dimensions, their outcomes—in terms of the actual degree of autonomy exhibited by the central bank—were nonetheless quite different. Why the setup of the Mexican central bank did not duplicate that of the Chilean central bank warrants further investigation. Chapter 7 will explore this in more detail.

CHAPTER 7

# Ambiguous Threat, Ambivalent Response

## The 1993 Mexican Central Bank Reform

The 1988 national elections demonstrated the extent of dissatisfaction with Mexico's ruling party and its neoliberal reform agenda. In particular, they pointed to the rise of a center-left movement with the potential to threaten the electoral hegemony of the PRI. As with Chile, we appeared to be witnessing the prelude to a decisive insulation response.

But while up to here the Mexican and Chilean cases look more or less similar, this is the crucial point where they part company. For while both authoritarian governments faced a threat of regime change, in Chile that threat was imminent, whereas in Mexico it was considerably more distant.

This chapter explores the implications of this difference for the amount of autonomy afforded the Mexican central bank. In brief, I argue that because pressures for democratization were still in their incipient stages, Mexico's authoritarians lacked the incentives to make the central bank fully autonomous. Rather, knowing that they were likely to remain in office for the next several years, they were careful to design an institution that would not overly restrict their own margin of maneuver within the foreseeable future.

The chapter unfolds as follows. In the first section, "The 1993 Mexican Central Bank Reform: An Overview," I demonstrate the key differences between the Mexican and Chilean reforms on the dependent variable. In addition to noting the considerably slower pace at which the Mexican reform evolved, I highlight those specific aspects of the legislation—looser constraints on lending to the executive branch and weaker policy-making tools—that rendered the resulting institution less autonomous than Chile's. In the second section, "Assessing the Degree of Threat: Mexico 1988–93," I then proceed to locate the source of this difference in the independent variable: the degree of threat. I show that while the Mexican government had a number of reasons to fear a leftward rotation of power in the future, a full-fledged transition was not yet under way. Though the ruling party did face growing internal tensions and mounting political competition, the most likely outcome in the short run still seemed to be one of regime continuity.

The third section, "Splitting the Difference: The Logic of Partial Insulation," links this diminished threat of democratization to the correspondingly weaker degree of autonomy observed. On the one hand, there was enough possibility of political change to prompt the authoritarians to use autonomy as an insulation tactic. On the other hand, knowing that they—and not their adversaries—were likely to retain power in the near future, they deliberately loosened the legislation to manipulate monetary policy when needed.

The chapter concludes with a postscript examining the central bank's role in the peso crisis. While some have argued that the lax monetary policy pursued by the Bank of Mexico in 1994 casts doubt on the significance of the autonomy initiative, I offer a variety of different types of evidence to suggest that the reform did, in fact, matter. More important, I also note that as pressures for democratization increased in Mexico, so too did efforts to enhance the autonomy legislation, thus reinforcing the central argument offered in this book about the relationship between democratization and institutional change.

## The 1993 Mexican Central Bank Reform: An Overview

### Reform Process: The Build-up to the 1993 Reform

The first contrast that emerges when comparing the central bank reforms of Chile (1989) and Mexico (1993) is the pace of the reform once the threat of democracy was on the table. Rather than being executed in a relatively short period of time, as had been the case in Chile, the Mexican reform instead incubated over a period of five years. Right off the bat, this difference signals a lack of urgency on the part of Mexico's incumbent authoritarian regime.

The idea for a central bank reform in Mexico surfaced early on in the Salinas sexenio. While individuals closely involved with the reform were not specific about its exact timing, most dated the initial discussions to shortly after Salinas took office.[1] All concurred that the idea was the brainchild of Finance Minister Pedro Aspe. In his own words, "the idea was in my mind since the beginning of the sexenio . . . as a way to 'lock in' our package of [fiscal] reforms so that Mexico would not revert to inflationary financing in the future."[2] After discussing the idea with the president of the central bank, Miguel Mancera, Aspe went to Salinas in order to bring the president on board.

1. Based on a series of tape-recorded interviews by the author with government officials closely involved with the central bank reform in Mexico City, Mexico, during November 1994–February 1995. Because of the sensitive nature of some of the material included in this chapter, all names of interviewees have been concealed, except where otherwise noted.

2. Pedro Aspe, Mexican finance minister (1988–94), interview by the author, tape recording, Mexico City, Mexico, January 30, 1995.

But while the initial idea for a central bank reform thus coincided closely with the onset of the democratic threat, the authoritarians did not move immediately to put it into practice. Rather, they proceeded to turn the notion over in their heads for the next three to four years. As one central bank economist closely involved with the initiative commented, "the idea would come up from time to time ever since the sexenio began."[3] Indeed, central bank autonomy was just one of several different commitment strategies being considered as a means of locking in tight monetary policy. In the early years of the Salinas administration, the economic team was also pondering at least two other candidates: "dollarizing" the economy by establishing a one-to-one parity between the Mexican peso and the U.S. dollar; or forming a western hemispheric currency zone akin to the European Monetary System.[4] Both options were ultimately discarded on the grounds that they would render Mexico too vulnerable to economic decisions made in other countries.[5]

The decision to get serious about central bank reform did not occur until 1992. At an annual meeting of the economic cabinet early that year, Aspe announced that it was time to go ahead with the initiative. Aspe and Mancera established two study teams to work on the central bank reform—one in the Ministry of Finance and the other in the central bank, although the bulk of the legwork took place in the latter. Over the course of the year that followed, these teams studied various models of autonomy from other countries in order to come up with a set of guidelines for the Mexican law. Of particular note, they consulted with the former president of the Central Bank of Chile, Andrés Bianchi, who spent two months in Mexico as an informal adviser to the government.[6]

It was not until May 1993 that Aspe finally announced the initiative to the public. One week later, it was submitted to both chambers of the Mexican legislature, where a proposal to pass a constitutional amendment for central bank reform was approved by a wide majority.[7] As was typical in Mexico, this was a very top down reform, designed by a handful of high-ranking economic advisers without widespread public debate or dissemination. As one top

3. Confidential interview by the author, Mexico City, Mexico, January 30, 1995.

4. As noted by Patricia Armendariz, former Finance Ministry official, interview by author, tape recording, Mexico City, Mexico, July 23, 1993.

5. Augustín Carstens, former director of research at the Bank of Mexico and principal author of the 1993 reform, interview by the author, Mexico City, Mexico, July 30, 1993.

6. Based on tape-recorded interviews by the author with several senior officials involved in the autonomy initiative, Mexico City, Mexico, November 1994–February 1995. This was confirmed by Andrés Bianchi, interview by the author, tape recording, Santiago, Chile, June 5, 1995.

7. The decision to amend the Constitution passed with 385–17 in favor within the Chamber of Deputies and 62–2 in favor within the Senate. The actual amendment was approved and went into effect in August 1993.

official in the Salinas administration put it, "like many major legislative initiatives enacted by the technocrats, the process was basically one of first making the decision and then figuring out who would write up the press release."[8]

But even after the proposal for a constitutional amendment had been unveiled, the reform was still far from complete. While the proposed amendment noted the bare bones of autonomy, that is, "that the central bank would be autonomous in nature . . . with the primary goal of price stability. . . . no authority will be able to order the bank to give it financing," the specifics behind such mandates still needed elaboration (Ortiz 1994). While this vote thus permitted the government to annul the previous central bank law that had been in operation since 1985, the government still needed to draft a new law to establish the effective means through which the central bank's new authority would be carried out. As a result, a series of much more intense negotiations ensued between the study teams at the central bank and the Finance Ministry over the summer of 1993. It was in these negotiations where the nitty-gritty behind such delicate issues as exchange rate policy and interest rate policy would be hammered out (see the third section of the chapter, "Splitting the Difference: The Logic of Partial Insulation"), which would subsequently assume such importance in the wake of the peso crisis that ensued.

The reform's elaboration culminated with its legislation in the Mexican Congress in December 1993. As a result of the quite extensive preparation noted previously, the new central bank law was largely a fait accompli by the time it reached the legislature. While some changes were proposed and incorporated into the legislation, the autonomy initiative sailed through both chambers without major alterations. This was largely due to the PRI's impressive comeback in the 1991 midterm elections (see the second section of the chapter, "Assessing the Degree of Threat: Mexico 1988–93"), which furnished the government with a sufficient majority to guarantee the reform's passage. In addition, the initiative also won the support of the right-wing PAN, which had long championed the idea of an autonomous central bank (Calderón

8. Manuel Camacho, former mayor of Mexico City, interview by the author, tape recording, Mexico City, Mexico, August 19, 1997. Given the esoteric nature of central bank reform, however, the administration did make more of an effort to discuss it with select public audiences than was the norm. For example, once the basic ideas had been established, the government made a point of vetting the initiative before the economic cabinet, the members of the Pact (peak business and labor organizations), and the chairman of the Chamber of Deputies. The president himself ran the idea past the elite CMHN, and it was also discussed with various individuals in the financial community (see "Crecerá la Influencia del Consejo Mexicano de Hombres de Negocios, Afirma el Politólogo Roderic Camp," *El Financiero*, January 19, 1993). The ruling party would also subsequently organize a congressional delegation to other countries with autonomous central banks to expose PRI legislators to various models of autonomy in practice (Angel Aceves, former chairman of the Mexican Chamber of Deputies, interview by the author, tape recording, Mexico City, Mexico, January 23, 1995).

Hinojosa 1993). Though the reform did inspire vociferous criticism on the part of the left-wing political parties, this was not sufficient to overturn the bill or even to make major alterations. In light of such strong bipartisan support, the legislation passed with a 92 percent approval rating.[9]

In sum, while the Chilean central bank reform was also "in the wings" for many years, once the democratic threat became apparent, its timetable accelerated dramatically. The Mexican case, in contrast, exhibited a much more protracted reform process. While the idea for autonomy initially surfaced early on in the Salinas administration, it was bandied about within the administration for several years and evolved gradually over the period 1988 to 1993. Although the Mexican government seemed intent upon enacting the reform within the Salinas sexenio, it also seemed to be in much less of a rush. To be sure, this delay had something to do with the nature of the Mexican electoral calendar (see the third section of the chapter, "Splitting the Difference: The Logic of Partial Insulation"). But the drawn-out nature of the reform process in Mexico also suggests that, unlike in Chile, Mexico's authoritarians perceived themselves to be under less pressure.

## Reform Outcome: Evaluating the 1993 Reform

If the prolonged nature of the Mexican reform process indicated a more diffuse democratic threat, the resulting legislation certainly reinforced this interpretation. Unlike in Chile, where the central bank was granted full autonomy, in Mexico the autonomy afforded the central bank was only partial.

The partial nature of Mexico's central bank autonomy was most evident in two key dimensions of the reform. The first entailed those rules governing central bank lending to the executive. While under previous (1985) central bank legislation, all central bank financing of the executive had taken place at the behest of the Finance Ministry itself, the Constitution now clearly stated that "no authority may order the Bank of Mexico to grant financing, by credit of any sort or through the acquisition of assets" (Constitución de la Estados Unidos Mexicanos, art. 28). Despite this effort to strengthen the Bank of Mexico's hand, however, the new law continued to allow the central bank to finance the executive via both direct and indirect means (Banco de México 1993, art. 11).

That the 1993 law permitted indirect financing of the government was not so unusual. As indicated in chapter 3, most central banks (with Chile as the noted exception) are allowed to acquire government paper in the course

9. In the Chamber of Deputies, the vote was 238–11 in favor, with 22 abstentions, while in the Senate, it passed by a vote of 61–3. In addition to the PRD, the Socialist Party also voted against the legislation.

of their open market operations. The fact that such purchases had to take place at market interest rates was also a step in favor of autonomy (Banco de México 1993, art. 12). That said, the terms surrounding the bank's direct lending to the executive were suspect on a number of grounds.

In those countries where direct lending to the executive is permitted, it is ordinarily highly restricted. In Germany, for example, this amount is stipulated as a strict cash limit (Swinburne and Castello-Branco 1991, 425). In the Mexican case, in contrast, the stated limit on central bank financing was expressed as "1.5% of government expenditures" (Banco de México 1993, art. 12). One and a half percent may appear a rather modest sum. From a technical standpoint, however, any limit set in relation to government expenditures is generally thought to be accommodative to government spending proclivities (Cukierman 1992, 377). Were a populist government to come to power with a lavish expenditure program, the central bank would be legally justified in increasing its lending to the government proportionately. Ironically, in this regard the new law was actually a step backward from the 1985 legislation, which had set the limit on government lending at 1 percent of government revenues (Banco de México 1990, art. 9).

It is true that the law included a countervailing mechanism in the event that this limit was exceeded. If the debtor balance of the government were to exceed 1.5 percent of government expenditures, the central bank was authorized to issue debt on the government's current account to avoid a monetization of its deficit. But the legislation also allowed this provision to be waived under "extraordinary circumstances" (Banco de México 1993, art. 12), providing yet another avenue through which the government might ably finance its spending needs. More to the point, such limitations on central bank lending to the executive were not to go into effect until April 1997. Until that time, the central bank was still legally obligated to cover any checks written by the government, and the government could withdraw money from its account at the central bank without prior notice (Banco de México 1993, transitory art. 4).

A second area where the autonomy of the Mexican central bank also fell short of Chile's concerned its policy-making powers. To be sure, these constituted a significant improvement over the status quo. While under the 1985 legislation the central bank was obliged to act "in accordance with the directives of credit and monetary policy indicated by the Minister of Finance" (Banco de México 1990, art. 2), the new law rendered the central bank "an institution within the state with an autonomous character" (Banco de México 1993, art. 1). Moreover, as in Chile, while the finance minister was permitted to attend central bank board meetings, he or she was given no voting privileges.

But while the central banks of both countries thus benefited from nominal autonomy over monetary policy formulation, in Chile, this authority was buttressed by a series of additional powers that were largely absent in Mexico. For example, while the Chilean central bank played a role in external debt management, exchange rate policy, and various foreign trade and investment policies, in Mexico all such policy-making powers continued to reside with the Ministry of Finance. The extensive policy-making instruments afforded the Chilean central bank were further reinforced through a series of explicit conflict resolution mechanisms that enabled the central bank board to override the finance minister where it saw fit. The Mexican law contained no such provisions. By failing to stipulate how disputes between these two agencies would be resolved, the 1993 legislation left the door open for backdoor influence from the executive. In a country where the Finance Ministry and central bank were "for all intents and purposes, Siamese twins,"[10] a clear-cut division of labor would have seemed all the more warranted.

Indeed, the only area of policy-making where the relative weights of the two institutions were spelled out at all explicitly was exchange rate policy. The 1993 law established a "foreign exchange commission," in which exchange rate policy would be shared between the two agencies on a three-to-three basis (Banco de México 1993, art. 21). But even there, the Ministry of Finance had the last word. All resolutions passed by this body required at least one favorable vote from the Ministry of Finance, and in the event of stalemate between the two agencies, the finance minister had the decisive vote. It is certainly true that, with the notable exception of Chile, most countries leave exchange rate policy in the hands of the Treasury. But most such arrangements presuppose a floating exchange rate. At the time that the autonomy legislation was enacted, Mexico was operating under a crawling peg system, in which government intervention was used to keep the exchange rate pegged to the dollar within a narrow target band. For practical purposes, this was tantamount to having a fixed exchange rate system, as it was really the exchange rate—and not the domestic currency—that served as the anchor for price stability in the economy.[11] By depriving the central bank of control of exchange rate policy, then, the government was limiting the central bank's ability to determine interest rates as it saw fit, at least as long as the crawling peg remained in effect.

In fairness, the law was considerably stronger on the other two dimensions of autonomy—central bank objectives and the rules governing the cen-

10. As characterized by Mike Zellner, financial reporter for *America Economía,* during an interview with the author, Mexico City, Mexico, July 26, 1993.

11. Under a fixed exchange rate, any increase (decrease) in the domestic money supply has to be offset by a corresponding decline (increase) in the country's foreign reserves to keep the exchange rate in equilibrium.

tral bank board, although even these were not without their weaknesses. Under its 1985 charter, the central bank was authorized to obtain "the purchasing power of the peso, the development of the financial system, and the generally healthy growth of the national economy" (Banco de México 1990, art. 1). As in Chile, the new law sought to enhance autonomy by narrowing the focus of these objectives to give more weight to price stability. It constrained the central bank to pursuing the "primary goal of obtaining price stability" along with the secondary objectives of "facilitating the sound development of the financial system and the orderly operation of the payments system" (Banco de México 1993, art. 2).

While this change certainly went a long way toward enhancing the autonomy of the central bank along this dimension, three caveats are in order. First, by including the stability of the financial system as an objective, the law opened up the possibility that price stability might at some point be compromised to protect the health of the banking sector, a caveat not without relevance to the events of 1994 (see the chapter postscript). Second, the new legislation also put an end to the Bank of Mexico's prior practice of setting quantitative monetary stock targets—a projected amount of internal credit that it expected to circulate each year, commonly thought to facilitate a commitment to price stability (Cukierman 1992, 388). Finally, the fact that the Bank of Mexico's annual economic report followed—rather than preceded—that of the government served as an implicit constraint on the Bank of Mexico's ability to determine monetary policy free of executive branch influence.[12]

Accountability measures to ensure compliance with these new objectives were predictably weak (Banco de México 1993, arts. 51, 52). The 1993 law did establish certain basic oversight provisions. Like the U.S. Federal Reserve and the German Bundesbank, the Mexican central bank was obliged to produce three reports annually on the state of monetary policy, and both chambers of the legislature were afforded the right to regularly summon the central bank governor. Following a motion by the PAN during the December congressional hearings, a clause was also added stipulating that all central bank governors could be brought to trial (Banco de México 1993, art. 61). However, the central bank was also given considerable leeway in its reporting duties. Unlike in the United States or Germany, where the central bank was required either to publish its monetary targets or to make public the minutes of its meetings, in Mexico there were no such stipulations. And while the legislature was given veto power over the annual selection of an external auditor for

12. Among other things, the government's annual economic report also included a statement of projected inflation rates.

the central bank, the Congress could only review the final results of such an audit and lacked the authority to take actions based on those results.[13]

The 1993 law probably went furthest in enhancing the autonomy of the Bank of Mexico in its fourth and final dimension: those rules pertaining to the central bank board. Under prior legislation, the central bank board had been made up of eleven individuals drawn from a variety of executive branch agencies, as well as three "independent" representatives from various social sectors (Banco de México 1990, art. 23). These individuals were all presidential appointees with indefinite term lengths, all of whom could be removed at the executive's discretion. The board met on an irregular basis, and all of its members held other professional positions. The largely cosmetic nature of the former central bank board was reflected in the fact that many of its members were not even aware that an autonomy initiative was in the offing. As one former member of this board quipped, "I found out through the press that there was to be a constitutional amendment to modify the statute of the central bank!"[14]

The new legislation enacted an organizational structure much more conducive to autonomy (Banco de México 1993, arts. 38, 40). To begin with, it established a governing board of five members (one governor, four vice-governors) who would be named by the president of the republic, with confirmation either by both houses of the Congress or by a permanent congressional commission.[15] While not quite as lengthy as Chile's ten-year terms, board member terms did compare favorably with those of the German Bundesbank (six years for the governor and eight years for vice-governors) and were staggered to avoid undue politicization. As the argument presented in chapter 3 would predict, Salinas used this opportunity to appoint a central bank board entirely congruent with his own policy preferences.[16] And because the legislation allowed for renewable terms, it enhanced the probability that this conservative bias would be maintained in the future.

13. The PRD did attempt to introduce a number of measures to augment the accountability of the central bank, including a mechanism whereby, within forty-five days of the release of the Bank of Mexico's annual report, the Congress would have the ability to review, revise, and even veto projected monetary policy for the upcoming year. These measures were roundly defeated.

14. Urquidi, interview.

15. This was not an explicit feature of the 1993 law but was automatically guaranteed by Mexican law, which requires congressional approval for all presidential nominees to federal government ministries and agencies.

16. They included the following: Miguel Mancera (governor of the central bank since 1982), Francisco Gíl Díaz (former undersecretary of finance in charge of revenues under Salinas), Jesús Marcos Yacamán (former director of economic research at the Bank of Mexico), Ariel Buira (former director of international organizations and agreements at the Bank of Mexico), and Guillermo Prieto Fortún (former president of the government's chief regulatory body for the private banking sector, the National Banking Commission).

As in Germany, the new law stipulated largely technical criteria for board member dismissal, and, as in Chile, such dismissals also required Senate approval (Banco de México 1993, art. 43). But there was one notable exception. In a clause buried deep within Article 43 that does not even bear a number, the law stated that the central bank governor could be removed for failing to comply with the decisions of the exchange rate commission (Banco de México 1993, art. 43).[17] Such a clause posed a serious impediment to autonomy, as it effectively rendered the governor beholden to the views of the executive branch on a crucially important policy issue.

As in Chile, the Mexican government solidified its commitment to an autonomous central bank over the long haul by enshrining it in a constitutional amendment. Because a constitutional amendment requires a two-thirds majority in both chambers of the legislature in order to be overturned, this arguably constitutes an important piece of evidence for the "tying successors' hands" thesis advanced in this book. Unlike in Chile, however, where the entire central bank legislation formed part of an organic constitutional law, in Mexico it was only the three sentences in Article 78 that fell into this category. What this meant in practice was that the basic principles underlying central bank autonomy in Mexico—that is, a commitment to price stability and the inability to force the central bank to lend to the federal government—would be very difficult to reverse. In contrast, the actual central bank law—that is, all of the supporting details discussed in this section—could be overturned by a simple majority. As we will see, this point is of considerable significance for understanding the likely course of Mexico's central bank legislation in the future.

In short, Mexico's authoritarian leaders designed a central bank reform that can best be termed as partial. On the one hand, there is no question that it constituted a significant improvement over the status quo. Particularly in those rules pertaining to its governing board and statutory objectives, but also in what concerned its limitations on lending and policy-making powers, there were clear advances over what had existed previously. On the other hand, despite the fanfare surrounding its creation, the Mexican central bank was granted considerably less autonomy than its Chilean counterpart. Such

17. I am grateful to Isaac Katz, professor of economics, Autonomous Technological Institute of Mexico (ITAM), for pointing this out. Isaac Katz, interview by the author, tape recording, Mexico City, Mexico, August 12, 1997. The fact that this clause is not even numbered would suggest that it was either an error or was inserted into the reform at the very last minute. In light of its obvious import, as well as the technical competence of those writing the reform, I would tend to doubt that it was a mistake. Rather, I would include it among the numerous inconsistencies and ambiguities that characterized the final version of the legislation as its contents were battled out between the central bank and the Finance Ministry (see the third section of the chapter, "Splitting the Difference").

an outcome might appear curious to the casual observer. After all, the Mexican government openly acknowledged that the Chilean central bank reform had served as one of its models in drafting its own central bank legislation. The authoritarians had even gone so far as to request that senior officials in the Chilean central bank come to Mexico in order to brief them on the Chilean experience. We must, therefore, ask ourselves why Mexico's central bank reform did not end up looking more like Chile's. The next section will begin to shed light on why this was the case.

## Assessing the Degree of Threat: Mexico 1988–93

This section offers a plausible hypothesis for the observed disparity between the Chilean and Mexican reforms. In brief, I attribute it to a qualitative difference in their domestic political environments. Whereas the 1988 plebiscite in Chile meant that the onset of democracy was a "scheduled event," in Mexico the shape and speed of the democratization process were a moving target that would ebb and flow over the course of the next several years. While incumbent fears of a populist future were thus palpable in both countries, in Mexico, the incentives to fully insulate the central bank were simply not as clear cut.

### The Intensity of Threat: The Sources of Populist Pressures

In the years following 1988, populist pressures in Mexico emanated from three main sources. While it was unclear at the time which—if any—of these potential threats would ultimately prevail, their combined magnitude placed enough uncertainty on the table to call the longevity of the Salinas economic model into question.

### External Threat: The Cárdenista Alternative

The first threat to the longevity of the economic model lay in the left-wing Party of the Democratic Revolution (Partido Revolucionario Democrático [PRD]) and, in particular, its leader Cuauhtémoc Cárdenas.[18] Recall that as of 1988, the regime faced a divided opposition, in which the most powerful contenders were the right-wing PAN and what would shortly become the left-

18. In 1989, Cárdenas converted his left-wing movement into a full-fledged political party—the Party of the Democratic Revolution. Although he invited his former FDN coalition partners to merge with this new political party, only the Mexican Socialist Party (Partido Mexicano Socialista [PMS]) chose to join.

wing PRD. From a strictly economic perspective, the PAN did not pose a threat to the ruling clique's vital interests.[19] Combining a mixture of classic liberalism with Christian social doctrine, the PAN had long fought to reduce the influence of the state in all aspects of political and economic life (Partido Acción Nacional 1994). In contrast, the PRD's avowedly anti-neoliberal platform was clearly at odds with the technocratic dogma (Cárdenas 1993).[20] While based on an objective assessment of electoral performance, the PAN would appear to have been much more of a rival to continued PRI dominance (see the discussion that follows), from a subjective standpoint, the PRD constituted a much larger threat to interests of the outgoing regime and, in particular, to Salinas himself.

Cárdenas's threat potential had a variety of origins. To begin with, he had a tremendous amount of public visibility. His symbolic role as the legitimate victor of the 1988 elections continued to afford him an impressive public following and a certain moral authority within the electorate (Cothran 1994, 183; Dresser 1994b, 64). In an opinion poll conducted in May 1993, Cárdenas continued to be mentioned as the most prominent opposition candidate in the 1994 presidential elections—with approximately 80 percent name recognition.[21] Indeed, prior to the presidential debate of May 1994, Cárdenas was in second place (Domínguez and McCann 1996, 190). Because of such demonstrated renown, it was impossible for the ruling party to dismiss him as a real electoral threat. As one Mexican intellectual noted at the time, "regardless of what you think of Cuauhtémoc Cárdenas and his allies, you cannot deny his mobilizing draw. . . . everything seems to indicate that the PRD campaign will reconstitute itself as a fundamental reference point in the federal elections of 1994."[22]

A second set of factors rendering Cárdenas a live concern for the ruling party was, ironically, his credential as an "ex-Príista" (i.e., a former member of the PRI). On the one hand, his "revolutionary" origins as the descendant of the Cárdenas legacy enabled him to go after the PRI's traditional support base

19. The PAN did have a more populist faction as well, embodied in the 1988 presidential candidate, Manuel Clouthier. Throughout the Salinas sexenio, however, this wing was clearly subordinate to the "Neopanista" leadership that was firmly in the neoliberal camp. See Stansfield 1996, 132–33; Crespo 1995, 62.

20. There are those who emphasize a subtle transition in the Cardenista rhetoric, claiming that his anti-neoliberal message mellowed over time, most notably in his eventual acceptance of NAFTA (Dresser 1994b, 64–65; Domínguez and McCann 1996, 186–87). But if such a transition did, in fact, take place over the course of the sexenio, it was most likely for pragmatic reasons and certainly only mild at best.

21. See "Durante su Sexenio, Carlos Salinas Vivió Obsesionado por su Propia Imagen en Comparación con la de Cuauhtémoc," *Proceso* 1080 (July 13, 1994): 23.

22. Luis Sálazar C., "Rumbo a las Elecciones de 1994: El Retorno del Cardenismo," *Cuadernos de Nexos,* November 1993, v.

and appeal to its traditional symbols (Bruhn 1996, 24). On the other hand, precisely because he and other PRD leaders had such a long history in the party, they brought with them a tremendous amount of political experience and knowledge of the political system, much more than what an ordinary opposition party—such as the PAN—could muster (Crespo 1995, 54–56). On both counts, the ruling party needed to worry about Cárdenas's potential to lure away disgruntled Príistas (see "Internal Threat: The PRI Old Guard," which follows).

Above all, however, Cárdenas also clearly posed an ideological or policy-based threat to the Salinas clique. For while a vote for the PAN was not essentially different—in policy terms—than a vote for the PRI, a vote for the PRD was tantamount to a rejection of Salinismo, liberalization, and the entire economic model itself (Regalado 1996, 161–62). As one Mexican journalist astutely observed, "the most threatening thing about Cárdenas is that he is outside the system. More so than the PAN, he is the real threat because he is potentially a 'loose cannon.'"[23] This outsider status was particularly dangerous for the PRI in the poorer southern regions of the country as well as in its industrial heartland, where regional voting patterns suggested a growing frustration with the prevailing economic model and willingness to support a "kinder, gentler alternative" embodied in the PRD (see the section of this chapter titled "The Proximity of Threat"). To the extent that the PRI and the PRD were increasingly competing for the same vote share, there was good reason for the authoritarians to be concerned about stopping the PRD's advance at all costs. After all, a PRD victory only increased this party's credibility among the PRI's own electoral bases at a time when the main determinant of defection from the ruling party was the sense that another party could win in the next presidential elections (Domínguez and McCann 1996, 187).

There were several signs that the Salinas administration viewed the left as a powerful policy threat over the course of its term in office. The aggressive manner in which the PRI fought to win back the states of Michoacán and México in the state elections of 1989 and 1990, respectively—states in which the Cárdenista block had won twenty-nine electoral seats in 1988—betrayed its underlying paranoia about losing to a party on the left (Klesner 1994, 178). This fear was again underscored by the government's willingness to concede defeat to the PAN in the gubernatorial elections in Baja California in 1989 and Chihuahua in 1992 but not to the PRD in the municipal elections in Michoacán in 1989 and 1992.[24] The government's overt embrace of several

23. Carlos Ramirez, columnist, *El Financiero,* interview by the author, tape recording, Mexico City, Mexico, December 12, 1994.

24. The government was ultimately forced to reverse the 1992 decision in favor of the PRD candidate but only after a great deal of postelectoral conflict.

long-championed PAN reform initiatives across the sexenio was also interpreted as indicating a systematic effort to marginalize the PRD (Crespo 1995, 58–65; Bruhn 1996, 240–47; Reding 1989, 689–701). This was equally true of an electoral law prohibiting different political parties from endorsing the same candidate, which many saw as an attempt to prevent the smaller left-wing parties that had supported Cárdenas in 1988 from institutionalizing this electoral union in the future (Morris 1992, 39). Finally, the government also used its control over the media to launch a negative image campaign against the PRD by portraying it as violent, dangerous, and communistic (Morris 1995, 100).

It was clear that through all of these measures the ruling party was employing a strategy of "selective repression" on the electoral front to divide and weaken the left (Reding 1989; Morris 1995, 98–100).[25] Nowhere was such a strategy more evident than in the case of the National Solidarity Program (Programa Nacional de Solidaridad [Pronasol]), a massive social program unveiled in 1989 to deliver a wide range of public works to poor districts throughout the country. Funded through sales resulting from the privatization of major public enterprises, Solidarity encouraged citizens to design and implement community development programs with financial assistance from the government (Cornelius, Craig, and Fox 1994). After but two short years, Solidarity enjoyed an annual budget of U.S.$5.1 billion and accounted for 60 percent of all federal investment (Morris 1992, 32). In addition to whatever economic motivations it may have had, many have argued that the Solidarity program was largely an effort to buy back support for the PRI by strategically channeling funds to Cárdenista strongholds while simultaneously rewarding PRI loyalists (Dresser 1991; Molinar Horcasitas and Weldon 1994; Bruhn 1996, 260–70).[26]

But by far the most important indicator of the left's threat potential was the subjective fear of Cárdenas by Salinas himself. A set of public opinion polls conducted by the office of the presidency during the Salinas years revealed what one journalist called a veritable "obsession" with Cárdenas on the part of the president.[27] On nearly every poll that went out of his office

25. At times, this campaign also included real repression against the left, entailing arrests and intimidation tactics. The PRD also maintains that over the course of the sexenio, 250 of its militants were killed (Morris 1995, 100).

26. Morris (1995, 97) documents, for example, how the first full-fledged Solidarity experiment in January 1989 targeted Cárdenas's home state of Michoacán. Similarly, in Morelos—another state that Cárdenas won in 1988—public investments increased by 93 percent from 1988 to 1989. Molinar and Weldon's study provides more systematic empirical support for the claim that the assignment of Pronasol resources did not correspond to the distribution that would have occurred if poverty had been the sole criterion.

27. See "Durante su Sexenio," 20–26.

from the very beginning of the sexenio all the way to its end, there was always at least one question that asked, "If the 1988 elections were repeated tomorrow, who would you vote for?"[28] And once Cárdenas's candidacy for the 1994 presidential elections had been announced in early 1993, his campaign was followed with scrupulous detail through a series of polls that sought constantly to evaluate his popularity, his policy positions, his actions, even how he dressed. If, in fact, it were true—as some might wish to argue—that the PRD's electoral decline in these years removed Cárdenas as an objective policy threat to the regime, then there would have been no reason to have followed his campaign with such minute attention to detail. The explanation for such "obsessive" behavior can only be that Salinas greatly feared Cárdenas's continuing appeal. In the words of one of the president's closest friends and confidantes, Manuel Camacho, "my impression is that the President never stopped worrying about the possibility that Cárdenas' popularity might grow and that he might win in 1994. . . . this was true even after 1991 and continued right until the very end."[29]

For all of these reasons, it was Cárdenas—more than any other political leader or party—who was seen as the regime's key opponent throughout the sexenio (Domínguez and McCann 1996, 188). As one scholar of the Mexican left noted, "the PRD . . . differed from other opposition parties in one important respect: the special PRI hostility it attracted as a left party that criticized the Salinas project and competed with the PRI for a similar constituency" (Bruhn 1996, 241).

## Internal Threat: The PRI Old Guard

The second source of policy uncertainty for the authoritarians lay within the PRI itself. Recall from chapter 6 that the corporatist sectors of the ruling party were deeply dissatisfied with its leadership's embrace of neoliberalism in the early 1980s. Of these groups, the labor sector had been particularly hard hit. On the one hand, the official labor movement's economic power had been declining steadily over the 1980s, as real wages plummeted, massive employment cuts took hold, and social spending dropped precipitously (de la Garza Toledo 1994; Middlebrook 1995, 255–87; Teichman 1995, 159–93). On the other hand, labor also saw a corresponding decline in its political influence within the ruling party. As the CTM failed increasingly to deliver winning candidates in national elections, the party responded by allotting it fewer and

28. Ibid, 22. This was confirmed during a confidential interview by the author with two individuals who worked on Salinas's polling team, tape recording, Mexico City, Mexico, August 20, 1997.

29. Camacho, interview.

fewer seats (Baer 1993, 59; de Remes la Brely 1993). As an expression of their discontent at what was perceived as a twin assault on the PRI's historically most influential corporate sector, many labor union officials took out their frustration at the polls, throwing their support to Cuauhtémoc Cárdenas in the 1988 elections (Teichman 1995, 175; Middlebrook 1995, 293–94).

The existence of such malaise within the party's traditional sectors was dangerous for Salinas on two fronts. To begin with, even as corporatist interest groups constituted an obstacle to economic reform, the ruling elite still needed to rely on them as a fundamental instrument of political control (Craske 1996). Because these more traditional sectors controlled the party machinery, they had the ability to withhold support for the president's pet initiatives in the legislature. Particularly in a setting where the ruling party had lost its two-thirds majority in the Chamber of Deputies, party discipline and party loyalty had become more important than ever (Weldon 1997, 247). They were also crucially important for ensuring the viability of the presidential succession mechanism (Middlebrook 1995, 301).

More important, however, the real secret weapon held by the traditional groups was their ability to defect from the ruling party. In the words of one presidential pollster, "what 1988 showed us was the real inexistence of the corporatist vote. . . . even after 1991, the competitive nature of the electoral system convinced us that there was no 'hard vote' (voto duro) guaranteed."[30] And the government knew that the party that stood to benefit from such defections was not the right-wing PAN but the left-leaning PRD.[31] While the leftward "brain drain" had slowed considerably after the major 1987 party split, there continued to be a few high-visibility defections during the first years of the Salinas administration (Cothran 1994, 184; Morris 1992, 41), and the ever feisty oil workers maintained their ties to the Cárdenas camp (Teichman 1996, 159). To be sure, the possibility of an all-out split from the PRI by its leftist faction seemed unlikely. But it was not difficult to imagine a scenario whereby a severe economic downturn might induce a sufficient number of PRI activists to defect to the Cárdenista camp (Coppedge 1993, 135; Teichman 1996, 164). In a country where economic performance has historically been the main determinant of whether or not voters will vote for the left in Mexico (Brophy-Baermann 1994), this was not a scenario to be dismissed lightly.[32]

30. Ulíses Beltrán, chief pollster for President Salinas, interview by author, tape recording, Mexico City, Mexico, August 15, 1997.

31. This point was strongly emphasized during my interview with Manuel Camacho.

32. Note that as the decade wore on and the economic situation in Mexico deteriorated, local party bosses did begin increasingly to leave the PRI because of unhappiness with the national direction of the party, enabling the PRD to inherit entire *charros* (local political machines) at a time from the ruling party (Klesner 1997, 8).

The party hierarchy was well aware that much of the party machinery was unhappy and that recovering the lost PRI vote had to be a priority during the first half of the sexenio.[33] Awareness of this "internal threat" manifested itself in two ways. In the short run, Salinas sought to smooth over tensions with the old guard by offering them a number of important political positions, including cabinet posts, governorships, and a role in the national assembly (Morris 1995, 93). Much more so than De la Madrid, Salinas sought to balance the increasingly technocratic nature of decision making in Mexico with a role for the more statist sectors in the party. As Centeno and Maxfield so eloquently phrased it, "this was a techno-authoritarian cabinet that consisted of planners and policemen; the former determined policy and the latter ensured that it was carried out" (Centeno and Maxfield 1992, 72). In turn, perhaps the most important indirect measure taken to preempt defection from the labor camp was a steady increase in average real manufacturing wages throughout the first half of the sexenio (Magaloni 1998, 6–9).

In the long run, however, it was clear that Salinas saw traditional party interests as an obstacle to his programmatic agenda that needed to be removed. In this regard, a much more important signal about the threat posed by entrenched party leaders was a series of measures designed to bring the country's political institutions more directly into the service of Salinas's long-term neoliberal economic agenda. First, he sought to disempower traditional labor leaders and rebuild a new pact with labor outside the confines of the official labor movement. During his first year in office, Salinas led a highly public campaign against corruption within the PRI, in which he arrested the leader of the powerful oil workers' union and forced the head of the corrupt teachers' union into early retirement (Morris 1995, 85). Few doubted that this was a measure intended to punish the "turncoats" who had voted for Cárdenas in 1988 (Cothran 1994, 179), while at the same time eliminating some of the major enemies of his neoliberal reform agenda (Middlebrook 1995, 195; Grindle 1996, 93). This was complemented by a series of measures to deprive traditional labor unions of control over policy and, most notably, over the government-subsidized worker-housing fund (Middlebrook 1995, 296–97). But perhaps this strategy was most evident in the onset of the so-called New Syndicalism, through which Salinas sought to cultivate and institutionalize relations with labor unions much more favorable to his neoliberal program of economic restructuring (Morris 1995, 84–88).

The same could be said for Salinas's attempts to reconfigure the structure of the ruling party itself. For example, under the guise of "democratizing" candidate selection in the PRI by promoting local primaries and party

33. Beltrán, interview.

conventions, Salinas in fact pursued a variety of tactics to build a ruling coalition centered around the "Salinas family." By reducing the number of traditional sector nominations for public office, he made way for an increase in the number of candidates from the popular sector, particularly those in the federal and state governments tied to the Salinas team and members of the local business community (Craig and Cornelius 1995, 282–83; Morris 1995, 93).[34] A series of reforms to recast mass-actor incorporation into the PRI along more territorial lines was similarly viewed by many as an effort to remold the party in his own image by promoting new ties to grassroots movements heretofore unconnected to the governing elite (Craske 1996; Grindle 1996; Dresser 1994a).[35] This would certainly seem to have been the guiding logic behind Solidarity, where its organizational structure outside the confines of the ruling party ensured that its beneficiaries would have allegiance not to the party but, rather, directly to the president himself (Morris 1995, 85–86; Grindle 1996, 94).

Through all of these measures, Salinas appeared to be attempting to keep the label "PRI" but to shift its coalitional base to create a new support base for neoliberal reforms. The tremendous energy that Salinas poured into reshaping Mexico's political institutions over the six years he was in power would thus seem proof of the enormous threat that traditional vested interests posed to the sustained viability of his economic model. In the words of one Mexican political analyst, "his goal was to dismantle political constraints and construct bases of consensus that would allow for the continuation and deepening of this economic restructuring program" (Dresser 1997, 63).

## Societal Threat: Small and Medium-Sized Businesses

A third and final member of the populist coalition threatening the future of the technocrats' economic project was those portions of the industrial sector that had failed to reorient their production in the wake of Mexico's economic

34. Indeed, despite the rhetoric surrounding the reforms to promote local primaries for candidate selection, the reality is that only 4.3 percent of the PRI's 1991 candidates for the Chamber of Deputies and none of its candidates for the Senate were chosen through party primaries or nominating conventions (Domínguez and McCann 1996, 120). The remainder were handpicked by the PRI leadership and government officials close to the president by virtue of a "unanimity rule" that allowed waiving a nominating convention in the event that only one candidate came forward for a given office.

35. During the fourteenth assembly of the PRI in 1990, the party approved a reform package proposed by Salinas in which the PRI's sectoral structure was retained but that also added opportunities for individuals and groups not affiliated with any sectoral organization to join. This was followed in 1992 by a call for a "refoundation" of the party in which the labor, peasant, and popular sectors would be replaced by four new "support branches" that were much more community and territory based.

restructuring. As noted in the previous chapter, these were generally the small and medium-sized businesses in traditional industries that continued to produce for the internal market and, as a result, were largely left out of the process of economic opening (Alba Vega 1993b; Puga 1992). During the Salinas sexenio, their situation continued to deteriorate. Not only did the number of smaller and medium-sized firms registered in the manufacturing sector fall from 871 in 1988 to 401 in 1993—amounting to a loss of some forty-three thousand jobs (Pastor and Wise 1997, 432)—but even among those firms that did manage to stay afloat, manufacturing output and wages stagnated (Pastor and Wise 1997, 435; Dussell Peters 1996, 70).[36] To obtain some idea of the magnitude of this situation, note that in the manufacturing sector, only 1.3 percent of all firms accounted for 71.8 percent of aggregate value in 1990, while microenterprises—which accounted for 86.9 percent of all manufacturing entities—provided only 4.6 percent of its aggregate value (Puga 1992, 20). As one author put it, small and medium-sized enterprises had become one of the "social escape valves" for unemployment and the contraction of salaries during the process of neoliberal reform (Puga 1993a, 44).

But while these firms were not among the most economically powerful in the country, they were the most numerous. As such, even though their economic weight deprived them of much clout within the structure of organized business, they did have one enormously powerful weapon: their vote. As one analyst of Mexican politics noted at the time, "it is difficult to imagine that many groups that have been affected by the economic policies of the regime and whose lives will be disrupted by NAFTA will remain disorganized and divided" (Centeno 1994, 242).

And, indeed, the progressive marginalization of smaller and medium-sized enterprises from the outward-oriented development model did lead to their gradual political mobilization (Luna 1994). Toward the end of the 1980s, for example, large groups of small and medium-sized producers challenged the great concentration of power within the CCE in the hands of financial and industrial groups (Luna and Tirado 1992, 83). When a separate organization was subsequently created to represent business interests in NAFTA, smaller firms accused this institution of a similar bias toward the interests of large firms (Puga 1993b, 66–68).[37] By the end of the Salinas sexe-

36. It is true that average wages in the manufacturing sector had been steadily increasing. But because the manufacturing sector's growth was steadily shrinking over this period, wages were accruing to an increasingly smaller group of workers, largely found in the more competitive manufacturing branches where small and medium-sized firms were not dominant (Pastor and Wise 1997, 432–35).

37. I refer here to the Business Council for Foreign Trade (Coordinadora Empresarial para el Comercio Exterior [COECE]), which was established in 1990 in the wake of the NAFTA negotiations between Mexico and the United States.

nio, such criticisms translated directly into policy demands. Small and medium-sized firms began to call actively for an industrial policy to meet the needs of those firms not able to manage the transition to internationalization, lobbying for increased credit support and an economic strategy more concerned with domestic markets (Teichman 1995, 189; Luna 1995, 87–92; Shadlen 2000, 89–93). Were their dissatisfaction with the neoliberal economic model to continue, it was entirely conceivable that their preferred form of protest might escalate from benign calls for industrial policy to the choice to vote for an opposition party more sympathetic to their protectionist leanings (Serrano 1996, 15). Indeed, by the early 1990s there was already evidence of a deliberate strategy on the part of the PRD to court these small businesses who were openly disaffected from the neoliberal model (Shadlen 2000, 96–97).

Once again, there is strong evidence that Salinas was not only aware of the mounting grievances expressed by small and medium-sized enterprises but was also intent on fixing them. A former economic aide went so far as to describe the president as "obsessed" with their predicament.[38] Beginning in 1990, and with a dramatic acceleration in 1993 and 1994, Salinas launched a quiet campaign to pump money into the small and medium-sized businesses via the government development banks. From 1992 to 1993 alone, so-called second tier (discount) lending rose by 78.5 percent (Nacional Financiera 1993, 29). It was most egregious where nonbank financial intermediaries such as credit unions were concerned, which grew in number from 55 in December 1989 to 539 in May 1994 (Werner 1995, 22), an increase on the order of 1,000 percent.[39] While fancy accounting techniques enabled government officials to mask the mounting fiscal deficit produced by such official credit expansion, as one Finance Ministry official put it, "the growth was simply savage."[40]

To be sure, one could plausibly attribute Salinas's "obsession" with the

38. Confidential interview by the author, tape recording, Mexico City, Mexico, August 22, 1997.

39. Under regulations that were revised in the early 1990s, development banks could no longer lend directly to creditors but rather had to do so via an intermediate source, whether a commercial bank or a "nonbank" entity such as a credit union or a factoring company. See Werner 1995 for a description of these changes.

40. Francisco Meré, director of Development Banks in the Ministry of Finance under the Zedillo administration, interview by the author, tape recording, Mexico City, Mexico, August 22, 1997. In 1993, the Mexican government changed the way in which public finances were counted by eliminating the "financial deficit"—or the financial intermediation activities of state development banks—from its recording of the federal budget deficit. The government justified this decision on technical grounds, arguing that because development banks were no longer operating outside the market, there was no need to include this deficit in the formal accounting system. That said, the removal of the financial deficit was perceived by many as an effort to hide the government's efforts to stimulate the economy. See "Replanteará Zedillo la Estrategia Económica," *El Financiero,* December 24, 1995; "El Déficit en Cuestión," *Reforma,* February 15, 1995.

fate of small and medium-sized businesses purely to economic strategy. After all, small enterprises did frequently fail to qualify for the high interest rates charged on commercial bank loans and as a result often faced serious obstacles to obtaining financing.[41] There was also strong evidence from the East Asian experience that effective competition required a mix of large and small firms (Fishlow 1994), and the president was well aware of such debates. But the irresponsible nature in which such loans were carried out—in terms of both their magnitude and the corresponding lack of supervision—would suggest that the president was overwhelmingly guided by the imperative of securing electoral victory for the PRI in 1994 (Morris 1995, 82; Luna 1994, 209).[42] Such an interpretation seems borne out by the periodic public gatherings the president would hold during these years with as many as 8,000 people at a time, at which he would personally hand out credit to small businesses with but 2–10 employees.[43] As one senior member of the PAN leadership colorfully phrased it, "the 'fat' of the pork was transferred through the development banks."[44]

Salinas's extreme efforts to direct finance toward small and medium-sized businesses during his tenure in office suggests that he saw them, first and foremost, as an electoral liability whose sympathies he needed to win over, whatever the price. While such policies were sharply at odds with his otherwise technocratic image, they were also a realistic reflection of the broad divide that existed between the winners and losers in the neoliberal development model and of the president's perceived need to accommodate them politically if he were to preserve it (Dresser 1997, 59–61).[45]

In brief, policy-based threats to the long-term potential of the Salinas

---

41. See "Small Businesses in a Big Time Economy," *Business Mexico,* March 1993, 4–7.

42. And few in the current Zedillo administration would deny this. Who exactly is to blame for this exorbitant lending spree on the part of the credit unions has been the source of much discussion in Mexico in the wake of the peso crisis. In part, it can be attributed to the inexperience of the National Banking Commission, which had only recently gained its independence from the Finance Ministry as an autonomous oversight body. It was also clearly the product of irresponsible conduct by the officials at the state development bank Nafinsa (Nacional Financiera), who actively exhorted—over and above the protests of other government agencies—the widespread formation of credit unions, even when it was clear that such loans had no chance of being paid back. At the end of the day, however, the board of directors of Nafinsa responded to the orders of the finance minister, Pedro Aspe, who himself served as the president's financial agent (Federico Patiño, adjunct director of financing, Nafinsa, under the Zedillo administration, tape recording, Mexico City, Mexico, August 20, 1997).

43. One Mexican journalist referred to such gatherings as a "heroic feat." Alberto Barranca, columnist, *Reforma,* interview by author, tape recording, Mexico City, Mexico, August 13, 1997.

44. Augustín Navarro, director of public relations, National Action Party, interview by author, tape recording, Mexico City, Mexico, August 20, 1997.

45. Kessler (1998) offers a different assessment of the political power of small and medium-sized businesses during the Salinas era.

economic model stemmed as much from inside the authoritarian regime as from the nature of its political competition. While the nature of this populist coalition was much more diffuse than had been the case in Chile, any one of its three components—and certainly their combination—was sufficient to jeopardize the prevailing economic model. Moreover, as the evidence presented previously suggests, there was no question that these were all a source of concern to incumbent authoritarian elites. The relevant question, therefore, is not whether these different threats constituted a source of alarm—clearly, they did—but whether they were of a significant magnitude to warrant taking some form of institutional action. I argue that they were but that how much insulation would be required to fend off this threat would be dictated by how soon it was likely to materialize.

## The Proximity of Threat: Mexico's Liberalizing Authoritarian Regime

If we accept that uncertainty over the future course of policy in Mexico emanated from a variety of sources over the course of the Salinas sexenio, the key question was how soon—if at all—any of this was likely to come to a head. Here is where we begin to see particularly marked changes with respect to the Chilean case. For unlike in Chile, where a changing of the guard was imminent, in Mexico there were mixed signals as to the longevity of authoritarian rule. While an eventual transition seemed likely, it still looked a good way off.

The ruling party vastly improved its fortunes in the 1991 midterm elections, claiming over 60 percent of the national vote. With this apparent about-face in voter sentiment, PRI hegemony was restored in the Chamber of Deputies, and the ruling party even gained back one of the Senate seats it had lost in 1988. In contrast, support for the right-wing PAN held steady at around 18 percent of the national vote, while support for the left-wing PRD plummeted from over 30 percent to a mere 8 percent. While a variety of factors contributed to the PRI's revitalization at the polls, two major determinants were presidential popularity and the country's economic recovery during the first half of the Salinas sexenio (Domínguez and McCann 1996, 126–36; Buendía 1996; Kaufman and Zuckerman 1998). By the end of his first three years in office, Salinas could point to an economy experiencing low but steady growth, a dramatic decline in inflation, and a steady rise in average real wages. As two analysts of Mexican politics noted at the time, "if the national elections of August, 1991 are a reasonably accurate reflection of popular sentiment, Mexico's economic policy is restoring confidence in the management of the economy by the PRI government" (Weintraub and Baer 1992, 200).

But despite its strong showing in 1991, it was also clear that the PRI would not continue to dominate the electoral sphere indefinitely. The PRI's overall vote share had been declining steadily over the past thirty years, with the proportion of electoral districts dominated by the PRI dropping from over 84.5 percent in 1964 to 37.7 percent in 1991 (see table 7.1). While this was partly due to demographic changes, these figures also reflected the growing number of independents in the Mexican electorate, particularly after 1988 (Basañez 1991; Klesner 1994; Magaloni 1998). As a result of this trend, midway through the Salinas sexenio "the Mexican political electorate was less securely under the PRI's control than it had ever been" (Klesner 1994, 189). As one scholar characterized the situation: "[there were] . . . risk and uncertainty with just enough opportunity to create unpredictable patterns; so much so that in only three years, it has inspired both the shock of 1988 and the counter-shock of 1991" (Morris 1992, 46). For practical purposes, such volatility meant that, were the electorate to determine that the ruling party was not capable of making national policy, PRI supporters in 1991 might just as easily take their business elsewhere (Domínguez and McCann 1996, 78).

Such electoral dealignment was particularly dangerous for the govern-

**TABLE 7.1. Mexico: Electoral Competition in National Elections, 1964–94 (% of 300 federal electoral districts)**

| Election Year | PRI Monopoly | Type of Competition[a] Strong PRI Hegemony | Weak PRI Hegemony | Two-Party Competition | Multiparty Competition | Opposition Victory |
|---|---|---|---|---|---|---|
| 1964 | 28.1 | 52.2 | 4.5 | 14.0 | — | 1.1 |
| 1967 | 24.2 | 61.2 | 3.6 | 9.7 | — | 1.2 |
| 1970 | 27.0 | 53.9 | 1.7 | 17.4 | — | — |
| 1973 | 18.7 | 51.3 | 4.1 | 21.8 | 1.0 | 3.1 |
| 1976 | 35.8 | 44.6 | 6.7 | 11.9 | 0.5 | 0.5 |
| 1979 | 9.4 | 48.0 | 12.3 | 6.3 | 22.7 | 1.3 |
| 1982 | 1.3 | 51.7 | 6.3 | 26.1 | 14.0 | 0.3 |
| 1985 | 3.3 | 41.7 | 9.0 | 21.0 | 21.3 | 3.7 |
| 1988[b] | 1.0 | 19.0 | 15.0 | 8.3 | 34.0 | 22.7 |
| 1991 | — | 21.7 | 16.0 | 18.0 | 41.0 | 3.3 |
| 1994 | — | 2.3 | 8.3 | 26.0 | 55.4 | 8.0 |

*Source:* Cornelius 1996, 65.

[a]PRI monopoly = PRI vote > 95%; strong PRI hegemony = PRI vote < 95% but > 70; weak PRI hegemony = PRI vote < 70%, but the difference between PRI and second party in district is > 40 percentage points; two-party competition = PRI vote < 70%, difference between PRI and second party is < 40 percentage points, second party vote > 25%, and third party vote < 10%; multiparty competition = PRI vote < 70%, difference between PRI and second party is < 40 percentage points, and second party vote < 25%, or third-party vote > 10%; opposition victory = any party's vote > PRI vote.

[b]For 1988, opposition victories include those won by the Cardenista.

ment in light of the inordinate degree of importance it had placed on NAFTA as the key to solving Mexico's economic problems. In effect, such a strategy intimately linked the electoral fate of the ruling party to the fate of the free trade agreement and the continued performance of the economy more generally (Basañez 1993, 110; Baer 1993, 62). And unlike in previous sexenios, where the ruling party had a variety of political tools at its disposal with which to manage an economic downturn, now such a crisis would be taking place amid an increasingly competitive political environment. One analyst appropriately referred to economic growth as Mexico's "Containment Policy" for the 1990s, in that the government's ability to forestall the onslaught of the opposition hinged on its maintaining positive economic results (Dresser 1994a, 141).

Indicators of internal party cohesion during this period offered a similarly mixed picture of ruling party strength. In light of his early efforts to oust recalcitrant labor leaders and personally influence candidate selection in the PRI, Salinas had largely succeeded in biasing the ruling party in favor of his interests. In turn, his attempts to co-opt the PRI's more intransigent old-style politicians into his cabinet also served to quell internal restiveness (Centeno 1994, 142–43). Perhaps Salinas's ability to manage internal party divides was best demonstrated by the fact that he was still able to impose unilaterally his choice for the PRI presidential candidate in late 1993.

That said, this marriage of convenience was also only a short-term strategy at best. For while Salinas could still rely on the traditional sectors of the party to marshal their bases in support for his economic program, the cost of co-optation had risen. First, it required increasing concessions that undermined the very set of neoliberal policies Salinas sought to promote. The fact that Salinas never acted on the pledge to enact a labor reform, for example, was widely perceived as the price of keeping powerful labor union leaders on board (Middlebrook 1995, 298). Second, furnishing old guard elements with a voice in the regime also enabled them to criticize—if not resist—Salinas's political reform agenda. There is some evidence, for example, to suggest that the PRI was engaging in "conditional party loyalty" during the first half of the Salinas sexenio, withholding its support for the president on key legislative initiatives (Diaz and Magaloni 1997; Weldon 1997, 245). Efforts to replace the three corporate entities of the PRI with more direct citizen-based organizations were also successfully defeated by the old guard, who managed by the end of the sexenio to virtually undo Salinas's internal restructuring effort (Morris 1995, 93–95; Craske 1996). Finally, dissatisfaction with the president's candidate selection process also provoked a good deal of internal party protest at the local and regional levels, even leading to the occasional defection to the opposition (Crespo 1995, 109; Morris 1995, 94–96). By keeping the statist elements of the party alive, Salinas thus placed himself in a double bind. While he himself might not be faced with reconciling this contradiction, there was no question that he was keeping a lid on a precarious situation.

A similarly murky image emerges if we consider our final indicator of the proximity of threat: the power of the regime's political opposition. Unlike in Chile, where the outgoing authoritarians faced a well-organized and ideologically united opposition front, the Mexican political opposition was divided throughout the period in question. The opposition parties of the right and left had put aside their ideological differences in 1988 to unite around the common goal of democratization. But immediately after the 1988 elections, the nature of interparty relations began to change (Bruhn 1996, 240–47; Crespo 1995, 58–84). Beginning with a constitutional reform on electoral procedures and later expanding to a series of economic and social policy initiatives, the right-wing PAN began to distance itself from the left-wing PRD and to ally itself instead with the government.[46] Over time, the PAN came to assume an unofficial role as a "junior partner" of the government, while the PRD was increasingly cast in the role of outsider (Alcocer V. 1994, 151–53). As long as the opposition remained so divided, this helped to contain the political threat to the regime.

In addition to the lack of unity between the two principal opposition parties, each suffered from internal weaknesses. To begin with, neither party had a national vote share that came anywhere near rivaling that of the PRI. Despite a number of significant gubernatorial victories by the PAN and its demonstrated skill as a negotiator (Stansfield 1996), this party controlled only 18 percent of the electorate, while the PRD held a paltry 8 percent. In part, this reflected their identities as largely regional parties, with the PAN based predominantly in the northern states, while the PRD's support was concentrated in Mexico City, Cárdenas's home state of Michoacán, and the rural south. Both parties also suffered from internal divides between those who favored negotiating with the PRI and those who favored isolationism (Cornelius 1996, 67–75; Crespo 1995, 62; Castañeda 1993, 184–94; Bruhn 1996, 169–84). Finally, each party was also handicapped by its own idiosyncratic deficiencies. In the case of the PAN, this party lacked a charismatic candidate with which to vie for the presidency throughout most of the sexenio.[47] The

46. Among others, these included the 1989–90 electoral reforms (see the following discussion), the agricultural reform of the ejido system, the privatization of the banks, and the central bank reform itself.

47. This changed in 1994 when the PAN named Diego Fernandez de Cevallos as its candidate for the upcoming presidential elections. While prior to the presidential debate in May 1994, Cevallos had very little national political exposure, he performed so well in a set of televised presidential debates in May of that year that he catapulted overnight into first place. Shortly after this victory, however, he virtually disappeared from the public eye, leading many to suspect that he was either "bought out" by the PRI or simply lost his nerve. See Crespo 1995, 79–280, for details.

PRD, for its part, was also hurt by the public perception that it lacked a rigorous alternative program of governance, not to mention the negative portrait that the government had succeeded in painting of it since its inception (Bruhn 1996, 208–49).

But even while the country's major opposition parties continued to be divided, Mexico was gradually demonstrating a more competitive political environment in which elections and party politics assumed heightened importance. While the ruling party had regained its hegemony within the electoral system at the national level in 1991, the situation was quite different at the state and local levels (Rodríguez and Ward 1995; Pacheco Mendez 1997). In 1989, the PRI's sixty-year monopoly on state governorships was finally broken with the officially recognized victory of a PAN candidate in Baja California. The persistent strength of the opposition was also reflected in a series of highly publicized and embarrassing incidents in which the PRI was forced to reverse officially declared gubernatorial victories and concede these to the opposition (Crespo 1995, 169–96. In turn, the PRI continued to lose ground to the opposition in medium-sized and large cities, such that by 1994, nearly 15 million Mexicans (almost one-fourth of the population) lived under municipal governments led by opposition parties (Cornelius 1994, 56) and more than three-quarters of all municipalities nationally exhibited high rates of electoral volatility (Pacheco Méndez 1997, 345).

Perhaps the most ominous development for the shape of the competition to come was the growing regionalization of the vote in Mexico (Klesner 1998; Magaloni 1998). By the mid-1990s, a clearly discernible trend had emerged whereby the PRI and the PAN appeared to be competing for the north and west zones of the country, while the PRI and the PRD vied for the south and central zones (see table 7.2). Klesner (1998) attributes such "bipartisan" voting patterns to the way in which the process of regional economic integration affected different areas of the country. Simply put, those regions with a strong manufacturing base and better educated labor forces were more favorably predisposed toward the two parties that wanted economic integration (PRI and PAN), while those regions that were either adversely affected by or excluded from integration seemed torn between their traditional allegiance to the ruling party and the more protectionist policies of the PRD. The emergence of a more divided Mexico was alarming news for the ruling party, as it suggested that in the future the PRI would be highly vulnerable both to the right and to the left as it sought to maintain its hegemony.

A variety of different indicators suggest that the ruling party perceived itself as on increasingly shaky ground vis-à-vis its competitors. In this regard, one can interpret the extensive use of polling, younger and more professional candidates, and widespread "get out the vote" campaigns in the 1991 elec-

**TABLE 7.2. Mexico: Federal Deputy Election Results by State, 1991–97 (% of voter share)**

| | PAN | | | PRI | | | PRD | | |
|---|---|---|---|---|---|---|---|---|---|
| State | 1991 | 1994 | 1997 | 1991 | 1994 | 1997 | 1991 | 1994 | 1997 |
| North | | | | | | | | | |
| Baja California | 44.7 | 36.7 | 43.4 | 45.7 | 50.6 | 35.2 | 2.8 | 7.8 | 13.7 |
| BC Sur | 24.5 | 33.3 | 20.9 | 66.4 | 57.2 | 48.4 | 1.5 | 5.4 | 13.3 |
| Chihuahua | 32.3 | 28.4 | 41.5 | 58.4 | 59.6 | 41.4 | 2.2 | 5.8 | 10.5 |
| Coahuila | 21.1 | 29.3 | 30.7 | 63.0 | 51.0 | 47.3 | 7.2 | 11.4 | 14.8 |
| Durango | 16.5 | 25.2 | 25.4 | 62.1 | 51.7 | 38.3 | 5.8 | 9.0 | 10.7 |
| Nuevo León | 25.9 | 41.5 | 49.5 | 68.5 | 49.2 | 39.3 | 1.2 | 2.3 | 2.8 |
| Sinaloa | 25.4 | 28.9 | 30.5 | 65.5 | 54.5 | 41.8 | 4.8 | 13.2 | 22.9 |
| Sonora | 24.2 | 32.8 | 32.8 | 68.6 | 48.3 | 38.9 | 3.3 | 13.5 | 26.9 |
| Tamaulipas | 14.7 | 23.5 | 19.6 | 63.3 | 50.9 | 47.3 | 3.7 | 15.3 | 26.9 |
| Zacatecas | 9.0 | 21.9 | 26.1 | 75.7 | 61.4 | 49.7 | 7.1 | 9.6 | 14.3 |
| Bajio | | | | | | | | | |
| Aguascalientes | 19.6 | 35.9 | 36.8 | 66.4 | 48.0 | 41.1 | 2.6 | 8.7 | 13.4 |
| Colima | 14.2 | 25.9 | 38.1 | 66.5 | 55.3 | 36.6 | 8.6 | 12.6 | 20.9 |
| Guanajuato | 33.4 | 30.5 | 44.0 | 53.4 | 54.7 | 33.0 | 4.7 | 8.6 | 13.1 |
| Jalisco | 23.7 | 41.8 | 44.9 | 63.1 | 44.6 | 35.4 | 2.7 | 7.7 | 11.7 |
| Michoacán | 8.7 | 15.2 | 18.3 | 53.9 | 44.9 | 35.4 | 31.2 | 35.4 | 40.1 |
| Nayarit | 4.1 | 16.3 | 23.8 | 70.5 | 59.4 | 50.4 | 12.9 | 16.5 | 20.8 |
| Queretaro | 21.0 | 30.1 | 45.6 | 69.9 | 59.1 | 38.5 | 2.4 | 5.0 | 9.3 |
| San Luís Potosí | 30.3 | 25.1 | 39.1 | 63.9 | 61.1 | 42.5 | 1.3 | 8.8 | 11.1 |
| Center | | | | | | | | | |
| Hidalgo | 7.5 | 16.6 | 16.3 | 72.7 | 62.4 | 49.3 | 8.5 | 14.9 | 27.1 |
| Morelos | 7.5 | 20.6 | 17.5 | 65.8 | 52.4 | 34.2 | 12.3 | 19.4 | 39.8 |
| Puebla | 14.9 | 27.0 | 25.8 | 69.5 | 52.5 | 48.4 | 4.6 | 14.0 | 18.4 |
| Tlaxcala | 8.5 | 22.6 | 19.2 | 74.2 | 55.2 | 44.3 | 6.2 | 14.6 | 23.7 |
| Metro | | | | | | | | | |
| DF | 19.9 | 27.3 | 18.1 | 46.3 | 40.6 | 23.2 | 12.0 | 21.4 | 45.5 |
| Mexico | 16.7 | 25.9 | 20.0 | 53.4 | 46.6 | 34.6 | 10.3 | 18.5 | 34.4 |
| South | | | | | | | | | |
| Campeche | 3.4 | 16.4 | 8.3 | 78.6 | 56.0 | 46.4 | 4.2 | 21.3 | 36.9 |
| Chiapas | 6.2 | 10.9 | 13.3 | 76.3 | 49.6 | 50.3 | 5.9 | 33.2 | 29.9 |
| Guerrero | 2.9 | 9.5 | 8.0 | 63.0 | 49.8 | 45.8 | 24.7 | 34.3 | 42.3 |
| Oaxaca | 5.3 | 12.6 | 12.9 | 73.5 | 53.5 | 49.5 | 9.5 | 27.3 | 31.1 |
| Quintana Roo | 11.7 | 27.3 | 23.9 | 76.2 | 55.6 | 45.9 | 5.8 | 12.2 | 23.9 |
| Tabasco | 2.4 | 5.7 | 4.9 | 72.6 | 59.6 | 51.3 | 18.9 | 33.0 | 40.7 |
| Veracruz | 5.0 | 15.2 | 21.6 | 75.3 | 54.4 | 43.1 | 6.0 | 23.3 | 27.3 |
| Yucatan | 36.0 | 40.9 | 38.5 | 61.8 | 54.3 | 50.7 | 0.2 | 2.7 | 7.6 |
| Total | 17.7 | 25.8 | | 61.5 | 50 | | 8.3 | 17 | |

*Source:* Klesner 1998, table 1. Reprinted with permission.

tions as proof of the ruling party's awareness of this new atmosphere of heightened competitiveness and the need to address it (Baer 1993, 60). The government also saw the need to undertake a series of electoral reforms during this period that marginally increased the space for opposition participation (Gomez Tagle 1993; Molinar Horcasitas 1996).[48] Finally, the fact that charges of electoral fraud were still widespread at the state and local levels even as late as 1993 also reflected the PRI's continuing uncertainty about its own ability to win elections honestly and make the victories stick (Morris 1995, 97; Bruhn 1996, 274–84; Cornelius 1994, 58–59).

When all is said and done, however, the question on the table is how this atmosphere of political threat measured up when compared to the Chilean case. Perhaps the best way to sum up the distinction between these two cases is that while Chile's authoritarian regime found itself in the midst of a transition to democracy in 1988–89, Mexico was still best characterized during 1988–93 as a liberalizing authoritarian regime—that is, one that had extended certain freedoms to the populace without relinquishing control over the process of change (Loeza 1994; Whitehead 1994). To be sure, the Mexican political environment did embody some aspects of a transition, including a pervasive environment of uncertainty, divisions within the elite, and a persistent challenge to the rules of the game (O'Donnell and Schmitter 1986). It was also clear that the apparent recovery of Mexico's economic health in the first half of the Salinas sexenio had not reversed the decline of hegemonic one-party rule. In spite of the PRI's remarkable political recovery in the 1991 midterm elections, "the anti-incumbent sentiment of the 1980s would translate into continued pressure for a democratic transition in Mexico in the 1990s" (Weintraub and Baer 1992, 191).

But while serving to expedite the transitional process, this liberalizing climate was not yet sufficient to trigger a full-fledged change of regime. And

48. The Salinas administration enacted three electoral reforms during its six years in office. The 1989–90 reform entailed a series of changes to make it more difficult for the PRI and government officials to commit electoral fraud (i.e., photographed voting credentials, same-day announcement of voting results, etc.). A second series of electoral reforms in 1993 served to double the Senate's size from 64 to 128 members, while guaranteeing that opposition parties would control at least one-quarter of the total seats, as compared with 5 percent during 1988–93. The final set of reforms, enacted in early 1994, included an external audit of voter registration lists, the creation of a special prosecutor for electoral crimes, a lower ceiling on party campaign financing, and fairer political party access to the media. It also set up an independent body—the Federal Electoral Institute (Instituto Federal de Elecciones [IFE])—to oversee elections. Many analysts have argued that the PRI has used such piecemeal changes in the electoral code over time in order to distract the public from reforming the core elements of Mexican authoritarianism (Reding 1991; Lujambio 1993; Loeza 1994). Be that as it may, there is no question that such changes moved Mexico in the direction of a more pluralistic political system, particularly after 1994 (Domínguez and McCann 1996, 193–97; Serrano 1996).

because of the in-between stage in which Mexico's rulers found themselves, the incentives for the incumbent authoritarian regime to fully insulate were less compelling than they had been in Chile.

## Splitting the Difference: The Logic of Partial Insulation

In the wake of the ambiguous nature of the democratic threat that surfaced in Mexico over the course of 1988–93, Salinas responded in kind. On the one hand, since simply handpicking his own successor might no longer be enough to guarantee the longevity of his preferred policies, some kind of institutional response was in order. On the other hand, it was also incumbent upon him to choose these rules carefully. Since he and his cohort were likely to be those affected in the immediate future, it was important that their control over the economy not be unduly restricted.

### Taking out Insurance: The Drive to Insulate

I argue that the Mexican government, in choosing to enact the central bank reform when it did, was motivated primarily by the need to take out some sort of "institutional insurance" on its economic program in the wake of an uncertain future. For while the magnitude of the threat facing Mexico's authoritarian government was lower than that in Chile, it was far from absent. Rather, there was enough uncertainty surrounding both the short-term outcome of the 1994 presidential elections and the long-term course of political change to warrant some degree of insulation.

The 1994 presidential elections marked a turning point in the time-honored Mexican tradition of the dedazo. For the first time in history, the designation of the PRI presidential candidate coincided with increasing signs of democratic political competition. While it was clear that "presidential control over the process of transition of the change of command will try to be as ironclad as ever, . . . the weight of the unforeseen . . . internal and external factors that are no longer in control of the president [is] much greater than before."[49] As one noted Mexican intellectual commented in late 1993, "until 1988 the central characteristic of the Mexican political system was the predictability of the electoral process for the change of command—today that is no longer the case. . . . in the mechanics of the end of the sexenio something new has been introduced: uncertainty."[50] As a result of this climate of

49. Lorenzo Meyer, "Mexico 1994 o el Difícil Camino de Un Cambio Sin Reglas," *Nexos,* August 1993, 53.
50. Ibid, 50.

increased uncertainty, "midway through the sexenio, when normally the most dangerous ghosts of our political authoritarianism tend to flourish . . . the government continues without being able to normalize the extraordinary situation that emerged with the celebrated elections of 1988."[51] As one of Mexico's leading political analysts succinctly summed this up, "without being democratic, the Mexican successor tradition was operating in a democratizing context."[52]

While Salinas could thus be reasonably confidant that his handpicked successor would emerge victorious in the presidential elections of 1994, he could not be absolutely sure. Indeed, by late 1993, "it was neither an exaggeration nor out of context to contemplate a PRI defeat and government by one or more parties" (Regalado 1996, 157). Several PRI officials admitted as much, confessing that while the party had done much better than had ever been imagined in 1991, "we knew that we might not win in 1994 and that . . . we could no longer take anything for granted."[53] As evidence of such fear, note that the government front-loaded the federal budget considerably in late 1993, loosening spending controls and stimulating demand in classic political business-style fashion (Ramírez de la O 1994, 4; Leiderman and Thorne 1996, 6–12).[54] Particularly noteworthy in this regard was the launching in late 1993 of Procampo—a rural relief effort modeled on Solidarity—precisely at a time when, as we have seen, rural groups seemed increasingly favorably disposed to the left-leaning PRD (Ramírez de la O 1996, 53). Certainly, the rampant and unsupervised lending via the public sector development banks described earlier could have no other reading than an electoral one. The fact that all such measures were planned for and programmed into the budget even before the tumultuous events of 1994 suggests that despite its seemingly comfortable position vis-à-vis its competitors, the ruling elite was actually quite insecure about its own ability to win the upcoming elections.

Because of this uncertainty over whether or not he faced a change within regime (to a continuation of authoritarian rule under a new leader) or a change of regime (to democracy and, if so, what sort), Salinas could not afford to take any risks. To be sure, the worst case scenario from the government's standpoint was a populist future centered on a revived left-wing alternative. But even if the PAN were to prevail in 1994, it was impossible to predict what might happen down the road. In the words of one analyst of Mexican politics,

51. Luis Sálazar C., "La Gran Asignatura Pendiente: Democracia y Legaldad," *Cuadernos de Nexos* 53 (November 1992): vi.

52. Hector Aguilar Camín, "La Pieza Perdida y El Paisaje en Tres Tiempos," *Nexos,* August 1993, 68.

53. Beltrán, interview.

54. Ministerio de Hacienda, *Informe Hacendario* 1, no. 3 (July–September 1993): 24–28.

"even if the victory went to a pragmatic Cárdenas or a dogmatically liberal Panista [member of the PAN], no one in the government believed that any group could manage the economy as competently as Salinas" (Coppedge 1993, 132). In order to grapple effectively with these multiple layers of uncertainty, Salinas would need to shift from merely pursuing policies as his predecessors had done to protecting them in an institutional form.

The 1993 central bank reform reflected precisely such a strategy. As one Mexican political scientist phrased it, "all reforms, such as central bank autonomy, NAFTA, etc. were done as if the government were preparing for a disaster. . . . in effect, it had to ask itself 'what if?'"[55] In this way, Mexico's 1993 central bank reform formed part of a larger set of institutional reforms that one Mexican journalist aptly termed the "trans-sexenial project" of the Salinas administration.[56] Through such reforms, Salinas sought to maintain influence over policy under future governments through a strategy of "imposed continuity." For example, Mexico's entry into NAFTA in November 1993 was arguably an effort to lock in the country's trade and investment policies with its largest trading partner for the next fifteen years (Basañez 1993, 98). The creation of an autonomous antitrust commission in December 1992 could likewise be interpreted as an attempt to make sure that the administration's emphasis on competition and free markets would be respected by future administrations.[57] As one journalist noted when observing this pattern of institutional change, "It seems obvious that these reforms condition—if not limit—the range of options for any party other than the PRI that accedes to the government in 1994."[58]

This more strategic interpretation of the central bank reform's timing was reflected in the criticism put forth by the left-wing opposition when the initiative was first announced. According to the PRD, the government was trying "to perpetuate, at least through the next sexenio, an economic and monetary policy focus . . . so that the group presently in power can continue to direct economic policy tomorrow from today."[59] PRD legislators considered the reform a clear attempt to "maintain control despite the next change

55. Juan Molinar, political scientist, El Colegio de México, interview by the author, tape recording, Mexico City, Mexico, December 15, 1994.

56. See, for example, Carlos Ramírez, "Indicador Político," *El Financiero,* August 16, 1993.

57. I refer here to the federal Law on Economic Competition, which set up an independent commission to police anticompetitive practices in the public and private sectors. This commission was governed by five commissioners, appointed by the president for ten-year renewable terms.

58. José Galindo López, "El Capital Político y los Plazos Largos: El Congreso del PRD," *Cuadernos de Nexos* (July 1993): xii.

59. "Frentes Políticos," *El Excelsior,* May 25, 1993.

of federal government,"[60] accusing the Salinas administration of trying to convert the Bank of Mexico into a "technocratic-financial nucleus, without social, legislative, or executive control."[61] In the words of the party's president, "there is no re-election, but there is continuity of the same economic policy, through mechanisms that exclude the fundamental decisions from popular sovereignty and even the organizations of political representation."[62] The net effect of such a strategy was that "while the Bank of Mexico would gain autonomy in relation to the next president, it would become dependent on the present head of the executive."[63]

Suggestive evidence for how the threat of political change might have influenced the reform's timing was also evident in select comments made by various government officials both during and after its legislation. Aspe himself hinted at such a motive when he unveiled the reform, noting that "for the first time ever, there will be no uncertainty regarding a possible change in the economic course of the country associated with a sexenial change of government."[64] A political motive was explicitly invoked by one central bank economist involved in drafting the reform who noted, "if with a non-autonomous central bank one already has fiscal balance and inflation under control, then there are no immediate incentives to authorize autonomy. *The only reason for autonomy under such circumstances might be to eliminate any future temptation to adopt expansionary polices*" (Roubli-Kaiser 1996, 13) (italics added).

Others corroborated this version of events. In the words of one of the president's leading political advisers, "The process of modernization that had begun in the sexenio allowed us to see an alternation in power in the future . . . and this was new as of this sexenio. In part this contributed to the timing of this reform."[65] Manuel Camacho also agreed that political variables had entered into Salinas's decision-making calculus. In his words, "the president . . . thought of everything in terms of the victory of the PRI, his own personal victories, and the competence of the presidential succession. . . . all of this intervened in even the most minuscule of decisions. So this reform was a way not to eliminate such uncertainty, but, yes, to reduce it."[66] It is possible that even Colosio himself was viewed as a potential risk for the policy preferences

60. "Respalda PAN la Iniciativa; La Oposición de Izquierda Pide Investigación Previa," *El Sol de México,* May 25, 1993.

61. "Frentes Políticos."

62. Porfirio Muñoz Ledo, president and senator of the PRD, *Statement to El Senado de México, June 22, 1993, Diario de Los Debates* 20, 12.

63. "Opinión de Partidos," *El Economista,* May 25, 1993.

64. "Frentes Políticos."

65. Confidential interview by the author, tape recording, Mexico City, Mexico, August 15, 1997.

66. Camacho, interview.

of the outgoing regime. As one member of Aspe's team in the Finance Ministry confessed, "we saw political changes coming—not just alterations between political parties but also within the ruling party itself. . . . I wasn't very sure that Colosio himself—who was not a very orthodox person when it came to the economy—would support an anti-inflationary policy with sufficient vehemence."[67]

But even if it is true that political considerations served as the underlying inducement for the central bank reform, we still need to understand its precise evolution and timing. Recall that while the idea initially surfaced at the beginning of the Salinas administration, it was not actually set into motion until early 1992. Why did the president wait three full years before beginning to work on this reform in earnest? Here, a variety of factors come into play. To begin with, there was a simple question of votes. Given the results of the 1988 elections—and, in particular, the lack of a PRI majority in the Chamber of Deputies—it was not wise to push ahead with a major reform initiative until the regime was on more solid footing politically.[68] The president thus made a calculated decision that it was more important to consolidate the ruling party's electoral base in the first half of the sexenio and wait until the second half of the administration to institutionalize its pet legislative initiatives.

More generally, the six-year calendar that characterizes presidential elections in Mexico is also relevant in explaining the reform's timing. One can imagine, for example, that had this been a parliamentary system, in which the legislature is effectively free to "fire" the prime minister at a moment's notice, Salinas might have tried to insulate the central bank right off the bat (see chap. 8). But because he knew that he had six years until he would have to step down from power, he chose instead to bide his time. On the one hand, and consistent with the logic of insulation outlined in chapter 3, it was only natural that he would put off as long as possible a reform that would limit his

67. Confidential interview by the author with former member of Finance Ministry, tape recording, Mexico City, Mexico, August 22, 1997. Some of those individuals interviewed for this study argued that it was, in fact, the "Colosio threat" that was driving the central bank reform. According to this logic, the reason the central bank reform surfaced in mid-1992 had less to do with an electoral logic (see the following discussion) than with the fact that by mid-1992, everyone was fairly certain that Colosio would become the next PRI presidential candidate. This argument is somewhat persuasive in that Colosio was certainly far less economically orthodox than his fellow presidential contender, Pedro Aspe. That said, he also had a very clear reputation as Salinas's "good son" and someone unlikely to deviate from the script (see, e.g., "Perspective on Mexico: Salinas Bets All on the 'Good Son,' " *Los Angeles Times*, November 30, 1993, p. B7). Thus, unlike Manuel Camacho—the third competitor for the throne—who, by his own admission, really was viewed by the technocrats as a "closet populist," Colosio was much less likely to "rock the boat" (Camacho, interview). Perhaps the biggest proof of Colosio's willingness to continue the economic model was his naming of Ernesto Zedillo—a tried and true technocrat—as his campaign manager.

68. Interviews, Beltrán; Camacho.

own discretion. On the other hand, and consistent with the story outlined earlier in this chapter, he also wanted to wait and see how the threat evolved before deciding exactly how much flexibility he would be willing to yield. The Mexican electoral cycle thus not only affected the timing of the reform but its shape as well (see the next subsection, "Autonomy 'A Medias': Retaining Executive Controls").

Rather than waiting until the very end of his term, however, Salinas had a strong incentive to have the central bank reform in place before the end of 1993. During the sixth and final year of his term, the government's priorities would shift toward ensuring the electoral victory of his successor. If Salinas were to avoid this "lame duck" scenario, he would need to complete all major institutional reforms before the electoral cycle resumed in 1994.[69] And because, as noted in chapter 3, central bank reforms take some time to mount and implement when they are done "from scratch," he would have needed to have begun working on the legislation as early as 1992 in order to have it ready by this date. However one chooses to interpret the precise timing of the initiative, it is clear that it was important that it take place before Salinas left power. According to one aide, he charged his staff to "guarantee me this before I go. . . . don't leave it undone for the next president."[70]

Mexican presidents have always tried to exert influence beyond their own sexenio by handpicking their successors. But this particular conjuncture was different: the dominance of a particular set of interests in power (embodied in Salinas) had also coincided with increasing signs that political change was on the horizon. Mere continuity in personnel would no longer be sufficient for protecting the president's preferred policies. Rather, it would also require institutional reform.

### Autonomy "A Medias": Retaining Executive Controls

But while there was thus enough uncertainty about the future course of events to warrant some degree of insulation in late 1993, the question was how much policy-making authority the incumbent government should yield to this independent agency. An earlier section of this chapter ("Reform Outcome: Evaluating the 1993 Reform") detailed the myriad ways in which the 1993 reform failed to result in a fully autonomous central bank. This section links such partial autonomy to the more ambiguous political threat confronting incumbent authoritarian elites. For unlike in Chile, where an imme-

69. I am grateful to Enrique Quintana, columnist, *Reforma,* for this point. Enrique Quintana, interview by the author, tape recording, Mexico City, Mexico, December 10, 1994.

70. Former Aspe aide, confidential interview by the author, tape recording, Mexico City, Mexico, August 22, 1997.

diate challenge to the regime's power met with a fully insulating response, in Mexico there was not enough risk of imminent democratization to warrant the complete abdication of executive control. Because of this cloudier overall picture, the resultant autonomy afforded the institution was watered down accordingly.

Exchange rate policy is particularly instructive in this regard. The question of which agency would control the exchange rate was one of the most contentious of those debated between the Finance Ministry and the central bank in the wake of their summer 1993 negotiations over the central bank law. Noting the quasi-fixed exchange rate regime that prevailed in Mexico at the time, many individuals within the central bank argued that exchange rate policy and monetary policy were effectively "two sides of the same coin." Accordingly, they argued in favor of the Chilean model, whereby the central bank would set exchange rate policy.[71] But despite their protestations to the contrary, the exchange rate policy dispute was ultimately decided in favor of the executive in the form of an exchange rate commission with the deciding vote for the finance minister. And the central bank, for its part, would supervise the country's reserves.

While the government justified its decision on two grounds—Chilean exceptionalism and unresolved theoretical debates (Roubli-Kaiser 1996, 17–21)—there was good reason to suspect that the actual motivation might have had much more to do with political calculations. For one thing, in addition to its purely monetary effects on the financial stability of the currency, the exchange rate is a price that affects the real component of the economy through its impact on the volume of trade. To the extent that the government was concerned with controlling policy instruments that would enable it to generate employment and, hence, votes, it was only logical that it would not wish to yield exchange rate policy to the central bank, particularly during an upcoming election year.[72] Also, because cyclical devaluations in Mexico had become such a politically charged issue (Frieden 1998; Kessler 1998), this was all the more reason for the government to be reluctant to yield control over this crucial element of policy. Were a devaluation to become necessary in the future, the government wanted to make sure that it—and not the central bank—would be in charge of determining its timing.

---

71. This view was expressed repeatedly to the author in the course of meetings with various officials at all levels at the central bank, Mexico City, Mexico, November 1994–February 1995. It was also shared by many in the academic community. See, for example, Katz 1993; Trigueros 1993.

72. I am grateful to Luis Alberto Giorgio for this point. Luis Alberto Giorgio, assistant director, Center for Latin American Monetary Studies (Centro de Estudios Monetarios Latinoamericanos [CEMLA]), interview by the author, tape recording, Mexico City, Mexico, December 8, 1994.

In short, given that certain individuals in the current Salinas administration expected to play an important role in the next administration's Finance Ministry, there was a short-term personal incentive to retain as many policy-making instruments as possible for this ministry. It was no secret, for example, that Salinas's chief of staff, José Córdoba, was hoping to capitalize upon his close ties to Colosio as a means of maintaining policy influence in the next sexenio (Centeno 1994, 170). Not surprisingly, a "strong form" of autonomy for the Bank of Mexico—including relinquishing control over exchange rate policy—had always been resisted by the members of the Córdoba camarilla within Salinas's economic cabinet.[73]

However one chooses to interpret the exchange rate policy decision, what is clear is that the executive branch was not yet ready to cede control over a policy instrument that would tilt the institutional balance of power in favor of the central bank. This was not only true of exchange rate policy but also of other areas of the law where the rules came up short. A faction within the central bank that had fought to impede any sort of lending whatsoever to the executive branch was also roundly defeated.[74] And while the idea of having the annual economic forecasts of both institutions emerge contemporaneously was also discussed, this idea was also rejected by the Finance Ministry in favor of having the government's projections come out first.[75] As noted earlier, this decision only increased the likelihood of executive branch influence over central bank policy decisions.

A positive spin on what took place in the course of these negotiations was that the executive had simply tried to "maintain a balance" between the powers of the two agencies.[76] With hindsight, however, a more accurate description would seem to be that autonomy "had been diluted" between May and December, as the Finance Ministry fought to keep control over a

73. Individual closely involved in the autonomy initiative, confidential interview by the author, tape recording, Mexico City, Mexico, August 22, 1997. While Córdoba himself was barred from running for president due to his French citizenship, his team included Undersecretary of Finance Guillermo Ortiz and Secretary of Trade and Development Jaime Serra. Both men had good reason to suspect that they would be given important positions in the next cabinet. In fact, Serra was the first finance minister named under the Zedillo administration, though he ultimately resigned in the wake of the peso crisis, only to be replaced by Ortiz. Of the two, Ortiz was very involved in the May–December negotiations over the precise content of the central bank law and was rumored to have been a key figure in retaining a variety of privileges for the executive branch.

74. Central bank official, confidential interview by the author, tape recording, Mexico City, Mexico, January 26, 1995.

75. Individual closely involved in the reform's negotiation, confidential interview by the author, tape recording, Mexico City, Mexico, January 31, 1995.

76. This opinion was expressed by one central bank official. Confidential interview by the author, tape recording, Mexico City, Mexico, January 23, 1995.

variety of policy arenas.[77] The desire to keep the central bank's power in check was reflected in the comments of several individuals closely involved in the reform. Salinas himself was said to have made it known that while he wanted it to be "a good reform . . . I don't want the government to wash its hands entirely."[78] Aspe also admitted that "the central bank was already getting a lot anyway. The pragmatic thing was not to give them everything at once, but rather, to wait and see how they handled this [degree of autonomy] first."[79] As one member of the central bank team cynically characterized the attitude of the Finance Ministry during the negotiations, "It was as if they said, sure, run . . . but we will cut off your legs."[80] Perhaps the best evidence that the reform's bark was worse than its bite was that even the reform's most vocal left-wing critics confided that "it was not as bad as they expected" when they saw the final product.[81]

In addition to reducing the central bank's discretionary powers, the law was also noteworthy for its manifest ambiguity. Consider the clause governing central bank lending to the executive. Whereas in most instances such a clause would be worded in its simplest form—that is, "the central bank cannot lend to the executive"—here the wording was much more convoluted: while the finance minister could no longer instruct the central bank to provide the federal government with a loan, the bank was perfectly free to do so of its own volition. A similar vagueness characterized those rules governing the lender of last resort function, which states that the central bank cannot lend to the banking system "except for purposes of monetary regulation" (Banco de México 1993, art. 14). In practice, it is quite difficult to interpret what, exactly, constitutes "monetary regulation," thus affording the Bank of Mexico a fair amount of discretion in this arena. Finally, there was even some confusion in the bill's language as to the precise nature of the central bank's jurisdiction over exchange rate policy. For example, Article 3 stated that the central bank would, among other things, regulate "foreign exchange." But this can be interpreted either as the power to regulate international reserves or to regulate the country's exchange rate policy more broadly. In light of the Finance Ministry's predominant role on the Foreign Exchange Commission, it is highly unlikely that the authorities intended the latter, but using this ter-

77. Former central bank official, confidential interview by the author, tape recording, Mexico City, Mexico, January 9, 1995.

78. Aspe, interview.

79. Ibid.

80. Confidential interview by the author, tape recording, Mexico City, Mexico, January 30, 1995.

81. Senior economic adviser to the PRD, confidential interview by the author, tape recording, Mexico City, Mexico, December 6, 1994.

minology—as opposed to simply stating "international reserves"—does leave this clause open to some speculation.

Many of those interviewed regarding the precise wording of the law concurred that the principal explanation for its apparent vagueness was that it had been written by a mix of lawyers (representing the Finance Ministry's/presidency's interests) and economists (representing the Bank of Mexico's interests). As one newspaper put it, "Definitively, the December 1993 reform, far from providing a solid, efficient and effective central bank, translated instead into a mumbo-jumbo elaborated by economists mixed in with lawyers and lawyers mixed in with economists."[82] As one Mexican economist quipped, "I have no doubt that if Gíl Díaz and Carstens had written this law themselves, [the Bank of Mexico] would have ended up much more autonomous both politically and economically."[83] But one also has to wonder whether such nebulous language was not, in fact, intentional. After all, Mexico adheres to a system of Roman law, in which—unlike in the common law system of the United States—there is no interpretation of the law by the courts. The government is thus obliged to interpret all laws exactly as they are written down. In light of the strong incentives that such a legal system provides to be precise, it seems difficult to interpret the manifold ambiguities within the central bank law as an accident.

To the contrary, much like the overt limitations on central bank discretion noted earlier, the imprecise nature of the legislation's language would seem to point to what one administration official aptly described as a deliberate effort by the Salinas administration to construct a series of "escape valves."[84] According to a variety of officials close to the Salinas cabinet, all laws written during the Salinas sexenio were designed to maintain some margin of security for the president.[85] Since all legislation inevitably made its way through José Córdoba's office upon completion, if these pockets of protection had not already been built in at the ministerial stage, they were guaranteed to be added in Córdoba's office, before the final product emerged.[86]

82. "Autonomía del Banco de México?" *Reforma*, February 15, 1995.

83. Katz, interview. Gíl Díaz and Carstens are both University of Chicago–trained technocrats in the central bank who were deeply involved in the drafting of the final legislation.

84. High-ranking official in the Ministry of Finance, confidential interview by the author, tape recording, Mexico City, Mexico, August 22, 1997.

85. Former political adviser to Salinas, confidential interview by the author, tape recording, Mexico City, Mexico, August 15, 1997.

86. Former political adviser to the president, confidential interview by the author, tape recording, Mexico City, Mexico, August 22, 1997. To be sure, one might interpret the reform's partial nature as an effort to send a cosmetic signal of credibility to the international community, all the while designing an institution that might allow the authoritarians to continue to win elections handily. But as I showed in chapter 6, the Mexican government did not really need to demonstrate its credibility to the international economic community in the

To be sure, in designing an institution that was only partially autonomous, the authoritarians were pursuing a strategy that posed both opportunities and risks. On the one hand, it would permit them to have an institution that was up and running in anticipation of an eventual turnover of power. This institutional "shell" could then be fine-tuned and strengthened over time should a more forceful democratic threat materialize. In the meantime, it would also permit them some room to manipulate policies to their advantage until complete delegation became absolutely necessary. On the other hand, if they lost the 1994 elections, they would also be "stuck" with a central bank that was not fully autonomous. And even if they did manage to stay in power, they would from here on out be at least partially constrained in their own policy-making abilities.

The reform that was ultimately crafted reflected the Mexican government's probabilistic assessment of its odds of staying in power as it approached the end of the Salinas sexenio. In proceeding as it did, the government must have reasoned that it was not only likely to win in 1994 but that it could always come back and fine-tune this reform later. The 1993 Mexican central bank reform thus effectively amounted to the first round of a long-term investment, one that would gain force over time. In the meantime, the important thing was to leave this institution "fertilized with [the government's] own people."[87]

As Mexico's authoritarians sat around debating the finer points of the central bank legislation in mid-1993, they had no idea what awaited them around the corner. As history would have it, political change came much sooner than the government had anticipated. These events would prove to have both short- and long-term ramifications for the Bank of Mexico's incipient autonomy.

## POSTSCRIPT: AUTONOMY TESTED—THE PESO CRISIS IN RETROSPECT

Over the course of 1994, the Mexican government witnessed a series of political and economic shocks that seriously jeopardized the ruling party's

latter half of the Salinas sexenio. This sort of argument also presumes that markets are easily fooled by a cosmetic reform, an observation that would seem to be out of sync with the savvy, well-informed nature of the international financial community. Finally, if the reform were designed purely for window-dressing purposes, implying that its rules were actually meaningless, then one also has to wonder why the authoritarians would not have gone ahead and designed a fully autonomous institution? I return to this latter issue in the chapter postscript.

87. Juan Molinar, Instituto Federal de Elecciones, interview by the author, tape recording, Mexico City, Mexico, August 15, 1997.

prospects in the upcoming presidential elections. In the wake of this challenge to the government's continued hold on power, the newfound autonomy of the Mexican central bank was quickly put to test. Exactly what triggered the cataclysmic denouement to the fabled "Mexican miracle" has been the subject of ongoing debate within academic and policy-making circles alike. Whichever hypothesis one chooses to privilege, however, one irrefutable feature of government policy in 1994 was an expansionary monetary policy by the central bank and a corresponding inability to defend the level of its international reserves. While some have interpreted this evidence as raising doubts about how much the reform really mattered in the first place, I argue that there are several reasons to believe that in fact it did and that its importance will be increasingly evident as Mexico moves toward democracy.

## The Threat Intensifies: Mexico, 1994

Throughout 1994, Mexico was rocked by a series of political and economic events that would place the incumbent party on increasingly unsure footing (Castañeda 1994; Edwards and Naím 1997). The "year of living dangerously" began on January 1, 1994, with the outbreak of an armed indigenous rebellion in the southwestern state of Chiapas that would continue throughout the year. Calling for an end to neoliberal economic reforms and political rights for indigenous peoples, the so-called Zapatistas' pleas for greater democratization and social services for the poor generated an outpouring of domestic and international support. In a country known for its political stability above all else, the Zapatista revolt was a clear and unequivocal sign that the social peace on which the Mexican revolution had long prided itself was beginning to show severe signs of strain (Crespo 1995, 197–239). More to the point, it raised the possibility that disgruntled voters in the south—already hostile to the neoliberal economic model—might seize upon the conflict as a justification for supporting a left-wing alternative in the upcoming elections (Klesner 1995, 147).

Close on the heels of the Chiapas revolt came a series of political murders that undermined the ruling party's unity in new and unprecedented ways (Smith 1997, 35–38). In March 1994, the PRI presidential candidate—Luis Donaldo Colosio—was abruptly assassinated while on the campaign trail. Five months later, a senior official in the ruling party followed suit.[88] In both cases, the targets of the murders had spoken of the need for further

88. I refer here to José Francisco Ruiz-Massieu, who was slated to become the head of the PRI delegation in the Chamber of Deputies.

democratic reform, particularly within the ruling party itself (Shultz and Wilson 1995, 13–20). And in both cases, rumors surfaced that important elements of the PRI leadership might have been involved (Cornelius 1996, 3). The sudden reappearance of political assassinations in Mexico—a phenomenon not exhibited since the prerevolutionary power struggles in the early part of the century—was yet another ominous sign that the country's much-vaunted stability was unraveling. The subsequent imposition of the staunchly technocratic Ernesto Zedillo as Colosio's replacement only served to lend fuel to the fire, generating considerable resistance from within the party's old guard and raising doubts about his ability to appeal to the masses (Smith 1997, 38).

Alongside its internal feuds, the ruling party was also confronting unexpected external competition that called into question its ability to win the presidential elections of August 1994. In February of that year, rumors began to surface that former mayor of Mexico City and one-time presidential contender Manuel Camacho might announce an independent bid for election.[89] Camacho had recently been appointed as commissioner for peace in the Chiapas conflict, following which he emerged as one of the most popular—and highly visible—politicians in the country (Domínguez and McCann 1996, 182). In addition to the symbolic importance of a Camacho candidacy as an unprecedented break with the dedazo tradition, it was also dangerous in that it had the ability to divide the party into two camps (Whitehead 1994, 337; Morris 1995, 106–7). Many feared that Camacho might find support not only among those in the PRI who had originally backed him as a candidate for the presidency but also among the opposition—and, in particular, the PRD.[90]

But no sooner had the "Camacho factor" receded as a principal source of alarm for the ruling party than a second external threat presented itself, this time from the right. In May 1994, a nationally televised presidential debate was held in which the unequivocal winner was the Panista candidate, Diego Fernandez de Cevallos. Cevallos's impressive performance in the debate underscored the weaknesses of the "official" candidate, Ernesto Zedillo, and the two men subsequently entered into a dead heat for the next several weeks (Domínguez and McCann 1996, 189–91). While Cevallos subsequently all but disappeared from the public eye, the ruling party could only assume at the time that it would need to battle it out with Cevallos until the bitter end.

89. See "Unintended Revolution in Chiapas: Passed over by Salinas, Camacho Is Tempted to Ride His New Image into an Independent Run for the Presidency," *Los Angeles Times,* March 2, 1994.

90. While Camacho eventually removed himself from the race, he did manage to pose a major threat to the security of the ruling elite for the better part of four months. See "Durante su Sexenio," 26.

Ongoing political instability was accompanied by economic chaos. There was a massive outflow of foreign capital over the course of the year, as the country's foreign reserves plummeted from almost U.S.$30 billion in January to just over U.S.$6 billion in December (Banco de México 1995, 41). By the end of the year, the combined effect of these multiple political and economic shocks was simply too much for the government to handle. On December 19, 1994, the newly elected government of Ernesto Zedillo was forced to devalue the Mexican peso by 19 percent, under a "managed float" system. One day later, after an additional $4 million left the country, the government announced that it would go to a free float. As the world watched in shock, Mexico plunged into a major financial crisis.

Any one of these events might have been potentially lethal in an election year. But to experience them all at once was beyond the pale. In the wake of this unprecedented political and economic threat to the sitting government, it was unclear if the PRI would weather the storm. Such conditions posed a clear test for Mexico's central bank: could it maintain its autonomy when the government needed it now more than ever?

## The Central Bank Responds: Assessing the Evidence

In the years since 1994, a veritable cottage industry has emerged around delineating the exact causes of the peso crisis.[91] For the present purposes, however, we are less concerned with the sequence of events culminating in the December 1994 devaluation per se than with the extent to which the Bank of Mexico's behavior in the wake of this crisis was consistent with that of an autonomous central bank.

Over the course of 1994, the Bank of Mexico pursued a monetary policy that can only be termed "expansionary." While in 1993 the monetary base grew at an average nominal rate of 7.3 percent, this figure rose to 20.6 percent in 1993, representing an increase of more than 200 percent (Banco de México 1994, 302). This was reflected in an unprecedented expansion of credit to the financial system, which grew at a rate of 41 percent in real terms over the

91. Among those explanations most commonly advanced are an overvalued exchange rate (Dornbusch and Werner 1994); improper fiscal and monetary policy (Krugman 1995; Lustig 1995; Sachs, Tornell, and Velasco 1995; Leiderman and Thorne 1996); failure to relay information in a timely and transparent manner (International Monetary Fund 1995); the vulnerability of the banking system (Calvo and Mendoza 1995); and a politically triggered speculative attack (Gíl Díaz and Carstens 1997). Others attribute it to underlying weaknesses in the Mexican economy, including low growth, a declining savings/investment ratio, and a large and growing current account deficit, which were only exacerbated by the events and policies of 1994 (Ramírez de la O 1996; Edwards 1997).

course of the year (Giorgio 1996, 11). Of particular note, net credit creation by public sector development banks increased by 35 percent between mid-1993 and mid-1994, equivalent to an increase of 3 percent of GDP (Leiderman and Thorne 1996, 11).[92] And while interest rates on three-month treasury bills did spike following the murder of Colosio, rising from around 10 percent in February to 18 percent in March, this differential showed a declining trend, due partly to hikes in corresponding U.S. rates (Sachs, Tornell, and Velasco 1995, table 3).

The government justified this injection of liquidity into the economy as a means of counteracting the pronounced drop in foreign reserves that took place over 1994.[93] According to this logic, they were not pursuing an "expansionary" policy so much as a "compensatory" one (Gíl Díaz and Carstens 1997, 178–80). Moreover, given the fixed exchange rate regime that was in place at the time, any rise in interest rates would have necessarily entailed forcing the exchange rate to the floor. And because all political and economic shocks were thought to be transitory, there was consequently no need to raise interest rates and/or risk a devaluation (Buira 1996, 316). Once Zedillo got elected, the situation was expected to normalize, and foreign capital would return to Mexico of its own volition.[94]

Nearly any economics textbook would argue, however, that in the wake of falling investor confidence, the appropriate policy to pursue in order to prevent capital from fleeing one's borders is to raise interest rates, even if this means weakening the domestic currency (Edwards 1995, 298). This was all the more true following the rise in U.S. interest rates in February 1994, mak-

92. This was in no small part the result of the deliberate expansion of lending to small and medium-sized producers that began in 1992 noted in the previous chapter. It should be noted that the central bank did repeatedly warn the Finance Ministry about the dangers of such lending practices, particularly those channeled through the credit unions (confidential interviews by the author with a variety of central bank officials, tape recordings, Mexico City, Mexico, August 1997). But despite its dissatisfaction with such lending, it is not clear that there was really much the central bank could do to stop it. Even if central bank officials had raised interest rates in an attempt to offset them, it was not clear that this measure would have had the desired effect, whether because the development banks had their own (subsidized) interest rates or because the loans simply had no chance of being repaid. Ultimately, the problem was one of supervision, and these powers did not reside with the Bank of Mexico but, rather, with the Finance Ministry itself. And as one central bank official observed matter-of-factly, "the development banks have always been 'off limits'" (central bank official, confidential interview by the author, tape recording, Mexico City, Mexico, August 7, 1997).

93. See, for example, Miguel Mancera's op-ed, "La Política Monetaria de México en 1994," *Reforma,* January 31, 1995.

94. Interviews by the author, tape recordings, Mexico City, Mexico, with central bank vice-governors Jesús Yacamán, August 12, 1997; José Sidaui, August 14, 1997; and Francisco Gíl Díaz, August 18, 1997.

ing investment in U.S. treasury bills even more attractive. Throughout the course of the year, there were several additional telltale signs that investors were increasingly nervous about the government's ability to stave off a devaluation. Between December 1993 and December 1994, foreign investors switched from peso-denominated bonds (*cetes*) to dollar-denominated bonds (*tesobonos*) almost in full, suggesting that they did not trust the stability of the exchange rate and predicted a run on the peso (Lustig 1995, 13; Edwards 1997, 113). A variety of other economic indicators—including the weekly foreign exchange risk, the weekly country (default) risk, and the daily position of the exchange rate relative to the ceiling of the exchange rate band—also suggested that the markets perceived Colosio's death as a permanent shock (Leiderman and Thorne 1996, 23–26). Finally, given that there were no reserve requirements in Mexico, the relatively high ratio of M2 to reserves at the end of 1993 meant that a bank run could easily have translated into a currency run (Sachs, Tornell, and Velasco 1995, table 8).

In subsequent years, a number of hypotheses have been put forth to explain the government's dogged refusal to raise interest rates. One such concern was the health of the banking system (Gruben and Welch 1996; Kildegaard 1997). Several officials interviewed for this study confessed that they deliberately eschewed an interest rate hike on the grounds that it might seriously endanger Mexico's commercial banks, which were already in bad shape due to overdue loans (see fig. A7.1).[95] Between 1987 and 1994, outstanding bank credit for consumption (credit cards and durable consumer goods) had grown in real terms by 457.7 percent, while credit for housing had increased by 966.4 percent (Ramírez de la O 1996, 53). By November 1994, overdue loans already comprised an estimated 96 percent of the total capital of the banking industry (Kildegaard 1997, 959). In light of the dire nature of the situation in the banking sector, protecting the banks from a solvency crisis was a top priority throughout 1994 (Calvo and Mendoza 1996).

There was also some speculation that Salinas's judgment—and, hence, the central bank's policy—was clouded by his own postelectoral ambitions, whether a short-term desire to head the World Trade Organization (Smith 1997, 39–43) or the longer-term ambition of one day ruling Mexico once again.[96] Because the credibility of the government's economic program was

95. Confidential interviews by the author with high-ranking central bank officials, tape recordings, Mexico City, Mexico, August 12, 1997.

96. Jorge Castañeda, political commentarist and professor of political science, Universidad Nacional Autónoma de Mexico (UNAM), interview by the author, Mexico City, Mexico, tape recording, August 11, 1997. Salinas did little to hide his ambition of one day returning to office and, indeed, even attempted to propose an amendment to the Constitution to allow for this, although such a measure was defeated by the old guard of his party (Centeno 1994, 1).

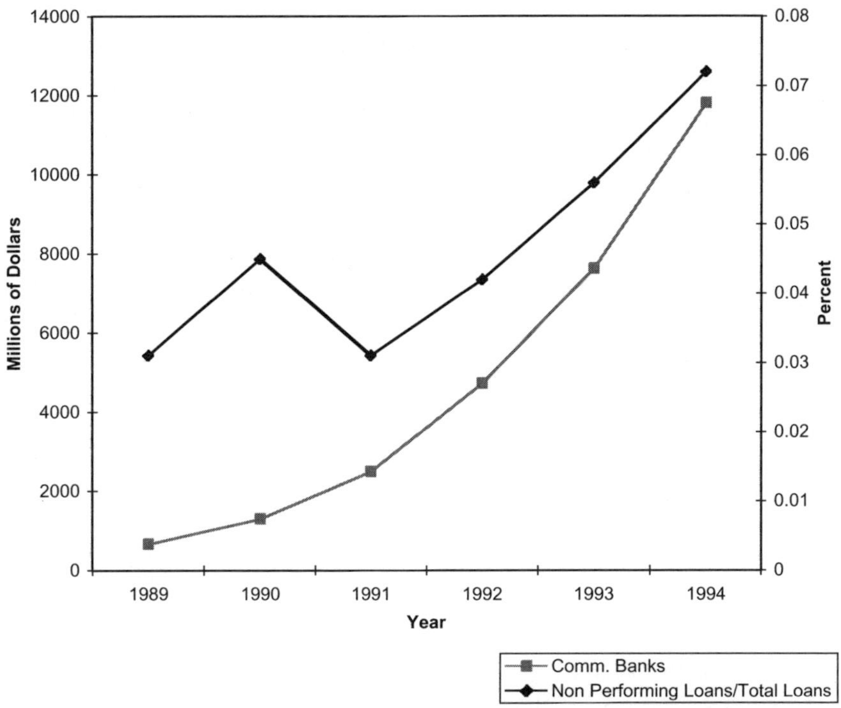


**Fig. A7.1. Mexico: Nonperforming loans, 1989–94. (From Sachs, Tornell, and Velasco 1995, table 10a.)**

intimately tied to adhering to the preannounced exchange rate, any tampering with existing macroeconomic variables was thus deemed out of bounds insofar as it might blemish his reputation at home and abroad (Sachs, Tornell, and Velasco 1995, 19–20). Indeed, Salinas appears to have faced some explicit pressure from one group of foreign investors to take all measures possible to manage the crisis, short of altering the exchange rate itself (Smith 1997, 41; Naím 1997, 305).

Finally, electoral motives were also almost assuredly at play. By ensuring ample credit to the private sector, the government sought to avoid an explosion of interest rates that might have contributed to the demise of PRI candidate Ernesto Zedillo in the 1994 presidential elections (Sachs, Tornell, and Velasco 1995, 21; González Gómez 1998, 48–49; Lustig 1995, 14–15). In the words of one expert on central banking in Latin America, “the central bank judged that it was better to have Zedillo than Cárdenas or Cevallos and adopted a monetary policy accordingly."[97] For while the ruling party would arguably have an incentive to make credit abundant in any electoral year, in 1994 these incentives were particularly acute for all of the reasons outlined earlier. According to one analysis, had the central bank not modified its orthodox monetary policy as it did, the electoral results in the presidential race would have been much closer.[98] The remarkable 4.7 percent average growth rate observed in the months leading up to the elections (see fig. A7.2)—not to mention the fiscal expansion due to development bank lending noted earlier— would certainly seem to corroborate a "political business cycle" reading of events. Perhaps these electoral pressures were best summed up by a former member of the Bank of Mexico's board of governors, who said,

> We were making decisions during a . . . politically difficult year in which the party that had been in power for so many years was beginning to question whether it would remain in power. So this meant that some decisions were made with fear, because no one wanted to alter any variable that might increase this fear or affect the outcome of the elections.[99]

None of this is to suggest, of course, that the central bank's failure to raise interest rates caused the peso crisis. It certainly played a role, although how much—and exactly why—is disputed by the experts.[100] Nor does it mean that had the central bank chosen to raise interest rates as early as March, the entire crisis could have been averted. Finally, given the fixed exchange rate that was in place at the time, it is difficult to separate the decision not to raise interest rates from the decision not to devalue. And because of the institutional rules governing the makeup of the Foreign Exchange Committee, it was the Finance Ministry—and not the central bank—that was ultimately responsible for exchange rate policy. Rather, the point I wish to underscore here is merely that in not raising interest rates, the central bank failed to comply with a fundamental element of its autonomy: the ability to preside over a pool of international reserves that can guarantee—over all other objectives—the stability of the currency (Banco de México 1993, art. 18).

97. Confidential interview by the author, tape recording, Mexico City, Mexico, August 15, 1997.

98. See "Relajar la Política Monetaria: Origen de la Crisis Financiera," *El Financiero,* January 25, 1995.

99. Confidential interview by the author, tape recording, Mexico City, Mexico, August 11, 1997.

100. See, for example, Krugman 1994; Sachs, Tornell, and Velasco 1995; Calvo and Mendoza 1996.

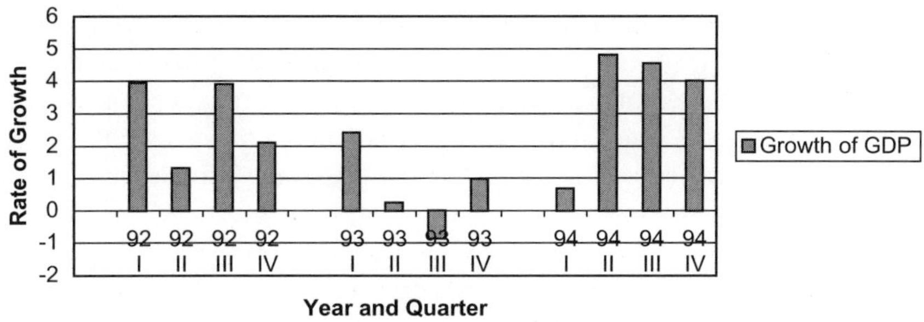


**Fig A7.2. Mexico: Quarterly growth of GDP, 1992–94. (From Gíl Díaz and Carstens 1998, 183.)**

### Revisiting the Rules: Does Autonomy Matter?

In the aftermath of the peso crisis, the Bank of Mexico came under heavy criticism for having failed to act in an autonomous fashion. As one editorial declared harshly, "the devaluation showed that autonomy was merely a formality . . . that the 'independence' of the central bank functioned exactly like the 'independence' of the Chamber of Deputies: servile, surreal and very Mexican."[101] The image of the central bank's president, Miguel Mancera, was particularly damaged by the events surrounding the peso crisis. As one newspaper noted when reporting the reactions of a group of Mexican entrepreneurs, "What hurt them most was to have been betrayed by Miguel Mancera, whom only 12 years earlier they had applauded for not collaborating with the president who . . . nationalized the banks. They could not conceive of how . . . [Mancera] could now buckle in front of Salinas . . . and Aspe."[102] Perhaps this general disillusion was best captured in the words of one of Mexico's most prominent businessmen, who commented, "we just assumed that if you created an autonomous organization, it would behave as such. . . . now we are very disappointed."[103]

What such comments collectively underscore is that the public viewed the peso crisis as definitive proof that the central bank's autonomy was meaningless. But was it? There is no question that—by virtue of their very flexibility—the rules themselves governing autonomy partly facilitated the irresponsible policy-making decisions that came to characterize 1994. For example, by

101. "Balance de Un Año Negro," *El Economista,* December 29, 1994.

102. "Asunto: Aplausos, Silbidos," *El Heraldo de México,* February 2, 1995.

103. Ernesto Rubio del Cuento, president, Cementos Mexicanos (CEMEX), interview by author, telephone, Mexico City, Mexico, January 20, 1995.

obliging the central bank to take the financial sector's "sound development" into account as one of its primary objectives, there was arguably some legal justification for the central bank's decided unwillingness to raise interest rates in 1994. Similarly, because some central bank lending to the executive was permitted, the Finance Ministry continued to have some latitude with which to intervene in interest rate policy.[104]

But are we to conclude that the rather fluid nature of the Bank of Mexico's autonomy throughout 1994 invalidates the reform effort entirely? In other words, if the central bank failed to constrain adequately an expansionary monetary policy during the first year of its existence, should we continue to expect this sort of behavior in the future? While it is easy to see how one might arrive at the conclusion that the law did not really matter, I would challenge such a line of reasoning from a variety of angles.

To begin with, if the autonomy legislation were entirely without basis, why did the authoritarians go to so much trouble to create the law in the first place? The fact that the central bank's autonomy was enshrined in the Constitution suggests that the government was intent on giving this law a certain pride of place. The vast majority of financial legislation in Mexico was traditionally done through bylaws, which are much easier to overturn should the circumstances warrant it. While it is true that the central bank law itself fell under such a statute, the basic commitment to price stability was permanently enshrined in the Constitution. If nothing else, the constitutional entrenchment of this fundamental objective suggests that the authoritarians had a long-term lock-in strategy in mind.

A second and related reason to believe that the rules mattered was, ironically, their partial nature itself. If the rules governing autonomy had not mattered, then it would have been far easier for the Salinas government simply to have created a fully autonomous institution and then proceed to violate it as it saw fit. It was, after all, an authoritarian government, and "in a country where personalities count more than institutions, laws are not enough" (Naím 1997, 297). But the interesting aspect of the Mexican case was not the

104. Technically speaking, the law granted the central bank complete freedom to decide the amount and terms of its internal credit. In reality, however, because the central bank acted as financial agent for the government in the weekly auction of its public debt, the Finance Ministry reserved the right to decide whether or not to participate in such an auction and on what terms. And, at times, rather than letting the market freely determine the price at which these bonds would be purchased, the government would set a limit above which it was not willing to sell them. The Bank of Mexico would then use this as a benchmark in the course of carrying out its open market operations. In colloquial terms, this strategy is known as *tirar la rayita* (line-drawing). Over the course of 1994, the Finance Ministry used this technique to impose an informal interest rate ceiling. This was acknowledged in a series of confidential tape-recorded interviews by the author with former and current central bank officials, Mexico City, Mexico, November 1994–February 1995.

out-and-out violation of an otherwise strong set of rules, as Naím suggests, but, rather—as I have demonstrated in detail in the preceding chapters—the deliberate creation of an autonomous institution that was only partial to begin with. This does not negate the fact that the authoritarian political context in which this legislation was born invariably made these already porous rules all the easier to penetrate. But the great deal of time and energy that the technocrats poured into carefully crafting the precise wording of this legislation to increase its autonomy in some respects and diminish it in others suggests that the rules did, in fact, matter a great deal and that the authoritarians were acutely aware of this.

But even if we do believe that the rules did matter in some broader sense, we must still come to terms with the fact that they proved to be quite malleable in 1994. Here I would raise a number of considerations. To begin with, 1994 was a truly exceptional year. None of the bizarre events that characterized 1994—from the Chiapas rebellion on the very first day, to the political assassinations, to the U.S. interest rate hike—could have been anticipated by the authorities and certainly not in conjunction with one another. In some sense, then, it may not be fair to judge Mexico's central bank autonomy by what was by all accounts an extraordinary year. As Lohmann (1992) has forcefully argued, we should not expect central banks to pursue price stability at all costs in the wake of unforeseen external shocks. Even if Mexico's central bank had looked exactly like Chile's on paper, then, it is not at all clear that it would have responded differently to the events of 1994.

A second reason to believe that the reform should work better post-1994 is that some of the very rules that rendered certain aspects of the original legislation weak have subsequently changed. Take exchange rate policy. At the time the reform was begun, the country was still operating under a fixed exchange rate system. In some sense, 1994 ultimately came down to weighing the trade-off between allowing interest rates to rise to whatever level was deemed appropriate and abandoning this key component of the government's economic program. And it is arguably the case that this was not—in the final analysis—the central bank's decision to make. But with the devaluation of December 1994, a floating exchange rate regime was put into place. As long as this system remains in effect, it grants the central bank complete freedom to determine interest rates as it sees fit, independent of the desires of the executive branch. In similar fashion, the three-year period of exception exempting the federal government from any limitations on lending by the central bank expired in April 1997. As a result of such changes, the government can no longer borrow from the central bank free of charge.

At times, there has also been open conflict between the central bank and the Finance Ministry on a given policy issue. On at least two important occasions in late 1994, for example, Mancera did choose to challenge the executive branch over exchange rate policy. First, in a highly secretive meeting on November 30, 1994, between important figures in the outgoing Salinas and incoming Zedillo administrations, Mancera purportedly threatened to resign if international reserves were to fall below 10 million dollars without an accompanying "free float."[105] Second, in the famous meeting to decide the fate of the peso on December 19, Mancera advocated going directly to a free float rather than widening the band but was overruled by then finance minister Jaime Serra.[106] To be sure, such actions arguably came late in the game, and because exchange rate policy ultimately fell under the purview of the Finance Ministry, there was not much that Mancera could do. But if the central bank proved capable of asserting whatever autonomy it had at what was arguably the country's most delicate moment, we can only surmise that it has been all the more able to do so in the years that followed.

And, indeed, in the ensuing years since the peso crisis, there have been other instances of conflict between the two ministries, again serving as indirect proof that the autonomy legislation was not entirely trivial. On a number of instances, for example, and particularly when Mancera was still in charge of the central bank, the two ministries clashed privately over interest rate policy, and the central bank won out.[107] They also disagreed publicly over the appropriate level of central bank intervention in the exchange rate market, with the administration favoring a gradual devaluation of the exchange rate and the Bank of Mexico fighting successfully to maintain the float, arguing that a weak peso would merely generate inflation.[108]

But perhaps the best evidence of the ongoing significance of the autonomy legislation was the outcome of the explosive controversy that erupted in Mexico in 1998 regarding the creation of a $61 billion government-sponsored stabilization fund (Bank Fund for Savings Protection [Fobaproa]) for the financial sector. The new fund was to be operated by the Bank of Mexico and thus fell under the jurisdiction of its newly appointed governor, Guillermo Ortiz, who had also supervised the initial privatization of the banks as an undersecretary of finance under Salinas. But because both the PAN and the PRD viewed Ortiz as partly responsible for the banking crisis, they refused to approve the authorization of Fobaproa unless Ortiz were to

105. See "La Historia Secreta," *Reforma,* March 17, 1995.

106. See "Línea Financiera," *Uno Más Uno,* December 22, 1994. This was also confirmed in a series of confidential interviews by the author.

107. Private e-mail communication by the author with central bank official in the operations department, December 2, 1998. Mancera stepped down in December 1997 and was replaced by then finance minister Guillermo Ortiz.

108. See "Peso Debate Flares up, but Zedillo Not Likely to Devalue Currency," *Lagniappe Letter,* October 11, 1996.

step down.[109] Even as the controversy raged on for months, the government remained firm in its defense of Ortiz, asserting that "Ortiz' continued presence in the Bank of Mexico is not a subject of negotiation" and underscoring that the autonomy of the institution made such a move impossible.[110] Given that the dismissal of a central bank governor can only be realized for technical reasons, Ortiz's premature removal from office for political reasons would have constituted a grave blow to autonomy. The government's intransigence in this regard thus served as concrete proof of its willingness to uphold the central bank's autonomy at all costs.[111]

In short, it is true that as they were initially crafted, the rules governing autonomy in Mexico were not nearly as strong as they might have been. By the same token, however, nor were they entirely meaningless. Not only will incoming governments face a central bank board entirely of Salinas's choosing, but they will also be constitutionally obliged to privilege price stability above all else, face real limits on their ability to borrow from the central bank, and confront a system in which interest rates are not subject to the vicissitudes of exchange rate policy. In short, incoming democratic governments will still be more constrained than they would otherwise have been had the law never been created in the first place.

## Conclusion

In closing, it is worth speculating about what, if anything, the hypothesized link between democratization and institutional change put forth in this book can tell us about the subsequent course of central bank reform in Mexico. The logic of the analysis suggests that as the democratic threat in Mexico intensified, there should have been a strong incentive for the authoritarian government to attempt to strengthen the existing autonomy legislation where it was weak.

In the years following the peso crisis, there is no question that such conditions began to emerge, as social unrest, elite divides, and electoral challenges from the opposition escalated (Kaufmann Purcell and Rubio 1998). In

109. See "Exige PRD Juicio Político Contra Ortiz, Gurria y Mancera," *La Jornada,* October 27, 1998; "Ortiz y Fernández Fuera o No Hay Fobaproa," *El Economista,* November 11, 1998.

110. "Labastida: La Renuncia de Ortiz, Tema Excluido de Toda Negociación," *La Jornada,* December 8, 1998.

111. The stalemate was ultimately resolved in an eleventh-hour deal brokered between the Zedillo administration and the right-wing PAN , in which Ortiz's role as head of the central bank went unaffected. See "In Mexico, Rival Parties Pass Accord on Bank Aid," *New York Times,* December 13, 1998.

particular, Cuauhtémoc Cárdenas's victory in the 1997 Mexico City mayoral elections and the corresponding loss of the PRI majority in both chambers of the legislature demonstrated in bold relief that pressures for democracy were only likely to intensify (Klesner 1997). What Cárdenas's victory made exceedingly clear is that more than ever before, there was a real possibility that Mexico might be ruled in the future by a group of individuals with a very different economic ideology than the technocrats that had been in power since 1982.

It is perhaps not surprising, then, that following on the heels of the Cárdenas victory in July 1997 rumors began to surface of a possible additional reform to the existing central bank law. While not proposing a radical overhaul of existing legislation, a number of individuals in the current government did express an interest in tying up a number of its loose ends.[112] This idea was subsequently formalized in a proposal submitted by President Zedillo to the Congress in 1998, in which the central bank would assume not only exclusive control over exchange rate policy but also oversight of the banking system (Starr 1998, 43).

Such a step was deemed important, as one senior government official put it, "not because Cárdenas will win in 2000, but because it is now a real possibility."[113] As one prominent member of the banking community phrased it, "the government needs to be very careful, precisely because it might find itself before an executive branch that . . . might try to prevent the central bank from bringing about an orthodox monetary policy."[114] This sentiment was echoed in somewhat starker terms by a high-ranking member of the central bank itself, who warned somewhat ominously, "In light of the changing political situation, we cannot afford to think in the short term any more."[115] The appointment of fiscal conservative Guillermo Ortiz as the governor of the Bank of Mexico in December 1997 would certainly seem to underscore this new line of thinking.[116]

Ultimately, it became clear that an additional central bank reform was not politically feasible in Mexico's new electoral environment. To the contrary, it would appear that Mexico's authoritarian elites misjudged the

112. Confidential interviews by the author with a number of central bank officials, August 1997, Mexico City, Mexico. Recall that autonomy was based on two legal frameworks: a constitutional amendment and the accompanying central bank law, and that it was the latter where all of the loopholes lay.

113. Confidential interview by the author, tape recording, Mexico City, Mexico, August 15, 1997.

114. José Madariaga, president, Probursa, interview by the author, tape recording, Mexico City, Mexico, August 8, 1997.

115. Confidential interview by the author, tape recording, August 18, 1997, Mexico City, Mexico.

116. See "Mexico's Budget: A Vote for Stability," *New York Times,* December 16, 1997.

timetable of political change in their country and missed their golden opportunity to strengthen this legislation once and for all. But had such a measure eventually come to pass, it would have been entirely consistent with the basic thrust of the argument advanced in this book. As pressures for democratization assumed a heightened importance, the authoritarians were forced to reevaluate how much longer they could safely expect to remain in power. They were forced to realize that if they did not act quickly to make their monetary policy truly insulated, they might lose this opportunity for good. Were the Zedillo administration to have enacted a central bank reform before leaving power, it thus would have been because now, as never before, it knew that its back was truly against the wall.

CHAPTER 8

# Central Bank Reform in Comparative Perspective

As noted in chapter 1, regime change is not the only impetus for central bank autonomy in the developing world. There is no question, for example, that the external credibility logic that Maxfield (1997) and others highlight also plays a central role in a number of recent cases. The 1991 Argentine central bank reform, for example, in which the Menem government set up a quasi-currency board that effectively tied the austral to the dollar, would seem to correspond more closely to this latter rationale (Williamson 1995). But without denying the salience of such international pressures, I have suggested that a number of cases may be better explained through the lens of domestic politics and, specifically, the threat of policy change. To develop this argument, I have focused on one class of countries of considerable importance in the developing world: democracies in transition from authoritarian rule.

The previous four chapters explored the dynamic between democratization and institutional change in two such transitional democracies: Chile and Mexico. This chapter supplements these in-depth case studies with an "in comparative perspective" dimension, in which I examine three additional cases of central bank reform under authoritarian rule that are broadly similar to those already examined: South Africa, Pakistan, and South Korea. What renders these cases particularly appealing is that they are drawn from outside Latin America, thereby speaking to the more general nature of the argument at hand. They also include one null case—South Korea—which allows us to explore a fuller range of outcomes on the dependent variable.

This discussion in this chapter is necessarily far from conclusive in terms of the empirical evidence it provides. Rather, it is meant to suggest the plausibility of the argument for addressing a wider range of cases than those contemplated in detail within this book. While the basic contours of my theoretical framework appear to be broadly consistent with the data at hand, there is of course some variation across the individual cases. In the chapter conclusion, I suggest how such variation might lay the groundwork for future comparative work on the politics of central bank reform in a variety of different institutional contexts.

### South Africa: Reform from Above

Let us begin with the South African case, which corresponds most closely to our ex ante expectations about central bank reform in the transition from authoritarian rule.

Our story begins in the late 1980s, when the apartheid system on which South Africa's authoritarian rule was based began showing signs of increased strain (Price 1991; Sisk 1995; O'Meara 1996; Lotter 1997). Over the course of the decade, antiapartheid political strikes, guerrilla attacks, and school boycotts rose to an unprecedented scale (Price 1991, 194). Many South Africans adopted a strategy of "nonparticipation," joining opposition groups outside the mainstream political parties. Business leaders facing intense economic pressures from white consumer groups and black workers also began pressuring the Botha government for political reform (Lotter 1997, 50–62). Finally, economic boycotts and diplomatic isolation by the international community made it clear that foreign governments had lost patience with apartheid rule (O'Meara 1996, 399). These combined tensions eventually took their toll on the ruling National Party (NP), as splits emerged between those soft-liners who favored black enfranchisement and the hard-liners who opposed allowing the black majority any say in government at all (O'Meara 1996, 374–77; Sisk 1995, 56–70). Even though the NP managed to keep its majority in the 1987 general elections with 52 percent of the vote, it was increasingly clear that the status quo was no longer tenable.

But while the prospect of political participation by South Africa's black majority directly threatened the NP's continued hold on power, it was also worrisome on economic grounds. Over the course of the 1980s—and under decided pressure from the business community (Davies, O'Meara, and Dlamini 1985, 23–31)—the NP had become increasingly committed to a neoliberal economic program rooted in an unfettered market, trade liberalization, and reduced government spending (CEAS 1993; Kentridge 1993). The leaders of the then-outlawed black African National Congress party (ANC) had, in contrast, long advocated an economic model centered around extensive regulation, an expanded public sector, and wide-scale redistribution (ANC 1990; MERG 1993; Michie and Padayachee 1997). The ANC leadership did soften its rhetoric over time and, once elected to office, went on to pursue a much milder set of economic reforms (Habib 1998). Ex ante, however, NP leaders and conservative business groups repeatedly expressed doubts about the ANC's ability to resist pressures for higher wages and welfare transfers from its more radical support base (Kentridge 1993). Indeed, as it became increasingly clear toward the end of the decade that apartheid rule would not last indefinitely, business elites acted on these fears, pressuring successive NP governments to step up their efforts to privatize the economy (Price 1991, 289).[1]

In 1989, three bombshells hit that would bring these concerns to a climax. In February, and for the first time in decades, an extreme right-wing candidate nearly succeeded in winning the presidential elections over the NP candidate (F. W. De Klerk). This was followed in April by the creation of a left-wing opposition political party calling for nonracial democracy and the rule of law, specifically targeted at garnering electoral support among the NP's predominantly English-speaking middle- and upper-class urban base (O'Meara 1996, 387). But the reality of the NP's deteriorating political position was finally driven home in the legislative elections of September, when the NP made its worst showing in thirty years, garnering only 6 percent of the voting age population. Although it still retained 93 of 166 seats, the ruling party that had dominated South African politics for the better part of a century had lost a majority of white support (Sisk 1995, 81–82). What this legislative defeat brought home was that if De Klerk wanted to prevent the further erosion of support on both the right and the left, a clear launch onto the reform path was needed (Lotter 1997, 75–90). On February 2, 1990, De Klerk made his landmark speech calling for sweeping political reform in South Africa—including the release of jailed ANC leader Nelson Mandela and other political prisoners—thus setting the country on a crash course with democratization.

But while both sides saw a negotiated transfer of power as inevitable as of 1990 (Sisk 1995, 75–82; Herbst 1997–98, 598–603), the question was when it would occur and under what terms. De Klerk made it clear from the beginning that the basic constitutional framework for democracy would have to be negotiated before elections were held (Sisk 1995, 82). A series of protracted negotiations thus ensued between the NP and the ANC, ultimately culminating in the CODESA (Conference for a Democratic South Africa) negotiations of 1993, which formally brought an end to apartheid rule. For our purposes, the significance of these negotiations lay in the myriad ways in which incumbent elites sought to protect white minority interests under the ensuing democratic regime (Herbst 1997–98, 603–607). To this end, the NP placed a number of nonnegotiable demands on the table, including a voting system based on proportional representation, a power-sharing mechanism within executive agencies, a set of powerful regional governments with large bud-

1. Business representatives demonstrated remarkable unanimity in favoring the liberalization of the economy, despite the fact that many firms would not fare well under international competition. Wood (1999, 27) attributes this to the fact that South African firms were increasingly integrated into overarching conglomerates and that individuals held highly diversified wealth through the Johannesburg Stock Exchange, lessening the sorts of sectoral concerns highlighted in chapter 3.

gets, and tenure security for white officials in the public bureaucracy.[2] In turn, the government also sought various protections for its economic model, including the constitutional guarantee of private property and independence for the South African Reserve Bank (Habib 1998, 6).

In fact, the Reserve Bank had already been strengthened considerably in 1989, a date not without significance for our larger political story. Prior to 1989, South Africa's central bank had lacked any real statutory independence (Joubert 1976, 411–15). Over the course of the 1980s, however, it had adopted a highly market-oriented monetary policy, relying heavily on the interest rate as the cornerstone of its anti-inflation efforts (Botha 1997). The 1989 Reserve Bank Act enshrined this commitment in law. Among other things, the act served to prioritize price stability as the institution's primary objective, allowed for greater freedom of action in its day-to-day operations, and formally eliminated a large number of distortionary credit practices (e.g., interest rate ceilings, reserve requirements, and consumer credit controls) (Stals 1993). The 1993 reform did little to change the 1989 legislation but did augment the Reserve Bank's strength in two significant respects. First, while the Reserve Bank's extensive policy-making powers had previously been carried out under the implicit and/or explicit control of the Finance Ministry, the 1993 law authorized the central bank to "exercise its powers and perform its functions independently" (Constitution of the Republic of South Africa, clause 196). Second, the Reserve Bank's commitment to price stability was also elevated to the constitutional level.[3]

The ANC adamantly opposed this legislation, arguing that the Reserve Bank should be placed more firmly under political control to ensure that "monetary policy is determined by and accountable to the democratic gov-

2. An additional provision for minority veto over policy-making was dropped from the list of demands. As Murray (1994, 194) notes, the NP negotiators came to realize that Afrikaner dominance of private enterprise together with an NP-appointed civil service, security establishment, and judiciary would serve as a more effective protection for minority interests than any numerical formula.

3. The reform has generally been viewed as fairly constraining in practice (Stals 1995; Schmulow and Greyling 1996; Maxfield 1997, 68), although its formal/legal underpinnings would appear to lie somewhere between the Mexican and Chilean cases. As noted, the legislation is considerably stronger on those dimensions concerning policy-making powers and central bank objectives. It appears to be less stringent on those provisions governing central bank lending to the executive, which seem somewhat vaguely defined, as well as on the makeup of the central bank board. The latter combines both a mini–governing board of five individuals with five-year renewable terms and a larger nine-person board elected by its shareholders for three-year terms (Reserve Bank of South Africa 1993, Articles 13f and 4). This somewhat unusual structure would seem to reflect the fact that the Reserve Bank is listed on the South African Stock exchange and has some seven hundred shareholders. More research is needed to evaluate its implications of this quasi-public structure for the bank's independent operation and governance.

ernment" (MERG 1993, 261). The ANC was particularly opposed to the preeminent role accorded anti-inflation in the new Constitution, maintaining that the monetary policy should also entail "the expansion of money supply commensurate with real GDP growth, and . . . strengthening the orientation of the financial system toward financing growth and development" (MERG 1993, 263). Such protestations notwithstanding, the ANC was overruled, and autonomy became permanently enshrined in the South African Constitution.

The 1993 South African central bank reform bears a number of similarities to the Chilean case. For starters, the NP's avowedly free-market private sector support base resembles that of Pinochet. The fact that business pressures to prioritize price stability had been present for more than a decade before the reform took place similarly casts doubt on credibility-based reasoning to explain the reform's timing.[4] As in Chile, the outgoing regime was visibly frightened by the more interventionist proclivities of its would-be successor. Finally, the economic content of the transitional negotiations—including central bank reform—was decisively influenced by the interests of the outgoing regime (Herbst 1997–98, 607).

Taken together, these factors add up to yet one more illustration of how conservative authoritarian elites use central bank reform to ward off the populist menace intrinsic to new democracies. The net result is that as the ANC embarked upon its historical ascent to power, it found itself confronted with an independent central bank, not because it wanted one there but because it had no choice.

## Pakistan: Reform in the Interim

While South Africa constitutes a fairly clear-cut case of institutional insulation in the wake of a transition from authoritarian rule, a more complicated story unfolds in the case of Pakistan.

Since its inception in 1948, Pakistan's postcolonial state was characterized by periodic bouts of democratic rule followed by sustained periods of military intervention (Burki and Baxter 1991; Dharamdasani 1994; Shafqat 1997). When military rule officially came to an end in 1985, the military

4. It is true that capital flight had provoked some decline in the country's external accounts throughout the 1980s, opening up the possibility that the reform was motivated by the need for international credibility. But such behavior by investors was primarily caused by domestic political instability and the international embargo against apartheid, rather than by some overriding failure on the part of the government to demonstrate its economic credentials (Smit and Mocke 1991, 114).

retained a strong say in politics through two primary avenues. First, it oversaw the creation of the so-called partie military, an informal aggregation of interest groups that would attempt to co-opt the leadership of Pakistan's political parties to protect the military's hegemony and advocate its interests (Shafqat 1997, 191). This strategy was targeted specifically at weakening the hand of the Pakistani People's Party (PPP), whose mass-based mobilization in the early 1970s under then prime minister Zulfikar Ali Bhutto was seen as a direct threat to the interests of the military, business, and the bureaucracy (Waseem 1992, 619). Second, the military also sought to weaken the formal powers of elected representatives through the notorious Eighth Amendment to the Constitution (Waseem 1992). This amendment not only empowered the president to dissolve elected assemblies but also removed the government's ability to appoint top military officials and high court judges.[5] In short, military elites assented to a transition to democracy, but it was only to a protected form of parliamentary rule in which the army was "generally accepted as the final arbiter in any political conflict" (Waseem 1994, 25).

Concurrent with changes in Pakistan's political environment in the mid-1980s were ongoing changes to its economic model. By the late 1980s, years of undisciplined spending by both military- and party-led governments had created a fiscal and monetary crisis marked by high inflation, soaring external debts, and plummeting international reserves (Shafqat 1997, 208–10). In the wake of the failed economic policies of PPP prime minister Benazhir Bhutto (1988–90), incoming prime minister Nawaz Sharif implemented an economic reform package emphasizing privatization, deregulation, and currency reform (Shafqat 1997, 227–47; Reza Nasr 1992, 530–37). Handpicked and groomed by the military as part of their "partie military" strategy, Sharif was the head of the Pakistan Muslim League (PML) party representing new business and industrial elites (SAARC-NGO 1995, 101–2).

But while Sharif's liberalization measures were carried out more swiftly and systematically than those of the Bhutto regime, persistent quarrels with the president, ongoing political unrest, and allegations of corruption led to a military shutdown of the Sharif government in April 1993 (Waseem 1994). In his place, a little known technocrat named Moeen Qureshi who had spent the bulk of his career at the World Bank was named caretaker prime minister pending elections in October. During his three-month stint in power,

5. The 1985 Constitution created a parliamentary system of government with a president (head of state) and a prime minister (head of government). Under this system, the president was elected through an electoral college consisting of members of the Senate and national assembly and members of the provincial assemblies. The prime minister was appointed by the president from among the members of the national assembly.

Qureshi dramatically accelerated the liberalization program begun under Sharif, enacting—among other things—an ordinance to increase the autonomy of the central bank (Waseem 1994, 58–74).[6]

While Pakistan's State National Bank (SNB) had once commanded a great deal of independent influence over monetary policy, over the course of the 1970s and 1980s it had gradually come to serve the interests of the government of the day (Meenai 1984, 162–72). This behavioral lack of autonomy was reinforced in the provisions of the law itself: all central bank governors were appointed for five-year renewable terms; there were no limitations on central bank lending to the executive; and the government had the right to override the central bank on important policy decisions (Mahmood and Shaukat 1995, 177–223). The 1993 reform constituted an abrupt about-face in this state of affairs. Among other things, it made all governor terms nonrenewable, allowed the central bank to recruit staff without federal government clearance, gave the bank new power to control the money supply and to regulate commercial banks, and set limits on the amount of credit that could be extended to the government.[7]

The first question to ask, then, is why the Pakistani government chose to suddenly create a substantially autonomous central bank in 1993, knowing that it would only be in power for three months? The conventional wisdom holds that Qureshi was merely buckling to pressures from international financial institutions, who capitalized upon his long-standing ties to Washington to pressure him to undertake a set of reforms in line with the so-called Washington Consensus (Singh 1994, 206–8).[8] Although we cannot deny that the Pakistani economy was highly vulnerable to the dictates of the international financial community in the early 1990s, a variety of factors cast doubt upon the notion that this was the exclusive motivation at work.

To begin with, while both the World Bank and IMF had outlined a series of "desirable" policy reforms for Pakistan in the early 1990s, they had only set out broad-gauged targets and left the specifics up to individual governments to determine (Shafqat 1997, 249). While a host of economic liberalization measures might have been consistent with these prescriptions, there was no reason to expect that central bank autonomy would necessarily form part of them. Second, if these international considerations were so predominant, then one must also question why the reform was not adopted earlier. The

6. See "Caretakers' Cost-Cutting Campaign: Tribal Confrontation with Bureaucrats," *Pakistan and Gulf Economist,* August 14–20, 1993; "Counting the Costs: The Prime Minister's Economic Package," *Pakistan and Gulf Economist,* August 28–September 3, 1993.

7. See "Legal Autonomy for State Bank: Fixing Limits of Budgetary Support to Government," *Pakistan and Gulf Economist,* October 23–29, 1993, 21–23.

8. See also "Mixed Reaction to Economic Package: Caretakers said to Exceed Mandate," *Pakistan and Gulf Economist,* August 28–September 3, 1993, 12.

World Bank and the IMF had been pressuring successive Pakistani governments to reform their economies since as far back as 1987.[9] More to the point, a former NBP vice-governor had been advocating central bank autonomy as a means of fighting the country's perennial budget deficits since the early 1980s (Meenai 1984, 162–66). In light of such preexisting pressures, and especially given what would appear to be the army's instrumental role in Qureshi's selection (Waseem 1994, 54), the more relevant question would thus seem to be why the military viewed 1993 as a propitious moment for central bank reform.[10]

Here, I would argue that a host of domestic political factors came into play, in particular the fact that the military foresaw the inevitability of democratization in Pakistan and what this might mean for its continued ability to protect its interests. What were those interests? The Pakistani military had always maximized political stability above all else, defining this as a desire to avoid "mass politics" (Waseem 1992, 619). But it had also always been decidedly pro-business, a position stemming from its strong ties to Pakistan's financial-industrial groups (Shafqat 1997, 34–37, 118, 201–8). While it was not clear in mid-1993 who was likely to win the scheduled elections, one of two main contenders was Benazhir Bhutto, whose mass-based PPP had long been viewed as the principal threat on both of these fronts (Waseem 1992, 619).

While Bhutto had distanced herself considerably from her father's socialist legacy, she continued to inspire fear among military and business elites alike, who were wary of what she might do to the economy once elected.[11] Perhaps these fears were best expressed by the interim central bank governor himself, who declared that "the major reason for wanting to increase the autonomy of the bank . . . has been the abnormal monetary expansion of the past three or four years," pointing specifically to rampant inflation under the PPP.[12] As one business editorial noted at the time, "the ordinance to increase the autonomy of the SBP . . . is no doubt an attempt . . . to make doubly sure that, on top of the conditionality package, as much economic power as possible is devolved away from the politicians."[13]

9. See "The New Prime Minister's Financial Handcuffs," *Pakistan and Gulf Economist*, September 11–17, 1993, 34.

10. Technically speaking, Qureshi was chosen through an army-sponsored negotiation between outgoing prime minister Sharif and PPP opposition leader Benazir Bhutto. But while the military did not have any overt constitutional role in such deliberations, it had long been generally accepted in Pakistan that the military was the key player in the formation and dismissal of governments (Waseem 1992, 630).

11. See "Benazir's Primary Concern: Smooth Functioning of the Democratic Process," *Pakistan and Gulf Economist*, October 23–29, 1993, 8.

12. See "SBP Governor Sets Targets for Himself," *Pakistan and Gulf Economist*, August 7–13, 1993, 50–51.

13. See "New Prime Minister's Financial Handcuffs," 56.

In light of its pervasive influence over the country's democratic institutions, the Pakistani military traditionally had not needed to worry very much about the threat of policy change implied by one given political administration or another. But a variety of factors in late 1993 combined to suggest that such controls might no longer be as effective as they once had been. On the one hand, it was becoming increasingly apparent that the "partie military" strategy was not working very well. While Sharif's 1990 victory had originally been seen as a triumph on this front, Sharif quickly distanced himself from the army once in office, which suggested that even handpicked politicians could not be trusted to carry out the military's interests (Waseem 1992, 630). On the other hand, growing domestic pressures for free and fair elections, changing attitudes within the military itself (Waseem 1992, 634), and explicit threats of U.S. economic sanctions (Waseem 1994, 56) made it increasingly difficult to imagine a future that would not be marked by greater democratic freedoms. In light of the PPP's vow to repeal the Eighth Amendment (SSARC-NGO 1995, 99), the military knew that if it was going to move to insulate business interests, this would have to occur before the 1993 elections took place.[14]

A few months after the Pakistani central bank ordinance went into effect, the incoming Bhutto administration amended it to provide the government with one-time authority to nominate the central bank board of directors with a three-year renewable term.[15] While this manifest weakening of the SBP's autonomy would seem to fly in the face of the institutional persistence logic offered in this book, there are a number of mitigating factors to be considered. First, as I point out in chapter 3, there are no guarantees that the authoritarians' institutional creations will necessarily "stick." Rather, they do the best that they can. At least at the time when the law was enacted, the Qureshi government seemed fairly confident about its durability. As one high-ranking government official noted, "given that the reform package is

14. It is true that the army indirectly aided Bhutto's victory in the 1993 elections by helping to depose Nawaz Sharif. This outcome is generally attributed to a temporary armistice between the PPP and the military, during which time Bhutto deliberately sought to provide assurances to the military that she was no longer a threat to its interests (Singh 1994, 210). This does not, however, remove the uncertainty surrounding her policy choices noted earlier. Rather, the army's shifting loyalties would seem to suggest that it had come to realize that it could not trust any politicians to carry out its will. Under such circumstances, its best strategy was to play the two parties off one another, thereby maintaining a divided parliament and precluding the two-thirds majority necessary to repeal the Eighth Amendment. (In fact, the Eighth Amendment was used for the last time to oust Bhutto in November 1996 and was definitively repealed in late 1997.)

15. See "A Minor Rumpus over SBP's Powers," *Pakistan and Gulf Economist,* January 15–21, 1994.

largely backed by the World Bank, the IMF, and the Pakistan Army, there is a high probability that a new elected government will retain [it]."[16] Second, when Bhutto was subsequently criticized for having placed the country's economic credibility in jeopardy, she was quick to emphasize that despite other changes, the bank retained the important power to limit credit to the federal and provincial governments (Maxfield 1997, 66). Her actions thus effectively amounted to a partial—not a full—repeal of the legislation. Finally, it is worth noting that these were only one-time changes, as opposed to a permanent rescinding of the ordinance.

However one chooses to slice it, there is no question that the existence of the central bank ordinance alone was not sufficient to prevent some ex post tampering by subsequent Pakistani administrations. Therefore the 1993 Pakistan central bank reform does not fit the argument advanced in this book with the same precision as other cases we have seen. But even with its multiple complications and intrigues, it is still a case where the timing of the central bank reform cannot be divorced from domestic political events and, in particular, the defensive motivations of a military regime under siege.

## South Korea: Failed Reform

The South Korean case provides a window into one variant of the null case contemplated in this book: one where, despite a compelling threat of political change, incumbent authoritarian leaders lack the corresponding economic incentives to undertake central bank reform.

The story of South Korea's transition to democracy really begins in the late 1970s, when an economic crisis of massive proportions rocked the political stability of the military-backed Democratic Justice Party (DJP), which had ruled the country since the early 1960s (Haggard 1994). Not only did the decline in exports, devaluation, and attendant inflation unleash political unrest within the country's working class and middle class, it also galvanized the country's fledgling opposition political parties (Sohn 1989). While the regime was able to survive the crisis by temporarily imposing martial law, the economic instability of the early 1980s had two important consequences. First, the government was forced to embark on a program of stabilization and trade reform that imposed heavy costs on the working class (Y. H. Kim 1994; Woo-Cummings 1997). Second, in taking steps to reform the country's con-

16. See "Counting the Costs," 7; and "Economic Reforms: The Caretakers' Legacy: Will the Bhutto Government Toe the Line?" *Pakistan and Gulf Economist,* October 23–29, 1993, 11.

stitution to allow for the indirect election of the president, the government inadvertently established a focal point for subsequent opposition efforts to secure direct election of the president (Haggard and Kaufman 1995, 94).[17]

But while the DJP was thus able to reassert its control over the political system in the aftermath of the 1980 crisis, it became increasingly apparent that this was not a stable equilibrium. Over time, popular resentment of semimilitary rule, delayed constitutional reform, and the perceived toll of adjustment on workers and the less developed segments of the economy combined to provide newfound momentum for opposition to authoritarian rule (Lee 1990; Han and Park 1993; Kong 1997). Above all, however, the prodemocracy movement constituted a decided effort to break up the cozy relationship that existed between the South Korean government and large industrial conglomerates (*Chaebol*) (Kong 1997, 100). For despite the decidedly export-oriented nature of the Korean development strategy, the state had played a considerable role in guiding the nature and pace of economic development within it (Choi 1993; Haggard and Collins 1994; Woo-Cummings 1997). A strategic interdependence had thus emerged over time between business and government, wherein the government used credit policy to induce big business to invest in selected sectors of the economy in exchange for its political support (Choi 1993, 38–39; Cho 1990, 237).

Popular dissatisfaction stemming from these multiple grievances was brought home in the legislative elections of 1985. While ostensibly held to shore up legitimacy for the DJP, they instead resulted in a stunning upset in which the ruling party won but 35 percent of the vote, despite electoral and campaign laws systematically biased in its favor (Haggard and Collins 1994, 93).[18] Although the DJP was able to maintain a slim legislative majority, its continued refusal to bow to popular demands for direct presidential elections provoked an explosion of political protests, street demonstrations, and clashes with the government, particularly by student and labor groups. While the government initially responded with repression, growing divides within its own ranks together with overt pressures from foreign governments ultimately led DJP presidential candidate Roh Tae-Woo to call for direct elections of the president (Haggard and Kaufman 1995, 93–95). Although a divided opposition enabled the DJP to retain the presidency in 1987, Roh's

17. Prior to 1980, the president was recruited from military institutions of the state (Lee 1995, 39).

18. Until the late 1980s, the electoral system in South Korea was based on a combination of two member districts and a national list that heavily favored the ruling party. The two-member district allowed the government to capture two seats in rural conservative districts where it had majority support and a second seat in urban centers where a divided opposition was represented by a single list. In addition, district boundaries were also drawn to favor conservative and rural voters (Haggard and Kaufman 1995, 123, 233).

pledge to undertake political and constitutional reform was widely seen as the beginning of a protracted transition to democracy that would culminate in 1993 with the election of Korea's first civilian president since 1961 (Kong 1997).

In the wake of the DJP's increasingly tenuous hold on power, incumbent elites were forced to enter into negotiations with a variety of opposition forces in late 1987 to reform the South Korean Constitution.[19] While Roh engaged in a greater degree of bargaining than is typical of most "top down" transitions, the resultant Constitution was nonetheless biased strongly in favor of the interests of ruling elites (Haggard and Kaufman 1995, 96). Not surprisingly, the government focused on protecting its three pillars of support: safeguarding its rural support base, ensuring the institutional integrity of the military, and limiting labor's ability to threaten capital. Thus, for example, electoral laws that favored conservative rural voters based on gerrymandered districts and proportional representation were retained (Haggard and Kaufman 1995, 96, 119).[20] The military was also subjected to very little civilian oversight, enabling it to engage in extensive civilian surveillance and the occasional use of force (Haggard and Kaufman 1995, 114). Finally, broad restrictions on labor militancy allowed the government to limit the formation of competing unions, restrict the role of third parties in resolving labor disputes, and curtail the unions' ability to strike (Haggard and Kaufman 1995, 123).

But even while the regime took a series of steps to strengthen executive control over economic policy (Haggard and Kaufman 1995, 97),[21] the government made no effort to augment the autonomy of the central bank. This is noteworthy, given that throughout the transition, a wide-ranging debate was unfolding simultaneously over whether or not to grant independence to the Korean central bank (Maxfield 1997, 115–19). The original 1950 Bank of Korea Act had actually delegated a fair amount of authority to the bank's seven-member Monetary Board (Ro 1994; Soon 1994). But this autonomy quickly evaporated following the military coup of 1962. In the first round of

19. At this time, there were essentially three main opposition parties: the center-left Peace and Democracy Party led by Kim Dae Jung, the centrist Reunification and Democracy Party of King Young Sam, and the conservative New Democratic Republic Party of Kim Jon Pil. The latter two parties would subsequently form a conservative alliance with the ruling DJP in 1990 under the banner of the Democratic Liberal Party.

20. In the course of these negotiations, the two-member district was replaced by a single-member district, and the share of the total number of seats allocated to the national list was reduced from one-third to one-quarter—both of which responded to opposition party demands. At the time, the government agreed to single-member districts only because it thought that these would divide the opposition, although they proved ultimately to be wrong on this point (Haggard and Kaufman 1995, 96).

21. Note, for example, that while the national assembly could debate an existing budget bill, it had no power to raise expenditures or to authorize changes.

revisions, the number of board members was increased to nine, and the governor himself was appointed by the minister of finance, who in turn presided over the seven remaining members, each of whom represented a distinct sectoral portfolio (Ro 1994; P. J. Kim 1994). In subsequent amendments to the act, the minister of finance was given veto power over all Monetary Board decisions, including the ability to oversee Bank of Korea bookkeeping (Maxfield 1997, 113). Thereafter, while the Bank of Korea's primary duty was to regulate the money supply, this effectively translated into making sure that seignorage revenues were channeled into low-interest loans in keeping with the government's overall industrialization policy (Soon 1994, 141; Woo-Cummings 1997, 62; Maxfield 1994, 561).

By 1987, and consistent with the broader pro-democracy rhetoric at the time, a group of Bank of Korea employees began to champion the cause of an autonomous central bank as a means of severing the historic link between government and big business. While initially more of a populist rebellion in the Bank of Korea's rank and file, the initiative gradually gained the support of its board of directors. Over the course of the next two years, the Ministry of Finance and Bank of Korea heatedly debated issues such as the appropriate level of executive branch veto power over monetary policy and jurisdictional authority for bank regulation (Maxfield 1997, 116) The reform initially received the support of two out of three of the country's opposition political parties, including the center-left Peace and Democracy Party, which viewed autonomy as enhancing checks on centralized political control (Maxfield 1997, 117).[22] But while Roh promised that securing the Bank of Korea's independence would be a priority during his first term, he ultimately used back-door channels to convince both the central bank and the political opposition to back the Finance Ministry's position (Maxfield 1997, 117–18). At the end of the day, authority over monetary policy and financial supervision continued to reside with the Ministry of Finance, and a constitutional change in the central bank's authority was deemed unnecessary (Ro 1994, 147).

In light of the militant strike activity and anti-business rhetoric that characterized South Korea's process of democratization, it is worth asking why the Korean government refused to support the central bank autonomy initiative of 1987–88. While Maxfield argues that government's disinterest can be explained by its lack of a need to shore up credibility with foreign capital (Maxfield 1997, 119), I would argue that a more complete explanation lies in its economic policy preferences and, in particular, the nature of its domestic constituency base. Because of their highly diversified presence within a variety of sectors in the economy, the number of Chaebol-owned firms benefiting

22. The ruling DJP as well as the more conservative New Democratic Republican Party opposed the initiative.

from preferential credit by the end of the 1980s had grown immense (Choi 1993, 39). The government could ill afford to undertake any measure—such as the elimination of credit subsidies—that would strike at the very heart of its political support base (Cho 1990, 237). Even modest attempts at financial liberalization in the 1980s had been limited by business resistance to any restrictions on its continued access to cheap credit (Choi 1993; Haggard and Collins 1994; Woo-Cummings 1997). While it is true that the Roh government did take some symbolic measures to reduce Chaebol domination soon after taking office (Soon 1994), its policies remained decidedly pro-business overall, reflected in its increasingly pro-management stance with respect to labor disputes (Haggard and Kaufman 1995, 232, 238–39).

Finally, a word is also in order on the democrats in this tale. If the Korean government itself lacked a compelling policy interest in establishing an autonomous central bank, such preferences were largely mirrored in its political opponents. Even while the democratization movement was accompanied by a huge upsurge in labor strikes and protests, much of the middle and working classes saw themselves as beneficiaries of import substitution industrialization (ISI) (Haggard and Kaufman 1995, 96, 232). This inherent conservatism in the electorate was reflected in the fact that despite the abundance of opposition parties at the moment of the transition, there was no real programmatic alternative to advocating anything other than the status quo (Kong 1997, 100; Haggard and Kaufman 1995, 230). Even the nominally center-left PDP—which had initially supported the autonomy initiative on purely political grounds—was in fact much more regionally based than ideologically based, and its own rhetoric grew increasingly conservative as the 1990s wore on (Haggard and Kaufman 1995, 138). In short, and in keeping with our idea of the intensity of threat, the outgoing authoritarians had little to fear where major issues of economic policy were concerned.

The South Korean case of nonreform thus corresponds quite closely to our ex ante expectations about the likelihood of central bank autonomy in the transition from authoritarian rule. Where ruling elites are backed by business groups with more decidedly interventionist policy preferences, the demand for central bank reform is not likely to surface. To put it simply, the short-lived movement for central bank reform in South Korea never really got off the ground because it was in no one's interest for it to do so.

## Conclusion

This chapter can do no more than establish the plausibility of the argument within the countries at hand. More research is needed to explore the particular nuances of each case. But through this brief foray into comparative work,

I hope to have accomplished two important tasks. First, to demonstrate that there have been a number of significant cases in recent years where the insulation logic of central bank reform advanced in this book seems to have some applicability. Second, to establish a general theoretical baseline upon which future scholars interested in understanding the politics of central bank reform might draw.

In this regard, it is worth speculating upon how one might appropriate the basic theoretical framework developed here and apply it to a democratic political context. One interesting implication of the argument in this regard has to do with the timing of bureaucratic reform. One of the central claims underpinning this book's logic is that because insulation is costly, authoritarian governments ought to wait until it is absolutely clear that they will need to step down from power before delegating authority to an independent agency. The question is how such incentives might vary once we introduce different types of democracies.

I would submit that, like their authoritarian counterparts, reform-minded politicians in political systems with a fixed term in office—such as all presidential democracies—ought to wait until the last possible instant before seeking to entrench their interests. After all, if they attempt to insulate their policy preferences too soon before leaving power, it is only they who stand to lose, as they are the ones who will suffer the related slippage effects, loss of flexibility, and the like. It therefore makes sense for them to delay assuming such costs as long as possible and thus to insulate only at the very end of their terms in office when they can pass these costs along to their successors.

The same is not true for many parliamentary regimes. Because the legislature in such a system is effectively free to fire the prime minister at a moment's notice, reform-minded politicians must always be on guard against the possibility that they may be unexpectedly ousted from power. This is especially true in multiparty parliamentary systems, which—because of the number of and ideological distances between government partners—are prone to votes of no confidence at the slightest provocation. Because the coalitions in such governments tend to be so fragile, a "carpe diem" mentality is thus likely to prevail among reformers, on the principle that if they do not act quickly, they may lose the opportunity for good.

The key factor determining the timing of insulation across different democratic political systems, then, would seem to be the time horizons of elected officials within them. In those systems where incumbent elites can predict with close to 100 percent certainty when they are likely to leave office, they are unlikely to assume the costs of insulation until the very last minute. In those political environments in which one has good reason to expect that one's hold on power may be curtailed inopportunely, governments are much more likely to be proactive early on. As a general rule, then, the more unstable a government's time horizons, the sooner we are likely to see governments taking measures to reform their bureaucracies (Boylan 2000).

Institutional nuances of this sort are well worth exploring in more detail, and they should also be tested across a wider set of cases. For present purposes, however, I am less concerned with providing definitive answers to such questions than with demonstrating the extent to which the basic contours of the argument can travel across a variety of different institutional contexts. I leave it to future research to probe these interesting—and, as yet, largely unexamined—aspects of comparative institutional design.

PART 3

# Conclusions

CHAPTER 9

# Democratic Consolidation and Institutional Theory

## Broadening the Debate

This book has sought to elucidate the pivotal role of institutional insulation in countries undergoing the transition from authoritarian rule. I have argued that once they know the writing is on the wall, authoritarian governments on the brink of losing power give democracy away with one hand while taking it back with the other.

Specifically, where exiting elites fear the populism that may be endemic to new democracies and know that a change of regime is imminent, they attempt to make monetary policy resilient to the distributional pressures that accompany democracy by creating an autonomous central bank. To the extent that they place themselves in charge of this institution, they in turn carve out a niche of power in what is arguably one of the most important public-policy-making bodies in the developing world. And incoming democratic governments have no choice but to accept this institutional inheritance, thereby removing a key aspect of economic decision making from their control.

To analyze the plausibility of this argument, this study examined two transitional democracies where central bank reforms took place—Chile (1989) and Mexico (1993). While both reforms reflected an attempt by authoritarian elites to deflect the policy uncertainty embedded in democratic rule, the cases differed noticeably in the amount of autonomy afforded the central bank. Through a paired comparison in which the need for external credibility and the expected policy distance between the authoritarians and the democrats were held constant, I showed how variation in the proximity of the democratic threat explained the observed difference in outcome (see table 9.1).

We began by looking at the strong case of transitional insulation: the Chilean central bank reform of 1989. General Pinochet's dramatic loss in the 1988 plebiscite was a devastating blow for Chile's conservative authoritarian regime. Not only did the victorious Concertación coalition pose a programmatic challenge to the authoritarians' neoliberal policy agenda, but these leaders also knew that their hold on power was finite. In order to fend off this pronounced and imminent threat, they crystallized their preferences for low inflation in a highly autonomous central bank.

We then turned our attention to a middle-range case: the Mexican central bank reform of 1993. Unlike in Chile, where the definitive knowledge of Pinochet's political fate prompted an all-out insulation offensive, the democratic threat facing Mexico's technocratic elite was considerably more tenuous. Although internal party splits and the growing strength of the opposition could no longer be ignored, the momentum for regime change had yet to definitively jeopardize Salinas's market-oriented agenda. While anticipation of an eventual change of rule thus mandated some sort of institutional response, Mexico's authoritarians did not need to create a fully autonomous central bank—at least not yet.

What this comparison ultimately underscores is the difference between a reform undertaken in the wake of a transition to democracy and one carried out under a liberalizing authoritarian regime. Whereas the former environment offers incentives to create as autonomous an institution as possible, the latter provides incentives to leave some leeway in institutional design. By comparing these two instances of central bank autonomy, this study thus illuminates the broader relationship between democratization and institutional change set out in the introduction to this book. Chapter eight confirmed this general relationship across a number of additional cases and also suggested how the basic framework might be extended to accommodate a variety of democratic political settings.

This chapter further addresses the generalizability of the argument at hand and assesses its ramifications for the study of democratization and institutional theory. The first section ("Generalizing the Argument: Other Insulation Strategies") speculates as to the possibilities for applying the logic to

**TABLE 9.1. Chile versus Mexico**

| | Chile | Mexico |
|---|---|---|
| Intensity of threat | Strong<br>market-oriented regime<br>center-left future | Strong<br>market-oriented regime<br>populist threats:<br>PRI/PRD/small business |
| Proximity of threat | Imminent<br>loss in plebiscite<br>united opposition | Distant<br>PRI dominant<br>divided opposition |
| Degree of autonomy | Full<br>CB cannot lend to government<br>full policy discretion<br>10-year terms (president=5 years)<br>price stability/stable payments system | Partial<br>CB can lend to government<br>moderate policy discretion<br>8-year terms (president=6 years)<br>price stability/stable payments system |

insulation strategies beyond central bank reform. The second section ("Insulated Transitions: Prospects for Democratic Consolidation") examines the consequences of these authoritarian institutional legacies for the process of democratic consolidation. The third section ("Implications for the Study of Institutional Design"), as its title indicates, contains a brief discussion of the argument's implications for the study of institutional design. I conclude by mapping out future avenues for research.

## Generalizing the Argument: Other Insulation Strategies

### The Empirical Universe

In the previous chapter, we examined the extent to which the argument presented in this book can be used to explain cases of central bank reform across other institutional contexts. A second way to extend the model at hand is to explore its application to other institutional forms. In the introductory chapter, I noted that central bank autonomy is but one of several institutional mechanisms through which outgoing authoritarian elites attempt to protect themselves against the onset of democracy. They also frequently employ a host of other electoral, constitutional, and military arrangements in order to tie the hands of their successors. In what follows, I elaborate on some of these other insulation strategies to flesh out the relevant empirical universe. This is followed by an assessment of the argument's ability to speak to these additional institutional forms.

One way that exiting authoritarian elites attempt to entrench their preferences before leaving power is by creating pockets of impunity for certain actors deeply identified with authoritarian rule. In Latin America and Africa, this actor is often the military. This protection assumes a number of different forms. Above all, military regimes seek to prevent retribution. Perhaps more consistently than any single other posttransition institutional guarantee, amnesty clauses are introduced that preclude former rulers of military regimes from being tried for human rights abuses carried out under military rule. Since 1978 and with the exception of Argentina and isolated instances in Chile, El Salvador, and Bolivia, the Latin American military involved in coups and subsequent human rights abuses have all been amnestied (Loveman 1998, 128).

In turn, military regimes also seek to make sure that the armed forces remain on solid financial footing. In the Chilean transition, for example, they automatically received 10 percent of the income from state copper sales, the nation's number one export. In Brazil, the military was given autonomous control over various defense sector industries, such as informatics and telecommunication, in order to afford it a privileged position in areas of technological development. Military regimes also frequently set up mechanisms that allow for their representation in top policy-making bodies and/or shield military officials from dismissal or oversight. In Portugal, Turkey, Chile, and Brazil, exiting elites created powerful military-dominated institutions to control national security. In Chile, the chief executive was given no power over the promotion or dismissal of high-ranking military officials but was instead forced to defer to a series of nonelected bodies on such matters. More generally, most Latin American constitutions in the 1990s continue to afford the armed forces broad scope to impose what is known as a "state of exception." This can be used to justify a variety of different forms of intervention in civilian affairs ranging from suspending ordinary rights and liberties, to delegating extraordinary powers to the president, to—in the ultimate instance—staging a coup (Loveman 1998, 134–39). By institutionalizing this array of different privileges for the military, the scope of authority afforded elected officials in new democracies is greatly reduced.

Moving away from the strictly military realm, another vehicle through which authoritarian elites seek to preserve their interests is by biasing the political arena for or against certain groups. At the extreme, the authoritarians may bar certain actors from even entering politics, such as political parties representing allegedly extremist elements. In both Turkey and South Korea, for example, legal restrictions were placed on labor militancy and political dissidence, thereby limiting contestation over certain crucial social policy issues. Voter registration procedures can also be created that discourage widespread popular participation, as occurred in Brazil. Or the authoritarians might appoint certain individuals to an otherwise elected post, as Pinochet did when he personally named nine of the country's forty-seven senators, or when the outgoing regime in Brazil stipulated that six out of twenty-two members of the cabinet would be uniformed officers.

In a similar vein, electoral rules can also be designed to disproportionately advantage certain partisan interests over others. The Communist Party in Poland sought and obtained the right to control 65 percent of all seats in the lower house of parliament before leaving power. Outgoing military officials in Turkey also set electoral thresholds that helped the conservative Motherland Party gain large legislative majorities under democratic rule. In a slightly different twist on this theme, successor governments in Nigeria were obliged to include a certain set of (neoliberal) policies in their programmatic agendas when running for office. More generally, Geddes (1995) has noted how outgoing elites in several Eastern European countries initially favored strong presidencies and majoritarian legislatures as a means of bolstering the influence of Communist Party leaders in the posttransition polities. In South Africa, in contrast, proportional representation was set up to favor the white minority political parties following the end of apartheid rule.

A third strategy available to exiting authoritarian elites seeking to leave their imprint on democratic rule is to remove certain governmental arenas from the vagaries of democratic politics. We have already noted a variety of cases where central bank autonomy served this purpose. To the extent that the supreme court can be appointed by the outgoing regime and given expanded powers, it offers a similarly potent form of policy insulation in this regard. Another example comes from the transitions in Chile, Thailand, and South Korea, where chief executives were empowered to establish spending ceilings that could not be raised by the legislature (cf. Baldez and Carey forthcoming). At other times, institutions may be used to enfranchise certain societal interests within the new regime. Nicaragua's Sandanistas, for example, were able to successfully institutionalize the gains from land reform before ceding office in 1990.

Finally, authoritarian regimes can also employ the power of appointment to entrench their preferred policies within the new democracy. In the Chilean case, the authoritarians not only appointed all but 16 of the country's 325 mayors but also made it legally impossible for the new government to appoint all but the top level of incoming state officials (Valenzuela 1992, 66). Job guarantees were similarly provided for civil servants affiliated with the outgoing (white) National Party in South Africa. In Brazil, traditional political elites allied with the military regime commandeered certain key ministries and administrative jobs at the federal and state levels that afforded them extensive control over state patronage (Hagopian 1990, 1996). In Poland, exiting elites ensured that bureaucracies in charge of external defense and internal order would remain in Communist hands throughout the first term of democratic rule. More generally, former nomenklatura in Eastern Europe and the former Soviet Union were able to secure fairly widespread control over the management and administration of various state-owned enterprises to assure themselves a dominant position in the emerging capitalist economy (Stark 1990).

Through all of these institutional tactics, the authoritarians seek to guarantee the survival of their policies long after they leave office. If they, themselves, cannot remain in power, both their people and their programmatic agendas will endure.

## A Note on Institutional Persistence

In principle, there should be no problem in applying the basic argument about institutional choice developed in this book to a wider set of insulation strategies. As noted in chapter 3, both the intensity of threat and the proximity of threat are meant to serve as general conditions under which authoritarian elites will seek to entrench their interests. While these two dimensions of threat might require some operational modifications when applied to different institutional forms, there is no reason to believe that the expected policy distance and the timing of democratization will cease to be relevant factors. Rather, as Moe and Caldwell (1994, 176) note, "the basic forces at work are generic."

Where one might have greater cause to challenge the broader applicability of the model at hand is on the question of institutional persistence and, more specifically, the extent to which we should expect all authoritarian enclaves to be equally "sticky." This is less of an issue for central bank reform, where the market-induced constraint privileged in this study should serve as a fairly powerful guarantee of institutional stability. That said, one could reasonably argue that biased electoral rules and/or bureaucratic appointment strategies might be more easily overturned in a newly democratic setting. It is certainly the case that not all of the examples furnished in the previous pages managed to survive the onset of democratic rule.

The transitions literature has been fairly vague on the topic of institutional persistence to date. Earlier scholarship assumed that all enclaves were the product of explicit negotiations between the outgoing and incoming democratic regimes and were thus necessarily self-enforcing (O'Donnell and Schmitter 1986; Hagopian 1990; Karl 1990). While exactly what rendered such agreements credible was not always fully spelled out, it presumably hinged on the exiting regime's ability to threaten a return to authoritarian rule (cf. Valenzuela 1992). Although a number of authors have subsequently cautioned against assuming that such bargains necessarily endure forever (e.g., Przeworski 1992; Haggard and Kaufman 1995; Geddes 1998), few have actually speculated as to the precise conditions that might affect their endurance.

An important exception in this regard is Hunter (1997), who argues that electoral incentives facing democratic politicians in Latin America to redistribute public resources and maintain greater autonomy over policy-making may push these leaders toward reducing the military's power over time. While an important corrective to the earlier literature, Hunter's argument does not really lend itself to generalizable propositions that could be further tested across a larger set of cases. To begin with, the two conditions she identifies as explaining when democratic governments will be willing to "cross" the military are very loosely defined.[1] More precise inferences are also rendered difficult by the fact that she includes a wide array of different insu-

1. The first of these, which has to do with the relative fluidity of institutional rules, is overly general. In the case she focuses on most closely (Brazil), it hinges on the relative weak-

lation strategies under the general heading "military prerogatives," ranging from military representation in policy-making bodies to electoral rules to constitutional reform, which in turn do not always covary. Finally, because she focuses exclusively on military regimes, it is not clear how much we can extrapolate from her data about a broader range of (nonmilitary) transitions.

In short, Hunter is on the right track, but her explanation as to those factors that facilitate the staying power of authoritarian institutional legacies requires further refinement. In my opinion, future analysis should attempt to parcel out insulation strategies along more narrowly defined lines of inquiry such as a particular feature of the electoral system or a specific institution such as the supreme court, as opposed to attempting to generalize about the catchall category "military prerogatives." In order to make more systematic claims, one could then evaluate the extent to which institutional entrenchment strategies vary by country, by issue area, or by some core feature of the institutional environment such as the number of veto players.

It is also possible that different institutions will be associated with different persistence rationales. Toward the end of chapter 3, I enumerated a variety of domestic political factors that might cause autonomous central banks to remain under democratic rule. To reiterate, I noted the power of vested interests, the existence of supramajority rules, respect for the rule of law, veto gates, the role of shared expectations, and path dependence. Following this line of reasoning, one might hypothesize, for example, that the maintenance of biased electoral laws hinges on the presence of supramajority rules, while military veto powers are more likely to depend on the existence of powerful domestic constituencies. At the very least, the two countries contemplated in detail within this study—Chile and Mexico—could serve as an excellent basis upon which to begin testing such propositions in a controlled environment.

Understanding exactly how all of this works would be an important contribution to the transitions literature. It is entirely possible that once we move beyond the credibility-based explanation that I privilege in the case of central banks, explaining institutional persistence becomes more tenuous. Alternatively, it may also be the case that the earlier literature was not necessarily wrong in positing the longevity of these authoritarian enclaves but perhaps

ness of the party system, although she alludes to a host of other institutional variables that might conceivably fall under this rubric (e.g., presidential versus parliamentary rule, internal party procedures, etc.). Her second variable—which has to do with the legitimacy of the military to intervene in politics—is arguably less a variable than it is a parameter in the sense that the armed forces' ability to exert influence over democracy has uniformly diminished in the current era. These conceptual problems are compounded by the fact the declining power of the military in the three additional cases she examines does not seem to depend on the presence/absence of these two variables but rather on broader power alignments and the general effectiveness of civilian governments.

underspecified with respect to the precise mechanisms and the conditions under which these apply. This is ultimately an empirical question and one that cannot be resolved without further investigation.

## Insulated Transitions: Prospects for Democratic Consolidation

In sum, there exist a myriad of mechanisms through which authoritarian regimes may seek to protect their interests once they know that they are losing power. How the authoritarians choose to do this will depend upon what arenas of policy they care about most and what institutional forms of protection are most readily available to them. The bulk of this book has been devoted to the motive, design, and implementation of these insulated structures. In conclusion it is worth touching on some of the implications they may have for the new democracies of the third world.

### Insulated Institutions: Why All the Fuss?

One set of issues that inevitably arises in this regard concerns how we are to distinguish the institutional insulation described in this book from "normal" forms of delegated authority found in established democracies.[2] After all, many polities remove specific policy domains from the hands of elected officials without marring their democratic credentials. The very essence of consociational democracies, for example, is to limit the influence of electoral majorities in areas of policy that are of particular concern to minorities (Lijphart 1977). Economic policy is also highly insulated in the small European democracies, where major decisions about wage and incomes policy are made through private corporatist negotiations between key interest groups and the government (Katzenstein 1986). The U.S. government itself has a long tradition of abdicating regulatory powers to semiautonomous agencies, such as the Securities and Exchange Commission (SEC), which monitors activities in the securities market.

One may question—as we did in chapter 2—whether institutional insulation in established democracies may also share some inequitable characteristics (cf. Moe 1990a, 1990b). That said, it is still important to clarify why the institutional enclaves in a transitional polity are particularly anti-democratic. One reason lies in their distorting effects upon the representativeness of these democracies. The authoritarians do not create these institutional footholds in

2. The following examples draw heavily from Valenzuela (1992).

order to promote a balance among the interests of different societal groups, as is the case in consociationalism. These institutions are instead designed to artificially preserve the influence of former rulers and their associated allies who have been permanently removed from office by the will of the people. Rather than protecting the interests of a minority with a legitimate claim to representation, they thus grossly overrepresent an illegitimate minority.

Second, these insulated structures also skew the institutional balance of power within new democracies. Traditionally, we are accustomed to thinking of autonomous agencies as at least in part a corrective against excess discretion in the hands of the chief executive. Many have interpreted the Mexican central bank reform of 1993, for example, as facilitating democratization by reducing the authority of the Mexican president over the economy (Maxfield 1997, 148). But this is an erroneous interpretation of the role that insulated institutions play in transitional polities. For while they do wrest control away from the chief executive by placing it in the hands of a decentralized, autonomous agency, that agency is in turn under the direction of a small elite with no legitimate claim on the state apparatus. Far from reducing the concentration of political power in the political system, these institutions arguably serve to exacerbate it.

This brings us to a third and final liability associated with such institutional forms: their consequences for the ability of incoming democratic governments to freely exercise their authority. For unlike the policy insulation that flows out of corporatism—which emerges from a set of negotiated agreements—the institutional forms to which this study refers are largely the product of imposition.[3] They are not created through voluntary actions taken by the democrats themselves but instead form part of a larger institutional inheritance that is thrust upon them. Although the new power holders would like to control these areas of policy in order to carry out their programs, they are instead precluded from even considering this as an option.

One might argue that even in established democracies, policymakers are frequently denied the opportunity to set policy within certain arenas. But there is a crucial difference in transitional polities: in many cases, this prohibition is reinforced by the veiled or explicit threat of a return to authoritarian rule. Precisely because these institutions have been imposed by actors with "privileged access to crucial elements of state power to make credible their threat of destabilization" (Valenzuela 1992, 65), they are often backed by a degree of coercion not present in most democratic settings.

As S. Valenzuela sums up the nefarious consequences of such authoritarian enclaves, "they undermine both the *end* of the democratic process—

3. This is true even where they may be the product of explicit understandings between the authoritarians and the democrats, as I argue subsequently.

i.e., the authority of democratically elected governments, and . . . detract from its *means*—i.e., the fairness and centrality of the electoral mechanism as a route to forming governments" (Valenzuela 1992, 62) (italics added). While this is arguably also true of certain forms of insulation in established democracies, the difference is one of both degree and kind. For while insulation in first world countries may compromise certain aspects of the democratic process, the institutions considered in this study have the potential to imperil the democratic system as a whole.

Consider the case of Chile. Despite several significant advances, Chile's democracy continued to be haunted in the 1990s by an electoral system that did not allow the majority to rule, a military not subject to civilian control, and an amnesty clause that precluded the definitive resolution of the human rights controversy. What all of these institutions pointed to was the continuing behind the scenes influence of various political actors who were not themselves subject to electoral accountability but had the ability to hold Chile's democratic future hostage. As long as such reserved domains of authoritarian influence remain, they cast reasonable doubt as to whether or not Chile's transition has actually ended. Indeed, one author went so far as to say that the Aylwin government was no further along the "transitional" continuum between authoritarianism and democracy when it stepped down from power in 1994 than it was when it began to rule four years earlier (Garretón 1993).

This is undoubtedly an overstatement, although not too far out of step with the views of some noted scholars of democratic consolidation (cf. Linz and Stepan 1996, 207–17).[4] Even Londregan (2000), who wishes to argue that the agenda-setting powers of the presidency have gradually eroded the policy constraints imposed by Chile's various institutional enclaves, admits that the effectiveness of this strategy was limited to issue areas where the authoritarians had less of a stake. And even there he concludes that change occurred at a pace that was "slow to glacial" at best (Londregan 2000, 212). He thus pre-

4. Despite modest improvements, the pervasive influence of the enclaves could still be felt in several realms of Chilean politics under Aylwin's successor, Eduardo Frei. In the electoral realm, for example, a movement in 1995 to abolish the institution of the designated senators was defeated. While the government was able to appoint two of their four replacements, the other two were named by governing bodies outside of executive control. Of particular note—and despite widespread popular protest—Pinochet was able to assume the position of "senator for life" upon stepping down from his role as commander in chief of the armed forces. Progress toward bringing certain former military officials to trial for human rights violations carried out under military rule was similarly limited. The prominent exception—the jailing of Pinochet's former head of secret police, Manuel Contreras—was enforced only after extensive delay and by offering concessions to the military, including a pay hike and a commitment to bring closure on remaining court cases (Hunter 1997, 155). And while Pinochet's right to diplomatic immunity as a for-life senator was revoked early in 2000—thereby enabling him to stand trial for human rights abuses carried out under military rule—it has yet to be seen whether or how this issue will be resolved by the Chilean courts.

dicts that the executive branch's ability to move certain policies in the direction preferred by the majority may take more than a generation to be realized, leaving Chile woefully shy of the responsiveness threshold set by established democracies.

To be sure, not all new democracies come as well insulated as Chile's. But most do share at least some of the institutional constraints described earlier. Unless and until these constraints can be removed, most authors seem to agree that the transitional polities of the third world are condemned to exist as "partial," "incomplete," or "unconsolidated" democracies.[5]

## Assessing the Future: Insulation as a Necessary Evil

Of course, this discussion necessarily begs the final question of what—if anything—these new governments can do to avoid the institutional legacies of their authoritarian predecessors. Unfortunately, the answer would seem to be "not much." While few scholars of democratization would extol the virtues of these institutional forms, most would agree that they constitute a necessary evil.

Regardless of their potentially perverse consequences for new democracies down the road, insulated institutions do serve an important function in the early stages of the transition. Some credit the enclaves with fostering an otherwise elusive consensus among contending factions by providing a supraconstitutional basis for dispute resolution (Godoy 1994, 18). More generally, they are thought to play a pivotal role in limiting the uncertainty of the transition by extending guarantees to those who formerly supported authoritarian rule (Karl and Schmitter 1994, 56). As Przeworski (1992) argues, a transition is only possible if some sectors within the dictatorship can expect to have a significant political presence under democratic conditions (Przeworski 1992, 126). For all of these reasons, the very success of the transition arguably hinges on the existence of institutions that are necessarily conservative—if not out-and-out anti-democratic—in nature.

The problem is that, once there, these insulated institutional forms place their democratic heirs in a double bind. For despite their integral role in facilitating the initiation of the transition, these pockets of authoritarian control are not easily uprooted. Rather, for all of the reasons noted earlier, they are in fact quite difficult to reverse. It is perhaps not surprising, then, that O'Donnell speaks of two transitions—one that entails the installation of a democratic government and a second more complex transition to an institutional-

5. For a conceptual discussion of democratic consolidation, see the various contributions found in Mainwaring, O'Donnell, and Valenzuela 1992; Linz and Stepan 1996; Diamond et al. 1997.

ized democratic regime (O'Donnell 1992, 18). Ironically, those enabling conditions most conducive to the first transition may prove to be the very factors that are most detrimental to its subsequent democratic evolution (Hagopian 1990; Karl 1990).

This is not to imply that change is out of the question. There is, after all, no a priori reason why democratization "cannot prove to be an ongoing process of renewal" (Karl 1990, 16). It may well be the case, as suggested earlier, that some authoritarian enclaves are simply less "entrenchable" than others are and/or certain institutional environments render them less resilient. It may also be the case that once a climate of trust has been established between the authoritarians and the democrats, the enclaves will become obsolete (Godoy 1994). But such a halcyon scenario seems unlikely. Particularly if Chile is to serve as any sort of model, the outlook for modifying the institutional structure of new democracies does not look promising. If these countries are ultimately to shake their authoritarian pasts, it is unlikely to happen any time soon.

## Implications for the Study of Institutional Design

In addition to its relevance to the study of democratic transitions and consolidation, the argument presented in this book also speaks to a host of other issues germane to modern political economy. Above all, it has attempted to make a contribution to the burgeoning literature on central banks. While the past few years have witnessed a growing body of literature on the causes and effects of central bank autonomy in the advanced industrial democracies, there has been relatively little corresponding research on central bank reform in the developing world. And where such work does exist (e.g., Maxfield 1997), it has tended to borrow heavily from economics, typically casting central bank independence as an efficient solution to a commitment problem that leaves politicians objectively better off. This book has put forth an alternative, more overtly political explanation for central bank reform and its related distributional effects. I raise the possibility that politicians who create autonomous central banks do so not so much to commit themselves to a future of low inflation but, rather, to bind the policy choices of future governments, who may well view this institutional inheritance as costly.

But while central banks have constituted the principal substantive focus of this book, my argument can also be read as a broader comment on the study of institutions. For as with the credibility literature, there has been a tendency within the social sciences in recent years to view institutions as efficient vehicles for welfare improvement. This bias has been most evident within that body of literature known as the new economics of organization (NEO) (Williamson 1985; Milgrom and Roberts 1992). In a nutshell, the NEO argues that institutions arise in order to overcome market failures, thereby helping actors to bargain their way toward mutually beneficial gains from trade. Like the credibility literature, it employs an essentially economic-based reasoning, with a focus on bargaining and Pareto-improving outcomes. While initially confined to economics and, in particular, to theories of the firm, this efficiency-based view of institutional design has rapidly become a dominant paradigm in political science as well (Steinmo, Thelan, and Longstreth 1992; Hall and Taylor 1996).

The hegemony of the NEO paradigm has recently been challenged on two grounds. First, it ignores the role that power may play in the process of institutional creation. Rooted as it is in the analysis of the firm in Coase 1937, the NEO posits a state of nature in which actors of equal strength engage in voluntary exchange. It is assumed that as actors enter into contractual agreements, they will jointly structure an authority relationship to serve their mutual needs—whether this is the firm (as in the case of economics) or the legislature (the most common example in politics). What is not clear is how well this marketlike depiction extends to the political environment (Moe 1984). While there are undoubtedly settings where political actors stand on equal footing, there are also many cases where the initial allocation of property rights privileges the interests of certain actors over others (Levi 1990; Knight 1992). Whether by virtue of their ability to exercise agenda control (Shepsle and Weingast 1989), to alter the game's payoff matrix (Conybeare 1987), or to induce cooperation by unilaterally shifting the status quo (Gruber 2000), more powerful actors are likely to be favored in the process of institutional design. In short, what the NEO characterizes as bargaining may more aptly be termed coercion when transposed to the political realm.

A second and related problem with the NEO is that it tends to overstate the welfare-enhancing effects of institutional outcomes. For while this paradigm acknowledges that politicians may have divergent interests, it is assumed that whatever institutional outcome is ultimately chosen will necessarily benefit all parties equally. But if it is true that politics is best characterized by power asymmetries, then it is not so clear that the resultant institutions—and the policies they embody—will necessarily serve all actors to the same degree. It seems more likely that outcomes will be skewed in favor of the interests of he or she who holds power, leaving some actors more advantaged than others.

This is certainly the thrust of Moe's work (1990a, 1990b), discussed in chapter 2, which is all about the ways in which incumbents use the power of office to impose their preferences on their successors, who may be left worse off. A redistributive air also infuses much of the literature in international relations over the past decade, which seeks to explain how actors choose an institutional equilibrium when there is more than one path to cooperation. The argument is that where such multiple equilibria exist, power and resources may determine the choice of solution (Krasner 1991; Garrett and Weingast 1993). Thus, for example, the bargains struck in the European internal market are said to reflect the preferences of the most powerful states (Garrett 1991; Moravscik 1991).

If there is good reason to argue for a more redistributive understanding of institutions in the developed world, such a critique would seem all the more compelling in the developing world. Hall and Taylor (1996), for example, have argued that the NEO seems best suited to those political settings where actors of roughly equal power are accustomed to interacting strategically within a mutually agreed upon set of rules. But does this sound like the political reality of the everyday developing country? At the very least, this set of analytical tools would seem particularly ill suited to one institutional environment of growing empirical significance: democracies in transition from authoritarian rule. After all, the transitional setting is one in which there exist glaring asymmetries of power, strategic interaction is far from routine, and the rules of the game are—by definition—in flux.

Despite this fact, a great deal of emphasis has been placed to date on the role of bargaining as the primary mechanism through which most transitions occur (O'Donnell and Schmitter 1986; Karl 1990; Przeworski 1992). Although undeniably some element of bargaining takes place in nearly all transitions that are not a product of out-and-out revolution, it may be misleading to overemphasize this dynamic as the transition's dominant leitmotiv. For these are generally not bargains among equals, at least in the sorts of top down, elite-led transitions where insulation tends to be most prevalent. In such cases, enclaves are frequently not the object of negotiation but rather are presented as a condition for withdrawal, without which the authoritarians are not willing to yield power (Przeworski 1992, 118). And even where these arrangements are the product of explicit understandings between exiting authoritarian and incoming democratic leaders, it is the authoritarians who—by virtue of their first mover advantage—have the ability to set the terms of this debate.

To state this somewhat differently, it may prove more fruitful to conceive of the transitional bargains so commonly referred to in the literature less in terms of what the democrats "give" the authoritarians (cf. Bates 1991) than what the authoritarians "take." For while it is true that the democrats do, in some sense, get democracy in exchange for these institutional constraints, they do not relish inheriting these enclaves and would overturn them if they could. While few scholars would disagree with this assertion, their emphasis on bargaining and negotiation tends to obscure the fundamental power asymmetries that lie at the heart of most transitions.

## Paths for Future Research

This study lends itself to a number of different avenues for future research. I have already speculated as to how the present argument might be extended to explain central bank reform under other institutional contexts and/or other forms of insulation. In closing, I raise two additional possibilities.

First, it might be interesting to examine the extent to which the insulation argument presented here holds across transitions over time. We know, for example, that during the first wave of transitions at the turn of the century, European governments created proportional systems of representation in order to maximize the influence of smaller, liberal parties under future democratic rule (Rokkan 1970; Boix 1999). In the second wave of transitions following the end of World War II, one could presumably study the differing ways in which colonial powers used institutions to try to shape the course of political and economic developments in the newly independent countries of the third world. Thus, for example, the franc-backed monetary union in the countries of West Africa has often been viewed as an attempt by France to remove monetary sovereignty from her colonies before relinquishing formal political control (Collier 1991; Van de Walle 1991). Other colonial institutional structures that illustrate a similar principle must surely also exist. Were we to find systematic evidence of such a trend, this would further underscore the empirical robustness of the argument at hand.

A second way to extend the argument might be to develop a fuller model of how authoritarian governments optimize across a range of different potential insulation strategies. The basic thrust of this book is that exiting authoritarians ought to try to "spread their DNA" across as many institutional domains as conform to their interests. Above a certain threshold, however, there must surely be some trade-off between allocating resources in one institutional arena versus another. The model presented here does not allow me to address this question, as the view of the world I am offering constitutes only a partial equilibrium. One future course of research might thus be to model how authoritarian governments go about calculating such trade-offs across the entire range of potential insulation domains and then to test this hypothesis across a wider set of countries.

Whatever the institutional form or historic moment at hand, the basic point is that insulation constitutes a central part of politics in any context and reflects the essence of strategy by outgoing elites in the transition from authoritarian rule. The bottom line is that these insulated institutions are created by authoritarian regimes who know they are losing power and who respond to this threat by willfully imposing their policy preferences on those who inherit the throne. The rules are not fair, nor are the opponents equally matched. But it is the price of democracy, and it is the only game in town.

# References


Acuña, Carlos H. 1994. Politics and Economics in the Argentina of the Nineties (Or, Why the Future No Longer Is What It Used to Be). In *Democracy, Markets, and Structural Reform in Latin America: Argentina, Bolivia, Brazil, Chile, and Mexico,* ed. William C. Smith, Carlos H. Acuña, and Eduardo A. Gamarra, 31–74. New Brunswick, NJ: Transaction Books.

Agénor, Pierre-Richard. 1994. Credibility and Exchange Rate Management in Developing Countries. *Journal of Development Economics* 45 (October): 1–16.

Agüero, Felipe. 1992. The Military and the Limits of Democratization in South America. In *Issues and Prospects of Democratic Consolidation: The New South American Democracies in Comparative Perspective,* ed. Scott Mainwaring, Guillermo O'Donnell, and J. Samuel Valenzuela, 153–98. Notre Dame, IN: University of Notre Dame Press.

Aguilar Camín, Hector, and Lorenzo Meyer. 1993. *In the Shadow of the Mexican Revolution.* Austin, TX: University of Texas Press.

Alba Vega, Carlos. 1993a. El Empresariado Mexicano ante el Tratado del Libre Comercio en América del Norte. In *Liberación Económica y Libre Comercio en América del Norte,* ed. Gustavo Vega Cañovas, 213–38. Mexico City, Mexico: El Colegio de México.

———. 1993b. La Microindustria Ante la Liberalización Económica y El Tratado del Libre Comercio. *Foro Internacional* 33, no. 3 (July–September): 453–83.

Alcocer V., Jorge. 1994. Party System and Political Transition in Mexico: A Pragmatic Approach. In *The Politics of Economic Restructuring: State-Society Relations and Regime Change in Mexico,* ed. Maria Lorena Cook, Kevin J. Middlebrook, and Juan Molinar Horcasitas, 149–58. La Jolla: University of California at San Diego, Center for U.S.-Mexican Studies.

Alcocer V., Jorge, and Rodrigo M. Morales. 1991. Mitología y Realidad del Fraude Electoral. *Nexos* 166 (October): 27–33.

Alesina, Alberto. 1988. Macroeconomics and Politics. In *NBER Macroeconomics Annual.* Cambridge, MA: National Bureau of Economic Research.

———. 1994. Political Models of Macroeconomic Policy and Fiscal Reforms. In *Voting for Reform: Democracy, Political Liberalization, and Economic Adjustment,* ed. Stephan Haggard and Steven B. Webb, 37–57. Washington, DC: World Bank.

Alesina, Alberto, and Allan Drazen. 1991. Why Are Stabilizations Delayed? *American Economic Review* 81:1170–88.

Alesina, Alberto, and Roberta Gatti. 1995. Independent Central Banks: Low Inflation at No Cost? *American Economic Review* 85, no. 2 (May): 196–200.

Alesina, Alberto, and Howard Rosenthal. 1995. *Partisan Politics.* New York: Cambridge University Press.

Alesina, Alberto, and Jeffrey D. Sachs. 1988. Political Parties and the Business Cycle in the U.S., 1948–84. *Journal of Money, Credit, and Banking* 20:63–82.

Alesina, Alberto, and Lawrence H. Summers. 1993. Central Bank Independence and Macroeconomic Performance: Some Comparative Evidence. *Journal of Money and Banking* 25 (May): 151–62.

Alesina, Alberto, and Guido Tabellini. 1990. A Positive Theory of Fiscal Deficits and Government Debt. *Review of Economic Studies* 57:403–14.

Altimir, Oscar. 1995. Distributive Implications of Adjustment and Economic Reforms in Latin America. Paper presented at the Conference on Development Strategy after Neoliberal Economic Restructuring in Latin America, March 24–25, North-South Center, University of Miami, Miami, FL.

Alvarez, R. Michael, Geoffrey Garrett, and Peter Lange. 1991. Government Partisanship, Labor Organization, and Macroeconomic Performance. *American Political Science Review* 55:539–56.

Ames, Barry. 1987. *Political Survival: Politicians and Public Policy in Latin America.* Berkeley: University of California Press.

ANC (African National Congress). 1990. *Recommendations on Post-Apartheid Economic Policy.* Proceedings of a workshop, April 28–May 1, Harare, South Africa.

Angell, Alan, and Benny Pollack. 1990. The Chilean Elections of 1989 and the Politics of Transition to Democracy. *Bulletin of Latin American Research* 9, no. 1:1–23.

Arrellano, José Pablo. 1988. Crisis y Recuperación Económica en Chile en los Años 80. *Colección Estudios Cieplan* 24 (June): 63–84.

———. 1989. Comentarios al Proyecto de Ley del Banco Central. *Cuadernos de Economía* 26, no. 77 (April): 91–96.

Arriagada, Genaro. 1985. *La Política Militar de Pinochet.* Santiago, Chile: Salesianos.

Arriagada, Genaro, and Carol Graham. 1994. Chile: Sustaining Adjustment during Transition. In *Voting for Reform: Democracy, Political Liberalization, and Economic Adjustment,* ed. Stephan Haggard and Stephen B. Webb, 242–86. Washington, DC: World Bank.

Arthur, W. B. 1989. Competing Technologies, Increasing Returns, and Lock-in by Historical Events. *Economic Journal* 99 (March): 116–31.

Aspe, Pedro. 1993. Iniciativa de Reforma Constitucional para Dotar de Autonomía al Banco de México. Address to the Mexican Chamber of Deputies, May 24. Typescript.

———. 1990. *Programa de Gobierno de la Concertación.* Santiago, Chile: Fundación Aylwin.

Bade, Robin, and Michael Parkin. 1980. Central Bank Laws and Monetary Policy. Manuscript, Department of Economics, University of Western Ontario.

Baer, M. Delal. 1993. Mexico's Second Revolution: Pathways to Liberalization. In *Political and Economic Liberalization in Mexico: At a Critical Juncture?* ed. Riordan Roett, 51–68. Boulder, CO: Lynne Rienner Publishers.

Balcerowicz, Lesnek. 1995. Understanding Post-communist Transitions. In *Economic Reform and Democracy,* ed. Larry Diamond and Marc F. Plattner, 86–100. Baltimore, MD: Johns Hopkins University Press.

Baldez, Lisa, and John M. Carey. Forthcoming. Pinochet's Constitution and Executive Agenda Control: Budgetmaking in Chile. In *The Structure of Fiscal and Regulatory Policy,* ed. Stephan Haggard and Matthew D. McCubbins. Washington, DC: World Bank.

Ball, L. 1994. What Determines the Sacrifice Ratio? In *Monetary Policy,* ed. N. G. Mankiw, 155–82. Chicago: University of Chicago Press.

Ball, L., N. G. Mankiw, and D. Romer. 1988. The New Keynesian Economics and the Output-Inflation Trade-off. *Brookings Papers on Economic Activity* 1:1–65.

Banco de México. 1990. *Ley del Banco de México.*

———. 1993. *Ley del Banco de México.*
———. 1994. *The Mexican Economy.* Mexico City, Mexico: Banco de México.
———. 1995. *The Mexican Economy.* Mexico City, Mexico: Banco de México.
Banian, King, Leroy O. Laney, and Thomas D. Willet. 1986. Central Bank Independence: An International Comparison. In *Central Bankers, Bureaucratic Incentives, and Monetary Policy,* ed. Eugenia Toma and Mark Toma, 199–218. Dordrecht: Martinus Nijhoff.
Barro, Robert, and D. Gordon. 1983a. Rules, Discretion, and Reputation in a Model of Monetary Policy. *Journal of Monetary Economics* 12 (July): 101–22.
———. 1983b. A Positive Theory of Monetary Policy in a Natural Rate Model. *Journal of Political Economy* 91:589–610.
Bartell, Ernest. 1992. Business Perceptions and the Transition to Democracy in Chile. Working paper 184, Helen Kellogg Institute for International Studies, University of Notre Dame, December.
Basañez, Miguel. 1991. Encuesta Electoral 1991. *Este País* 5 (August): 3–6.
———. 1993. Is Mexico Headed Toward its Fifth Crisis? In *Political and Economic Liberalization in Mexico: At a Critical Juncture?* ed. Riordan Roett, 95–115. Boulder, CO: Lynne Rienner Publishers.
Batarce, Jaime A. 1993. Los Efectos de la Deuda Subordinada y la Solución de Mercado. Serie Documentos de Trabajo 201, Centro de Estudios Públicos, Santiago, Chile, October.
Bates, Robert H. 1991. The Economics of Transitions to Democracy. *PS: Political Science and Politics* 24, no. 1 (March): 24–27.
———. 1994. Comments. In *The Political Economy of Policy Reform,* ed. John Williamson, 29–34. Washington, DC: Institute for International Economics.
Bates, Robert H. et al. 1998. *Analytic Narratives.* Princeton, NJ: Princeton University Press.
Bates, Robert H., and Anne O. Kreuger. 1993. Generalizations Arising from the Country Studies. In *Political and Economic Interactions in Economic Policy Reform,* ed. Robert H. Bates and Anne O. Krueger, 444–72. Oxford: Basil Blackwell.
Bawn, Kathleen. 1997. Choosing Strategies to Control the Bureaucracy: Statutory Constraints, Oversight, and the Committee System. *Journal of Law, Economics, and Organization* 12:101–26.
Bazdresch, Carlos, and Santiago Levy. 1991. Populism and Economic Policy in Mexico, 1970–1982. In *The Macroeconomics of Populism in Latin America,* ed. Rudiger Dornbusch and Sebastián Edwards, 223–62. Chicago: University of Chicago Press.
Beck, Nathaniel. 1982. Presidential Influence on the Federal Reserve in the 1970s. *American Journal of Political Science* 26 (August): 415–45.
Bernanke, Ben, and Alan Blinder. 1992. The Federal Funds Rate and the Channels of Monetary Transmission. *American Economic Review* 82, no. 4:901–21.
Bernhard, William T. 1998. A Political Explanation of Variations in Central Bank Independence. *American Political Science Review* 92, no. 2 (June): 311–27.
Bizberg, Ilán. 1996. Restructuración Productiva y Transformación del Modelo de Relaciones Industriales: 1988–1994, *Foro Internacional* 36, nos. 1–2 (January–June): 80–106.
Blackburn, Keith, and John Christenson. 1988. Monetary Policy and Policy Credibility: Theories and Evidence. *Journal of Economic Literature* 27 (March): 1–45.
Bohn, Henning, and Robert Inman. 1996. Balanced Budget Rules and Public Deficits:

Evidence from US States. Working paper 5533, National Bureau of Economic Research, Cambridge, MA.

Boix, Carles. 1999. Setting the Rules of the Game: The Choice of Electoral Systems in Advanced Democracies. *American Political Science Review* 93, no. 3 (September): 609–24.

Bosworth, Barry P., Rudiger Dornbusch, and Raúl Labán. 1994. *The Chilean Economy: Policy Lessons and Challenges.* Washington, DC: Brookings Institution.

Botha, P. J. J. 1997. The South African Reserve Bank and the Rate of Interest. *South African Journal of Economics* 65, no. 4 (December): 532–67.

Boylan, Delia M. 1996. Taxation and Transition: The Politics of the 1990 Chilean Tax Reform. *Latin American Research Review* 31, no. 1:7–31.

———. 2000. Bureaucratic Delegation in Comparative Perspective: Constitutional Structure and Reform Timing. Paper presented at the Twenty-second International Congress of the Latin American Studies Association, March 16–18, Miami, FL.

Bresser Pereira, Luiz Carlos. 1993. Economic Reforms and Economic Growth: Efficiency and Politics in Latin America. In *Economic Reforms in New Democracies: A Social-Democratic Approach,* ed. Luiz Carlos Bresser Pereira, José María Maravall, and Adam Przeworski, 15–76. New York: Cambridge University Press.

Bresser Pereira, Luiz Carlos, Jose María Maravall, and Adam Przeworski. 1993. *Economic Reforms in New Democracies: A Social-Democratic Approach.* New York: Cambridge University Press.

Briones Espinosa, Ramón. 1989. Informe Sobre El Proyecto de Ley Sobre El Banco Central en Trámite en la Junta del Gobierno. Manuscript, Comité de Reformas Políticas de la Concertación, Santiago, Chile.

Brophy-Baermann, Michelle. 1994. Economics and Elections: The Mexican Case. *Social Science Quarterly* 75, no. 1 (March): 125–35.

Broz, J. Lawrence. 1998. The Origins of Central Banking: Solutions to the Free-Rider Problem. *International Organization* 52, no. 2 (spring): 231–68.

Bruhn, Kathleen. 1996. *Taking on Goliath: The Emergence of a New Left Party and the Struggle for Democracy in Mexico.* University Park: Pennsylvania State University Press.

Buendía, Jorge. 1996. Economic Reform, Public Opinion, and Presidential Approval in Mexico, 1988–1993. *Comparative Political Studies* 29, no. 5 (October): 566–91.

Buffie, Edward, and Allen Sangines Krause. 1989. Mexico 1959–1986: From Stabilizing Development to the Debt Crisis. In *Developing Country Debt and the World Economy,* ed. Jeffrey D. Sachs, 393–552. Chicago: University of Chicago Press.

Buira, Ariel. 1996. Reflections on the Mexican Crisis of 1994. In *Private Capital Flows to Emerging Markets after the Mexican Peso Crisis,* ed. Guillermo A. Calvo, Morris Goldstein, and Edward Hochreiter, 307–20. Washington, DC: Institute for International Economics.

Burki, S. J., and Craig Baxter. 1991. *Pakistan under the Military.* Boulder, CO: Westview Press.

Butler, David, and Donald Stokes. 1974. *Political Change in Britain: The Evolution of Electoral Choice.* London: MacMillan.

Calderón, Alvaro, and Stephany Griffith-Jones. 1994. Los Flujos de Capital Extranjero en la Economía Chilena: Renovado Acceso y Nuevos Usos. Working paper 37, CEPAL, Santiago, Chile.

Calderón Hinojosa, Felipe. 1993. Hacia Una Real Autonomía del Banco de México. *Quórum: Publicación Mensual del Instituto de Investigaciones Legislativas* 11, no. 16 (July): 29–36.

Callaghy, Thomas M. 1989. Toward State Capability and Embedded Liberalism in the Third World: Lessons for Adjustment. In *Fragile Coalitions: The Politics of Economic Adjustment,* ed. Joan M. Nelson, 115–38. New Brunswick, NJ: Transaction Books and the Overseas Development Council.

Calvo, Guillermo A. 1995. Varieties of Capital Market Crises. Manuscript, Department of Economics, University of Maryland.

Calvo, Guillermo A., and Enrique G. Mendoza. 1996. Mexico's Balance of Payments Crisis: Chronicle of a Death Foretold. *Journal of International Economics* 41:235–64.

Camp, Roderic. 1985. The Political Technocrat in Mexico and the Survival of the Political System. *Latin American Research Review* 20, no. 1:97–118.

———. 1989. *Entrepreneurs and Politics in Twentieth Century Mexico.* New York: Oxford University Press.

———. 1990. Camarillas in Mexican Politics: The Case of the Salinas Cabinet. *Mexican Studies* 1 (winter): 87–107.

———. 1995. *Political Recruitment across Two Centuries: Mexico 1884–1991.* Austin: University of Texas Press.

Campero, Guillermo. 1988. Los Empresarios Ante la Alternativa Democrática: El Caso de Chile. *Proposiciones* 16:48–61.

———. 1991. Entrepreneurs under the Military Regime. In *The Struggle for Democracy in Chile: 1982–1990,* ed. Paul W. Drake and Iván Jaksić, 128–60. Lincoln: University of Nebraska Press.

Cárdenas, Cuarhtémoc. 1993. The False Hopes of the Economic Reform. In *Political and Economic Liberalization in Mexico: At a Critical Juncture?* ed. Riordan Roett, 149–54. Boulder, CO: Lynne Rienner Publishers.

Carr, Barry. 1989. The Left and Its Potential Role in Political Change. In *Mexico's Alternative Political Futures,* ed. Wayne Cornelius, Judith Gentleman, and Peter H. Smith, 361–90. La Jolla: University of California at San Diego, Center for U.S.-Mexican Studies.

Castañeda, Jorge. 1993. *La Utopía Desarmada.* Mexico City, Mexico: Joaquín Mortiz/Planeta.

———. 1994. *Sorpresas Te da la Vida: México 1994.* Mexico City, Mexico: Aguilar.

Cavallo, Ascanio. 1992. *Los Hombres de la Transición.* Santiago, Chile: Editorial Andrés Bello.

CEAS (Central Economic Advisory Service). 1993. The Key Issues in the Normative Economic Model. Manuscript, Johannesburg, South Africa.

Centeno, Miguel Angel. 1994. *Democracy within Reason: Technocratic Revolution in Mexico.* University Park: Pennsylvania State University Press.

Centeno, Miguel Angel, and Sylvia Maxfield. 1992. The Marriage of Finance and Order: Changes in the Mexican Political Elite. *Journal of Latin American Studies* 24 (February): 57–85.

Central Bank of Chile. 1989. *Seminar: Experiences with Central Bank Autonomy.* Monetary Studies 11. Santiago, Chile: Central Bank of Chile.

———. 1990. *Constitutional Organic Act of the Central Bank of Chile.* Santiago, Chile: Central Bank of Chile.

Cheyre, Hernán. 1988. Proyecciones Económicas para el Periodo 1989–1997: Bajo Escenarios Políticos Alternativos. *Estudios Públicos* 32 (spring): 239–61.

Cho, Y. J. 1990. Financial Policy in Korea and Taiwan. In *Korean Economic Development,* ed. Jene Kwon, 225–44. New York: Greenwood Press.

Choi, Byung-Sun. 1993. Financial Policy and Big Business in Korea: The Perils of Financial Regulation. In *The Politics of Finance in Developing Countries,* ed. Stephan Haggard, Chung H. Lee, and Sylvia Maxfield, 23–54. Ithaca, NY: Cornell University Press.

Cieplan. 1982. *El Modelo Económico Chileno: Trayectoria de una Crítica.* Santiago, Chile: Editorial Aconcagua.

Clark, William Roberts. 1994a. Party Structure, Regime Stability, and Governmental Supply of Central Bank Independence in Developing Countries. Paper presented at the annual meeting of the American Political Science Association, September 1–4, New York.

———. 1994b. Asset Specificity, Collective Action, and the Societal Demand for Central Bank Independence in Developing Countries. Paper presented at the annual meeting of the International Studies Association, March 28–April 1, Washington, DC.

Clark, William Roberts, and Sylvia Maxfield. 1996. Credible Commitments, International Investment Flows, and Central Bank Independence in Developing Countries: A Signaling Model. Paper presented at the annual meeting of the American Political Science Association, August 29–September 1, San Francisco, CA.

Clark, William Roberts, Usha Nair Reichert, Sandra Lynn Lomas, and Kevin L. Parker. 1998. International and Domestic Constraints on Political Business Cycles in OECD Economies. *International Organization* 52, no. 1 (winter): 87–120.

Coase, Ronald. 1937. The Nature of the Firm. *Economica* 4 (November): 386–405.

Collier, Paul. 1991. Africa's External Economic Relations: 1960–1990. *African Affairs* 90:339–56.

Collier, Ruth Berins, and David Collier. 1991. *Shaping the Political Arena.* Princeton, NJ: Princeton University Press.

———. 1991. *A Nation of Enemies.* New York: W. W. Norton.

Conybeare, John A. C. 1987. *Trade Wars: The Theory and Practice of International Commercial Rivalry.* New York: Columbia University Press.

Coppedge, Michael. 1993. Mexican Democracy: You Can't Get There from Here. In *Political and Economic Liberalization in Mexico: At a Critical Juncture?* ed. Riordan Roett, 127–40. Boulder, CO: Lynne Rienner Publishers.

Corbo, Vittorio, and Stanley Fischer. 1994. Lessons from the Chilean Stabilization and Recovery. In *The Chilean Economy: Policy Lessons and Challenges,* ed. Barry P. Bosworth, Rudiger Dornbusch, and Raúl Labán, 29–67. Washington, DC: Brookings Institution.

Cordera, Rolando, and Carlos Tello. 1981. *La Disputa por la Nación: Perspectivas y Opciones del Desarrollo.* Mexico City, Mexico: Siglo Veintiuno Editores.

Cordoba, José. 1994. Mexico. In *The Political Economy of Policy Reform,* ed. John Williamson, 232–84. Washington, DC: Institute for International Economics.

Cornelius, Wayne A. 1994. Mexico's Delayed Democratization. *Foreign Policy* 95 (summer): 53–71.

———. 1996. *Mexican Politics in Transition: The Breakdown of a One-Party Dominant*

*Regime.* Monograph Series 41. La Jolla: University of California at San Diego, Center for U.S.-Mexican Studies.

Cornelius, Wayne A., and Anne Craig. 1991. *The Mexican Political System in Transition.* La Jolla: University of California at San Diego, Center for U.S.-Mexican Studies.

Cornelius, Wayne A., Anne Craig, and Jonathon Fox. 1994. *Transforming State-Society Relations in Mexico: The National Solidarity Strategy.* U.S.-Mexico Contemporary Perspectives Series. La Jolla: University of California at San Diego, Center for U.S.-Mexican Studies.

Cornelius, Wayne A., Judith Gentleman, and Peter H. Smith. 1989. Overview: The Dynamics of Political Change in Mexico. In *Mexico's Alternative Political Futures,* Monograph Series 30, ed. Wayne Cornelius, Judith Gentleman, and Peter H. Smith, 1–54. La Jolla: University of California at San Diego, Center for U.S.-Mexican Studies.

Correa, Enrique. 1993. La Estrategia Político-Institucional Para la Transición en Chile. Speech at International Seminar on Chilean Democratization in Comparative Perspective, July 20, FLACSO—Programa Chile, Santiago, Chile. Typescript.

Cortázar, René. 1990. El Proceso de Cambios y la Concertación Social. In *Transición a la Democracia: Marco Político y Económico,* ed. Oscar Muñoz, 69–84. Santiago, Chile: Cieplan.

Cothran, Dan A. 1994. Carlos Salinas and the Revolutionary Regime. In *Political Stability and Democracy in Mexico: The "Perfect Dictatorship"?* ed. Dan A. Cothran, 177–207. Westport, CT: Praeger.

Cottareli, Carlo, and Curzio Giannini. 1998. Inflation, Credibility, and the Role of the International Monetary Fund. Policy Analysis and Assessment paper 98/12, International Monetary Fund, Washington, DC.

Craig, Anne, and Wayne Cornelius. 1995. Houses Divided: Parties and Political Reform in Mexico. In *Building Democratic Institutions: Party Systems in Latin America,* ed. Scott Mainwaring and Timothy R. Scully, 249–97. Stanford, CA: Stanford University Press.

Craske, Nikki. 1996. Dismantling or Retrenchment? Salinas and Corporatism. In *Dismantling the Mexican State?* ed. Rob Aitken, Nikki Craske, Gareth A. Jones, and David E. Stansfield, 78–91. New York: St. Martin's Press.

Crespo, José Antonio. 1995. *Urnas de Pandora: Partidos Politicos y Elecciones en el Gobierno de Salinas.* Mexico City: Espasa Calpe.

Cukierman, Alex. 1992. *Central Bank Strategy, Credibility, and Independence: Theory and Evidence.* Cambridge, MA: MIT Press.

———. 1994. Commitment through Delegation, Political Influence, and Central Bank Independence. In *A Framework for Monetary Stability,* ed. J. A. H. de Beaufort Wijnholds, Sylvester C. W. Eijffinger, and L. H. Hoogdin., 55–74. Boston: Kluwer Academic Publishers.

———. 1996. The Economics of Central Banking. Working paper 36–96, Sackler Institute for Economic Studies, Tel Aviv University, Tel Aviv, Israel.

Cukierman, Alex, Pantelis Kalitzidakis, Lawrence H. Summers, and Steven B. Webb. 1993. Central Bank Independence, Growth, Investment, and Real Rate. *Carnegie-Rochester Conferences Series on Public Policy* 39 (December): 95–140.

Cukierman, Alex, Miguel A. Kiguel, and Nissan Liviatan. 1992. How Much to Commit to an Exchange Rate Rule? Balancing Credibility and Flexibility. World Bank Policy Research Working Papers on Macroeconomic Adjustment and Growth, World Bank, Washington, DC, July.

Cukierman, Alex, and Mariano Tomassi. 1998. When Does It Take a Nixon to Go to China? *American Economic Review* 88, no. 1:180–97.

Cukierman, Alex, and Stephen B. Webb. 1995. Political Influence on the Central Bank: International Evidence. *World Bank Economic Review* 9, no. 3:397–423.

Cukierman, Alex, Steven B. Webb, and Bilin Neyapti. 1993. Measuring the Independence of Central Banks and Its Effect on Policy Outcomes. *World Bank Economic Review* 6, no. 3:353–98.

David, Paul A. 1988. The Future of Path-Dependent Equilibrium Economics: From the Economics of Technology to the Economics of Almost Everything? Technical Report, Stanford University, Institute for Mathematical Studies in the Social Sciences, Stanford, CA, August.

Davies, Rob, Dan O'Meara, and Sipho Dlamini. 1985. *The Struggle for South Africa.* London: Zed Books.

Debelle, Guy, and Stanley Fischer. 1994. How Independent Should a Central Bank Be? In *Goals, Guidelines, and Constraints Facing Monetary Policymakers,* ed. J. Fuhrer, 195–221. Conference Series 38. Boston: Federal Reserve Bank of Boston.

de Figuereido, Rui J. 1998. Political Uncertainty and Policy Insulation: Testing the Formal Theory with State Line-Item Veto Adoption. Manuscript, Haas School of Business, University of California at Berkeley.

De Haan, Jakob, and Clemens L. J. Siermann. 1994. Central Bank Independence, Inflation, and Political Instability. Manuscript, Department of Economics, University of Groningen.

De Haan, Jakob, and Jan-Egbert E. Sturm. 1992. The Case for Central Bank Independence. *Banca Nazionale del Lavoro Quarterly Review* 182:305–27.

De Haan, Jakob, and Gert Jan Van't Hag. 1995. Variation in Central Bank Independence across Countries: Some Provisional Empirical Evidence. *Public Choice* 85:335–51.

De la Cuadra, Sergio. 1987. Panel Sobre "La Independencia del Banco Central." *Colección Estudios Cieplan* 22 (December): 177–91.

De la Garza Toledo, Enrique. 1994. The Restructuring of State-Labor Relations in Mexico. In *The Politics of Economic Restructuring: State-Society Relations and Regime Change in Mexico,* ed. Maria Lorena Cook, Kevin J. Middlebrook, and Juan Molinar Horcasitas, 195–218. La Jolla: University of California at San Diego, Center for U.S.-Mexican Studies.

De Remes la Brely, Alain. 1993. Hegemonía y Clientelismo en el Sistema Electoral Mexicano. Master's thesis, Departamento de Ciencias Sociales, Instituto Tecnológico Autónomo de México.

DeLong, J. Bradford, and Lawrence H. Summers. 1992. Macroeconomic Policy and Long-Run Growth. *Federal Reserve Bank of Kansas City Economic Review* (fourth quarter): 5–30.

Dharamdasani, M. D., ed. 1994. *Pakistan under Democratic Regime.* Varanasi, India: Shalimar Publishing House.

Diamond, Larry et al., eds. 1997. *Consolidating the Third Wave Democracies: Theories and Perspectives.* Baltimore, MD: Johns Hopkins University Press.

Díaz, Alberto, and Beatriz Magaloni. 1997. Presidential Agenda Setting under Hegemonic Party Rule: Executive and Legislature in Mexico. Manuscript, Departamento de Ciencias Sociales, Instituto Tecnológico Autónomo de México and Centro de Docencia Económica.

Domínguez, Jorge I., ed. 1996. *Technopols: Ideas and Leaders in Freeing Politics and Markets in Latin America in the 1990s.* University Park: Pennsylvania State University Press.

Dominguez, Jorge I., and James McCann. 1992. Whither the PRI? Explaining Voter Defection in the 1988 Mexican Presidential Elections. *Electoral Studies* 11, no. 3:207–22.

———. 1996. *Democratizing Mexico: Public Opinion and Electoral Choices.* Baltimore, MD: Johns Hopkins University Press.

Donor, Richard. 1992. The Limits of State Strength: Towards an Institutionalist View of Economic Development. *World Politics* 44 (April): 398–441.

Dornbusch, Rudiger, and Sebastián Edwards. 1991. *The Macroeconomics of Populism.* Chicago: University of Chicago Press.

———. 1994. Exchange Rate Policy and Trade Strategy. In *The Chilean Economy: Policy Lessons and Challenges,* ed. Barry P. Bosworth, Rudiger Dornbusch, and Raúl Labán, 81–103. Washington, DC: Brookings Institution.

Dornbusch, Rudiger, and Steven Marcus. 1991. *International Money and Debt.* San Francisco: International Center for Economic Growth.

Dornbusch, Rudiger, and Alejandro Werner. 1994. Mexico: Stabilization, Reform, and No Growth. *Brookings Papers on Economic Activity* 1:253–97.

Downes, Patrick, and Reza Vaez-Zadeh. 1991. *The Evolving Role of Central Banks.* Washington, DC: International Monetary Fund.

Drake, Paul W. 1990. *The Money Doctor in the Andes: The Kemmerer Missions, 1923–1933.* Durham, NC: Duke University Press.

Dresser, Denise. 1991. *Neopopulist Solutions to Neoliberal Problems: Mexico's National Solidarity Program.* Current Issue Brief Series 3. La Jolla: University of California at San Diego, Center for U.S.-Mexican Studies.

———. 1994a. Embellishment, Empowerment, or Euthanasia of the PRI? Neoliberalism and Party Reform in Mexico. In *The Politics of Economic Restructuring: State-Society Relations and Regime Change in Mexico,* ed. Maria Lorena Cook, Kevin J. Middlebrook, and Juan Molinar Horcasitas, 125–48. La Jolla: University of California at San Diego, Center for U.S.-Mexican Studies.

———. 1994b. Five Scenarios for Mexico. *Journal of Democracy* 5, no. 3 (July): 57–71.

———. 1997. Falling from the Tightrope: The Political Economy of the Mexican Crisis. In *Mexico 1994: Anatomy of an Emerging Market Crash,* ed. Sebastián Edwards and Moisés Naím, 55–80. Washington, DC: Carnegie Endowment for International Peace.

Dugan, William E., and Alfredo Rehren. 1990. Impacto del Régimen Político en la Intermediación de Intereses: Instituciones Públicas y Grupos Empresariales en Chile. *Política* 22–23 (June): 117–36.

Dussell Peters, Enrique. 1996. From Export-Oriented to Import-Oriented Industrialization: Changes in Mexico's Manufacturing Sector, 1988–1994. In *Neoliberalism Revisited: Economic Restructuring and Mexico's Political Future,* ed. Gerardo Otero, 63–83. New York: Westview Press.

Edwards, Sebastián. 1990. The Sequencing of Economic Reform: Analytical Issues and Lessons from Latin American Experiences. *World Economy* 13, no. 1:1–14.

———. 1995. *Crisis and Reform in Latin America: From Despair to Hope.* New York: Oxford University Press.

———. 1997. Bad Luck or Bad Policies? An Economic Analysis of the Crisis. In *Mexico 1994: Anatomy of an Emerging Market Crisis,* ed. Sebastián Edwards and Moisés Naím, 95–124. Washington, DC: Carnegie Endowment for International Peace.

Edwards, Sebastián, and Alejandra Cox Edwards. 1991. *Monetarism and Liberalization: The Chilean Experiment.* 2d ed. Cambridge, MA: Ballinger.

Edwards, Sebastián, and Moisés Naím. 1997. *Mexico 1994: Anatomy of an Emerging Market Crash.* Washington, DC: Carnegie Endowment for International Peace.

Edwards, Sebastián, and Guido Tabellini. 1991. Explaining Fiscal Deficits and Inflation in Developing Countries. Working paper 3493, National Bureau of Economic Research, Cambridge, MA.

Eijffinger, Sylvester C. W., and Jakob De Haan. 1996. The Political Economy of Central Bank Independence. Special Papers in International Finance 19, Department of Economics, International Finance Section, Princeton University, May.

Eijffinger, Sylvester C. W., and Eric Schaling. 1993. Central Bank Independence: Theory and Evidence. Center Discussion Paper Series 9325, Tilburg University.

Elizondo, Carlos. 1993. The Making of a New Alliance: The Privatization of the Banks in Mexico. Documento de Trabajo 5, Centro de Investigación y Docencia Económica, Mexico City, Mexico.

Epstein, David, and Sharyn O'Halloryn. 1994. Administrative Procedures, Information, and Agency Discretion. *American Journal of Political Science* 38, no. 3:697–722.

Escobar Toledo, Saúl. 1987. Rifts in the Mexican Power Elite, 1976–1986. In *Government and Private Sector in Contemporary Mexico,* ed. Sylvia Maxfield and Ricardo Anzaldúa Montoya, 65–88. La Jolla: University of California at San Diego, Center for U.S.-Mexican Studies.

Eyzaguirre, Nicolás. 1989. Una Visión Crítica de la Ley Orgánica del Banco Central. Manuscript, CEPAL, Santiago, Chile, September.

Fernandez, Raquel, and Dani Rodrik. 1991. Resistance to Reform: Status Quo Bias in the Presence of Individual-Specific Uncertainty. *American Economic Review* 81:1146–85.

Ffrench-Davis, Ricardo. 1989. Modificaciones Posibles a la Ley del Banco Central. Manuscript, CEPAL, Santiago, Chile, December.

———. 1991. Desarrollo Económico y Equidad en Chile: Herencias y Desafíos en el Retorno a la Democracia. *Colección Estudios Cieplan* 31 (March): 31–51.

Ffrench-Davis, Ricardo, Manuel Agosín, and Andras Uthoff. 1995. Capital Movements, Export Strategy, and Macroeconomic Stabilization in Chile. In *Coping with Capital Surges: The Return of Finance to Latin America,* ed. Ricardo Ffrench-Davis and Stephany Griffith-Jones, 99–144. Boulder, CO: Lynne Rienner Publishers.

Ffrench-Davis, Ricardo, and Oscar Muñoz. 1990. Desarrollo Económico, Inestabilidad y Desequilibrios Políticos en Chile: 1950–1989. *Colección Estudios Cieplan* 28 (June): 121–56.

Figari Oxley, Augustín. 1989. El Banco Central de Chile: Su Autonomía en el Contexto de la Constitución Política de 1980. Master's thesis, Departamento de Economía, Universidad Católica de Valparaiso, Valparaiso, Chile.

Fishlow, Albert, et al. 1994. *Miracle or Design? Lessons from the East Asian Experience.* Washington, DC: Overseas Development Council.

Flaño, Nicolás. 1992.On Solid Ground: Chile's Economy Today. Lecture to the Smithsonian Campus on the Mall, Washington, DC, February.

Flisfisch, Angel. 1994. La Gestión Estratégica de un Proceso de Transición y Consolidación: El Caso Chileno, *Proposiciones* 25 (October): 20–33.

Fontaine, Juan Andrés. 1989. Banco Central: Autonomía Para Cautelar la Estabilidad. *Cuadernos de Economía* 26, no. 77 (April): 65–74.

———. 1993. Transición Económica y Política en Chile: 1970–1990. *Estudios Públicos* 50 (autumn): 229–79.

Foxley, Alejandro. 1985. *Para una Democracia Estable.* Santiago, Chile: Cieplan.

———. 1986. The Neoconservative Economic Experiment in Chile. In *Military Rule in Chile: Dictatorship and Oppositions,* ed. J. Samuel Valenzuela and Arturo Valenzuela, 13–50. Baltimore, MD: Johns Hopkins University Press.

———. 1990. La Política Económica para la Transición. In *Transición a la Democracia: Marco Político y Económico,* ed. Oscar Muñoz, 101–20. Santiago, Chile: Cieplan.

Frank, Voker. 1997. Growth with Equity: A Marriage That Works? Chilean Labor Organizations' Experience in the New Democracy 1990–1996. Paper presented at the Twentieth International Congress of the Latin American Studies Association, April 17–19, Guadalajara, Mexico.

Franzese, Robert J. Jr. 1994. Central Bank Independence, Sectoral Interests, and the Wage Bargain. Working paper 56, Center for European Studies, Harvard University.

———. 1996. The Political Economy of Public Debt: An Empirical Examination of the OECD Post-War Experience. Chap. 8 in The Political Economy of Over-Commitment: A Comparative Study of Democratic Management of the Keynesian Welfare State. Ph.D. diss., Department of Government, Harvard University.

———. 1999. Two Hands on the Wheel: Independent Central Banks, Politically Responsive Governments, and Inflation. *American Journal of Political Science* 43, no. 3 (July): 681–706.

Frei, Eduardo. 1994. *Un Gobierno Para Los Nuevos Tiempos: Bases Programáticas del Segundo Gobierno de la Concertación.* Santiago, Chile.

Frieden, Jeffry. 1991a. *Debt, Development, and Democracy: Modern Political Economy and Latin America: 1965–85.* Princeton, NJ: Princeton University Press.

———. 1991b. Invested Interests: The Politics of National Economic Policies in a World of Global Finance. *International Organization* 45, no. 4 (autumn): 425–51.

———. 1998. The Politics of Exchange Rates. In *Mexico, 1994: Anatomy of an Emerging-Market Crash,* ed. Sebastián Edwards and Moisés Naím, 81–94. Washington, DC: Carnegie Endowment for International Peace.

Frieden, Jeffry, and Ronald Rogowski. 1996. The Impact of the International Economy on National Policies: An Analytical Overview. In *Internationalization and Domestic Politics,* ed. Robert O. Keohane and Helen Milner, 25–47. New York: Cambridge University Press.

Fry, Maxwell J. 1982. Models of Financially Repressed Developing Economies. *World Economy* 10, no. 9:731–50.

———. 1984. Saving, Financial Intermediation, and Economic Growth in Asia. *Asian Development Review* 2, no. 1:82–91.

———. 1997. *Emancipating the Banking System and Developing Markets for Government Debt.* New York: Routledge.

Fukuyama, Francis. 1991. *The End of History and the Last Man*. New York: Free Press.

Garretón, Manuel Antonio. 1986. Political Processes in an Authoritarian Regime: The Dynamics of Institutionalization and Opposition in Chile, 1973–1980. In *Military Rule in Chile: Dictatorship and Oppositions,* ed. J. Samuel Valenzuela and Arturo Valenzuela, 144–83. Baltimore, MD: Johns Hopkins University Press.

———. 1989. *La Posibilidad Democrática en Chile*. Cuadernos de Difusión. Santiago, Chile: FLACSO.

———. 1991. La Redemocratización Política en Chile: Transición, Inauguración, y Evolución. *Estudios Públicos* 42 (autumn): 101–33.

———. 1992. El Aprendizaje Político en la Redemocratización Chilena. Documento de Trabajo, Serie Estudios Políticos 24, FLACSO—Programa Chile, Santiago, Chile, November.

———. 1993. La Dimensión Política de los Procesos de Transformación en Chile. Documento de Trabajo, Serie Estudios Políticos 29, FLACSO—Programa Chile, Santiago, Chile, August.

———. 1998. *Partisan Politics in the Global Economy*. New York: Cambridge University Press.

Garrett, Geoffrey, and Peter Lange. 1996. Internationalization, Institutions, and Political Change. In *Internationalization and Domestic Politics,* ed. Robert O. Keohane and Helen V. Milner, 48–75. New York: Cambridge University Press.

Garrett, Geoffrey, and Barry R. Weingast. 1993. Ideas, Interests, and Institutions: Constructing the European Community's Internal Market. In *Ideas and Foreign Policy: Beliefs, Institutions, and Political Change,* ed. Judith Goldstein and Robert Keohane, 173–206. Ithaca, NY: Cornell University Press.

———. 1993. Liderazgo Empresarial y Reforma Económica Estructural en México: La Perspectiva del Proceso a Principios de los Noventa. In *Ajuste Estructural y Actores Sociales,* ed. Enrique de la Garza, 1–38. Mexico City, Mexico: Universidad Nacional Autónoma de México, Editorial El Cabanito.

———. 1994a. New Circuits, Markets, and Actors in the Mexican Financial System. Manuscript, Department of Economics, UAM-Azcapotzalco.

———. 1994b. Grupos Privados Nacionales en México, 1987–1993. *Revista de la Cepal* (August): 159–75.

———. 1997. El Liderazgo de las Grandes Empresas Industriales Mexicanas en los Noventa. In *Las Grandes Empresas Privadas Nacionales en América Latina en los Noventa,* ed. Celso Garrido and Walker Peres, 1–33. Mexico City, Mexico: UAM-Cepal.

Garrido, Luis Javier. 1987. El Partido del Estado Ante la Sucesión Presidencial en México, 1929–1987. *Revista Mexicana de Sociología* 49, no. 3 (July–September): 59–82.

———. 1989. The Crisis of Presidencialismo. In *Mexico's Alternative Political Futures,* ed. Wayne Cornelius, Judith Gentleman, and Peter H. Smith, 417–34. La Jolla: University of California at San Diego, Center for U.S.-Mexican Studies.

Geddes, Barbara. 1994a. *Politician's Dilemma: Building State Capacity in Latin America*. Berkeley: University of California Press.

———. 1994b. The Politics of Economic Liberalization. *Latin American Research Review* 30, no. 2:195–214.

———. 1995. A Comparative Perspective on the Leninist Legacy in Eastern Europe. *Comparative Political Studies* 28, no. 2 (July): 239–74.

———. 1998. What Do We Know about Democratization after Twenty Years? Paper presented at the annual meeting of the American Political Science Association, September 3–6, Boston, MA.

George, Alexander L. 1982. Case Studies and Theory Development. Paper presented at the Second Annual Symposium on Information Processing in Organizations, October 15–16, Carnegie-Mellon University.

Giavazzi, Francesco, and Alberto Giovannini. 1989. *Limiting Exchange Rate Flexibility: The European Monetary System.* Cambridge, MA: MIT Press.

Giavazzi, Francesco, and Marco Pagano. 1994. The Advantage of Tying One's Hands: EMS Discipline and Central Bank Credibility. In *Monetary and Fiscal Policy,* ed. Torsten Persson and Guido Tabellini, 1:225–46. Cambridge, MA: MIT Press.

Gibson, Edward L. 1997. The Populist Road to Market Reform: Policy and Electoral Coalitions in Mexico and Argentina. *World Politics* 50, no. 3 (April): 339–70.

Gíl Díaz, Francisco, and Augustín Carstens. 1997. Pride and Prejudice: The Economics Profession and Mexico's Financial Crisis, 1994–95. In *Mexico 1994: Anatomy of an Emerging Market Crash,* ed. Sebastián Edwards and Moisés Naím, 165–200. Washington, DC: Carnegie Endowment for International Peace.

Giorgio, Luis Alberto. 1997. *Banking Distress and Crisis: Lessons from Selected Experiences in Latin America.* Washington, DC: The World Bank.

Godoy, Oscar. 1994. La Cuestión de la Transición. *Revista de Ciencia Política* 16, nos. 1–2:11–20.

Golob, Stephanie R. 1996. Making Possible What Is Necessary: Pedro Aspe, the Salinas Team, and the Next Mexican Miracle. In *Technopols: Ideas, Leaders, and Their Impact on Freeing Politics and Markets,* ed. Jorge I. Dominguez, 95–144. University Park: Pennsylvania State University Press.

Gómez Tagle, Sylvia. 1993. Electoral Reform and the Party system, 1977–90. In *Mexico: Dilemmas of Transition,* ed. Neil Harvey, 64–90. London: The Institute of Latin American Studies, University of London, and British Academic Press.

Gonzáles Casanova, Pablo, and Aguilar Camín, Hector, eds. 1985. *México ante la Crisis: El Contexto Internacional y la Crisis Económica,* vol. 1. Mexico City, Mexico: Siglo Veintiuno Editores.

González-Gómez, Mauricio. 1998. Crisis and Economic Change in Mexico. In *Mexico Under Zedillo,* ed. Susan Kaufman Purcell and Luis Rusio, 37–65. Boulder, CO: Lynne Rienner Publishers.

Goodman, John B. 1991. The Politics of Central Bank Independence. *Comparative Politics* 23, no. 2 (January): 329–49.

———. 1992. *Monetary Sovereignty: The Politics of Central Banking in Western Europe.* Ithaca, NY: Cornell University Press.

Grilli, Vittorio, Donato Masciandaro, and Guido Tabellini. 1991. Political and Monetary Institutions and Public Financial Policies in the Industrial Countries. *Economic Policy* 13 (October): 341–92.

Gridle, Merilee. 1996. *Challenging the State: Crisis and Innovation in Latin America and Africa.* New York: Cambridge University Press.

Gruben, William, and John Welch. 1996. Distortions and Resolutions in Mexico's Financial System. In *The Changing Structure of Mexico,* ed. Laura Randall. New York: M. E. Sharpe.

Gruber, Lloyd Gerard. 2000. *Ruling the World: Power Politics and the Rise of Supranational Institutions.* Princeton, NJ: Princeton University Press.

Habib, Adam. 1998. South Africa: The Politics of Economic Policy-Making. Paper presented at the annual meeting of the American Political Science Association, September 3–6, Boston, MA.

Haggard, Stephan. 1994. From the Heavy Industry Plan to Stabilization: Macroeconomic Policy 1976–1980. In *Macroeconomic Policy and Adjustment in Korea, 1970–1990,* ed. Stephan Haggard et al., 49–74. Cambridge, MA: Harvard Institute for International Development and Korean Development Institute.

Haggard, Stephan, and Susan Collins. 1994. The Political Economy of Adjustment in the 1980s. In *Macroeconomic Policy and Adjustment in Korea, 1970–1990,* ed. Stephan Haggard et al., 75–110. Cambridge, MA: Harvard Institute for International Development and Korean Development Institute.

Haggard, Stephan, and Robert R. Kaufman. 1989. Economic Adjustment in New Democracies. In *Fragile Coalitions: The Politics of Economic Adjustment,* ed. Joan M. Nelson, 57–78. Washington, DC: Overseas Development Council.

———. 1995. *The Political Economy of Democratic Transitions.* Princeton, NJ: Princeton University Press.

Haggard, Stephan, and Chung H. Lee. 1993. The Political Dimension of Finance in Economic Development. In *The Politics of Finance in Developing Countries,* ed. Stephan Haggard, Chung H. Lee, and Sylvia Maxfield, 3–22. Ithaca, NY: Cornell University Press.

Haggard, Stephan, and Sylvia Maxfield. 1993. Political Explanations of Financial Policy in Developing Countries. In *The Politics of Finance in Developing Countries,* ed. Stephan Haggard, Chung H. Lee, and Sylvia Maxfield, 293–326. Ithaca, NY: Cornell University Press.

———. 1996. Financial Internationalization and the Developing World. *International Organization* 50, no. 1 (winter): 35–68.

Haggard, Stephan, and Matthew D. McCubbins, eds. Forthcoming. *The Structure of Fiscal and Regulatory Policy.* Washington, DC: World Bank.

Haggard, Stephan, and Stephen B. Webb, eds. 1994. Introduction to *Voting for Reform: Democracy, Political Liberalization, and Economic Adjustment,* ed. Stephan Haggard and Stephen B. Webb. Washington, DC: World Bank.

Hagopian, Francis. 1990. "Democracy by Undemocratic Means"? Elites, Political Pacts, and Regime Transition in Brazil. *Comparative Political Studies* 23, no. 2 (July): 147–70.

———. 1996. *Traditional Politics and Regime Change in Brazil.* New York: Cambridge University Press.

Hall, Peter A. 1994. Central Bank Independence and Coordinated Wage Bargaining: Their Interaction in Germany and Europe. *German Politics and Society* 31 (spring): 1–23.

Hall, Peter A., and Robert J. Franzese Jr. 1998. Mixed Signals: Central Bank Independence, Coordinated Wage Bargaining, and European Monetary Union. *International Organization* 52, no. 3 (summer): 505–35.

Hall, Peter A., and Rosemary Taylor. 1996. Political Science and the Three New Institutionalisms. *Political Studies* 44, no. 5 (December): 936–57.

Hallerberg, Mark, and Jurgen von Hagen. 1997. Electoral Institutions, Cabinet Negotiations, and Budget Deficits in the European Union. Working paper 6341, National Bureau of Economic Research, Cambridge, MA.

Han, Sung-joo, and Yung Chul Park. 1993. South Korea: Democratization at Last. In

*Driven by Growth: Political Change in the Asia-Pacific Region,* ed. James Morley, 163–92. Armonk, NY: M. E. Sharpe.

Hastings, Laura A. 1993. Regulatory Revenge: The Politics of Free-Market Financial Reforms in Chile. In *The Politics of Finance in Developing Countries,* ed. Stephan Haggard, Chung H. Lee, and Sylvia Maxfield, 201–29. Ithaca, NY: Cornell University Press.

Held, David. 1996. *Models of Democracy.* 2d ed. Stanford, CA: Stanford University Press.

Hellman, Joel. 1998. Winners Take All: The Politics of Partial Reform in Post-Communist Transitions. *World Politics* 50, no. 2 (January): 203–34.

Herbst, Jeffrey. 1997–98. Prospects for Elite-Driven Democracy in South Africa. *Political Science Quarterly* 112, no. 4:595–615.

Heredia, Blanca. 1992. Mexican Business and the State: The Political Economy of a "Muddled Transition." Working paper 182, Helen Kellogg Institute for International Studies, Notre Dame University, October.

———. 1994. Making Economic Reform Politically Viable. In *Democracy, Markets, and Structural Reform in Latin America,* ed. William C. Smith, Carlos H. Acuña, and Eduardo A. Gamarra, 265–96. Miami: North-South Center Press.

———. 1996. State-Business Relations in Contemporary Mexico. In *Rebuilding the State: Mexico after Salinas,* ed. Mónica Serrano and Victor Bulmer-Thomas, 131–50. London: Institute of Latin American Studies.

Hernández Rodriguez, Rogelio. 1988. Los Hombres del Presidente de la Madrid. *Foro Internacional* 28, no. 1 (July–September): 5–38.

Heyman, Timothy. 1991. *Investing in Mexico: Mexican Economy and Financial Markets.* Mexico City, Mexico: Editorial Milenio.

Hibbs, Douglas A. Jr. 1977. Political Parties and Macroeconomic Policy. *American Political Science Review* 71 (December): 1467–87.

Hojman, David. 1990. Chile after Pinochet: Aylwin's Christian Democrat Economic Policies for the 1990s. *Bulletin of Latin American Research* 9, no. 1:25–47.

Horn, Murray J., and Kenneth A. Shepsle. 1989. Commentary on "Administrative Arrangements and the Political Control of Agencies": Administrative Process and Organizational Form as Legislative Responses to Agency Costs. *Virginia Law Review* 75 (March): 499–508.

Horowitz, Donald. 1985. *Ethnic Groups in Conflict.* Berkeley and Los Angeles: University of California Press.

Huber, John, and Charles R. Shipan. 2000. The Costs of Control: Legislators, Agencies, and Transactions Costs. *Legislative Studies Quarterly* 25, no. 1 (February): 25–52.

Huneeus, Carlos. 1985. La Política de la Apertura y sus Implicancias para la Inauguración de la Democracia en Chile. *Revista de Ciencias Políticas* 12, no. 1:25–84.

———. 1986. La Inauguración de la Democracia en Chile: Reforma en el Procedimiento y Ruptura en el Contenido Democrático? *Revista de Ciencia Política* 8, nos. 1–2:23–87.

———. 1988a. La Democracia en Chile: Un Enfoque Institucional. *Pensamiento Ibero-Americano* 14 (July–December): 93–108.

———. 1988b. El Ejército y la Política en el Chile de Pinochet: Su Magnitud y sus Alcances. *Opciones* 14:89–136.

———. 1994. En Defensa de la Transición: El Primer Gobierno de la Democracia en Chile. Working paper 18, Universität Heidelbert, Institut für Politische Wissenschaft, Lateinamerikaforschung, December.

Huneeus, Carlos, and Jorge Olave. 1987. La Participación de los Militares en los Nuevos Autoritarismos: Chile en Una Perspectiva Comparada. *Opciones* 11:119–62.
Hunter, Wendy. 1997. *Eroding Military Influence in Brazil: Politicians against Soldiers.* Baltimore, MD: Johns Hopkins University Press.
Hunter, Wendy, and David S. Brown. 1998. Democracy and Social Spending in Latin America, 1980–1992. Manuscript, Department of Political Science, Vanderbilt University; and Department of Political Science, Rice University.
International Monetary Fund. 1992. *Exchange Rate Agreements and Exchange Rate Restrictions.* Washington, DC: International Monetary Fund.
———. 1995. *Developments in 1994: World Economic Outlook Annex I, Factors behind the Financial Crisis in Mexico.* Washington, DC: International Monetary Fund.
Iversen, Torben. 1998. Wage Bargaining, Central Bank Independence, and the Real Effects of Money. *International Organization* 52, no. 3 (summer): 469--504.
Jensen, Michael C. 1983. Organization Theory and Methodology. *Accounting Review* 8 (April): 319–87.
Johnson, David R., and Pierre L. Siklos. 1992. Political Effects on Central Bank Behavior: Some International Evidence. In *Varieties of Monetary Reforms: Lessons and Experiences on the Road to Monetary Union,* ed. P. L. Siklos, 133–64. Boston: Kluwer Academic Press.
Jordan, Thomas J. 1997a. Central Bank Independence and the Trade-off between Inflation and Output Stabilization. *Journal of Institutional and Theoretical Economics* 153:366–83.
———. 1997b. Disinflation Costs, Accelerating Inflation Gains, and Central Bank Independence. *Weltwritschaftliches Archiv* 133, no. 1:1–21.
Joubert, W. A. 1976. *The Law of South Africa.* Vol. 1. Durban: Butterworths.
Kane, Edward J. 1980. Politics and Fed Policymaking: The More Things Change the More They Remain the Same. *Journal of Monetary Economics* 6:199–211.
Karl, Terry. 1986. Petroleum and Political Pacts: The Transition to Democracy in Venezuela. In *Transitions from Authoritarian Rule: Prospects for Democracy.* Vol. 2, *Latin America,* ed. Guillermo O'Donnell, Philippe C. Schmitter, and Laurence Whitehead Jr., 196–220. Baltimore, MD: Johns Hopkins University Press.
———. 1990. Dilemmas of Democratization. *Comparative Politics* 23, no. 1 (October): 1–21.
Karl, Terry, and Philippe C. Schmitter. 1994. Democratization around the Globe: Its Opportunities and Risks. In *World Security: Trends and Challenges at Century's End,* 2d ed., ed. Michael T. Klare and Dan Thomas, 43–62. New York: St. Martin's Press.
Katz, Isaac. 1993. *El Nuevo Entorno Económico e Institucional: La Autonomá del Banco de México.* Manuscript, Departamento de Economía, Instituto Tecnológico Autónomo de México.
Katzenstein, Peter. 1986. *Small States in World Markets: Industrial Policy in Europe.* Ithaca, NY: Cornell University Press.
Kaufman, Robert R., Carlos Bazdresch, and Blanca Heredia. 1994. Mexico: Radical Reform in a Dominant Party System. In *Voting for Reform: Democracy, Political Liberalization, and Economic Adjustment,* ed. Stephan Haggard and Stephen B. Webb, 360–410. Washington, DC: World Bank.
Kaufman, Robert R., and Leo Zuckerman. 1998. Attitudes toward Economic Reform in

Mexico: The Role of Political Mediations. *American Political Science Review* 92, no. 2 (June): 359–76.

Kaufman Purcell, Susan, and Luis Rusio, eds. *Mexico under Zedillo.* Boulder, CO: Lynne Rienner Publishers.

Keefer, Philip, and David Stasavage. 1998. When Does Delegation Improve Credibility? Central Bank Independence and the Separation of Powers. Paper presented at the annual meeting of the American Political Science Association, September 3–6, Boston, MA.

———. 1999. Bureaucratic Delegation and Political Institutions: When Are Central Banks Irrelevant? Paper presented at the annual meeting of the American Political Science Association, September 2–5, Atlanta, GA.

Kentridge, Matthew. 1993. Turning the Tanker: The Economic Debate in South Africa. CPS Social Contract Series, Research report 32, Centre for Policy Studies, Johannesburg, South Africa.

Kessler, Timothy P. 1998. Political Capital: Mexican Financial Policy under Salinas. *World Politics* 51, no. 1 (October): 36–66.

Kildegaard, Anne. 1997. Foreign Finance and the Collapse of the Mexican Peso. *Journal of Economic Issues* 31, no. 4 (December): 951–67.

Kim, P. J. 1994. Financial Institutions. In *Korea's Political Economy: An Institutional Perspective,* ed. Lee-Jay Cho and Yoon Hyung Kim, 273–319. Boulder, CO: Westview Press.

Kim, Yoon Hyung. 1994. An Introduction to the Korean Model of Political Economy. In *Korea's Political Economy: An Institutional Perspective,* ed. Lee-Jay Cho and Yoon Hyung Kim, 45–62. Boulder, CO: Westview Press.

King, Gary, Robert O. Keohane, and Sidney Verba. 1994. *Designing Social Inquiry: Scientific Inference in Qualitative Research.* Princeton, NJ: Princeton University Press.

Kinney-Giraldo, Jeanne. 1996. Development and Democracy in Chile: Finance Minister Alejandro Foxley and the Concertación Project for the Nineties. In *Technopols: Ideas, Leaders, and Their Impact on Freeing Markets and Politics in Major Latin American Countries in the 1980s and 1990s,* ed. Jorge I. Domínguez, 229–75. Pittsburgh: Pennsylvania State University Press.

Klesner, Joseph L. 1994. Realignment or Dealignment? Consequences of Economic Crisis and Restructuring for the Mexican Party System. In *The Politics of Economic Restructuring: State-Society Relations and Regime Change in Mexico,* ed. Maria Lorena Cook, Kevin J. Middlebrook, and Juan Molinar Horcasitas, 159–94. La Jolla: University of California at San Diego, Center for U.S.-Mexican Studies.

———. 1995. The 1994 Mexican Elections: Manifestation of a Divided Society? *Mexican Studies* 11, no. 1 (winter): 137–49.

———. 1997. Dissolving Hegemony: Electoral Competition and the Decline of Mexico's One-Party-Dominant Regime. Paper presented at the annual meeting of the American Political Science Association, August 28–31, Washington, DC.

———. 1998. Economic Integration and Regional Electoral Dynamics in Mexico. Manuscript, Department of Political Science, Kenyon College.

Knight, Jack. 1992. *Institutions and Social Conflict.* New York: Cambridge University Press.

Kong, T. Y. 1997. Democratization and Its Aftermath: Transition and Continuity in South Korea. In *The Korean Peninsula in Transition,* ed. D. H. Kim and T. Y. Kong, 91–115. Oxford: MacMillan Press.

Krasner, Stephen D. 1991. Global Communications and National Power: Life on the Pareto Frontier. *World Politics* 43, no. 3 (April): 336–66.

Kreps, David M. 1990. *A Course in Microeconomics.* Princeton, NJ: Princeton University Press.

———. 1991. Corporate Culture and Economic Theory. In *Positive Perspectives on Political Economy,* ed. James E. Alt and Kenneth A. Shepsle, 90–143. New York: Cambridge University Press.

Krugman, Paul. 1995. Emerging Market Blues. *Foreign Affairs* 74, no. 4 (July–August): 28–44.

Kydland, Finn, and Edward Prescott. 1977. Rules Rather than Discretion: The Inconsistency of Optimal Plans. *Journal of Political Economy* 85:473–92.

Lange, Peter, and Geoffrey Garrett. 1985. The Politics of Growth: Strategic Interaction and Economic Performance in the Advanced Industrial Democracies, 1974–1980. *Journal of Politics* 47:792–827.

Larraín, Mauricio. 1989. How the 1981–1983 Chilean Banking Crisis Was Handled. Policy, Planning, and Research Working Papers, World Bank, Washington, DC.

Lee, Manwoo. 1990. *The Odyssey of Korean Democracy: Korean Politics 1987–1990.* New York: Praeger.

———. 1995. South Korea's Politics of Succession and the December 1992 Presidential Election. In *Politics and Policy in the New Korean State: From Roh Tae-woo to Kim Young Sam,* ed. James Cotton. New York: St. Martin's Press.

Leiderman, Leonardo, and Alfredo E. Thorne. 1996. The 1994 Mexican Crisis and its Emerging Aftermath: What Are the Main Lessons? In *Private Capital Flows to Emerging Markets after the Mexican Peso Crisis,* ed. Guillermo A. Calvo, Morris Goldstein, and Eduard Hochreiter, 1–43. Washington, DC: Institute for International Economics.

Levi, Margaret. 1990. A Logic of Institutional Change. In *The Limits of Rationality,* ed. Karen Schweers Cook and Margaret Levi, 402–18. Chicago: University of Chicago Press.

Lijphart, Arend. 1975. The Comparable-Cases Strategy in Comparative Research. *Comparative Political Studies* 9, no. 2 (July): 158–77.

———. 1977. *Democracy in Plural Societies: A Comparative Exploration.* New Haven, CT: Yale University Press.

Lindblom, Charles. 1977. *Politics and Markets.* New York: Basic Books.

Linz, Juan J. 1975. Totalitarian and Authoritarian Regimes. In *Handbook of Political Science,* ed. Fred Greenstein and Nelson Polsby, 187–411. Reading, MA: Addison-Wesley.

———. 1990. Transitions to Democracy. *Washington Quarterly* 13, no. 3:143–63.

Linz, Juan J., and Alfred Stepan. 1996. *Problems of Democratic Transition and Consolidation: Southern Europe, South America, and Post-communist Europe.* Baltimore, MD: Johns Hopkins University Press.

Loeza, Soledad. 1989. The Emergence and Legitimization of the Modern Right, 1970–88, trans. William B. Heller. In *Mexico's Alternative Political Futures,* ed. Wayne A. Cornelius, Judith Gentleman, and Peter H. Smith. La Jolla: University of California at San Diego, Center for U.S.-Mexican Studies.

———. 1994. Political Liberalization and Uncertainty in Mexico. In *The Politics of Economic Restructuring: State-Society Relations and Regime Change in Mexico,* ed.

Maria Lorena Cook, Kevin J. Middlebrook, and Juan Molinar Horcasitas, 105–24. La Jolla: University of California at San Diego, Center for U.S.-Mexican Studies.

Lohmann, Susanne. 1992. Optimal Commitment in Monetary Policy: Credibility versus Flexibility. *American Economic Review* 82, no. 1 (March): 273–86.

———. 1997. Is Japan Special? Monetary Linkages and Price Stability. *Monetary and Economic Studies* (December): 63–79.

———. 1998a. Federalism and Central Bank Independence: The Politics of German Monetary Policy, 1957–1992. *World Politics* 51, no. 3 (April): 401–46.

———. 1998b. Reputational versus Institutional Solutions to the Time Inconsistency Problem in Monetary Policy. In *Positive Political Economy: Theory and Evidence,* ed. Sylvester C. W. Eijffinger and Harry Huizinga, 9–22. New York: Cambridge University Press.

Londregan, John. 2000. *Faustian Bargains: Legislative Institutions and Chile's Democratic Transition.* Cambridge University Press.

Londregan, John, and Keith T. Poole. 1990. Poverty, the Coup Trap, and the Seizure of Executive Power. *World Politics* 42, no. 2 (January): 151–83.

Lotter, H. P. P. 1997. *Injustice, Violence, and Peace: The Case of South Africa.* Atlanta: Rodopi.

———. 1993. The Political Left in Chile, 1973–1990. In *The Latin American Left: From the Fall of Allende to Perestroika,* ed. Barry Carr and Steve Ellner, 23–40. Boulder, CO: Westview Press.

———. 1995. The Transition to Civilian Government in Chile, 1990–1994. In *The Struggle for Democracy in Chile: 1982–1990,* ed. Paul W. Drake and Iván Jaksić, 305–37. Lincoln: University of Nebraska Press.

———. 1998. When You Wish upon the Stars: Why the Generals (and Admirals) Say Yes to Latin American "Transitions" to Civilian Government. In *The Origins of Liberty: Political and Economic Liberalization in the Modern World,* ed. Paul W. Drake and Matthew D. McCubbins, 115–45. Princeton, NJ: Princeton University Press.

Luders, Rolf J. 1991. Massive Divestiture and Privatization: Lessons from Chile. *Contemporary Policy Issues* 9, no. 4 (October): 1–19.

Lujambio, Alonso. 1993. Presidentes y Congresos: Estados Unidos, la Experiencia Latinoamericana, y el Futuro Mexicano. *Foro Internacional* 33, no. 3 (July–September): 317–60.

Luna, Matilda. 1994. Los Retos de la Globalización: La Reforma Microeconómica. In *Los Empresarios Ante la Globalización,* ed. Ricardo Tirado, 194–221. Mexico City, Mexico: Universidad Nacional Autónoma de México, Instituto de Investigaciones Sociales.

———. 1995. Entrepreneurial Interests and Political Action in Mexico: Facing the Demands of Economic Modernization. In *The Challenge of Institutional Reform in Mexico,* ed. Riordan Roett, 194–221. Boulder, CO: Lynne Rienner Publishers.

Luna, Matilda, and Ricardo Tirado. 1992. *El Consejo Coordinador Empresarial: Una Radiografía.* Proyecto Organizaciones Empresariales en México, Cuaderno 1. Mexico City, Mexico: Universidad Nacional Autónoma de México, Facultad de Ciencias Políticas y Sociales y el Instituto de Investigaciones Sociales.

Luna, Matilda, Ricardo Tirado, and Francisco Valdés Ugalde. 1991. Los Empresarios y La Política en México, 1982–1986. In *Las Empresas y Los Empresarios en el México*

*Contemporáneo,* ed. Ricardo Pozas and Matilda Luna, 21–87. Mexico City, Mexico: Grijalvo.

Lustig, Nora. 1992. *Mexico: The Remaking of an Economy.* Washington, DC: Brookings Institution.

———. 1995. The Mexican Peso Crisis: The Foreseeable and the Surprise. Brookings Papers in International Economics 114. Washington, DC: Brookings Institution, June.

Magaloni, Beatriz. 1998. Electoral Consequences of the Peso Crisis: Last Gasp for the PRI? Paper presented at the 1998 Latin American Studies Convention, September 28–30, Chicago.

Mahmood, S., and N. Shaukat. 1995. *The Law of Banks.* Lahore: Legal Research Centre.

Mainwaring, Scott, Guillermo O'Donnell, and J. Samuel Valenzuela, eds. 1992. *Issues and Prospects of Democratic Consolidation: The New South American Democracies in Comparative Perspective.* Notre Dame, IN: Kellogg Institute with the University of Notre Dame Press.

Mansell Carstens, Catherine. 1992. *Las Nuevas Finanzas en México.* Mexico City, Mexico: Editorial Milenio.

———. 1994. The Internationalization of the Mexican Financial System. Paper presented at the Global and Comparative Analysis of Financial Institutions, May 9–13, Rockefeller Foundation Bellagio Conference and Study Center, Bellagio, Italy.

Martin, Lisa L. 1993. Credibility, Costs, and Institutions: Cooperation on Economic Sanctions. *World Politics* 45 (April): 406–32.

Masciandaro, Donato, and Guido Tabellini. 1988. Monetary Regimes and Fiscal Deficits: A Comparative Analysis. In *Monetary Policy in the Pacific Basin Countries,* ed. H. Cheng, 125–52. Boston: Kluwer Academic Publishers.

Mashaw, Jerry. 1990. Explaining Administrative Process: Normative, Positive, and Critical Stories of Legal Development. *Journal of Law, Economics, and Organization* 6:267–98.

Massad, Carlos. 1989. La Función Técnica y la Función Política del Banco Central: Anatomía Prenatal. *Cuadernos de Economía* 26, no. 77 (April): 75–90.

Maxfield, Sylvia. 1993. The Politics of Mexican Financial Policy. In *The Politics of Finance in Developing Countries,* ed. Stephan Haggard, Chung E. Lee, and Sylvia Maxfield, 230–58. Ithaca, NY: Cornell University Press.

———. Bankers' Alliances and Economic Policy Patterns: Evidence from Mexico and Brazil. *Comparative Political Studies* 23, no. 4 (January): 419–58.

———. 1989. International Economic Opening and Government-Business Relations. In *Mexico's Alternative Political Futures,* ed. Wayne A. Cornelius, Judith Gentleman, and Peter H. Smith, 215–36. La Jolla: University of California at San Diego, Center for U.S.-Mexico Studies.

———. 1994. Revenue Imperatives and Central Bank Authority in Industrializing Nations. *World Politics* 46, no. 4 (July): 556–88.

———. 1997. *Gatekeepers of Growth: The International Political Economy of Central Banking in Developing Countries.* Princeton, NJ: Princeton University Press.

Maxfield, Sylvia, and Ricardo Anzaldúa Montoya, eds. 1987. *Government and Private Sector in Contemporary Mexico.* La Jolla: University of California at San Diego, Center for U.S.-Mexican Studies.

McCubbins, Matthew D., Roger G. Noll, and Barry R. Weingast. 1987. Administrative

Procedures as Instruments of Political Control. *Journal of Law, Economics, and Organization* 3, no. 2 (autumn): 243–77.

———. 1989. Structure and Process, Politics and Policy: Administrative Arrangements and the Political Control of Agencies. *Virginia Law Review* 75:431–82.

McKinnon, Ronald I. 1973. *Money and Capital in Economic Development.* Washington, DC: Brookings Institution.

———. 1991. *The Order of Economic Liberalization: Financial Control in the Transition to a Market Economy.* Baltimore, MD: Johns Hopkins University Press.

McRae, Duncan. 1977. A Political Model of the Business Cycle. *Journal of Political Economy* 85:239–86.

Meenai, S. A. 1984. *Money and Banking in Pakistan.* Karachi: Oxford University Press.

Meller, Patricio. 1984. Los Chicago Boys y el Modelo Económico Chileno: 1973–1983. *Apuntes Cieplan* 43 (January).

———. 1992. La Apertura Comercial Chilena: Lecciones de Política. *Colección Estudios Cieplan* 35 (September): 9–54.

Méndez, Roberto, Oscar Godoy, Enrique Barros, and Arturo Fontaine Talavera. 1989. Por Qué Ganó el No? *Estudios Públicos* 33 (summer): 83–134.

MERG (Macroeconomic Research Group). 1993. *Making Democracy Work: A Framework for Macroeconomic Policy in South Africa.* Bellville, South Africa: Centre for Development Studies.

Michie, Jonathon, and Vishnu Padayachee, eds. 1997. *The Political Economy of South Africa's Transition.* London: Dryden Press.

———. 1995. *The Paradox of Revolution: Labor, the State, and Authoritarianism in Mexico.* Baltimore, MD: Johns Hopkins University Press.

Milgrom, Paul R., Douglas C. North, and Barry R. Weingast. 1990. The Role of Institutions in the Revival of Trade: The Law Merchant, Private Judges, and the Champagne Fairs. *Economics and Politics* 2, no. 1 (March): 1–22.

Milgrom, Paul, and John Roberts. 1992. *Economics, Organization, and Management.* Englewood Cliffs, NJ: Prentice-Hall.

Millán, René. 1988. *Los Empresarios Mexicanos ante el Estado y la Sociedad.* Mexico City, Mexico: Universidad Nacional Autónoma de México, Siglo Veintiuno/Instituto de Investigaciones Sociales.

Moe, Terry M. 1984. The New Economics of Organization. *American Journal of Political Science* 28:739–77.

———. 1987. Interests, Institutions, and Positive Theory: The Politics of the NLRB. *Studies in American Political Development* 2:236–39.

———. 1990a. The Politics of Structural Choice: Toward a Theory of Public Bureaucracy. In *Organization Theory: From Chester Barnard to the Present and Beyond,* ed. Oliver E. Williamson, 116–53. New York: Oxford University Press.

———. 1990b. Political Institutions: The Neglected Side of the Story. *Journal of Law, Economics, and Organization* 6 (December): 213–53.

Moe, Terry M., and Michael Caldwell. 1994. The Institutional Foundations of Democratic Government: A Comparison of Presidential and Parliamentary Systems. *Journal of Institutional and Theoretical Economics* 150, no. 1:171–95.

Molinar Horcasitas, Juan. 1989. The Future of the Electoral System. In *Mexico's Alternative Political Futures,* ed. Wayne Cornelius, Judith Gentleman, and Peter H. Smith, 265–90. La Jolla: University of California at San Diego, Center for U.S.-Mexican Studies.

———. 1993. *El Tiempo de la Legitimidad: Elecciones, Autoritarismo, y Democracia en México.* Mexico City, Mexico: Cal y Arena.

———. 1994. Changing the Balance of Power in a Hegemonic Party System. In *Institutional Design and Democratization,* ed. Arendt Lijphart and Carlos Waisman, 137–60. Boulder, CO: Westview Press.

———. 1996. Renegotiating the Rules of the Game: The State and Political Parties. In *Rebuilding the State: Mexico after Salinas,* ed. Mónica Serrano and Victor Bulmer-Thomas, 25–39. London: Institute for Latin American Studies, University of London.

Molinar Horcasitas, Juan, and Jeffrey Weldon. 1994. Electoral Determinants and Consequences of National Solidarity. In *Transforming State-Society Relations in Mexico: The National Solidarity Strategy,* ed. Wayne Cornelius, Anne Craig, and Jonathon Fox, 123–42. U.S.-Mexico Contemporary Perspectives Series. La Jolla: University of California at San Diego, Center for U.S.-Mexican Studies.

Montecinos, Veronica. 1988. Economics and Power: Chilean Economists in Government 1958–1985. Ph.D. diss., Department of Political Science, University of Pittsburgh.

Montero, Cecilia. 1990. La Evolución del Empresariado Chileno: Surge un Nuevo Actor? *Colección Estudios Cieplan* 30 (December): 91–122.

———. 1993. El Actor Empresarial en Transición. *Colección Estudios Cieplan* 37 (June): 37–68.

Moravcsik, Andrew. 1991. Negotiating the Single European Act: National Interests and Conventional Statecraft in the European Community. *International Organization* 45, no. 1 (winter): 19–56.

Morris, Stephen D. 1992. Political Reformism in Mexico: Salinas at the Brink. *Journal of Interamerican Affairs and World Affairs* 34, no. 1:27–57.

———. 1995. Political Reformism in Mexico: An Overview of Contemporary Mexican Politics. Boulder, CO: Lynne Rienner Publishers.

Moulian, Tomás. 1992. El Gobierno Militar: Modernización y Revolución. Documento de Trabajo. Serie Estudios Políticos 23, FLACSO—Programa Chile. Santiago, Chile, November.

———. 1993. Los Actores Políticos de Gobierno y Oposición: El Caso Chileno. Paper presented at the International Seminar on Chilean Democratization in Comparative Perspective, July 19–21, FLACSO—Programa Chile, Santiago, Chile.

Muñoz, Oscar. 1985. Chile: El Colapso de un Experimento Económico y sus Efectos Políticos. *Colección Estudios Cieplan* 16 (June): 101–22.

———. 1992. Economie et Société au Chili: Un Développement Historique Marqué par la Frustration et le Changement. *Revue Internationale des Sciences Sociales,* UNESCO—Paris, November.

Murray, Martin. 1994. *The Revolution Deferred: The Painful Birth of Post-Apartheid South Africa.* New York: Verso.

Nacional Financiera, SNC. 1993. *Annual Report 1993.* Mexico City, Mexico.

Natella, Stefano, and Justin Manson. 1991. *The Mexican Banking System.* New York: First Boston.

Nelson, Joan M. 1993. The Politics of Economic Transformation: Is Third World Experience Relevant in Eastern Europe? *World Politics* 45, no. 3 (April): 433–63.

———. 1994. *Intricate Links: Democratization and Market Reforms in Latin America and Eastern Europe.* New Brunswick, NJ: Transaction Books.

Nordhaus, William. 1975. The Political Business Cycle. *Review of Economic Studies* 42:169–90.

North, Douglas C., and Barry R. Weingast. 1989. Constitutions and Commitment: The Evolution of Institutions Governing Public Choice in Seventeenth-Century England. *Journal of Economic History* 49 (December): 803–32.

O'Donnell, Guillermo. 1992. Transitions, Continuities, and Paradoxes. In *Issues and Prospects of Democratic Consolidation: The New South American Democracies in Comparative Perspective,* ed. Scott Mainwaring, Guillermo O'Donnell, and J. Samuel Valenzuela, 17–56. Notre Dame, IN: Kellogg Institute with the University of Notre Dame Press.

O'Donnell, Guillermo, and Philippe C. Schmitter. 1986. *Tentative Conclusions about Uncertain Democracies.* Baltimore, MD: Johns Hopkins University Press.

Offe, Claus, and Helmut Wiesenthal. 1980. Two Logics of Collective Action: Theoretical Notes on Social Class and Organizational Form. *Political Power and Social Theory* 1:67–115.

Oks, Daniel, and Sweder van Wijnbergen. 1993. Mexico in the International Financial System. In *Mobilizing International Investment for Latin America,* ed. Colin Bradford, 203–34. Paris: OECD.

O'Meara, Dan. 1996. *Forty Years Lost: The Apartheid State and the Politics of the National Party 1948–1990.* Athens, OH: Ohio University Press.

Ortega Riquelme, Ernesto. 1985. *El Pequeño Empresario de la Clase Media.* Santiago, Chile: Instituto de Estudios Humanísticos.

Muñoz, Ernesto, and Ernesto Tironi. 1988. *Pobreza en Chile.* Santiago, Chile: Centro de Estudios de Desarrollo.

Ortiz, Guillermo. 1994. *La Reforma Financiera en México.* Mexico City, Mexico: Fondo de Cultura Económica.

Ossa, Fernando. 1993a. Políticas de Fomento al Sector Exportador Chileno. In *El Modelo Económico Chileno,* ed. Daniel Wisecarver, 359–400. Santiago, Chile: Instituto de Economía, Pontificia Universidad Católica.

———. 1993b. La Creación del Banco Central de Chile en 1925: Antecedentes Previos y los Primeros Años de Operación. *Estudios de Economía* 20, no. 1:177–91.

Pacheco Méndez, Guadalupe. 1997. Un Caleidoscopo Electoral: Ciudades y Elecciònes en México, 1986–1994. *Estudios Sociólogos Mexicanos* 15, no. 44: 319–50.

Pardo V., Lucia. 1989. Un Diagnóstico Acerca de la Situación de la Pequeña, Mediana y Micro Empresa: Problemas de Organización y de Financiamiento. Manuscript, Departamento de Economía, Universidad de Chile.

Parkin, Michael. 1987. Domestic Monetary Institutions and Deficits. In *Deficits,* ed. J. M. Buchanan et al., 310–37. New York: Basil Blackwell.

Partido Acción Nacional. 1994. *Plataforma Política.* Marzo.

Pastor, Manuel, and Carol Wise. 1997. State Policy, Distribution, and Neoliberal Reform in Mexico. *Journal of Latin American Studies* 29, no. 4 (May): 419–56.

Pastor, Robert. 1990. Post-Revolutionary Mexico: The Salinas Opening. *Journal of Interamerican Studies and World Affairs* 32, no. 3 (autumn): 1–24.

Peñaloza, Tomás W., and Celso Garrido. 1994. Sistema Financiero y Bancos Mexicanos en Perspectiva Internacional. In *Transiciones Financieras y TLC: Canadá, México, y Estados Unidos,* ed. Antonio Gutiérrez Pérez and Celso Garrido Noguera, 29–74. Mexico City, Mexico: Editorial Ariel.

Persson, Torsten, and Lars Svensson. 1989. Why a Stubborn Conservative Would Run a Deficit? Policy with Time Consistent Preferences. *Quarterly Journal of Economics* 104:325–45.

Persson, Torsten, and Guido Tabellini. 1993. Designing Institutions for Monetary Stability. *Carnegie-Rochester Conference Series on Public Policy* 39 (December): 53–84.

———, eds. 1994. *Monetary and Fiscal Policy.* Vol. 1, *Credibility.* Cambridge, MA: MIT Press.

Petras, James, and Fernando Ignacio Leiva. 1994. *Democracy and Poverty in Chile: The Limits to Electoral Politics.* Boulder, CO: Westview Press.

Piñera, José. 1994. Chile. In *The Political Economy of Policy Reform,* ed. John Williamson. Washington, DC: Institute for International Economics.

Pollard, Patricia S. 1994. Central Bank Independence and Economic Performance. *Federal Reserve of Saint Louis Monthly Review* (July–August): 21–36.

Posen, Adam S. 1993. Why Central Bank Independence Does Not Cause Low Inflation: There Is No Institutional Fix for Politics. In *Finance and the International Economy,* ed. R. O'Brien: 7:40–65. Oxford: Oxford University Press.

Poterba, James. 1994. State Responses to Fiscal Crises: The Effects of Budgetary Institutions and Politics. *Journal of Political Economy* 102, no. 4:799–821.

Price, Robert M. 1991. *The Apartheid State in Crisis: Political Transformation in South Africa, 1975–1990.* New York: Oxford University Press.

Przeworski, Adam. 1986. Some Problems in the Study of the Transition to Democracy. In *Transitions from Authoritarian Rule.* Vol. 3, *Comparative Perspectives,* ed. Guillermo O'Donnell, Philippe C. Schmitter, and Laurence Whitehead Jr., 47–63. Baltimore, MD: Johns Hopkins University Press.

———. 1991. *Democracy and the Market: Political and Economic Reforms in Eastern Europe and Latin America.* New York: Cambridge University Press.

———. 1992. The Games of Transition. In *Issues and Prospects of Democratic Consolidation: The New South American Democracies in Comparative Perspective,* ed. Scott Mainwaring, Guillermo O'Donnell, and J. Samuel Valenzuela, 105–52. Notre Dame, IN: Kellogg Institute with the University of Notre Dame Press.

Przeworski, Adam, and Henry Teune. 1982. *The Logic of Comparative Social Inquiry.* Malabar, FL: Krieger Publishing Company.

Puga, Cristina. 1992. *Empresarios Medianos, Pequeños y Micro: Problemas de Organización y Representación.* Projecto Organizaciones Empresariales en México, Cuaderno 3. Mexico City, Mexico: Universidad Nacional Autónoma de Mexico, Instituto de Investigaciones Sociales.

———. 1993a. *Mexico: Empresarios y Poder.* Mexico City, Mexico: Universidad Nacional Autónoma de México, Facultad de Ciencias Políticas y Sociales/Porrúa.

———. 1993b. *Organizaciones Empresariales y Tratado de Libre Comercio.* Proyecto Organizaciones Empresariales en México, Cuaderno 7. Mexico City, Mexico: Universidad Nacional Autónoma de Mexico, Instituto de Investigaciones Sociales.

Puryear, Jeffrey. 1994. *Thinking Politics: Intellectuals and Democracy in Chile, 1973–1988.* Baltimore, MD: Johns Hopkins University Press.

Quintana, Enrique. 1992. Las Negociaciones Corporativas y la Política Neoliberal. In *Relaciones Corporativas en un Periodo de Transición,* ed. Matilda Luna and Ricardo Pozas, 181–87. Mexico City, Mexico: Universidad Nacional Autónoma de Mexico, Instituto de Investigaciones Sociales.

Ramírez de la O, Rogelio. 1994. El Informe del Banco de México para 1993: Nulo Crecimiento. *Encanal: Informe Especial No. 2* (Junio): 1–26.

———. 1995. The Mexican Peso Crisis and Recession of 1994–1995: Preventable Then, Avoidable in the Future? In *The Mexican Peso Crisis: International Perspectives,* ed. Riordan Roett, 11–32. Boulder, CO: Lynne Rienner Publishers.

———. 1996. Comment. In *Private Capital Flows to Emerging Markets after the Mexican Crisis,* eds. Guillemo A. Calvo, Morris Goldstein and Eduard Hochreiter, 50–55. Washington, DC: Institute for International Economics.

Reding, Andrew. 1988a. Mexico at the Crossroads: The 1988 Election and Beyond. *World Policy Journal* 6, no. 5:615–49.

———. 1988b. The New Democratic Current: A New Era in Mexico. *World Policy Journal* 5, no. 2:323–66.

———. 1989. Mexico under Salinas: A Facade of Reform. *World Policy Journal* 6, no. 4:688–729.

———. 1991. Mexico: The Crumbling of the "Perfect Dictatorship." *World Policy Journal* 8, no. 2:55–84.

Regalado, Jorge. 1996. The Opposition and the 1994 Presidential Elections in Mexico. In *Dismantling the Mexican State?,* ed. Nikke Craske, Gareth A. Jones, David Stansfield, 152–68. New York: St. Martin's Press.

Rehren, Alfredo. 1995. Empresarios, Transición, y Consolidación Democrática en Chile. Manuscript, Instituto de Ciencia Política. Pontificia Universidad Católica de Chile, Santiago, Chile.

Remmer, Karen. 1990. Democracy and Economic Crisis: The Latin American Experience. *World Politics* 42, no. 3 (April): 315–55.

Reserve Bank of South Africa. 1993. *South African Reserve Bank Act.*

*Revista Cieplan.* 1988. El Consenso Económico-Social Democrático es Posible. *Revista Cieplan* 14 (November): 36–44.

Reyes del Campillo. 1996. *Modernización Política en México: Elecciones, Partidos, y Representación (1982–1994).* Mexico City, Mexico: Universidad Autónoma Metropolitana.

Reza Nasr, Syyed Vali. 1992. Democracy and the Crisis of Governability in Pakistan. *Asian Survey* 32, no. 6 (June): 521–37.

Ro, Sung-Tae. 1994. Korean Monetary Policy. In *Macroeconomic Policy and Adjustment in Korea: 1970–1990,* ed. Stephan Haggard et al., 145–84. Cambridge, MA: HIID and Korean Development Institute.

Roberts, Kenneth. 1995. Neoliberalism and the Transformation of Populism in Latin America: The Peruvian Case. *World Politics* 48 (October): 82–116.

Rodriguez, Victoria E., and Peter M. Ward. 1995. *Opposition Government in Mexico.* Albuquerque: University of New Mexico Press.

Rodrik, Dani. 1994. The Rush to Free Trade in the Developing World: Why So Late? Why Now? Will It Last? In *Voting for Reform: Democracy, Political Liberalization, and Economic Adjustment,* ed. Stephan Haggard and Steven B. Webb, 61–88. Washington, DC: World Bank.

———. 1996. Understanding Economic Policy Reform. *Journal of Economic Literature* 34 (March): 9–41.

———. 1997. *Has Globalization Gone Too Far?* Washington, DC: Institute for International Economics.

Rogoff, Kenneth. 1985. The Optimal Degree of Commitment to an Intermediate Monetary Target. *Quarterly Journal of Economics* 100:1169–90.

Rokkan, Stein. 1970. *Citizens, Elections, Parties: Approaches to the Comparative Study of the Processes of Development.* New York: McKay.

Ronfeldt, David. 1989. Prospects for Elite Cohesion. In *Mexico's Alternative Political Futures,* ed. Wayne Cornelius, Judith Gentleman, and Peter H. Smith, 435–52. La Jolla: University of California at San Diego, Center for U.S.-Mexican Studies.

Ros, Jaime. 1987. Mexico: From the Oil Boom to the Debt Crisis, An Analysis of Policy Responses to External Shocks, 1978–1985. In *The Latin American Debt Crisis,* ed. Rosemary Thorp and Laurence Whitehead Jr. London: MacMillan.

———. 1994. Mexico in the 1990s: A New Economic Miracle? Some Notes on the Economic and Policy Legacy of the 1980s. In *The Politics of Economic Restructuring: State-Society Relations and Regime Change in Mexico,* ed. Maria Lorena Cook, Kevin J. Middlebrook, and Juan Molinar Horcasitas, 67–104. La Jolla: University of California at San Diego, Center for U.S.-Mexican Studies.

Rosende, Francisco. 1993. La Autonomía del Banco Central de Chile: Una Evaluación Preliminar. *Cuadernos de Economía* 91 (December): 293–326.

Roubli-Kaiser, Federico. 1996. Autonomía bajo Tensión Financiera. La Experiencia Reciente de México. Cuadernos de Investigación 36, Centro de Estudios Monetarios Latinoamericanos, Mexico City, Mexico. Junio.

Rubio, Luis. 1993. El Talón de Aquiles de la Reforma Económica. *Vuelta* 200 (July): 36–69.

SAARC-NGO. 1995. *Electoral Politics in Pakistan: National Assembly Elections 1993.* Report of the SAARC-NGO Observers. Delhi: Vikas Publishing House.

Sachs, Jeffrey D. 1990. *Social Conflict and Populist Policies in Latin America.* San Francisco: ICS Press.

Sachs, Jeffrey D., Aarón Tornell, and Andrés Velasco. 1995. The Collapse of the Mexican Peso Crisis: What Have We Learned? Working paper 5142, National Bureau of Economic Research, Cambridge, MA.

Sandbrook, Richard. 1985. *The Politics of Africa's Economic Stagnation.* Cambridge: Cambridge University Press.

Schmulow, D., and Lorraine Greyling. 1996. Monetary Policy in the New South Africa: Economic and Political Constraints. *South African Journal of Economics* 64, no. 3 (September): 175–92.

Schneider, Ben Ross. 1997. Big Business and the Politics of Economic Reform: Confidence and Concertation in Brazil and Mexico. Paper presented at the Latin American Studies Convention, April 17–19, Mexico City, Mexico, Guadalajara, Mexico.

Schultz, Donald E., and Edward J. Williams. 1995. Crisis or Transformation? The Struggle for the Soul of Mexico. In *Mexico Faces the 21st Century,* ed. Donald E. Schultz and Edward J. Williams, 1–28. Westport, CT: Greenwood Press.

Serrano, Monica. 1996. The Legacy of Gradual Change: Rules and Institutions under Salinas. In *Rebuilding the State: Mexico after Salinas,* ed. Mónica Serrano and Victor Bulmer-Thomas, 3–23. London: Institute of Latin American Studies.

Shadlen, Kenneth. 2000. Neoliberalism, Corporatism, and Small Business Political Activism in Contemporary Mexico. *Latin American Research Review* 35, no. 2: 73–106.

Shafqat, S. 1997. *Civil-Military Relations in Pakistan: From Zulfikar Ali Bhutto to Benazir Bhutto.* Boulder, CO: Westview Press.

Sheahan, John. 1997. Effects of Liberalization Programs on Poverty and Inequality: Chile, Mexico, and Peru. *Latin American Research Review* 32, no. 3:7–37.

Sigmund, Paul. 1977. *The Overthrow of Allende and the Politics of Chile.* Pittsburgh, PA: University of Pittsburgh Press.

Sikkink, Kathryn. 1991. *Ideas and Institutions: Developmentalism in Brazil and Argentina.* Ithaca, NY: Cornell University Press.

Siklos, Pierre L. 1995. Establishing Central Bank Independence: Recent Experiences in Developing Countries. *Journal of International Trade and Economic Development* 4, no. 3 (November): 351–84.

Silva, Eduardo. 1991. The Political Economy of Chile's Regime Transition: From Radical to "Pragmatic" Neo-Liberal Policies. In *The Struggle for Democracy in Chile: 1982–1990,* ed. Paul W. Drake and Iván Jaksić, 98–127. Lincoln: University of Nebraska Press.

———. 1996. *The State and Capital in Chile.* Boulder, CO: Westview Press.

Simmons, Beth A. 1996. Rulers of the Game: Central Bank Independence during the Interwar Years. *International Organization* 50, no. 3 (summer): 407–43.

Sims, Christopher. 1992. Interpreting the Macroeconomic Times Series Facts: The Effects of Monetary Policy. *European Economic Review* 26:975–1011.

Singh, Rai. 1994. Democracy in Pakistan: An Analysis of the 1993 Elections. In *Pakistan under Democratic Regime,* ed. M. D. Dharamdasani, 195–214. Varanasi, India: Shalimar Publishing House.

Sisk, Timothy D. 1995. *Democratization in South Africa: The Elusive Social Contract.* Princeton, NJ: Princeton University Press.

Smelser, Neil J. 1968. The Methodology of Comparative Analysis of Economic Activity. In *Essays in Sociological Interpretation,* ed. Neil J. Smelser, 62–75. Englewood Cliffs, NJ: Prentice-Hall.

Smit, B .W., and B. A. Mocke. 1991. Capital Flight from South Africa: Magnitude and Causes. *South African Journal of Economics* 59, no. 2:101–17.

Smith, Peter H. 1979. *Labyrinths of Power: Political Recruitment in Twentieth Century Mexico.* Princeton, NJ: Princeton University Press.

———. 1989. Presidencialismo and the Prospects for Political Reform. In *Mexico's Alternative Political Futures,* Monograph Series 30, ed. Wayne Cornelius, Judith Gentleman, and Peter H. Smith, 391–416. La Jolla: University of California at San Diego, Center for U.S.-Mexican Studies.

Smith, Peter H. 1997. Political Dimensions of the Peso Crisis. In *Mexico 1994: Anatomy of an Emerging Market Crisis,* Sebastian Edwards and Moisés Naím, 31–53. Washington, DC: Carnegie Endowment for International Peace.

Sohn, Hak-kyu. 1989. *Authoritarianism and Opposition in South Korea.* London: Routledge.

Soon, Cho. 1994. *The Dynamics of Korean Economic Development.* Washington, DC: Institute for International Economics.

Sørenson, Georg. 1993. *Democracy and Democratization.* San Francisco: Westview Press.

Stallings, Barbara. 1992. International Influence on Economic Policy: Debt, Stabilization, and Structural Reform. In *The Politics of Economic Adjustment: International Constraints, Distributive Conflicts, and the State,* ed. Stephan Haggard and Robert R. Kaufman, 41–88. Princeton, NJ: Princeton University Press.

Stals, C. L. 1993. What Financial Means Will Be Available for the Development of South Africa? *South African Quarterly Reserve Bank Bulletin.*

———. 1995. Monetary Policy in 1995. *South African Reserve Bank Quarterly Bulletin,* February.

Stansfield, David. 1996. The Pan: The Search for Ideological and Electorial Space. In *Dismantling the Mexican State,* ed. Rob Atken, Nikke Craske, Gareth A. Jones, and David Stansfield, 130–57. New York: St. Martin's Press.

Stark, David. 1990. *Negotiating the Institutions of Democracy: Contingent Choice and Strategic Interactions in the Hungarian and Polish Transitions.* Ithaca, NY: Cornell University Press.

Starr, Pamela. 1998. Monetary Mismanagement and Inadvertent Democratization in Technocratic Mexico. Paper presented at the Twenty-first International Congress of the Latin American Studies Association, September 24–26, Chicago, IL.

Steinmo, Sven, Kathleen Thelen, and Frank Longsteth. 1992. *Structuring Politics: Historical Institutionalism in Comparative Analysis.* New York: Cambridge University Press.

Stepan, Alfred. 1988. *Rethinking Military Politics: Brazil and the Southern Cone.* Princeton, NJ: Princeton University Press.

Stokes, Susan C. 1996. Public Opinion and Market Reforms: The Limits of Economic Voting. *Comparative Political Studies* 29, no. 5 (October): 499–519.

———. 2001. *Mandates, Markets, and Democracy: Neoliberalism by Surprise in Latin America.* New York: Cambridge University Press.

Stone, Randall. 1996. Russia and the IMF: Reputation and Unrestricted Bargaining. Paper presented at the annual meeting of the American Political Science Association, August 29–September 1, San Francisco, CA.

Swinburne, Mark, and Marta Castello-Branco. 1991. Central Bank Independence and Central Bank Functions. In *The Evolving Role of Central Banks,* ed. Patrick Downes and Reza Vaez-Zadeh, 414–44. Washington, DC: International Monetary Fund.

Tapia, Daniel. 1993. Experiencia del Banco Central Autónomo. *Cuadernos de Economía* 30, no. 91 (December): 349–55.

Teichman, Judith. 1995. *Privatization and Political Change in Mexico.* Pittsburgh, PA: University of Pittsburgh Press.

Teichman, Judith. 1996. Economic Restructuring, State-Labor Relations, and the Transformation of Mexican Corporatism. In *Neoliberalism Revisited: Economic Restruction and Mexico's Political Future,* ed. Gerado Otero, 149–66. Boulder, CO: Westview Press.

Tornell, Aarón, and Gerardo Esquivel. 1995. The Political Economy of Mexico's Entry into Nafta. Working paper 5322, National Bureau of Economic Research, Cambridge, MA.

Trigueros, Ignacio. 1993. La Autonomía del Banco de México: Algunos Cabos Sueltos. *Informe Mensual Sobre la Economía Mexicana* 11, no. 3 (Mayo): 21–29.

Tsebelis, George. 1997. Decision-Making in Political Systems: Veto Players in Presidentialism, Parliamentarism, Multicameralism, and Multipartism. *British Journal of Political Science* 25:289–325.

Valdés, Juan Gabriel. 1995. *Pinochet's Economists: The Chicago School in Chile.* New York: Cambridge University Press.

Valdés, Rodrigo. 1992. Cuantificación de la Reestructuración Sectorial Generada por la

Liberalización Comercial Chilena. *Colección Estudios Cieplan* 35 (September): 55–83.

Valdés Ugalde, Francisco. 1994. From Bank Nationalization to State Reform: Business and the New Mexican Order. In *The Politics of Economic Restructuring: State-Society Relations and Regime Change in Mexico,* ed. Maria Lorena Cook, Kevin J. Middlebrook, and Juan Molinar Horcasitas, 219–42. La Jolla: University of California at San Diego, Center for U.S.-Mexican Studies.

———. 1996. The Private Sector and Political Regime Change in Mexico. In *Neoliberalism Revisited: Economic Restructuring and Mexico's Political Future,* ed. Gerardo Otero, 127–47. New York: Westview Press.

Valenzuela, Arturo. 1978. *The Breakdown of Democratic Regimes: Chile.* Baltimore, MD: Johns Hopkins University Press.

———. 1991. The Military in Power: The Consolidation of One-Man Rule. In *The Struggle for Democracy in Chile: 1982–1990,* ed. Paul W. Drake and Iván Jaksić, 21–72. Lincoln: University of Nebraska Press.

Valenzuela, J. Samuel. 1992. Democratic Consolidation in Post-Transitional Setting: Notion, Process, and Facilitating Conditions. In *Issues and Prospects of Democratic Consolidation: The New South American Democracies in Comparative Perspective,* ed. Scott Mainwaring, Guillermo O'Donnell, and J. Samuel Valenzuela, 57–104. Notre Dame, IN: Kellogg Institute with the University of Notre Dame Press.

Van de Walle, Nicholas. 1991. The Decline of the Franc Zone: Monetary Politics in Francophone Africa. *African Affairs* 90:383–405.

———. 1994. The Politics of Non-Reform in Cameroon. In *Hemmed In: Responses to Africa's Economic Decline,* ed. Thomas Callaghy and John Ravenhill, 357–97. New York: Columbia University Press.

Varas, Augusto. 1987. *Los Militares en el Poder.* Santiago, Chile: FLACSO-Pehuén.

Vergara, Pilar. 1985. *Auge y Caída del Neoliberalismo en Chile.* Santiago, Chile: FLACSO.

———. 1993. Ruptura y Continuidad en la Política Social del Gobierno Democrático Chileno. *Revista Mexicana de Sociología* Año 55, no. 3 (July–September): 169–202.

———. 1994. Market Economy, Social Welfare, and Democratic Consolidation in Chile. In *Democracy, Markets, and Structural Reform in Latin America: Argentina, Bolivia, Brazil, Chile, and Mexico,* ed. William C. Smith, Carlos H. Acuña, and Eduardo A. Gamarra, 237–62. New Brunswick, NJ: Transaction Books.

———. 1997. In Pursuit of "Growth with Equity": The Limits of Chile's Free-Market Social Reforms. *International Journal of Health Services* 27, no. 2:207–15.

Walsh, Carl E. 1994. Is There a Cost to Central Bank Independence? *Federal Reserve Bank of San Francisco Weekly Letter* 94–05, February 4.

———. 1995a. Central Bank Independence and the Short-Run Output-Inflation Trade-off in the European Community. In *Monetary and Fiscal Policy in an Integrated Europe,* ed. Barry Eichengreen, Jeffry Frieden, and Jurgen von Hagen, 12–37. New York: Springer-Verlag.

———. 1995b. Optimal Contracts for Central Bankers. *American Economic Review* 85:150–67.

Waseem, M. 1992. Pakistan's Lingering Crisis of Dyarchy. *Asian Survey* 32, no. 7 (July): 617–34.

———. 1994. *The 1993 Elections in Pakistan.* Karachi: Vanguard Books.

Way, Christopher. 2000. Central Banks, Partisan Politics, and Macroeconomic Outcomes. *Comparative Political Studies* 33, no. 2 (March): 196–224.

Weintraub, Sidney. 1990. *Transforming the Mexican Economy: The Salinas Sexenio.* Washington, DC: National Planning Association.

Weintraub, Sidney, and M. Delal Baer. 1992. The Interplay between Economic and Political Opening: The Sequence in Mexico. *Washington Quarterly* (spring): 187–201.

Weldon, Jeffrey. 1997. Political Sources of *Presidencialismo* in Mexico. In *Presidentialism and Democracy in Latin America,* ed. Scott Mainwaring and Matthew Soberg Shugart, 225–58. New York: Cambridge University Press.

Werner, Martín. 1995. La Banca de Desarrollo: 1988–1994, Balances y Perspectivas. *El Mercado de Valores* 1 (Enero): 9–25.

Weyland, Kurt. 1997. "Growth with Equity" in Chile's New Democracy? *Latin American Research Review* 31, no. 1:37–67.

Whitehead, Laurence Jr. 1989. Political Change and Economic Stabilization: The Economic Solidarity Pact. In *Mexico's Alternative Political Futures,* Monograph Series 30, ed. Wayne Cornelius, Judith Gentleman, and Peter H. Smith, 181–214. La Jolla: University of California at San Diego, Center for U.S.-Mexican Studies.

———. 1994. Prospects for a "Transition" from Authoritarian Rule in Mexico. In *The Politics of Economic Restructuring: State-Society Relations and Regime Change in Mexico,* ed. Maria Lorena Cook, Kevin C. Middlebrook, and Juan Molinar Horcasitas, 327–46. La Jolla: University of California at San Diego, Center for U.S.-Mexican Studies.

Wiarda, Howard J. 1989. Mexico: The Unravelling of a Corporatist Regime? *Journal of Inter American Studies and World Affairs* 30, no. 4:1–28.

Williamson, John. 1995. *What Role for Currency Boards?* Policy Analysis in International Economics 40. Washington, DC: Institute for International Economics, September.

Williamson, John and Stephan Haggard. 1994. The Political Conditions for Policy Reform. In *The Political Economy of Policy Reform,* ed. John Williamson, 525–96. Washington, DC: Institute for International Economics.

Williamson, Oliver. 1985. *The Economic Institutions of Capitalism.* New York: Free Press.

Wisecarver, Daniel, ed. 1993. *El Modelo Económico Chileno.* Santiago, Chile: Instituto de Economía, Pontificia Universidad Católica.

Woo-Cummings, Meredith. 1997. Slouching toward the Market: The Politics of Financial Liberalization in South Korea. In *Capital Ungoverned: Liberalizing Finance in Interventionist States,* ed. Michael Loriaux et al., 57–91. Ithaca, NY: Cornell University Press.

Wood, Elisabeth Jean. 1999. The Stakes of the Game: The Politics of Redistribution in Democratic Transitions. Paper prepared for the Annual Meeting of the American Political Science Association. September 2–5, Atlanta, GA.

Wooley, John T. 1984. *Monetary Politics.* New York: Cambridge University Press.

Young, Crawford. 1993. *The Rising Tide of Cultural Pluralism.* Madison: University of Wisconsin Press.

Zahler, Roberto. 1989a. La Inserción Institucional del Banco Central de Chile. *Cuadernos de Economía* 26, no. 77 (April): 97–114.

———. 1989b. Comentarios a la Ley Orgánica Constitucional del Banco Central de Chile. Manuscript, CEPAL, Santiago, Chile.

Zielinsky, Jacub. 1995. Political Parties and Central Bank Autonomy. Paper presented at the Fifty-third Annual Meeting of the Midwest Political Science Association, April 6–8, Chicago, IL.

# Index